Anglo-Saxon Northumbria

John Edward Leigh

Peter Hunter Blair, 1912-1982

Peter Hunter Blair

Anglo-Saxon Northumbria

edited by
M. Lapidge and P. Hunter Blair

VARIORUM REPRINTS
London 1984

British Library CIP data   Hunter, Blair, Peter
                              Anglo-Saxon Northumbria – (Collected studies series;
                              CS192)
                              1. Great Britain – History – Anglo-Saxon period,
                              449-1066
                              I. Title   II. Hunter Blair, Pauline
                              III. Lapidge, Michael   IV. Series
                              942.01   DA135

                              ISBN 0-86078-141-0

Copyright © 1984 by   Variorum Reprints

942.01
B63a

Published in Great Britain by   Variorum Reprints
                                   20 Pembridge Mews London W11 3EQ

Printed in Great Britain by   Galliard (Printers) Ltd
                                   Great Yarmouth Norfolk

                                   VARIORUM REPRINT CS192

84-8585

CONTENTS

This volume contains a total of 338 pages.

FOREWORD

It is likely that anyone who has undertaken the study of Anglo-Saxon England during the past thirty years will have been guided in the early phases of this study by Peter Hunter Blair's eminently readable and authoritative book, *An Introduction to Anglo-Saxon England* (Cambridge: University Press, 1956; 2nd edn., 1977). This book has often been described as the standard work on the subject; and justifiably so, for it sets the standard for all books on Anglo-Saxon England by the breadth and interdisciplinary interest of its scope, embracing not only written, historical sources, but also geography, place-name studies, archaeology, architecture, economics, literature (in Latin and Old English) and palaeography. It presents a balanced and judicious assessment of all areas and periods of Anglo-Saxon England: Hunter Blair's intention was to view the Anglo-Saxon period as a continuous whole, from the period of Roman occupation until the Norman Conquest. His scholarly expertise ranged easily over this entire period. At an early stage of his career he had familiarised himself with the techniques of Romano-British archaeology, excavating one of the milecastles on Hadrian's Wall (the report of which, published in *Archaeologia Aeliana* 4th ser. 11 [1934], 103-20, was his first publication); his interest in the continuity between Roman Britain and early Anglo-Saxon England later issued in the full-length, popular study *Roman Britain and Early England 55 B.C. – 871 A.D.* (London: Thomas Nelson & Sons, 1963).

But it was to his native Northumbria – its origins, early history and intellectual achievements – that Hunter Blair's deepest scholarly interest was drawn. The twelve essays and lectures reprinted here all illustrate aspects of this one abiding interest. All of them reveal his procedure of minute and detailed analysis of the written, historical sources on which our knowledge of Anglo-Saxon Northumbria is based. It is the demonstration and elaboration of this scholarly procedure that is Hunter Blair's enduring contribution to Anglo-Saxon studies.

The procedure is evident in the earliest essay reprinted here (I), a study of the late Irish compilation known as the Three Fragments. The work had been used uncritically for many years by students of Viking and Northumbrian history. By comparing its account of certain ninth-century events with those in sources such as the *Historia Regum* attributed to Symeon of Durham, Hunter Blair demonstrated conclusively the unreliability of the Three Fragments as a witness to events in ninth-century Northumbria. His assessment of the text has been followed by subsequent historians; most recently, for example, by A. P. Smyth, *Scandinavian Kings in the British Isles, 850-880* (Oxford, 1977), pp. 108 ff.

The *Historia Regum* attributed to one Symeon (a twelfth-century precentor at Durham) had long been thought to contain much contemporary source-material for early Northumbrian history, but before Hunter Blair's time had never been studied critically. The exceptional importance and interest of the text was signalled in an early essay (II); then in a later, pioneering study (IX) Hunter Blair analysed the *Historia Regum* comprehensively in order to identify the various layers and constituent elements (drawn from a variety of sources) which it contains. His analysis has been followed by all later students of the text; indeed, his work is rich in suggestions which have yet to be explored properly. In particular, his suggestion that the first five sections of the compilation were the work of a single redactor active *c.* 1000 has received confirmation by more recent scholarship; it has now been demonstrated that the redactor in question was Byrhtferth of Ramsey who was active at that time (see M. Lapidge, 'Byrhtferth of Ramsey and the Early Sections of the *Historia Regum* attributed to Symeon of Durham', *Anglo-Saxon England* 10 (1981), 97-122). But the lines along which demonstration proceeded were drawn by Hunter Blair.

The written sources for the earliest period of Northumbrian history — principally Gildas, the anonymous *Historia Brittonum* and the early entries in the *Anglo-Saxon Chronicle* — were the subject of a series of four related and complementary papers, three of which were published in *Archaeologia Aeliana* between 1947 and 1949 (III, IV, V), the fourth in a volume published in collaboration with his Cambridge colleagues (VIII). These textual studies served to clarify the origins and geographical extent of Northumbria during the sixth to eighth centuries, and Hunter Blair's synthesis has been influential on modern scholarship, although it is only fair to note that the sources are now capable of more sophisticated analysis than was possible during the 1940's (see in general the remarks of D. N. Dumville, 'Sub-Roman Britain: History and Legend', *History* 62 [1977], 173-92, as well as his particular study, ' "Nennius" and the *Historia Brittonum*', *Studia Celtica* 10-11 [1975-6], 78-95).

The most important written source for the early history of Northumbria (as indeed for all of Anglo-Saxon England) is unquestionably Bede's *Historia Ecclesiastica*, and it was perhaps inevitable that Hunter Blair should have devoted so many years' scholarly energy to elucidating and evaluating Bede. His Bedan studies began in earnest with work on one of the two most important surviving manuscripts of the *Historia Ecclesiastica*, the so-called 'Moore Bede' (now Cambridge, University Library, MS Kk.5.16), a manuscript written in Northumbria shortly after Bede's death. Hunter Blair's study of this manuscript issued in his valuable facsimile edition: *The Moore Bede*, Early English Manuscripts in Facsimile IX (Copenhagen, 1959). An important by-product of his work on the Moore manuscript was his discussion and analysis of the so-called 'Moore Memoranda' (VI), a series of chronological entries copied at the end of the text of the *Historia Ecclesiastica* which are a unique witness to events in Northumbria after Bede's death.

Hunter Blair's long and intimate familiarity with Bede and his critical attempts to evaluate Bede as a historical source are seen to splendid advantage in two public lectures which are reprinted here — the Jarrow Lecture of 1959 (VII) and a lecture delivered in Spoleto in 1969 (X) — as well as in a brief but important analysis of the correspondence of Pope Boniface V concerning the Northumbrian mission as reported in Book II of Bede's *Historia Ecclesiastica* (XI). These essays in the critical evaluation of Bede culminated in 1970 in the publication of his book *The World of Bede* (London: Secker & Warburg), widely recognised as the best overall account in any language of Bede and his Northumbrian context. A similar work, intended for a wider public but containing

iv

mature and valuable insights on every page, is his *Northumbria in the Days of Bede* (London: Victor Gollancz Ltd., 1976).

In the final essay in this volume (XII), Hunter Blair turned his attention to the period following Bede's death. Beginning with the evidence for Bede's literary training and the books known to him, Hunter Blair proceeded to ask probing questions about the transmission of these books to later generations in Northumbria, in particular to the school of studies at York as described by Alcuin in his poem on 'The Bishops, Kings and Saints of York' (Alcuin's poem has recently been edited with translation by Peter Godman [Oxford, 1982]; Godman's commentary permits several corrections to be made to Hunter Blair's identifications of authors listed by Alcuin, such as Pompeius). In one important respect Hunter Blair's evaluation of Bede's literary training has been superseded. He argued that Bede knew Vergil only at second-hand; but in making this argument he underestimated the importance of Bede's own metrical *Vita S. Cuthberti*, which is deeply indebted to Vergilian diction at every point, and hence the argument that Bede knew no Vergil cannot stand (see N. Wright, 'Bede and Vergil', *Romanobarbarica* 6 [1981-2], 361-79). Nevertheless, in the questions it asks and the method it follows, the essay is a pioneering study of Latin learning in early Northumbria.

It will be seen that, although they stretch over a period of some forty years and bear on different aspects of scholarly problems, the essays collected here are unified by a single interest and purpose. They stand not only as a memorial to a loved and respected scholar, but as a major contribution to our understanding of Anglo-Saxon Northumbria.

MICHAEL LAPIDGE

Department of Anglo-Saxon,
Cambridge,
July 1983

PETER HUNTER BLAIR, 1912-1982

Peter Hunter Blair considered himself a Northumbrian by inclination as well as by birth. Born in Gosforth in 1912, he was sent at a tender age to Bow Preparatory School in Durham. ('There's Bow', he announced at intervals as we circled newly-routed Durham on an hilarious occasion trying to get in to the citadel.) Thence to Durham School. Matins and evensong at the Cathedral remained in his romantic soul for ever: and when in 1979 we slept in King James's faded four-poster in the deanery guest flat, with the hours (quartered) tumbling clamorously over the cloister from the great clock all night, the noise did not matter: it was *his* cathedral. He talked of childhood holidays in Galloway, Rothbury, Bamburgh, the Cheviots. When he introduced me to his own particular milecastle, known as number thirty-seven, near Housesteads on Hadrian's Wall, which he dug in 1932, he was remembering a magical long vacation spent at Chesterholm, now the site of the Vindolanda Museum.

The magic re-awoke; lecturing visits in the seventies were filled with equal ecstasy: 'great and glorious day', he records in his diary of his O'Donnell lecture, 'Edinburgh glittering with romance'. And a few weeks later: 'York all resplendent on a cold clear night with its walls and Minster alight'. And of St Andrews: ' . . . all glorious – how I should have loved it as an undergraduate!' No wonder he once said to me in a voice of bewildered protest: 'I have been exiled all my life in Cambridge'. When we tried to discover the rights of this life-long dichotomy by buying an old Manse near Duns (Berwickshire) for vacations and possible retirement, he wrote of it as his 'childhood's dream, a stone house in Scotland'. Here for five years we possessed the north, he renewing his devotion – for his first happy marriage to Joyce Thompson, his family and his college had kept him largely in the south for twenty years – I drunk with it for the first time. Here much of his last book, *Northumbria in the Days of Bede*, the distillation of his Northumbrian and Bede studies, was written, as its flavour attests. But he describes his joy as if the dice were too strongly loaded against it: ' . . . the wood seemed peopled by every kind of divinity and myself possessed by it all – a great longing to cut off from the south and stay in these northern parts – it has taken three summers to feel again the old magic, but I suppose it may not be'.

In the event and for many reasons the 'flat-lands' reclaimed us and if a proof of his devotion to his calling and his college were needed, it is here. His father indeed (Charles Hunter Blair, the esteemed Newcastle antiquary), in directing him to the university of the Cam ('that muddy stream' Peter would laugh, thinking of the beer-brown torrents of the north) had in effect laid the course of his life. He was nurtured by H. M. Chadwick, awarded the Scandinavian Studentship, elected after the war to a Fellowship at Emmanuel and a University Lectureship in the Department of Anglo-Saxon, Norse and Celtic, and served the university and his college for the rest of his life. At Emmanuel he was Tutor, Praelector, Senior Tutor (slightly against his will: he saw his own scholarship flying out of the window), Vice-Master and Archivist. Hundreds of young men remembered him as Senior Tutor (1951-65): he cudgelled his memory to recall them when they greeted him, and often succeeded. More easily they recalled him: sitting, for instance, below the college wall on a Bumps supper occasion, gravely wishing each wanderer goodnight by name as he (illicitly) climbed in.

But he was scholar as well as college man. He was gently but firmly pushed by Professor Whitelock towards a Litt.D., which he took in 1973 (he was often self-distrustful, though he seemed calm and confident enough to the younger students he taught) and became Reader in Anglo-Saxon History from 1974 until his retirement in 1978. A certain shy and humble childlikeness (at odds with the awe-inspiring presence) did not preclude a proper pride. When his gown was stolen off its college peg in 1974 he confided to his diary: ' – greatly distressed – it is my Litt.D. gown and I was proud of it'. His proposed election to Fellowship of the British Academy in 1980 he quite genuinely, at first, could not believe.

He was longing for total retirement (his re-indexing of the Emmanuel College archives being virtually complete) so that he could pursue further some new work on Hild of Whitby and double monasteries in early Northumbria, upon which he had lectured in vintage form in November 1981, and about which he was deeply excited (his posthumous essay, 'Whitby as a Centre of Learning in the Seventh Century', is forthcoming in a volume entitled *Learning and Literature in Anglo-Saxon England: Studies presented to Peter Clemoes*, edited by Michael Lapidge and Helmut Gneuss and printed by the Cambridge University Press). His first account of his research, as a young man in 1939, has in view a history of Northumbria, 'a large subject', he admits sagely. These essays, spanning his whole career, forays into realms after his own heart, form a part of that large subject, the subject of his working life.

PAULINE HUNTER BLAIR

Bottisham, Cambridge
July 1983

ACKNOWLEDGEMENTS

Acknowledgement is gratefully made to the following for permission to reproduce the essays in this collection: the University Museum of National Antiquities, Viking Ship Museum, Oslo (I); The Society of Antiquaries of Newcastle upon Tyne (II, III, IV, V); Cambridge University Press (VI, VIII, IX, X); the Rector of St Paul's Church, Jarrow (VII); the Centro italiano di studi sull'alto medioevo (X); and SPCK (XII). Acknowledgement is also made to the Master and Fellows of Corpus Christi College, Cambridge, for permission to reproduce Plate I (a) in Study IX; and to the Syndics of the University Library, Cambridge, for Plate XI in Study VI and Plate I (b) and (c) in Study XI. Miss Sarah Foot kindly compiled the Index.

OLAF THE WHITE
AND THE THREE FRAGMENTS
OF IRISH ANNALS

The source which is commonly known as the Three Fragments has been used by almost every writer on the viking age since it was first published together with an English translation in 1860[1]. It is a document written mainly in Irish, but with occasional sentences in Latin, and as its name indicates it consists of three distinct series of Irish annals of which the first stretches from 573 to 735, the second from 662 to 704 and the third from 851 to 913. The third of these, with which alone the following study is concerned, covers an important period of the viking age and one for which there is little evidence from the Scandinavian side. For this reason, and also because it has for long been accessible in an English translation, the evidence of the source has been freely used both by English and Scandinavian scholars, but usually without any understanding of what the source is or of the value of the evidence it provides. The only attempt to estimate the reliability of the source as a whole for the history of the vikings in the west seems to be that made by Jan de Vries in the Norsk Historisk Tidsskrift[2] and he comes to the conclusion that the source is far from being real history. He points out the marked contrasts in style which it contains. Long verbose accounts of battles and other events alternate with series of brief entries which are purely annalistic in style, and it at once becomes apparent that the source is composite and that there is no verdict which can be applied equally to all parts of it. The series of brief annalistic notices, as de Vries points out, frequently do not belong to the same year as the events described immediately before or after. Dates are seldom introduced and the Fragment at first sight appears to be without any chronological scheme. In addition to de Vries's article, there is a short paper in Révue Celtique[3], written by van Hamel, in which some entries of the Three Fragments relating to events which took place outside Ireland are critically examined. The author was well aware of the composite nature of the source but he confined his examination to only one very small part of it.

Close study of the third Fragment quickly removes the first impression that it is no more than a mass of material assembled without regard for order or chronology[4]. It can be clearly demonstrated that the foundation of the source consists of an annalistic history, composed of a series of brief annals similar to those found in the annals of Ulster and pursuing a regular chronological sequence. Dating by the Christian era or by the regular year of a king plays no part in this series, but the events of each year are defined by what for long seems to have been the normal method employed by the Irish chroniclers, a method which was still in use as late as 1102. This method consisted of inserting at the head of each year, not a date, but the letter "K" or the abbreviation "Kal.", standing for "Kalendae (Januarii)". The number of events recorded in each year varies considerably, from one in some years to as many as nine or ten in others. The style and contents of the brief annals which follow immediately after the abbreviation "Kal." suggests that they are the work of an annalist who was writing very soon after the events which he describes. Entries of this type form one distinct element in the source, and it seems clear that entries of at least two other types have been imposed at a later date upon this original material. Standing at the opposite extreme to the brief annals are several long passages which can only be described as saga. The contrast which they offer to the element described above is as strong as can be imagined. The author seems to have made it his object to use as many words as possible and the resulting stories cannot be described as history in any sense of the word. The third element stands somewhere between these two extremes and it consists of a series of annals which for some reason or other arouses suspicion. The following is an example of such an entry:

"In this year also, the sixth year of the reign of Maelsechlainn, Amhlaeibh Conung, i. e. the son of the king of Lochlann, came to Erin and he brought with him commands from his father for many rents and tributes, but he left suddenly. Imhar, his younger brother, came after him to levy the same rents." (Three Fragments 124—7.)[5]

There are at least three reasons for feeling suspicious about this entry. First, the assignation of an event to a regnal year is not usually found in contemporary annals. This is not the usage, for example, of the Anglo-Saxon chronicle or of the annals of Ulster. Second, the entry cannot be strictly contemporary with the events which it describes because it refers not only to Amhlaeibh's departure but also to the subsequent arrival of Imhar. Third, the word "Conung" applied to Amhlaeibh is a Norse loan-word and it would hardly be found in an annal which was written c. 850. For these reasons the entry cannot be accepted as a contemporary record. It is one example of many similar entries, which for convenience may be styled embellished annals. It remains only to remark now that the abbreviation "Kal." occurs in all twenty six times in the Fragment: in other words, the source is divided into twenty six sections each of which represents one year, though in practice it will be found that all the events recorded between two "Kal.s" do not necessarily belong to the same year. The sequence of years is fairly regular until 874, but after that there are long gaps in the source. With these preliminary remarks, we can now consider what use has been made of this source in the past, so far as concerns viking history, and whether that use is justified.

The Fragment contains several passages about a man called Amhlaeibh whom it generally describes as the son of the king of Lochlann. The name is an Irish form of the Norse Olaf which appears in Anglo-Saxon sources as Anlaf. Other Irish sources show that Amhlaeibh was one of the most prominent of the Norse vikings in Ireland, where he first arrived in 853. For some twenty years he was actively engaged in the west in association with a man called in Irish, Imhar, which is the Norse Ivar. It has long been a problem whether the man who is known in the Irish annals as Amhlaeibh is the same as Olaf the White, described in Norse sources as King of Dublin. The history of Olaf the White is briefly recounted in Landnamabok where it is said that he was the son of Ingjald, the son of Helgi, the son of Olof, the son of Godfrey, the son of Halfdan Whiteleg, king of the Uplanders[6]. The same pedigree is also found in Ari's Islendingabok, in Njal's saga and in the tract Af Upplendinga Konungum[7]. Landnamabok records that Olaf the White went on a piratical expedition to the west where he captured Dublin and Dublinshire and was made king over it. He married a famous woman, Aud the Deepminded, and they had a son called Thorstein the Red. Olaf was eventually killed in Ireland, after which Aud and Thorstein went to the western isles. There are three points in this Norse account which, it has been said, argue strongly against the identification of the Norse chief Olaf the White with the Irish Amhlaeibh. The genealogy of Olaf the White, the fact of his marriage with Aud the Deepminded and the fact that he was killed in Ireland, are all said to be contradicted by the evidence of the Fragment[8].

The arrival of Amhlaeibh in Ireland is recorded twice in the Fragment. One of the passages is that which is quoted above and the second is as follows:

"Amhlaeibh, son of the king of Lochlann, came to Erin and the Galls of Erin submitted to him."

(Three Fragments 134—5.)

Reasons have been given above for thinking that the first of the two entries recording Amhlaeibh's arrival is of late construction, and I do not think it can be regarded as anything more than a late, amplified version of the second. The Fragment also contains references to the marriage of a person called Amhlaeibh in two distinct places. The first passage is in the middle of year section ten (i. e. the section which follows the tenth "Kal.") where the record of a plundering expedition to the plains of Meath is prefaced with the following words "Aedh, son of Niall, and his son-in-law i. e. Amhlaeibh (the daughter of Aedh was wife to Amhlaeibh) set out with great forces of Gaeidhil and Lochlanns . . . . . ."[9]. The fact of this expedition is witnessed by entries in the annals of Ulster 861 and in the annals of the Four Masters 860. In these two places, however, Aedh is said to have been accompanied by the kings of the foreigners and their names are not mentioned nor is there anything to parallel the statement that Amhlaeibh was the son-in-law of Aedh. I do not think that this Amhlaeibh, described as Aedh's son-in-law, is to be identified with Olaf the White because a son of Aedh was at this time married to Gormflaith and the implication is that Gormflaith and Amhlaeibh were contemporaries. Gormflaith, however, died in 948 and Olaf the White within a year or two of 870.

The second passage about Amhlaeibh's marriage is found in year section 15 in the following context. The king of the Lochlanns had three sons called Amhlaeibh, Imhar, and Oisli. Oisli was the youngest of the three, but because he excelled the others in warlike pursuits, they resolved to kill him. Oisli came on one occasion to visit his brothers and

"he requested a thing which he did not think would be granted him. He first requested that freedom of speech should be granted him, and what he said was: 'Brother' said he 'if thou art not fond of thy wife the daughter of Cinaeth, why not give her away to me, and whatever dower thou hast given for her, I shall give to thee."

(Three Fragments 171—3.)

Amhlaeibh was seized with jealousy when he heard this and drawing his sword, he slew Oisli. One of the objections to the identity of Amhlaeibh and Olaf the White is based on this passage. It has been

5

said that because Amhlaeibh was married to a daughter of Cinaeth MacAilpin[10] at the same time as Olaf the White was married to Aud the Deepminded, the two cannot be identical. The passage has also been used to explain the invasion of Alba (western Scotland) in 866. Kenneth MacAlpin having died, Amhlaeibh was attempting to claim the lordship of certain lands through the right of his wife[11]. The story of Amhlaeibh, Imhar and Oisli is obviously a late construction of a type similar to other saga entries in the Fragment and the slight foundation of truth which underlies it cannot possibly bear the weight of the superstructure that has been built upon it. That there were three viking chiefs with the same names in Ireland at this period is shown by the annals of Ulster which in 862 record the plundering of the land of Flann by three kings of the foreigners "to wit Amhlaim and Imhar and Auisle". The same source records later that Auisle, the third king of the foreigners, was slain by his brothers (866). It is greatly to be doubted that these three vikings were in fact brothers. Such a relationship might easily have been given by an Irish annalist to chieftains of the same race who were closely associated with each other in Ireland, and the word "fratres" in the annals of Ulster 866 could just as well be translated "brethren", meaning to imply no more than affinity of race. Again the Fragment does not say that Amhlaeibh was married to a daughter of Kenneth MacAlpin, but only to a daughter of Cinaeth. Kenneth is, of course, only the modern form of the name Cinaeth, but it is a name which is very common in the Irish annals and there is no reason at all for supposing that this particular Cinaeth was Kenneth MacAlpin. The latter's death is recorded elsewhere in the Fragment which then gives the full name, "Cinaedh MacAilpin" and not merely "Cinaedh".

The most important of the passages relating to Amhlaeibh are to be found in the nineteenth year section. Following the abbreviation "Kal." at the head of this section, is a series of ten regular annals, all of which are shown by comparison with the annals of Ulster and the annals of the Four Masters to belong to 871. Amongst them there is an account of the return of Amhlaeibh and Imhar to Dublin after the successful attack on Dumbarton in the previous year. The remainder of the year section contains the two following passages:

1. "Amhlaeibh went from Erin to Lochlann to wage war on the Lochlanns and to aid his father Goffridh, for the Lochlanns had made war against him, his father having come for him; but as it would be tedious to relate the cause of this war, and besides it appertains but little to us, though we have a knowledge of it, we forbear writing it, for our business is not to write whatever may belong to Erin, nor even all these; for the Irish suffer evils, not only from Lochlanns but they also suffer injuries from one another.

2. In this year the tenth of the reign of Aedh Finnliath, Imhar son of Gofraidh son of Ragnall son of Gofraidh Conung son of Gofraidh, and the son of the man who went away from Erin, i. e. Amhlaeibh, plundered all Erin from west to east, and from north to south." (195)

Gustav Storm[12] seems to have been the first to suggest an interpretation of these two passages. His views which were published in 1880 were based on the belief that the passages in question provide reliable information about events which took place in the year 871 and this is a belief which does not seem ever to have been seriously challenged. There is a poem about the battle of Hafrsfirth which is preserved in Fagrskinna and in Heimskringla[13]. In the one place it is assigned to Tjodolfr of Hvin and in the other to Thorbjorn Hornklofi. The scaldic poems are at all times obscure and difficult to understand, nor is this one any exception to the general rule. Three of the combatants in the battle are mentioned by what seem to be nicknames. One of the leaders is called Kjøtvi the Wealthy and he is shown defending his land Lúfa, a king of noble lineage. Kjøtvi's followers are said to have carried "spears from the west and swords from France". The name given to the third combatant is Haklangr. He was fighting on the same

7

side as Kjøtvi and his death seems to have turned the tide of battle in Lúfa's favour. Lúfa (i. e. shock-head) is to be identified with Harald Fairhair. It was the name given to him because he had made a vow not to cut his hair until he was ruler of all Norway. The correctness of this identification cannot be disputed. The other two names are more difficult. Various accounts of the battle have been preserved in Icelandic literature and Storm shows[14] that in thirteenth century tradition, represented by Egil's saga, Snorre, Landnamabok and Gretti's saga, Haklangr has become Thorir Haklangr. Kjøtvi remains unaltered but in Vatnsdøla saga, which dates from c. 1400, it has become Asbjørn Kjøtvi. Storm argues that the older Icelandic accounts of the battle of Hafrsfirth are based on the poem preserved in Fagrskinna and Heims-kringla and, accordingly, information which is found in the sagas, but not in the poem, must be regarded as more than uncertain. He comes to the conclusion that all we can say about the battle of Hafrsfirth is that Harald's opponent was a king Kjøtvi and that amongst the fol-lowers of the latter were another king, with the name Haklangr, and companies of vikings of the western isles. Storm thus sweeps aside the whole of Norse tradition about the battle. Having thus cleared the ground, he turns to the viking kingdom of Dublin and its rulers Amhlaeibh and Imhar whom he describes as sons of Gudrød Ragnvaldsson, king in Lochlann. He quotes the Fragment's account of Amhlaeibh's return to Lochlann and says that since he is never heard of again he must have died on that expedition. The date of Amhlaeibh's recall was 871 according to the Fragment, and according to Are's reckoning, the date of the battle of Hafrsfirth was 871 or 872. Therefore, Storm concludes, the name Kjøtvi stands for Goffraidh and the name Haklangr for Amhlaeibh. Thus the Norse poem and the Irish Fragment together show how Guthfrith, a king in Lochlann, got help from his son king Olaf of Dublin. The latter would naturally bring his men with him and thus are the "spears from the west and swords from France" to be explained. Haklangr, according to the poem, was killed. The Irish account shows that the danger must have been very great because Guthfrith himself came to Ireland to fetch his son. The rise of Harald Fairhair to power would mean just such a danger to a king like Kjøtvi. Considering his hypothesis proved, i. e. that Haklangr = Olaf Guthfrithsson = Amhlaeibh of the Irish annals, Storm elaborates his theory and tries to show that the whole position of the vikings in the west was influenced by Harald's victory and the death of Olaf. The destruction of the royal house of Dublin in the person of Olaf and the consequent severing of the connection between Norway and Dublin may be taken to explain the period of forty years during which Ireland was "without ravage of foreigners"[15]. He thought that not only Ireland, but also parts of Scotland and the Scottish Isles were affected by the death of Olaf. The expedition made by Harald to the west soon after the battle of Hafrsfirth and the creation of the earldom of Orkney, led to a complete change in the relations between Norway and the Scandinavian settlements "west over seas".

Storm accepted the genealogy given in the second of the two entries in the Fragment as that of a royal family of Agder. Since then attempts have been made to connect it with the royal house of Vestfold whose genealogy is recorded by Ynglingatal. The following are four of the kings in the list preserved in Ynglingatal:

> Halfdan the Bounteous and Meat Grudging,
> Gudrød the Hunter king,
> Olaf of Geirstead,
> Rognvaldr Higher than the Hills.

Three of the names found here are in the genealogy given by the Fragment, but beyond this the two genealogies have no points in common. De Vries considered the Irish genealogy to be suspect, but he pointed out that Gudrød the Hunter King and Olaf of Geirstead ruled at about the same time as Goffraidh and Amhlaeibh and he suggested as a possible explanation of the differences between the two

9

genealogies that, although Ynglingatal records the names of the successive rulers, it need not be supposed that it was always the son who succeeded the father. The Irish genealogy is of considerable importance because, if it is accepted as representing the descent of Amhlaeibh, it is a serious argument against the identity of Amhlaeibh with Olaf the White. The descent of Olaf the White is well known from Norse sources and, as shown above, it is quite different from that given in the Fragment. Similarly, the evidence of the Fragment may be thought to conflict with Landnamabok which says that Olaf the White fell in battle in Ireland. It is true that the Fragment does not say that Amhlaeibh was killed in Lochlann, but since he is never heard of again in Ireland, almost all writers on the subject have assumed that he was.

It is obvious that any interpretation of the two entries in the Fragment must depend on an estimate of their authority. Storm's hypothesis was founded on the belief that the ninth century Irish annals must rank as higher authority than thirteenth century Icelandic tradition. This, of course, is true, but it in turn rests on the belief that these particular entries were in fact written in the ninth century. Analysis of the Fragment shows that the whole work is not all of the same value and we are not entitled to speak of it as a ninth century source. Parts of it are clearly much later, perhaps almost as late as the Icelandic traditions relating to the same period, and the entries, therefore, must be more closely examined.

Neither of the two is a contemporary annal. The contents and wording of the first show it to be not merely retrospective but also the work of a man who was consciously compiling a history which was confined within limits. The author could therefore omit facts which were not relevant to the subject with which he was dealing. The second entry has more the appearance of an annal but it is betrayed by its opening words. These are the words of a man anxious to demonstrate his knowledge of history and his skill in chronology.

Secondly, I do not know of any parallel in either Irish or Norse sources for the information which is given here. On two counts, therefore, the entries are to be considered suspect.

The first of the two entries seems to say that Amhlaeibh was recalled to Scandinavia by his father in order that he might help his father against the enemies who were making war against him. The name of Amhlaeibh's father is given as Goffridh, old Norse Guthfrith. The war in question was evidently one of considerable importance and the scribe had information about it but, because it did not strictly concern Ireland, he refrained from writing it down. This is a curious feature of the entry and one which gives a vivid glimpse of the scribe at work selecting his material. The second entry records the plundering of the whole of Erin by Imhar and the son of Amhlaeibh. The reference to Amhlaeibh as "the man who went away from Erin" shows that the two entries are intimately connected with one another and ought to be considered together. It is not surprising that there should be no record of this "plundering" in the other annals, as the description of it is so vague that it is hard to believe that such a plundering can ever have taken place. The chief interest of the second entry is the genealogy which it contains. It gives the descent of Imhar, carrying back his ancestry four generations. Three of the four names which it contains are the same, namely Goffraidh, and the fourth is Ragnall. Strictly speaking the genealogy belongs to Imhar and not to Amhlaeibh, but since the first of the two entries calls Amhlaeibh's father Goffridh, really the same as Goffraidh, and since the Fragment elsewhere calls Imhar and Amhlaeibh brothers, it can be applied to either or both of the two. The genealogy itself is quite unlike any other genealogy found in the Irish annals at this time. When the Irish annalists record anything about a man's descent, they give either the name of his father or else the name of his grandfather, but, at least so far as concerns the vikings, I do not recall a single instance other than the present, where the name of more than one ancestor is given. The recurrence

11

I

of the name Goffraidh is another curious feature. Calculating thirty years to a generation, the first Goffraidh should have been living about 750, but as de Vries points out[18] it is most unlikely that at this early period the name Goffraidh should occur three times in four generations of the same family.

There are other reasons of rather a different kind which can be brought against Storm's hypothesis. The battle of Hafrsfirth seems to mark the beginning of Norway's history as a single kingdom, and Harald Fairhair, at least in Snorre's eyes, was the first king of all Norway. He seems to have become a national hero to whom all kinds of achievements were assigned. Institutions which were probably in existence long before Harald's time were assigned to him as the first historical figure and, as a result, Harald's own person and the events connected with his life received an importance out of relation to reality. In recent years the evidence of other kinds of material has been brought to bear upon the history of Scandinavia during the viking age so that a better estimate can be formed of the value of thirteenth century tradition for ninth century history. There was evidently nothing odd to Storm, writing in 1880, in the circumstance that an Irish scribe should have had information about the battle of Hafrsfirth. News of a battle of such importance and of such far-reaching political consequences might be expected to reach the British Isles within a short time. Storm himself does not refer to the curious feature of the entry to which attention has already been drawn. The scribe says, in effect, that he knew all about the war which led to Amhlaeibh's recall to Scandinavia. The change of attitude is reflected in de Vries's article on the Three Fragments. He plainly realised that it was most unlikely that an Irish annalist could have known about the battle of Hafrsfirth, if the entry does in fact refer to that event, and he explains the difficulty by saying the annalist did not really know any more about the war, but was anxious to impress his readers with his learning[19]. Little or nothing seems to have been known in the British Isles about Scandinavia

12

before the reign of Alfred. The first authentic information is contained in the accounts of the voyages of Wulfstan and Ohthere which Alfred wrote in the introduction to his translation to Orosius. The points in which Alfred was interested were the geography of Scandinavia and the principal commodities in which its people traded. Nothing at all is said about political events. Even at a later date when there was some contact between the ruling houses of Norway and England, there is no reason to suppose that the earliest history of the Scandinavian kingdoms was ever a subject of interest to chroniclers in the British Isles. The Irish annals contain very few notices of foreign events and these are mostly confined to events which happened in England, Scotland, or Wales. They reveal an almost remarkable ignorance about the lands from which the vikings came, not even giving the names of the lands, much less details of their history. It is, therefore, impossible to believe that an Irish annalist in the ninth century could have known anything about the battle of Hafrsfirth and, even if he was writing in the tenth or eleventh centuries, it is most unlikely that he could have had any details about a war of which very little is known even in Icelandic tradition.

For these various reasons Storm's interpretation of the two passages must be rejected. The passages themselves are not reliable and therefore the whole hypothesis built upon them falls to the ground. The explanation which is put forward in the following pages to take the place of Storm's hypothesis has as its starting point the curious resemblance of the names in Imhar's genealogy to the names of the Scandinavian kings of Northumbria in the first half of the tenth century. In order to make this clear it will be necessary to review the history of Scandinavian Northumbria from about 876 as far as the battle of Brunanburh in 937.

The principal sources of Northumbrian history in the late ninth and early tenth centuries are the works ascribed to Symeon of Durham and in particular his Historia Regum, a work whose composite character has long been recognized. The Historia Regum begins in 616 and it contains fairly regular entries as far as 957 at which point a break is caused by the introduction of a long extract from William of Malmesbury. The history then returns to the year 851 and continues its account from there to 1129. There are therefore two accounts in it of events from 851 to 957[20]. Arnold, the editor of the works of Symeon of Durham in the Rolls Series[21], advanced reasons for believing that one section of Historia Regum "A", from 731 to 957, represents a separate compilation made by a monk of St. Cuthbert whom he styled "the Cuthbertine" and whom he supposed to have been writing in the late tenth or early eleventh century. Until 887 the Cuthbertine drew on the lost Northumbrian chronicle known as the Gesta Veterum Northanhymbrorum and Asser's life of Alfred, but after the end of Asser's work he was left to his own devices. His work contains some valuable information about the history of Northumbria during the first half of the tenth century and it embodies a short series of what seem to be almost contemporary annals. Historia Regum "B" was, according to Arnold, compiled by Symeon from Florence of Worcester and Eadmer with additions from other sources. In addition to the Historia Regum, there are the Historia Dunelmensis Ecclesiae, the anonymous Historia de Sancto Cuthberto and two tracts containing genealogies of the Anglo-Saxon kings and lists of bishops. The importance of the Irish annals for the history of Northumbria in this period was recognized as long ago as 1867 by D. H. Haigh who made use of the annals of Ulster, the annals of Clonmacnoise and the annals of the Four Masters[22].

Halfdene's division of the lands of Northumbria amongst his followers marked the beginning of the Danelagh. The circumstances of his death are not altogether clear, but he seems to have died in Ireland in 877 whilst attempting to etablish control over the Dublin Norse after the deaths of Olaf the White and Ivar. The next Scandinavian ruler of Northumbria whose name is known, was Guthred, a mysterious person about whom very little reliable information has been preserved. What is to be regarded as perhaps the most authentic statement about him is found in Aethelweard[23] and is to the effect that his death took place four years before the death of Alfred and that he was buried in York. The story how he came to be made king is told in Historia Regum "B"[24] where it is said that Eadred, abbot of Carlisle, was instructed in a vision to tell the Danish and English armies to redeem a certain Guthred, son of Hardecnut, who had been sold as a slave to a widow at Hwitingaham and to make him their king. This was done and Guthred, after being made king, bestowed numerous gifts upon the see of St. Cuthbert, including all the lands between Tees and Wear. The same story is also found in Historia Dunelmensis Ecclesiae[25]. This source lays considerable stress on Guthred's donations to the church and in addition it records that soon after Guthred's accession the Scots invaded Northumbria and destroyed Lindisfarne. Guthred prepared to resist them but just as battle was about to begin the Scottish army was swallowed in the earth. This event is recorded in the Irish annals[26] and also in the Historia de Sancto Cuthberto[27]. The dates of Guthred's reign are generally said to be 883—894. Neither of these two dates, which are derived from Symeon, is reliable. The second is contradicted by Aethelweard who places Guthred's death four years before Alfred's and also by the Annales Lindisfarnenses which give 893. There are also serious objections for the date 883 for Guthred's accession. This date is found in Historia Regum "A", but both the date and the accompanying record of Guthred's accession are interlineations in the manuscript. It is found also in Historia Regum "B", but the date is here followed, not by an annal recording the mere fact of Guthred's accession, but by a long descriptive entry which records the manner of Halfdene's death, the story of Guthred's election and the number of gifts which he made to the see of St. Cuthbert. In other words, the entry is a narrative which spreads over a number of years. It may therefore be permitted to doubt the authority of

Symeon's date 883. There is also a positive objection to it. The Irish version of the campaign in which the Scottish army was swallowed in the earth records that Constantine, son of Cinaedh, king of Alba, was killed on that occasion. Constantine, however, is known to have been dead by 877[28] and since the invasion took place during Guthred's reign, Symeon's date 883 for the accession of Guthred must be wrong. The tracts, mentioned above, give no dates with their list of kings but according to the order of succession which they give[29], Egbert was set up as king by the Danes over the Northumbrian survivors after the fall of York and it is said that he reigned five years. He was succeeded by Richsi who reigned two years and he by Egbert II who also reigned two years and was succeeded by Guthred. If Egbert I began to reign in 867, the year after the fall of York, Guthred according to this reckoning would have succeeded in 877 and this is in fact the date which is implied by the order of Symeon's narrative in Historia Regum "B". It is said there that the army which had been under the command of Halfdene remained without a leader after his death. "Jam subactis sibi indigenis terrae, dominium usurpavit ibique manere paravit, et vastatas Northumbriae provincias incolere."[30] Immediately after this follows the story of Eadred's vision and the election of Guthred. There is no suggestion in this narrative of any interregnum of seven years, during which the army remained without a leader, in itself a thing most unlikely to have happened.

Various attempts have been made to explain Guthred's identity and that which is most widely accepted is that Guthred was the same as a king Cnut whose name is found on large numbers of coins in the famous Cuerdale hoard[31]. This hoard which was found in a leaden chest near a difficult ford of the Ribble about two miles above Preston, contained, in addition to much other treasure, upwards of 7 000 coins. The first three of the six issues of Edward the Elder are represented in the hoard and from the fact that the third was current at the time of its deposit, the hoard may be dated between 909 and 912. It has been very reasonably suggested that it represents part of the treasure which was abandoned by the Northumbrian viking army in its hasty retreat after the battle of Tettenhall. More than 2000 of the coins were issues of Northumbrian ecclesiastical mints and 2534 of the rest belonged to a king Cnut. The historical sources do not record any king Cnut who ruled in Northumbria in this period, and, since there are no coins which are known to have been issued by Guthred, it is argued that the coins which bear Cnut's names are really Guthred's and that the name Cnut is to be explained as Guthred's baptismal name. There are two principal objections to this theory. It was a common practice for heathen kings to adopt another name after baptism, but that a heathen king would adopt after baptism another heathen name, such as Cnut, is most unlikely. Secondly it has been pointed out that Cnut's coins in the Cuerdale hoard were not only in better condition than any of the other coins in the hoard, but many of them were, when they were found, as fresh as if they had just come from the die[32]. Yet if Cnut was Guthred who died c. 894, all these coins should have been in circulation for seventeen years, if the deposit of the hoard is to be connected with the battle of Tettenhall in 911.

Guthred's origin evidently puzzled Symeon as it must continue to puzzle us. I have suggested that Guthred succeeded to the Northumbrian kingdom within about a year of Halfdene's death and it seems to me not unlikely that he may have come to Northumbria from Ireland. The Irish source which records Halfdene's death says that after that event some of the vikings were driven out of Ireland and went to Alba (i. e. Scotland) where they won a battle. Constantine the king of Alba was slain in this battle and, the source continues "it was on that occasion that the earth burst open under the men of Alba"[33]. This must surely refer to the invasion of Northumbria during Guthred's reign when, according to the Historia de Sancto Cuthberto[34], the Scottish army was swallowed in the earth, and there is at least a suggestion that Guthred may have been one of the leaders of those vikings who

17

left Ireland after Halfdene's death in 877, but of this more will be said later[35].

For a brief period after the death of Guthred, Northumbria was drawn back into the affairs of the rest of England. Coins indicate the existence of a ruler Siegfried or Sigeferth[36], but it is certain that the Scandinavian hold on York was temporarily weakened, otherwise the Northumbrians would hardly have accepted as their king a nephew of Alfred who had made a valiant but unsuccessful attempt to seize the kingdom of Wessex in opposition to the rightful heir, Edward the Elder[37]. In 906 the latter was in a position to dictate a peace to Northumbria which seems to have been observed for the next five years till it was broken by the advance of a Northumbrian army into Mercia[38]. The army was overtaken on its way home and severely defeated in the battle of Tettenhall in which two viking kings, Eowils and Halfdan, were slain together with a number of other distinguished people[39].

The next Scandinavian ruler of Northumbria was a famous viking called Ragnall whose name appears in English and Latin sources as Regnold, Reignuald, Inguald and Reginaldus and who in the Irish annals is described as a grandson of Imhar. Ragnall is first heard of fighting against Barid, son of Ottir, in a naval battle off the coast of Man in 914[40]. In 917 he was associated in warfare with Sihtric against Nial Glundubh, high king of Ireland[41]. This Sihtric is also described as a grandson of Imhar, a description which is given to many Norsemen in the Irish annals and which implies that Sithric was a brother or cousin of Ragnall. In the following year Ragnall, with two earls called Ottir and Graggaba, left Ireland and went to Alba. The men of Alba met them on the banks of the river Tyne. According to the account of this battle which is given in the annals of Ulster, the vikings divided themselves into four battalions, one with Gothfrith, one with the two earls and one with the young lords. Ragnall remained in ambush with the fourth. The men of Alba, attacking the three divisions which they saw, at first carried all before them, but Ragnall fell upon them from the rear and eventually won the day. Ottir and Graggaba were both killed. There is a reference to this campaign in a brief annal in Historia Regum "A" under the date 912:

Reignwald rex et Oter comes et Oswl Cracabam irruperunt et vastaverunt Dunbline.[42]

Where "Dunbline" is I do not know but there seems no reason beyond the similarity of names for its identification with Dunblane. Ottir (Oter) was the leader of a band of vikings who settled at Waterford on the south coast of Ireland. The Annales Cambria record that he was in Britain in 913, probably in Anglesey or Wales, and in the following year it was his son Barid who was defeated by Ragnall in the battle off the Isle of Man, with the result apparently that Ottir submitted to, or allied himself with, Ragnall. It is quite likely that Ottir had been in Wales some years earlier than this. The Annales Cambriae record under 906 "gueith Dinmeir et Miniu fracta est". Manuscript C has "bellum Dynerth" and the annal is evidently to be connected with a passage in Caradoc of Llancarfan which records the battle of Dinarth, following the destruction of St. Davids by a fleet under the command of "Uther" and "Rahald"[43]. It is said in this source that this "Rahald" was killed soon afterwards, so that he cannot have been the same as Ragnall. Nothing is known about Oswl Cracabam, the third of the three leaders in the entry quoted above, but his name suggests that he may have been English. The preservation of the names of these three leaders provides an instance of the curious contact between Historia Regum "A" and the Irish annals which is noticeable on other occasions at this date. There is more information about the invasion in the Latin sources. The Historia de Sancto Cuthberto[44] records how, during the reign of Edward, a king Regenwaldus came with a large force and seized the land of Aldred, son of Eadulf. Aldred fled to Scotland to get help from the king and together they met Regenwaldus at Corbridge. The Norsemen were completely victorious.

I

The date of the invasion given in Historia Regum "A" disagrees by five years with the date given in the annals of Ulster. It is a possibility that the two sources record two distinct invasions, but it seems unlikely that the three leaders Ragnall, Ottir, and Graggaba would have collaborated on two occasions with a gap of five years between. Moreover, the next entry in Historia Regum "A", dated 914, is demonstrably placed four years too early. The next recorded event in Ragnall's career is the capture of York in 919 and two years after that, he died, having in the year of his death acknowledged, together with other rulers in Britain, the overlordship of Edward the Elder[45].

Within a year or two of Ragnall's death there was a king Sihtric ruling in Northumbria and there can be very little doubt that he was the same as that Sihtric, brother or cousin of Ragnall, who was fighting in Ireland in 917. His reign was short and except that there was a meeting between him and Aethelstan at Tamworth and that he married one of Aethelstan's sisters[46], not much is recorded about him. After his death which the Anglo-Saxon Chronicle places in 926, the kingdom of Northumbria came under the control of Aethelstan. There are, however, one or two points of interest about Sihtric which invite discussion. Historia Regum "A" has two annals which refer to him and the first of them is as follows:

914 Niel rex occisus est a fratre Sihtrico . .

The annal is found also in texts E and F of the Anglo-Saxon chronicle under the year 921:

Her Sihtric cyng ofsloh Niel his brothor.[47]

The meaning of this annal has never been satisfactorily elucidated although it is known to refer to the death of Niall Glundubh, high king of Ireland. Niall Glundubh was the son of Aedh Finnliath the son of Niall Caille and he became high king of Ireland in 916. During his brief reign he conducted a vigorous warfare against the Norsemen led by Ragnall whose reign in Northumbria has already been discussed and that Sihtric whose reign is being discussed at the present moment. The battle in which Niall Glundubh, together with many other Irish kings, met his death was fought near Dublin in 919 and, though the annals of Ulster[48] only give the names of those kings who fell on the Irish side, it is clear from the preceding annal that Sihtric was one of the leaders on the Norse side. Both the annals of Clonmacnoise[49] and the annals of the Four Masters[50] give Sihtric and Imhar as the leaders of the vikings. The battle was an occasion of great sorrow for the people of Ireland and the annalists introduced several passages of verse into their accounts of it, some of them lamentations for the disaster which had befallen Ireland and some of them sayings said to have been uttered by various people at the time. Amongst the latter is a saying attributed to Gormflaith, the daughter of Flann and the wife of Niall Glundubh:

"Evil to me the compliment of the two foreigners who slew Niall and Cearbhall:
Cearbhall (was slain) by Hulb, a great deed: Niall Glundubh by Amhlaeibh."[51]

A number of poems attributed to Gormflaith have been edited by O. J. Bergin[52]. The poems are preserved in the O'Gara manuscript and in the Dean of Lismore's Book. Whether or not any of the poems were really written by Gormflaith must be considered doubtful. The Dean's Book shows that some of them were recited as early as the fifteenth century and Bergin states that in their original form they may well go back two or three centuries[53]. One of these poems is in the form of a lament in which Gormflaith calls to mind those people dear to her who are now dead. Amongst them is the son of a king of Innsi Gall.

"Dead the son of the king of Innsi Gall, he the son of Amhlaeibh (?) of Arann: Amhlaeibh's son used to be on . . . . of my fair knee like a beloved son."[54]

In the tenth year section of the third Fragment, quoted above, it will be remembered that there is a passage in which it is stated that

I

Amhlaeibh was the son-in-law of Aedh, son of Niall. I do not think that the Amhlaeibh who is thus described can have been Olaf the White for the reason which will be made most easily apparent by a genealogical table:

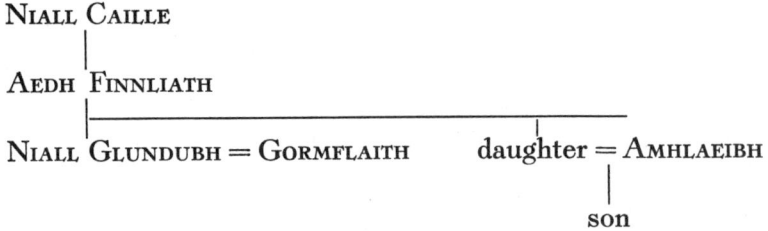

NIALL CAILLE

AEDH FINNLIATH

NIALL GLUNDUBH = GORMFLAITH   daughter = AMHLAEIBH

son

Niall Caille ... died 846 (annals of Ulster 845)
Aedh Finnliath died 879 (» » » 878)
Niall Glundubh died 919 (» » » 918)
Gormflaith .... died 948 (» » » 947)

The table shows that both Gormflaith and Amhlaeibh were married to children of Aedh Finnliath and the presumption is that they were contemporaries. Gormflaith, however, died in 948 which was almost eighty years after the death of Olaf the White. I would therefore suggest that the person whom the Fragment describes as Amhlaeibh, Aedh's son-in-law, is the same as that Amhlaeibh who, according to the saying attributed to Gormflaith, slew Niall Glundubh. We are now in a position to say that in the battle in which Niall Glundubh was killed, he was opposed by, amongst others, his own brother-in-law Amhlaeibh. The next question is to see whether there is any evidence to show that Amhlaeibh was related to Sihtric. The following passage is found in Adam of Bremen:

"Anglia ut supra diximus et in Gestis Anglorum scribitur, post mortem Gudredi a filiis ejus Amalaph, Sigtrih et Reginald per annos fere centum permansit in ditione Danorum."[55]

22

In general, Adam of Bremen can hardly be considered a good authority for Northumbrian history in the tenth century, but this passage seems worthy of some respect since Adam gives his authority for it. It is not known what the Gesta Anglorum was but it was evidently a chronicle which had some information about Northumbrian affairs and it is at least a possibility that it was the source from which some of the annals in Historia Regum "A" were derived. I do not know how literally the passage is to be interpreted but at the least it is some evidence that Sigtrih and Reginald, i. e. Sihtric and Ragnall, had a brother called Olaf or, in the Irish form, Amhlaeibh. On this evidence the genealogy can be amplified and it will be seen that Sihtric, king of York and successor of Ragnall, was related by marriage to Niall Glundubh and could be fairly described as his brother:

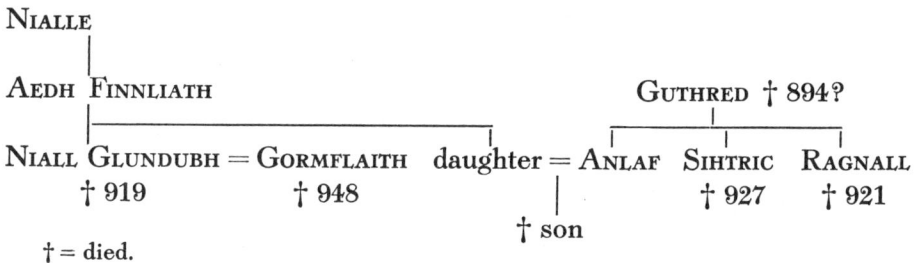

NIALLE
|
AEDH FINNLIATH   GUTHRED † 894?
| |
NIALL GLUNDUBH = GORMFLAITH   daughter = ANLAF   SIHTRIC   RAGNALL
     † 919   † 948 | † 927   † 921
                                     † son
† = died.

Except in the case of Guthred, all the "obits" will be found in the annals of Ulster under the annals previous to the date given here. Throughout this period, the chronology of the annals of Ulster appears to be one year behind the true date.

The successor of Sihtric was Guthfrith who, like his two predecessors, is also described in the Irish annals as a grandson of Imhar. His first visit to Northumbria was on the occasion when he commanded one of the four battalions of vikings in the battle which was fought against the men of Alba in 918. His second visit was less successful for he returned to Dublin within six months of his departure after being driven out of York by Aethelstan[56]. He was still in Ireland in 930[57] and four years later he died and the manner of his death is thus described in the annals of Ulster 933:

"Gothfrith a most cruel king of the Norsemen died of anguish".

It was Guthfrith's son, famous as Anlaf Guthfrithsson, who was one of the chief conspirators in the movement against Aethelstan which came to a head soon afterwards and which resulted in the great English victory at Brunanburh.

This discussion has led us a very long way from the Fragment, but before returning to that source it will be convenient to summarise briefly what has been said about the Scandinavian rulers of York. Halfdene, the son of Ragnar Lothbrok, died in Irland in 877 and was succeeded almost immediately by Guthred whose origin is obscure, but whose reign seems to have been long. Little or nothing is known of the kings in the earliest part of the tenth century, but between 918 and 927 three kings, Ragnall, Sihtric and Guthfrith, all described as grandsons of Imhar, ruled at different times. Guthfrith died in 934 and the leadership of the western vikings fell to his son Olaf, perhaps better known as Anlaf, who fought at Brunanburh and later became king in York. The relationship of these later kings to the earlier is a problem of some difficulty because I do not know how much weight can be laid on the evidence of the Irish annals about the descent of the vikings. It is clear that Olaf (Irish form Amhlaeibh) and Ivar (Irish form Imhar) were regarded as the founders of the Norse power in Dublin, and after their deaths the annals of Ulster refer, between 874 and 895, to one son of Olaf and two sons of Ivar. Between 895 and 934 there are references to no less than six grandsons of Ivar, whilst there is no mention of any grandson of Olaf. The absence of descendants of Olaf is probably to be explained by the migration of his family to Scotland and eventually to Iceland. It is rather a curious fact that members of the third generation of Norsemen in Ireland are always referred to as grandsons of so-and-so. The annals of Ulster never mention the father of any one of the six grandsons of Ivar. There is therefore a considerable gap in our knowledge of the second generation. The last occurrence of the phrase "grandson of Imhar" in the annals of Ulster is in annal 937 and after that the formula "son of" reappears. I have suggested that Guthred, like all his successors, came to York from the west and I think it not unlikely that he may belong to the missing second generation. The passage from Adam of Bremen records that he was in fact the father of Ragnall and Sihtric.

Now at last we are in a position to return to the two passages in the nineteenth year section of the Fragment which are quoted above. The first of these two passages is to the effect that a man called Amhlaeibh went from Erin to Lochlann at the request of his father Goffridh, the king of the Lochlanns, in order to help him against his enemies who were making war upon him. Storm maintained that this referred to the recall of Olaf the White from Ireland by his father in c. 871 in order to help against Harald Fairhair. I venture to suggest that the passage is a late interpolation and that it refers to an appeal by Goffridh, i. e. Guthfrith king of York, for the help of his son Amhlaeibh, i. e. Anlaf Guthfrithsson, against his English enemies and that the war in question was none other than that which culminated in the battle of Brunanburh in 937 Guthfrith was in Northumbria in 918 and he was driven out by Aethelstan in 926. He then went to Ireland and was still there in 930. What he did in the interval between then and his death in 934 is not known, but since his son was fighting at the battle of Brunanburh and later became king in York, it may well be that both father and son were in England attempting to regain possession of Northumbria some time in the 930's. Aethelstan led an army to Scotland in 934[58] and it is by no means unlikely that this campaign was connected in some way with an attempt of the vikings from Dublin to regain control of the north of England.

An entry which is found in the next year section of the Fragment seems to show that this is the correct interpretation of the passage. The section begins with a series of annals recording events which occurred in 872. The last entry but one is as follows:

"The king of the Lochlanns, i. e. Goffridh, died of an ugly sudden disease."

I have no doubt that this is another reference to that Guthfrith who was expelled from York by Aethelstan and whose death is recorded in similar words in the annals of Ulster 933:

"Guthfrith, grandson of Imhar, a most cruel king of the Norsemen, died of anguish."

Compare with these the entry in the annals of Clonmacnoise 929:

"Godfrey, king of the Danes, died a filthy and ill-favoured death."

The reason why the entry in the Fragment is placed in a year section dated 872 is that the annals of Ulster record in that same year the death of another famous Norseman, namely Ivar himself. I suspect that the entry in the Fragment may have referred originally to Ivar's death, and that the words "i. e. Goffridh" were inserted by someone, who having read the contents of the previous year section, could only think that the king of the Lochlanns was the Goffridh who is there mentioned.

The second of the two passages quoted above is clearly to be taken in close connection with the first and I think that the genealogy which it contains is not that either of Ivar or Olaf, but is nothing more than a list of Scandinavian rulers of York in the late ninth and early tenth centuries. It will be convenient to repeat the genealogy, placing the names in descending order and distinguishing between the different Goffraidhs:

> Gofraidh (I)
> Gofraidh Conung (II)
> Ragnall
> Gofraid (III)

The last of these four has been identified above with the Guthfrith who was expelled from York by Aethelstan and who died in 934. Ragnall, I suggest, is that king who ruled in York c. 918—921. Ragnall and Guthfrith, however, seem to have belonged to the same generation, a fact which suggests that this is a list of kings rather than a genealogy. It is probable that Gofraidh Conung (II) is that mysterious Guthred, perhaps father of Ragnall, who was ruling in York at the end of the ninth century. There remains Gofraidh (I). I know of only one viking ruler in the west who bore this name before the time of Guthred king of Northumbria. In the annals of the Four Masters under the year 851 there is recorded the death of Gofraidh the son of Fergus. He is there described as chief of the "Innsi Gall", which is the name given by the Irish to those islands off the west coast of Scotland which were occupied by the vikings.

In conclusion we may revert to the problem to which attention was drawn at the outset, namely whether Amhlaeibh of the Irish annals is the same as the man who is described in Norse sources as Olaf the White. There were three principal objections to the identification of these two vikings, namely that they were descended from different people, that they married different wives and that they died in different places. All these objections are based on the apparent conflict of evidence between Landnamabok and the Fragment. In the course of the above discussion I have tried to show that the evidence of the Fragment has been repeatedly used in a way which its contents do not justify. The evidence which it contains about Amhlaeibh's pedigree, his marriage and his alleged journey back to Lochlann will not stand the test of examination.

I

NOTES

[1] Annals of Ireland; John O'Donovan, Dublin 1860. All references are to this edition. [2] 5. rekke, 5. bind, 1924, s. 509—532. [3] Tome 36, 1915—16, p. 1—22. [4] This study was based mainly on O'Donovan's translation which is often inaccurate. I cannot claim to have studied the source in its original language. [5] All references are to O'Donovan's edition. [6] The Book of the Settlement of Iceland, Ellwood, Kendal 1898, p. 62—3. [7] A. O. Anderson, Early Sources of Scottish History, Edinburgh 1922, vol. 1, p. 306, note 1. [8] op. cit. vol. 1, p. 306—311. [9] Three Fragments p. 150—151. [10] That is Kenneth MacAilpin, founder of the Scottish kingdom, who ruled from 844 to 860. [11] T. D. Kendrick, A History of the Vikings, London, 1930, p. 304. [12] Historisk Tidsskrift, 2. rekke, 2. bind, 1880, p. 313—331. [13] N. Kershaw, Anglo-Saxon and Norse Poems, Cambridge 1922, p. 88—91, and notes 185—6. [14] Storm op. cit. p. 316 and ff. [15] The War of the Gaedhil with the Gaill, ed. Todd, London 1867, p. 27. [16] op. cit. p. 329. [17] de Vries op. cit. p. 521. [18] op. cit. p. 520. [19] de Vries op. cit. p. 522—3. [20] For convenience I distinguish these two as Historia Regum "A" and "B". [21] Published 1882—85, two vols. All references are to this edition. [22] Archaeologia Aeliana, new series, vol. vii, p. 21—77. [23] Aethelweard bk. iv, ch. 3. [24] sub anno 883. [25] Lib. II, cap. XIII. [26] The War of the Gaedhil and the Gaill, p. 27. [27] Paragraph 33. [28] W. F. Skene, Celtic Scotland, Edinburgh 1876, vol. 1, p. 327. [29] See the Libellus de Primo Saxonum Adventu. [30] The subject is "It", i. e. "exercitus" from the previous sentence. [31] Victoria County History, Lancaster, vol. 1, p. 258 and ff. [32] British Numismatic Journal, vol. 21, 1931—3, p. 188—9. [33] War of the Gaedhil and the Gaill, p. 27. [34] Paragraph 33. [35] For other views compare Saga Book of the Viking Club, vol. vii, 1911—2, p. 43—48. [36] Archaelogical Journal, vol. 91, 1934, p. 9. [37] Anglo-Saxon Chronicle, 901 A. [38] ibid. 906 A. [39] ibid. 911 A and D: 910 E. [40] Annals of Ulster 913. [41] ibid. 916. [42] Annals of Ulster 917. [43] The History of Wales by Caradoc of Llancarfan, Wynne, London 1697, p. 45. [44] Paragraph 22.

34

45 The chronology of the Irish annals is here preferred to that of the English sources.
46 Anglo-Saxon Chronicle 925 D.   47 Annals of Ulster.   48 sub anno 918.
49 sub anno 915.   60 sub anno 915.   51 Annals of the Four Masters 917.
52 A Miscellany presented to Kuno Mayer, ed. Bergen and Marstrander, Halle, 1912.
53 ibid. p. 343—5.   54 ibid. p. 358—9.   55 M. G. H. ed. Pertz. Scriptores VII, p. 314.
56 Annals of Ulster 926; Anglo-Saxon Chronicle 927 E, F; Historia Regum "A" 927.
57 Annals of Ulster 929   58 Anglo-Saxon Chronicle 934, E and F.

II

SYMEON'S HISTORY OF THE KINGS

Symeon's *History of the Kings* survives in only one manuscript, which is written in various hands and generally assigned to the end of the twelfth century. There is no need to dispute about who wrote this history which a rubric, composed some years after Symeon's death, ascribes to him, because what is called a history is in fact a mass of unedited material, most of it useless, some of it immensely valuable. Symeon was at one stage concerned with the accumulation of this mass, but he was neither the first nor the last to be so concerned, and his own original contribution is very slight. He was content for the most part to copy long passages from Asser, Florence of Worcester and others, but in so doing he did not fail to copy other material which was then available. The high-sounding title which a later scribe prefixed, cannot conceal the fact that the work which follows is in reality a collection of sources designed to form the basis of a history which Symeon, because of old age or some other reason, never wrote. His ability as a historian is revealed in his history of the church of Durham, and it will hardly be denied that if he had completed a political history, it would have held a high place in the list of mediæval histories of England; but we may be grateful for whatever chance it was that has preserved the material which he collected rather than that same material re-arranged, expanded and coloured with the opinions of his own times. The production of a satisfactory text was never difficult, principally because there is only one manuscript and that written in hands for the most part easily legible. Twysden's edition of 1652 was followed by that in *Monumenta Historica Britannica* in the middle of the nineteenth century. Hodgson Hinde made use of his topographical knowledge in an edition published by the Surtees Society in 1868, and this in turn was followed by Arnold's edition, completed in 1885, in the Rolls Series. Arnold wrote an important introduction embodying the results of work done by Stubbs on Roger of Howden. Scholars of still more recent times have not been blind to the value of Symeon's history, but much work has yet to be done before it can be used to the full.

Few details are known about Symeon's life. He was, of course, a monk at Durham, having come there from Jarrow late in the eleventh century, but it is not known when he was born or when he died, though he cannot have lived much, if at all, after 1130. His work, to which the term " history " has been applied loosely, is in fact written in the form of a chronicle, that is to say events are recorded year by year and not in the narrative form used by Bede, who was more concerned to arrange his material by subjects than years. The earliest of the Northumbrian kings form the natural starting point to a history which was continued with breaks of varying length to 957. The entry for this year was followed by an extract from William of Malmesbury which has no connection with what goes before or with what follows, and thereafter the history carries back to 848, whence it continues to 1129. There are therefore two parallel accounts of events from 848 to 957. After Symeon's death, as one may suppose, the history was continued for a further period to 1153 by John, prior of Hexham. Even if it were not for this Hexham continuation, there is clear evidence that at some period a Hexham hand made considerable additions to the history which we now have. The first stage, therefore, in analysing

Symeon's history must be the removal of the Hexham additions. This having been achieved, there still remains a history in two parts, of which the first extends to 957 and the second from 848 to 1129. Arnold's theory was that the first of these two histories was the work of a monk of St. Cuthbert writing at Chester-le-Street in the tenth century. This writer he styled for convenience, but not altogether euphoniously, " the Cuthbertine." The material available for this writer included, for the earliest period, Bede's history and thereafter a short chronicle reaching from 731, the date at which Bede's history ends, to 802. He could find nothing after the end of this chronicle until the middle of the ninth century, when he could draw upon Asser's life of Alfred, and this he continued to do for as long as possible. At about the year 900 the nature of his work changes abruptly, and from there to 957 extends a series of brief entries mostly concerned with the Scandinavian kingdom of York. They are irregular and in some places obscure, but nevertheless they form the most important single source for English political history in the first half of the tenth century. So much for the first of these two histories. Turning to the second, Arnold explained the repetition by suggesting that Symeon wrote his own account of Alfred, based partly on Asser and partly on Florence of Worcester, intending to substitute it for that of the Cuthbertine. From 900 till 1119 almost the whole of the history is derived from Florence. The survival of the two accounts of Alfred is to be explained by supposing that Symeon left his work in an unfinished state. Obviously in a finished work two such accounts would never have been left side by side in a single work.

This brief survey based on Arnold's work shows clearly that it is only the first part of the history which is important for the Anglo-Saxon period, because the second part where it deals with that period is all derivative and not original work. Turning, therefore, exclusively to the first part, we have seen that even this is not all original work, but contains, apart from a few unimportant quotations, material derived from three principal sources : Bede's *History,* Asser's *Life of Alfred* and an unknown Hexham hand. How much is derived from the first of these two is easily decided by direct comparison of the texts in question. Exactly how much was inserted by the Hexham hand is less easily determined. The additions by this hand, in Arnold's opinion, consisted of an account of the martyrdom of two Kentish princes put at the very beginning of the history, two passages relating to Acca and Alchmund respectively, both of whom were bishops of Hexham, and the extracts from William of Malmesbury noted above. The passage about Acca includes an account of his translation in about 1040 and a reference to one of the invasions of Malcolm Canmore, possibly that of 1079. A third episode concerns Aldred, the relic snatcher, a brother of the church of Hexham, who made valiant but unsuccessful attempts to steal a bone from one of Acca's little fingers. It is said of Aldred that as a young man he had been brought up in the church of Hexham in the days before that church was given by Thomas II, archbishop of York, to the canons who still served there in the writer's day. Thomas II held the see of York from 1108 to 1114, and in 1112 he handed over the church of Hexham, which had been reduced almost to a state of ruin, to certain canons regular. The date 1112, therefore, is a *terminus post quem* for the construction of the Acca insertion, and as a matter of fact the date can safely be put some years later than this. The writer explains that he was recording the miraculous repulse of Malcolm Canmore's invasion because, though the event was well known by common report, it was well to put it in writing before everyone forgot about it. The latest stage, therefore, in the manipulation of the manuscript is represented by the addition of certain passages betraying a Hexham influence at about the middle of the twelfth century or perhaps a little earlier.

The separation of the Hexham element can be achieved

II

largely by considerations of style, context and subject, but
these are not altogether sure means, and the further solution of the problem suggests a question. If there existed in
the second half of the tenth century a more or less consecutive history of Northumbria, is it not likely that traces
of it will be found in other post-conquest historians of the
north country? Stubbs seems to have been the first to
show that such traces do exist. The date of Symeon's death
is not known, but it may have been *c.* 1130. Between
twenty and thirty years later a work was compiled under
the name of *Historia Saxonum vel Anglorum post obitum
Bedae*, and at least two copies of this work, which is more
briefly known as the *Historia post Bedam*, still exist in
manuscript. This work, in the opinion of Stubbs, formed
the basis of the first part of Roger of Howden's history,
and its growth is traced by Stubbs in the following stages :

A. A short chronicle reaching from 731 to 802.
B. A continuation of this by an unknown person to some
   date after the middle of the tenth century.
C. The combination in a single work of " B " together
   with another history reaching from 848 to 1121 and
   derived almost entirely from Florence of Worcester.

Symeon's share in the growth of this history is not
altogether clear. Arnold believed that he was responsible
for combining the two chronicles (i.e. producing stage
" C "), but Stubbs wrote on this point, " I dare not decide "
(p. xxx RS ed. of Roger of Howden). The addition, however, of the annals from 1120 to 1129 is generally agreed to
have been Symeon's work. The important point is that
stage " C " was reached before these additional annals
1120-1129 existed, because the *Historia post Bedam* shows
acquaintance with the combined chronicles but not with the
additional annals. Therefore in this work and its offspring,
Roger's history, there survives a version of that chronicle
from early times to the middle of the tenth century which
we have already traced in Symeon's history. The two

versions are not derived directly one from the other, but are laterally related.

The existence of this other version ought to have some bearing on the problem before us, namely the exclusion of the Hexham additions from the first part of Symeon's history. Arnold was well aware of this, and while he showed comparison of the two versions to be useful, he showed also that the method had limitations because the compiler of the *Historia post Bedam* did not merely copy but tried to reduce the two conjoined chronicles, in the words of Stubbs, " to a reasonable chronological sequence " (*op. cit.* xxxi). He abbreviated everywhere, and for this reason it cannot certainly be said that because a particular statement does not occur in the *Historia post Bedam*, that it did not occur either in the work as it came into Symeon's hands. This other version, therefore, while useful, does not help as much as could be wished. Moreover, the information about Acca in the *Historia post Bedam* s.a. 740 suggests that this work was derived from a manuscript which already had the Hexham additions in it. We must accordingly look elsewhere.

One of the most valuable of post-conquest histories has until very recently been largely unusable for the general student because it survives in only one manuscript, the Cottonian MS., Faustina B IX, and the only available editions of it are full of mistakes. The publication of a facsimile edition of this manuscript in 1936 with a long and careful analytical introduction has overcome the difficulties of access. The manuscript contains what is commonly known as the chronicle of Melrose. The main stages in the growth of this monastic chronicle have been traced by the editors as follows. The first stage was a preliminary compilation of events from other sources, beginning with the end of Bede's history and continuing to 1171. Thereafter the chronicle continues without any break to 1263, and finally there is a brief continuation which closes in 1275. The editors find no certain evidence for the date when the first part was composed. It may have been between 1173 and 1174, but the better interpretation appears to be that the text was not written earlier than 1185. The principal source of this first part was material from the Northumbrian group represented by Symeon's history and the *Historia post Bedam*. This material includes a third version of that Northumbrian chronicle which originally ended at some date after the middle of the tenth century. The importance of this version is that it appears to lack those Hexham additions which make it so difficult to determine how much of the material in Symeon's history is older than the twelfth century. Expressed in another way the version in the chronicle of Melrose, though preserved in a later manuscript, appears nevertheless to be in an earlier form and it ought therefore to be possible to eliminate the Hexham additions from Symeon by its help with a fair degree of certainty. The achievement of this would carry the problem a stage further. All the derived material could be removed and there would remain two brief chronicles, one from 731 to 802 and the other from *c.* 900 to *c.* 950, each of them represented in at least three laterally related versions.

The next stage is to determine the authenticity of these two chronicles, to show if possible where and when they were compiled, and whether, in spite of surviving only in manuscripts of the twelfth and later centuries, they can be used as contemporary records. Traces of them are not confined to the sources already mentioned because they both appear in more or less similar form in certain texts of the Anglo-Saxon chronicle. Plummer pointed out that one of the respects in which text D of this work differs from A, B and C is by the inclusion of a body of annals relating to northern affairs from 733 to 806. There can be no doubt from their contents that they are an English version of the same short chronicle which we have found in Symeon, the *Historia post Bedam* and the chronicle of Melrose. Verbal comparison is, of course, impossible, but

their contents suggest that once again the relation is col-
lateral and not direct. The version in the Anglo-Saxon
chronicle, for example, mentions some points which Symeon
does not and vice versa. The widespread use to which
these chronicles were put by later historians serves to
emphasize the importance of examining them closely and
of establishing a text as free from corruption and late additions as possible. The existence of at least three Latin
versions as well as one English version ought to make this
latter task not altogether too difficult. Many scholars have
emphasized the importance of the chronicles, but none has
yet undertaken a critical and comparative examination of
all the surviving versions, and until this has been done
the fullest use cannot be made of the material which they
contain.

Bede's history ended in 731, but he himself did not die
till some four years later, and Plummer was of the opinion
that the brief annals for the years 731 to 734 which are
found in the earliest manuscripts of the history may have
been written by Bede himself. The plan which he had
adopted, a narrative history arranged in books and chapters according to subjects, was one which later writers did
not follow, and indeed it could not have been followed by a
scholar of much less ability than Bede. The first of the
two short chronicles was beyond doubt designed to begin
where Bede finished, and accordingly we find that the
annals for 731 to 734 which Plummer ascribes to Bede are
included in it. After 735 the chronicle reveals very little
connection with that other continuation of Bede which is
found in a group of later manuscripts of his history. It
follows its own course, recording mainly events of Northumbrian history, at first brief and rather irregular, and
gradually becoming fuller through the course of the eighth
century. Among its annals are two or three references to
eclipses, the actual occurrence of which can be checked by
calculation, and to other natural phenomena of a kind
which no chronicler would bother to record unless he was

writing at a date soon after the occurrence of the events themselves. A fact which points in a similar direction is that several events are recorded not only as to the day of the month on which they occurred, but also as to the day of the week. Such entries present an opportunity of checking the chronology, and a high degree of accuracy is apparent in this respect. The chronicle appears to be quite free from that kind of entry which betrays by its contents that it must have been written long after the event which it describes. A good example of this is found in the Anglo-Saxon chronicle, text A 787, which records the arrival of viking ships on the south coast and concludes by saying that this was the first time such ships had visited England, thereby showing that the writer was looking back on a series of such visits. Nothing of this kind is to be found in the chronicle at present being discussed. Turning to the kind of material found in the chronicle, the early annals are concerned mainly with the royal and episcopal successions in the various kingdoms and bishoprics throughout England. A study of the information about the episcopal succession reveals the remarkable fact that, excepting one detail about York and the demonstrably accidental omission of Whithorn, the annals from 731 to 745 contain a list of the deaths and consecrations of the bishops in nearly all the English sees during that period. The chronicle contains in addition a list of the first nine archbishops of Canterbury, as well as notices of three English bishops in the Irish see of Mayo. The eighth century was the great period of Northumbrian missionary activity on the continent, but it is little less than remarkable to find a series of English bishops holding an Irish see at this time. This emphasis on the episcopal succession may not be without importance in considering the growth of historical writing in England. Genealogies and lists of kings and other notable people seem to be amongst the earliest recorded history, and such lists continued to be kept at a time when other records were not. The earliest of these lists which now survives is that contained in the British Museum MS. Vespasian B VI. Internal evidence demonstrates that this list was originally compiled in about 812 and probably at Lichfield. Additions have been made to these lists at various times, but the entries in the original hand suggest that for most of the sees bishops consecrated shortly before or after 805 occupy the last place in the original hand. This may be significant when it is considered that Symeon's version of the chronicle ends in 802 and the Anglo-Saxon chronicle's version in 806. The bulk of the remaining material concerns Northumbrian history. There are a few entries which give important information on the relations between English, Britons, Picts and Scots in the lands south of Forth and Clyde. Entries which show contact with Ireland have already been mentioned. Another topic on which there is evidence is the state of monasticism in Northumbria. No less than eight entries refer to kings, queens and lay officials who gave up their positions and became monks or clerks. The Northumbrian nobility was no fit source of recruitment for the monasteries if the traditions of Bede and his age were to be maintained. These entries form a valuable link between the warnings of Bede about the state of Northumbrian monasticism in his letter to Ecgbert and the lament of Alfred over the decay of learning throughout England and especially in the north. They show, too, why Northumbria fell such an easy prey to the vikings. The chronicle records in addition to Northumbrian affairs a series of events in Carolingian history between 775 and 802, and in this the hand of Alcuin is perhaps to be detected.

Short though this chronicle is, it is only as one turns to study the last sixty years before the great Danish invasion that one realizes how valuable it is. Its information is not so meagre nor are its entries so brief but that they offer a contrast with the utter dearth of record which follows between c. 805 and 866. Neither Symeon nor any other writer of his age could find material to fill the gap. This is a point which deserves emphasis because failure to appreciate it has resulted in deductions of a historical kind which cannot fairly be made. The see of Whithorn, for example, has frequently been said to have come to an end *c*. 802, whereas the truth is that the list of bishops comes to an end, which is a very different matter. As a matter of fact there is record of a later bishop of Whithorn. The list fails not merely for Whithorn, but also for Canterbury, York, Hexham and Lindisfarne, and logically the argument of extinction would have to be applied to these as well as to Whithorn. What has happened seems to be that after the disturbances caused by the first viking onslaughts had passed, some attempt was made to bring the lists of bishops up to date again. Evidence for Canterbury would not be hard to find, nor would it be hard for a Durham writer to get information about Cuthbert's bishops. At a later period some of the gaps were filled, as marginal entries in Symeon's history show. Whithorn, however, lay in a remote part of Northumbria, and as a see it was chiefly important in the earlier period, so that evidence about it might not be available. There is no evidence to show when the see of Whithorn came to an end, but it was in a better position than any of the other northern sees to survive the invasion of 866.

The second of the two short chronicles offers fewer difficulties than the first because it appears to be in a less corrupt form. The entries are even briefer and individually they are not unlike the type of annal which contemporary Irish historians were composing. There is good evidence of close contact between Ireland and Northumbria in the first half of the tenth century so that the resemblance may not be altogether the result of chance. No more is attempted than the recording of events. The task of stringing these events into a connected narrative is left to the reader. The wildness of the times is fully reflected in this chronicle which records little else but the progress of the viking campaigns and the deaths of leaders on either side. Within these limits, however, it provides an account of the wars between the vikings and the English which is altogether more trustworthy and more accurate chronologically than the hopelessly confused version preserved in the Anglo-Saxon chronicle. Eric Bloodaxe was the last of the Scandinavian kings of Northumbria and thereafter the kingdom was governed by earls. Symeon's version of the short chronicle places this change in 952, and the version in the chronicle of Melrose two years earlier. Whichever of these two dates is right, the chronicle seems originally to have come to an end with the last of the Northumbrian kings, though in its various versions it was continued for a greater or lesser time, and the succession of the Northumbrian earls was kept up to date for as long as two hundred years in the form of an appendix to the original chronicle. The list of earls in Symeon's version, interpolated with one or two items of Northumbrian history, extends from Eric Bloodaxe to Henry I, but the list no longer occupies the place which we may be sure that it originally held, namely at the end of the short chronicle. Arnold found good reasons for believing that the section on the Northumbrian earls which in the now existing text of Symeon's history appears under 1072, ought properly to be placed under 952, in connection with the expulsion of Eric Bloodaxe. This is in fact the place which it occupies in Roger of Howden's work, and in the chronicle of Melrose it is found under 950 in immediate connection with Eric Bloodaxe. This latter version of the list of earls, though much briefer than Symeon's, nevertheless comes down to a later date, namely to Henry II. The extension of the list to the middle of the twelfth century does not in any way detract from the value of the short chronicle itself, nor is it any evidence that this chronicle was not constructed till the twelfth century. Every detail in it suggests that, as it now survives, it is a genuine record of the tenth century, untouched except for minor slips on the part of copyists.

The sources at present available for the study of Anglo-

Saxon history, though they are steadily increasing, are still far from plentiful. The destruction of documents and libraries in past times has made it impossible that they will ever be as plentiful as could be wished. Admirable editions of the major works of the period exist, such as Bede's history, the Anglo-Saxon chronicle, together with the laws and several lesser works besides, but there remains a field of evidence which as yet seems to be largely untouched. I mean the work of the historians who wrote in Latin after the Norman conquest. Each of these historians has his reputation, from Symeon at one end to, perhaps, Geoffrey of Monmouth at the other, but each in a greater or lesser degree has preserved material which could be put to use. In some the material may consist of old traditions told in the form of saga, in others it may consist of annals or chronicles copied from older sources. The two chronicles whose existence is revealed by analysis of Symeon's *History of the Kings* have long been known and recognized as valuable, but it is only when every entry, almost every word, in each of these two chronicles has been subjected to the closest scrutiny, and all the versions closely compared, that their historical information can be used without hesitation. There are several other problems in connection with these two chronicles which invite discussion. To Bede, one may suspect, much of the credit for the first of the two may be due. Presumably as he wrote his history some kind of machinery for collecting information automatically developed. One would hesitate to describe Jarrow as a news agency, but we know that Bede himself seldom left his monastery and he must have had messengers to keep him in touch with the outer world. The completeness of the information about the episcopal succession in the ten years following his death suggests that Jarrow may for a time have maintained the contacts which he had established. One would like to consider further the relation between this first chronicle and the ninth century lists of bishops. Is there any connection between these lists and the collection

II

of material for what we now know as the Anglo-Saxon
chronicle ? The continuity of this great work over five hundred years and more is perhaps its most remarkable feature,
and it tends to make one forget that in several monasteries
up and down the country chronicles were kept which might
in favourable circumstances have developed into works of
similar importance. The chronicles preserved in the Northumbrian group may be compared with the West Saxon
annals, the Mercian register, the additions to Nennius, the
annals of St. Neot and other similar short, historical chronicles, most of which eventually found their way into the
national chronicle.

III

THE ORIGINS OF NORTHUMBRIA

1. *The Gildas Tradition.*

The historian who sets out to make an inquiry into the origins of Northumbria is much in the position of a man who tries to journey by night across the sands from Holy Island to the mainland opposite. He knows that there are guide-posts which will help him on his way if he can find them, and he knows also that if he strays from the track which they mark, he will do so at the risk of being swallowed in quicksands. The kingdom of Northumbria[1] came into being about the year 600 through the forcible coalescence of two originally separate units, the kingdoms of Bernicia and Deira. Bernicia was founded in 547.[2] So much is beyond reasonable doubt, even if the circumstances of its foundation are mere conjecture. But when we seek to determine even the date, much less the circumstances, of Deira's foundation, we find ourselves leaving firm ground behind with an uneasy awareness that we shall not reach it again until we have been carried back beyond the last days of Roman Britain. To disregard this period of uncertainty between Roman Britain and English Northumbria might, indeed, be the easiest course, but it could not fail

---

[1] The substance of this paper was read at a meeting of the *Arch. Inst.* in Burlington House 3 April 1946. I am grateful to Dr. I. A. Richmond and Prof. C. F. C. Hawkes for helpful criticism on several points, though I have not always agreed with their views. My debt to Prof. H. M. Chadwick has accumulated for many years and is now unhappily beyond repayment. I alone, however, am responsible for the views I have expressed.

[2] Bede, *HE* v, 24. I hope to show elsewhere how this date was calculated.

to give a seriously distorted view of Northumbrian history
as a whole. There is no justification for assuming from the
comparative lack of evidence that this interval was a period
of quiescence or of political stagnation. On the contrary,
there is every indication that it was one of great vitality and
of profound political changes whose consequences could
not but greatly affect the course of later Northumbrian
history.

Opinions about the merits of Gildas as a historian have
varied greatly. For himself he never claimed that his work
De Excidio et Conquestu Britanniae[3] was anything more
than a letter or an admonishment (*admonitiuncula*).[4] Bede
called him *historicus*,[5] and many other writers of the middle
ages followed Bede's example. Modern writers have tended
to regard Gildas as prophet and preacher rather than as
historian,[6] but of late there has been a growing realization
that, whether prophet or historian, Gildas was a contemporary witness of a very obscure period in the history of
Britain, and that therefore his work deserves to be taken
seriously.[7] He was by far the earliest writer to attempt a
rational account of events in Britain between the end of the
Roman and the beginning of the English periods, and
furthermore his work served as the main source of information for later writers attempting the same task. To a large
extent its errors and obscurities are due to the efforts of its
author to produce a connected narrative despite the gaps in
his sources, especially the native sources, of which he himself complained.[8]

[3] Ed. T. Mommsen, *MGH Auct. Antiquiss.*, XIII, 1-85, also H.
Williams, with translation and notes, in *Cymmrodorion Record Series*,
no. 3. The work is cited hereafter as *Exc.*
[4] *Exc.* 1.
[5] *HE* I, 22.
[6] So Sir John Lloyd, *A History of Wales*, 3rd ed., 139.
[7] Cf. C. E. Stevens, *Gildas Sapiens*, EHR 56, 353-73, and F. M.
Stenton, *Anglo-Saxon England*, 2.
[8] *Exc.* 4—*quantum tam potuero, non tam ex scriptis patriae scrip-
torumve monimentis, quippe quae, vel si qua fuerint, aut ignibus hostium
exusta aut civium exilii classe longius deportata non compareant, quam
transmarina relatione, quae crebris inrupta intercapedinibus non satis
claret.*

The first stage in the inquiry must, therefore, be to consider what Gildas wrote about events in Britain, and more particularly in northern Britain, at the end of the Roman period. The expedition of Magnus Maximus to the continent, he wrote, robbed Britain of all her armed forces and the country, which was completely ignorant of the practice of war, was then left exposed for the first time to the ravages of two foreign tribes, the Scots from the north-west and the Picts from the north.[9] In answer to an urgent appeal for help the Romans sent a legion to Britain, and after driving off the invaders, they told the inhabitants to build a wall across the island between the two seas as a protection. This they did, but it was no use because it was built of turf.[10] As soon as the legions had gone, the old enemies came back across the sea and a second appeal for help was sent to the Romans. The appeal was answered, the enemies were again defeated and a second wall was built, but this time by the Romans themselves in their accustomed mode of structure.[11] At the same time towers were built along the southern shores of Britain as a protection against dangers threatening from that quarter. The Romans then urged the Britons to look to their own defence, and after leaving behind them patterns for the manufacture of arms, they departed as people who never intended to return.[12] As soon as the Romans had gone the Scots and Picts came back[13] and seized the whole northern part of the land as far as the wall. The Britons tried to hold back the enemy by manning their fortifications, but the invaders broke through and the Britons abandoned their wall and their cities. To these external disasters were added further troubles caused by tumults within, and in their distress they sent a third appeal to the Romans, addressing it to Aetius in his third consul-

[9] *Exc.* 14.
[10] *Exc.* 15.
[11] *Exc.* 18—*solito structurae more*, which may be taken to mean that this second wall was of stone.
[12] *Exc.* 17, 18.
[13] *Exc.* 19.

III

ship. The appeal was not answered. Some of the Britons gave up the fight, but others fought on and inflicted a severe defeat on their enemies.[14] Soon after, the Scots—or the shameless Irish attackers, as Gildas calls them here[15]—went home, to return again before long. Of the Picts he says that then and long afterwards they settled down in the furthermost part of the island with occasional pillaging and devastation.[16]

After their victory the Britons entered upon a period of prosperity. Gildas indicates that this period lasted a considerable time, and although it was not a kind of prosperity of which he could approve, he admits that it was an age of such wealth as none who came after could remember.[17] In due course the threat of invasion was renewed and was accompanied by a deadly pestilence. To meet these new perils the proud tyrant[18] and his councillors decided to invite the Saxons into Britain in order that they might repel the invaders from the north. Three shiploads of Saxons arrived, and on the instructions of the tyrant they first settled in the eastern part of the island. When news of the success of their expedition reached their homeland, another contingent was sent and the Britons supplied them with provisions as if they had been soldiers about to fight for their hosts. All went well for a time, but eventually there was a dispute about their rations, and finally the Saxons revolted, causing widespread destruction all over the island from sea to sea.[19] After a while some of the Saxons returned home and the Britons, led by Ambrosius Aurelianus, won

[14] Exc. 20.
[15] Exc. 21—impudentes grassatores Hiberni.
[16] Exc. 21—Picti in extrema parte insulae tunc primum et deinceps requieverunt, praedas et contritiones nonnunquam facientes. Williams, op. cit., translates, "began their successive settlements," implying that these Picts were new settlers from elsewhere. This is not in keeping with the interpretation which Bede seems to give to this passage, HE I, 14—Picti in extrema parte insulae tunc primum et deinceps quieverunt, praedas tamen nonnunquam exinde et contritiones de Brettonum gente agere non cessarunt.
[17] Exc. 21.
[18] Exc. 23—superbus tyrannus. Gildas does not give his name.
[19] Exc. 23-4.

a victory over those that remained.[20]   From that time sometimes the citizens, sometimes the enemy were victorious
until the siege of *Mons Badonicus*.

This narrative is sufficiently convincing in its broad outlines to justify the belief that it contains some truth, but in
its details it presents two major difficulties which have done
much to discredit it as a whole.   The turf wall is stated to
have been built after the departure of Magnus Maximus,
and the stone wall at some unstated time after the turf wall.
Gildas has certainly made a serious blunder, but his failure
to solve an archæological problem of which the solution is
scarcely complete even yet, is not an adequate reason for
rejecting all his information on other topics.   The correspondence of archæological and other evidence with
details in his account of the building of the two walls suggests with some force that he was less mistaken than he
appears to have been, and that the two appeals to Rome
and the results which flowed from them should be taken
to represent the reorganization of the Roman defences of
Britain in 369 and again after 383.[21]   The second difficulty
lies in the appeal which the Britons are alleged to have
addressed to Aetius in his third consulship.   Gildas does
not precisely state the cause of the trouble which led to the
sending of this third appeal for help, but the implication
from the order of his narrative is that the appeal was for
help against fresh incursions of the old enemies.   But the
consequences of this implication are difficult to accept.   The
appeal was not answered, some of the Britons gave up the
fight while others fought on and won a victory, a period of
prosperity followed, fresh dangers began to threaten, and
finally the Saxons were called in to help.   Gildas gives no
indication of the interval of time which elapsed between the
sending of the appeal to Aetius and the calling in of the
Saxons, but if all these separate events are considered without reference to other sources, it might not seem unreason-

[20] *Exc.* 25.
[21] C. E. Stevens, *op. cit.*, esp. 359-60.

able to suppose that they would have required a generation or more for their fulfilment. The appeal to Aetius cannot have been despatched earlier than 446, the first year of his third consulship, and if thirty years are added to this, Gildas seems to be saying that the Saxons did not come to Britain until after 475. The conclusion that there is some mistake in his narrative can only be avoided by virtually ignoring the item which seems to require the longest period of time, namely the phase of prosperity.[22] If Gildas had used figures to record the date of the third appeal to the Romans, a textual corruption might have been suspected, but he did not use figures, and therefore the date must be allowed to stand. Nor can it be denied that some serious trouble befell Britain in the third consulship of Aetius, because Gildas quotes from the letter which was sent to Aetius, and was therefore working ultimately from a written document. It is possible, however, to ask whether this great trouble was in fact the trouble which Gildas supposed it to be. William Skene, who seems to have been the first to pose this question, suggested that the trouble which was recorded in the document quoted by Gildas was not due to fresh incursions from the north, but to the revolt of the Saxons.[23] This suggestion has again been advanced by Mr. C. E. Stevens[24] who has brought additional arguments to its support. The details of the British recovery are not recorded by Gildas, but its results are, so far as they concerned the enemies from the north. The Scots went home, and although Gildas says that they returned later, he does not refer to them again in his narrative. The Picts apparently withdrew to the north and confined their activities to periodical raids. The remaining part of the narrative—the period of prosperity, the renewal of trouble, the arrival of the Saxons

[22] The difficulty is more readily apparent in Bede's narrative, *HE* i, 13-15, where he has left himself with only the three years 446-449 for the whole sequence of events from the appeal to Aetius to the arrival of the English.
[23] W. F. Skene, *The Four Ancient Books of Wales*, i, 35-6.
[24] *op. cit.*, 362-3.

III

and their eventual revolt—contains no inconsistencies in itself.

The blunder which Gildas made about the building of the walls is not a matter which need cause us any concern. He could not hope, any more than other historians or antiquarians down to the nineteenth century, to solve correctly a problem which could only be solved by scientific excavations. The problem raised by the appeal to Aetius is more serious. Are we entitled to suppose that Gildas made a mistake in the interpretation of one of his sources? The brief extract which he quotes from the letter to Aetius might refer equally well to a fresh incursion of the Picts and Scots or to the revolt of the Saxons, or perhaps even to a combination of the two. The question does not seem to admit of a proven answer, but I am inclined none the less to follow Skene and Stevens on the ground that it is difficult to make sense out of the narrative of Gildas without making some modification of this kind. There is no evidence that Gildas knew the dates of Aetius' third consulship, and he made no attempt to give a date for the arrival of the Saxons. The chronological difficulty raised by his own narrative may therefore never have occurred to him in the way in which it must surely have occurred to Bede, who knew both the initial date of Aetius' third consulship[25] and an approximate date for the arrival of the Saxons.[26] When it is recalled that the letter to Aetius need not have been dispatched until 453, the year before his fourth consulship, it will be seen that there is no chronological difficulty in the way of supposing the letter to have referred to the Saxon revolt. If this supposition is allowed, the phase of prosperity will have to be placed before, not after, the appeal to Aetius, and there will remain four points which are fundamental to the narrative of Gildas so far as it concerns northern Britain—that the troubles caused by the Roman withdrawal were followed by a phase of British recovery

[25] *HE* I, 13.
[26] *HE* I, 15.

and prosperity, that attendant upon this recovery the Scots were driven out and the Picts were driven back and finally that the Saxons were called in to help in the north at a time of renewed danger after the period of prosperity.

The second stage in this inquiry must be to consider certain later authorities who made use of Gildas, in order to determine what alterations they made to his narrative. Bede used Orosius for his account of the rebellion of Magnus Maximus,[27] and after drawing upon the same source for certain other events of imperial history which affected Britain, he turned to Gildas, using his entire narrative in direct quotation, in paraphrase or in abbreviation. He omitted none of the essential points, but he did make a number of small additions, most of which consisted of details connected with the building of the walls, and some of which arose from his knowledge of a third wall, where Gildas knew of only two, and of another builder, namely Severus. He describes the wall built by Severus as being, not a stone wall as some supposed, but a rampart of turves.[28] In describing the stone wall which was built in answer to the second appeal to the Romans, he says that it was built in the place where Severus had previously made his rampart.[29] With the first and last of the three walls thus identified with the *vallum*[30] and the Hadrianic Wall respectively, the middle one of the three, that is the turf wall built after the first appeal to the Romans, had to be equated with the only other wall of whose existence Bede was aware, namely the Antonine Wall. Bede must surely have seen both the *vallum* and the Hadrianic Wall, and although he is less likely to have seen the Antonine Wall, he would know about it because, as he says, it began at its eastern end near the monastery of Abercorn.[31] He knew more

[27] *HE* I, 9.
[28] *HE* I, 5.
[29] *HE* I, 12.
[30] We can hardly suppose that Bede meant the Hadrianic Turf Wall. At the most he could not have known more of this than the surviving two mile loop in the Birdoswald-Appletree sector.
[31] *HE* I, 12.

about the construction of the various walls than Gildas did, but this was the kind of information which he could get by going to look for himself or getting someone else to do so for him. The differences between Bede and Gildas on the walls are therefore no more than differences of interpretation and, Severus excepted, there is nothing to suggest that Bede knew any more about the political circumstances which led to their construction than Gildas did.

Another point on which Bede differs from Gildas is in his interpretation of the word *transmarinae*, which Gildas used of the Picts and Scots and which Bede borrowed from him. We use this word, he writes,[32] not because the Picts and Scots live outside Britain, but because they are separated from that part of the country held by the Britons by two arms of the sea which cut deep into the island from east and west. On the western side lies *Urbs Alcluith*, and on the eastern side lies *Urbs Giudi*. Bede seems to have felt that it was inaccurate to use the term *transmarinae* of people who did not in fact live across the sea from the main island of Britain, and he was therefore at pains to explain that he used the word only in a limited sense. The reason for his uneasiness is simply that conditions had changed. In the times of which Gildas wrote, that is the early fifth century, *transmarina* was a fairly accurate description of one at least of the two peoples in question, namely the Scots, but it was much less applicable to the Scots of Bede's own time because some of them had by then been firmly established north of the Clyde for two centuries. Bede's gloss on *transmarina* is not so much an addition to Gildas's narrative as a modification designed to make it in keeping with the changed conditions of later times.

The unsuccessful appeal to Aetius and the disasters which followed, the recovery of the Britons and their demoralization, the plague and the invitation to the Saxons— all these are incorporated by Bede in an abbreviated form. The only important point on which Bede differs from Gildas

[32] *HE* I, 12.

in this part of the narrative is that he identifies the *superbus tyrannus* of Gildas with Vortigern.[33]   In his description of what happened after the arrival of the Saxons in Britain, Bede seems to differ slightly from Gildas, but it is not easy to tell whether the difference is only one of style and language or whether it is due to the use of different sources. In response to the invitation from the Britons, Bede writes,[34] three shiploads of Saxons arrived, and at the king's orders they settled in the eastern part of the island, apparently for the purpose of fighting against its enemies, but actually with the intention of conquering it.   So much comes from Gildas mainly in direct quotation, but Bede goes on to say that the Saxons engaged in battle against the enemies who had come from the north, and were victorious.[35]   This is much more explicit than anything to be found in Gildas, who writes of the Saxons as having the apparent intention of fighting on behalf of the Britons, but not as having actually done so.   Gildas does, however, imply that the Saxons had some success, because it was news of this success which encouraged more of their countrymen to follow them.   Bede goes on to say that a larger band of armed men then came to Britain, that they too were given lands on which to settle and that an agreement was made whereby the Saxons should fight against Britain's enemies in return for wages to be paid them by the Britons.[36]   This also is more explicit than the account given by Gildas which mentions the supplying of provisions for the newcomers, but does not explicitly mention the granting of lands.   Bede may only have been rewriting the rather lurid passage in which Gildas had described these events, but his account does leave the impression that Gildas was not the only source from which it was drawn.   After recounting the origin of the various races which came to

[33] *HE* I, 14.
[34] *HE* I, 15.
[35] *HE* I, 15—*inito ergo certamine cum hostibus, qui ab aquilone ad aciem venerant, victoriam sumsere Saxones.*
[36] *HE* I, 15.

Britain and of the kingdoms which they founded, Bede then describes the revolt of the Saxons, deriving the greater part of his description in direct quotation from Gildas, but adding one statement of fact which is not found in Gildas—namely that after the Saxons had fought successfully against the Picts, they suddenly formed an alliance with them and turned against the Britons.[37]

This statement is of the greatest interest, because if it was not derived from Gildas, it seems to supply independent evidence in support of one of the most striking points in the narrative of Gildas, namely that the Saxons were first called in to help in dealing with dangers threatening in the north. It might be argued that, in referring to an alliance between Picts and Saxons, Bede has been influenced by Constantius' *Life of Germanus* which describes Picts and Saxons as having fought on the same side against the Britons in the Hallelujah battle.[38] Although it is true that in the order of his narrative Bede placed his account of the Hallelujah battle, which he derived from Constantius, after his account of the revolt of the Saxons which he derived from Gildas, yet he knew and stated that the Hallelujah battle had been fought some years before what he regarded as the *aduentus Saxonum* proper. Bede derived the greater part of *HE* I, 12-16, from Gildas. He refers to the alliance between Picts and Saxons and their joint attack on the Britons in I, 15. In I, 16, he describes the British victory at *Mons Badonicus*, and he concludes the chapter with the words *sed haec postmodum*. He then abandons the chronological order of his narrative and inserts a digression on the rise of Pelagianism and an account of the measures taken to combat it which he derived almost entirely from Constantius. This digression which forms I, 17-21, carries him back to the first visit of Germanus (429), and includes an account of the Hallelujah battle. He opens

[37] *HE* I, 15—*tum subito inito ad tempus foedere cum Pictis, quos longius iam bellando pepulerant, in socios arma vertere incipiunt.*
[38] Constantius' account is used by Bede, *HE* I, 20.

I, 17, with the words *ante paucos sane aduentus eorum annos heresis Pelagiana per Agricolam inlata etc.* *Eorum* here refers to the Saxons, and there can be very little doubt that this qualifying phrase applies to the whole insertion which forms I, 17-21. In I, 22, Bede returns to Gildas for his material, and resumes the narrative from the point at which it had been interrupted in I, 16. Bede thus leaves no room for doubt of his awareness that the alliance between Picts and Saxons at the Hallelujah battle was on an occasion which befell some years before the *aduentus Saxonum.* I am therefore of the opinion that his reference to an alliance between the Saxons and the Picts on the occasion of the Saxon revolt is not derived from Constantius or influenced by him and that it may accordingly be used as independent evidence in support of the testimony of Gildas that the Saxons were first called in to deal with troubles in the north of Britain. My impression that Bede had some source of information other than Gildas about the earliest settlements of the Saxons in the north and about their initial victories over the Picts is thereby strengthened.

Bede made one other major addition to the narrative of Gildas, namely the insertion of a number of dates. He placed the building of the turf and stone walls which resulted from the first two appeals to the Romans after 407[39] and before 423.[40] Gildas had placed the appeal to Aetius simply during the latter's third consulship. Bede adds that Aetius was consul for the third time in the twenty-third year of the reign of Theodosius, which began in 423.[41] The British recovery, the repulse of the Picts and Scots and the phase of prosperity he placed between the appeal to Aetius and the arrival of the Saxons which he assigned to some unspecified year during the joint reign of Marcian and Valentinian whose beginning he placed in 449.[42] The result of placing the narrative of Gildas within such a frame-

[39] *HE* I, 11, 12.
[40] *HE* I, 13.
[41] *HE* I, 13.
[42] *HE* I, 15. Marcian was not recognized in the west until 452.

work was to give the whole story a chronological rigidity which was entirely lacking in the original and to raise in an acute form the difficulty of interpreting the letter to Aetius as an appeal for help against the Picts and Scots. We ought not, however, to allow our estimate of the value of Gildas's narrative to be unduly influenced by Bede's chronological framework. The whole structure of Bede's *History* rested upon a chronological foundation, and when he embodied extracts from such writers as Gildas and Constantius the result was bound to be a somewhat artificial union.

The *Historia Brittonum* differs very greatly from both Bede and Gildas in its account of events in Britain between the departure of the Romans and the arrival of the English. It refers briefly to the rebellion of Magnus Maximus, to the attacks of the Picts and Scots and to the British appeals for help.[43] It then relates side by side what are really two separate stories, one concerning Hengest's invasion of Kent and the other the relations of Vortigern with Germanus. The latter has no bearing on the history of northern Britain, and there is therefore no need to discuss it. The story of Hengest's invasion of Kent[44] is of importance in two respects, first because the prominence which it gives to the Kentish settlement tends to obscure the earlier evidence of Bede and Gildas—a point which will be considered more fully below—and second because a small section of it deals directly with the north. Hengest, it is said, suggested to Vortigern, after the latter had consented to give him Kent, that he should send home for his son Octha and his nephew Ebissa, that these two should be set to fight against the Scots, and that they should be rewarded with lands in the north near the wall called *Guaul*. Octha and Ebissa arrived with forty ships, circumnavigated the lands of the Picts, ravaged the Orkneys, and finally took possession of very

---

[43] Cc. 29, 30. The references are to Mommsen's edition, *MGH Auct. Antiquiss.*, XIII, 111-222.

[44] Discussed in detail by H. M. Chadwick, *The Origin of the English Nation*, 36-44.

many districts beyond the *mare Frenessicum* as far as the borders of the Picts.[45] Several paragraphs later the *Historia Brittonum* adds that after the death of Hengest, Octha left the north of Britain to settle in Kent, and from him the kings of Kent were descended.[46] At first sight this story seems to lend powerful support to the evidence of Bede and Gildas that Saxon mercenaries were employed in the north at an early date, but there are points about it which suggest that it should be used with caution. According to the *Historia Brittonum* Octha was the son and successor of Hengest and came to be regarded as the ancestor of the kings of Kent. On two points this is in direct conflict with Bede who writes—*erat autem idem Aedilberct filius Irmin-rici, cuius pater Octa, cuius pater Oeric cognomento Oisc, a quo reges Cantuariorum Oiscingas cognominare. Cuius pater Hengist,* etc.[47] Bede thus makes Octha the grandson, not the son of Hengest, and reckons the Kentish kings to have been descended from Oisc, not from Octha. Bede is supported by the *Anglo-Saxon Chronicle* which, however, changes the name of Hengest's son to Aesc.[48] So far as I am aware the name Ebissa is not recorded elsewhere, a fact which suggests that, like so many other personal names in the *Historia Brittonum*, it is a corrupt form.[49] *Mare Frenes-sicum* (with variants *Fresicum, Frisicum*) is presumably to

[45] C. 38—*invitabo filium meum cum fratueli suo, bellatores enim viri sunt, ut dimicent contra Scottos, et da illis regiones, quae sunt in aquilone iuxta murum, qui vocatur Guaul. et jussit ut invitaret eos et invitavit: Octha et Ebissa cum quadraginta ciulis. at ipsi cum navigarent circa Pictos, vastaverunt Orcades insulas et venerunt et occupaverunt regiones plurimas ultra mare Frenessicum* (variants—*Fresicum, Frisicum*) *usque ad confinium Pictorum.*

[46] C. 56—*in illo tempore Saxones invalescebant in multitudine in Brittannia. mortuo autem Hengisto Octha filius eius transivit de sinistrali parte Britanniae ad regnum Cantorum et de ipso orti sunt reges Cantorum.*

[47] *HE* II, 5.

[48] Text A, *s.a.* 455, 457, 465, 473, 488.

[49] It is possible that *Ebissa* is a corruption arising from the two names *Eoppa* and *Oesa*, father and grandfather respectively of Ida of Bernicia. The relevant part of the Bernician genealogy in the additions to the *Historia Brittonum* runs . . . *genuit Aedibrith genuit Ossa genuit Eobba genuit Ida* (c. 57). The genealogies in the *Historia Brittonum* are closely related to those found in Cott. Vesp. B VI and CCCC 183 (see

be interpreted as the Frisian Sea. Jocelyn's *Life of Kentigern* refers to the Frisian Shore in a context which indicates that the shore of the Firth of Forth was meant.[50] The Durham group of MSS. of the *Historia Brittonum*, none of which is earlier than the late twelfth century, supply the gloss *qui* (quod) *inter nos Scottosque est* and thereby seem to agree with Jocelyn in identifying the Frisian Sea with the Firth of Forth.[51] But whether or not this identification is correct, the name *Mare Frenessicum* is not out of keeping with the age to which the expedition of Octha and Ebissa is referred by the *Historia Brittonum*. Procopius,[52] writing soon after the middle of the sixth century, names the *Frissones* as one of the three races inhabiting Britain, and there are linguistic grounds[53] which compel us to suppose that the Frisians played a substantial part in the settlement of Britain. For some centuries before the viking age much of the trade of north-western Europe seems to have been conducted by the Frisians.[54] Dorestad, their principal town, was known to the Ravenna geographer.[55] At one time the most prosperous part of Mainz is said to have belonged to them, and they are said to have been so numerous in Worms at a later date that they were charged with the duty of keeping part of the town wall in repair.[56] Bede

H. M. Chadwick, *op. cit.*, 41). Cott. Vesp. B VI, reads in the reverse order—*ida eopping eoppa oesing oesa aethelberhting*. With the names in this order the formation of *ebissa* from *eoppa oesing* would be no more difficult than many of the other corruptions in the *Historia Brittonum*. It is not without interest to note that in Geoffrey of Monmouth's richly embroidered account (Bk. VIII, ch. 18) of a Saxon expedition to the north, Octha's companion is called, not Ebissa, but Eosa. An early marginal gloss in the twelfth century Ushaw MS. of Geoffrey identifies *mons Damet* (*Damen* in other MSS.), the scene of one of their exploits, with Wingates, near Brinkburn (Northumberland), EHR, 58, 47-8.

[50] *Frisicum litus*—Jocelyn's *Life of Kentigern*, ch. viii, ed. A. P. Forbes, *Historians of Scotland*, vol. v, 176. The passage is discussed by Skene, *Celtic Scotland*, II, 183-5.

[51] Mommsen's C²DᵐGL. In MSS. of this place and date *Scottos* must refer to the Scots of Scotland, not to the *Scotti* of Ireland.

[52] *History of the Wars*, Loeb ed. VII, xx, 7.

[53] H. M. Chadwick, *op. cit.*, 58-60.

[54] E. Wadstein, *Norden och Väst-Europa i gammal tid*, 33-53.

[55] Ed. Pinder and Parthey, 228.

[56] Wadstein, *op. cit.*, 40.

refers to a Frisian merchant in London,[57] and there was a Frisian colony in York in the time of Alcuin.[58] In these conditions a part of the waters off Britain may well have come to be known as the Frisian Sea in the period between the Anglo-Saxon and Viking invasions, just as another part of the coast had previously come to be known as the Saxon shore.

The story of Octha and Ebissa contains three indications of the locality of their alleged settlements. Hengest's original suggestion was that they should be given the districts next the wall called *Guaul*, but the settlements themselves are said to have been beyond the Frisian Sea and reaching as far as the borders of the Picts, without reference to any wall. We have seen that Jocelyn and Durham tradition of the twelfth century and later identified the Frisian Sea with the Firth of Forth. If this identification is right—and we cannot discount it entirely—there can hardly be any doubt that the author of the story believed the districts concerned to have lain on the north side of the Firth of Forth and not far from the eastern end of the Antonine Wall, but in that case the story would be self-contradictory because the settlements would not merely have reached as far as the borders of the Picts but would have been inside those borders. The southern side of the Firth of Forth would have seemed a much more likely area, but we should then have to assume that the author of the *Historia Brittonum* was writing somewhere north of the Forth.[59] It has been suggested that the Frisian Sea should be identified with the Solway,[60] but even if the circumnavigation of the Picts is to be interpreted as meaning that Octha and Ebissa sailed south along the west coast of Scotland, which is in itself doubtful, the attack on the Orkneys

---

[57] *HE* IV, 20 (22). See F. M. Stenton, *op. cit.*, 56, for some numismatic evidence of trade between London and the Frisian coast.
[58] *Altfridi Vita Sancti Liudgeri*, c. 11, *MGH* SS II, 407.
[59] As F. Lot unconvincingly does, *Nennius et l'Historia Brittonum*, 65.
[60] O. G. S. Crawford, *Antiquity*, IX, 284.

is placed after this voyage and before the settlements which suggests that Octha and Ebissa made their way back to the North Sea before finally settling down.[61] If it is accepted that the settlements lay in the east rather than in the west, the Humber seems to be the only remaining possibility.[62] But are we bound to suppose that *ultra* refers to the standpoint of the author ? Might it not be interpreted as referring to the standpoint of Octha and Ebissa, meaning only that Octha and Ebissa crossed the sea and settled beyond it ? If this interpretation were allowed, the Frisian Sea would be no more than a name for the North Sea in general and the settlements would then lie somewhere towards the north of eastern Britain. Taken as a whole the story of Octha and Ebissa does not inspire confidence. It seems to be wrong about the ancestry of Octha, the name Ebissa looks like a corruption and the Frisian Sea cannot be certainly identified. But even if the story cannot be accepted in its details, it may none the less preserve a muddled tradition, independent of Bede and Gildas, that a Germanic settlement took place in the north-east of England or the south-east of Scotland at about the same time as the invasion of Kent, i.e. *c.* 449.

We have discussed the story of Octha and Ebissa at considerable length because it has a direct bearing on the beginnings of Northumbrian history. It is therefore the more necessary to remind ourselves that the position occupied by this story in the *Historia Brittonum*, so far from being a prominent one, is altogether subordinate to the matter relating to Hengest's invasion of Kent and to the dealings of Germanus with Vortigern. The space devoted to the invasion of Kent is seven or eight times as great as that devoted to Octha and Ebissa. In order to appreciate the consequences of this fact, we must now make a brief review of this discussion of the Gildas tradition. Gildas himself wrote

[61] As J. N. L. Myres points out, *History*, NS, 20, 262, n. 1.

[62] So Myres, *op. cit.*, 262, though I think he goes too far in describing the identification of the Frisian Sea with the Humber estuary as "virtually certain."

an account which was all but timeless, and which leaves a clear impression upon its readers that the outstanding achievement in Britain after the withdrawal of the Roman armies was the expulsion of the Picts and Scots and the establishment of British authority over a wide area of northern Britain. Gildas was, of course, in a position to look back and so to realize what a disastrous mistake from his point of view the introduction of the Saxons into Britain had been. Bede followed Gildas in his main outlines, and besides giving a clear impression of having known more about the Saxons in the north than Gildas did, he added a statement of fact about a treaty between the Saxons and the Picts at the time of the Saxon revolt which was certainly not derived from Gildas. At the same time he confined the story within a rigid chronological framework and made Vortigern responsible for the invitation to the Saxons. The *Historia Brittonum* made only the briefest of references to the Gildas tradition, and in its place added a long and detailed story about the invasion of Kent which contained a short digression on the adventures of Octha and Ebissa in the north. In this way the *Historia Brittonum* exaggerated the importance of what was, from the strictly contemporary point of view, merely a local affair and thereby seriously distorted the picture drawn by Gildas. Chance has preserved a detailed tradition about what was happening in Kent, but it is no more than chance which has failed to preserve similar traditions about what was happening in other parts of the country. This process of distortion was carried a stage further by the Parker text of the *Anglo-Saxon Chronicle* which omitted all reference to events in the north of Britain and confined itself to brief entries relating to the progress of the invasions in the south. It is natural enough that events which are well to the fore in the scene depicted by Gildas the Briton should recede with the passage of time and finally disappear altogether from the works of English writers, but the change is one of emphasis alone and must not be allowed to impugn the

THE ORIGINS OF NORTHUMBRIA   19

veracity of Gildas. Even at the risk of seeming to labour the point, it must be urged that the danger of gaining a distorted impression of these times is one that must be kept constantly in mind. The sum of all the available literary evidence for this period of cataclysmic change is small in the extreme, and even if it tells a part of the truth, it certainly does not tell more than a small fraction of the whole. To dismiss the story of the Kentish war as romance or to transplant Hengest to some other part of the country[63] is to forget that the fame of Hengest is accidental, to forget that the independent Ravenna geographer calls the leader of the Saxons not Hengest but Ansehis and to forget also that one more tradition might have given us yet a third name.

2. *The Veracity of Gildas.*

We have so far considered the accounts of those early writers who set out to compose a narrative which would cover the whole period from the last days of Roman Britain to the beginnings of English Northumbria. We are now in a position to discuss evidence which is independent of the Gildas tradition and which may be expected in part to serve as a check upon the veracity of Gildas and in part to throw light upon some of the episodes at which the Gildas tradition seems to hint. In order to find firm ground as a starting-point we must go back to the great disaster which overwhelmed Roman Britain in 367. Ammianus[64] names three peoples as playing an important part in the events of this year—the Picts, who are said to have been divided into two tribes called the *Dicalydonae* and the *Verturiones*, the Scots and the *Attacotti*. The Picts and Scots began to operate jointly against the defences of Roman Britain in the first half of the fourth century, and from then until the

---

[63] As would E. G. M. Fletcher, *Antiquity*, XVII, 91-3.
[64] XXVII, 8. Conveniently cited by R. W. Moore, *The Romans in Britain*, 94.

withdrawal of the Roman armies the military history of the province is very largely the record of their attacks and of the measures taken against them by successive Roman commanders. The events of 367, the fourth century rebuilding of the fort at Carnarvon and the construction of signal stations along the north-east coast—to note only a few details—are plain evidence that the Picts and Scots, either by themselves or with the help of allies, were not only able to carry a strong frontier by direct assault, but could also penetrate a very long way to its rear. It is difficult to believe that they could have achieved such things without being in control, and perhaps even in occupation, of a part of the country on the north side of the Tyne-Solway line. The third of these peoples, the *Attacotti*, are obscure. Ammianus describes them as a warlike people, and according to the *Notitia Dignitatum*[65] some of them served in the Roman armies in various parts of the western empire. There is no reference to any British tribes having taken part in the attack on the Wall from the north, unless the Attacotti were themselves of British origin. The political boundaries of these parts cannot again be drawn with any approach to certainty before the second half of the seventh century, and the situation which they then disclose is fundamentally changed. Abercorn was in English hands and Dumbarton was the capital of the British kingdom of Strathclyde. With the possible exception of a small area near the eastern end of the Antonine Wall, there is no good evidence for the presence of either Picts or Scots south of the Forth-Clyde line, the Attacotti have disappeared, and virtually the whole area between the two Walls is found to be divided between British and English peoples.

There are two ways in which it might be held possible to account for this revolutionary change in the political geography of northern Britain. The first which raises the very difficult question of the identity of the peoples living between the two Walls in the fourth century, is to suppose

[65] Cited by R. W. Moore, *op. cit.*, 194.

that Ammianus was mistaken in implying that the Britons took no major part in the operations of 367, and that many of those whom he calls Picts were in fact Britons. But even if this was the case (and we may note in passing that Bede was never in any doubt about the separate identities of the Britons and the Picts), it would not account entirely for the virtual disappearance of the Picts and Scots from the area south of the Antonine Wall or for the complete superiority which the Britons were able to establish in this area before the expansion of Northumbria towards the end of the sixth century. The second way, which does not necessarily exclude the first, is to suppose that at some period between 367 and c. 550 there was a phase of vigorous warfare which placed the Britons in complete control of the whole of Scotland as far north as the Forth-Clyde line. It cannot be supposed for one moment that the expulsion of the Picts and Scots was the work of the Northumbrian invaders of the sixth century. Northumbria was formed out of territory won by the English from the Britons, not from the Picts and Scots. If the English are excluded, there remain only the Roman army and the Britons, and therefore, even if the literary sources had contained no hint of any such northern success, we should have been compelled to postulate something of the kind in order to account for the facts as we find them in 367 and again some two centuries later. The testimony of Gildas on the fact of recovery, at least in the north, is therefore not to be doubted, but we may, indeed must, ask whether, in placing the recovery after the withdrawal of the Romans, he has placed it at the right time. The British domination of southern Scotland at the time of the foundation of Bernicia in 547 is not in dispute. The problem which concerns us now is how and when that domination was achieved. What sequence of events enabled the British so to recover from the disasters of 367 that they could not only overcome their old enemies, but could also offer a prolonged and vigorous opposition to the English invaders some two centuries later ? In his description of the

island of Britain Bede thought fit to refer to *Alcluith*, i.e.
Dumbarton, which he describes as *ciuitas Brittonum
munitissima usque hodie.*[66] What were the circumstances
which justified a reference to Dumbarton in such a way as
to imply that it was one of the most powerful strongholds
of Britain long before Bede's time, and what circumstances
justified a not dissimilar reference to *urbs Giudi*, at the
eastern end of the Antonine Wall?[67] There is not at
present enough evidence to give complete answers to all
these questions, but there is at least enough to justify an
attempt to give partial answers.

Gildas leaves no room for doubt that the British civiliza-
tion about which he wrote was Christian, and that is why
it has left so few material remains. The amount of archæological evidence which can at present be brought to bear on
these problems consists only of a small group of tombstones
which seem, on considerations of style and language, to
belong to this period. The entire group consists only of
eleven stones of which five are connected with ecclesiastical
establishments at Whithorn and Kirkmadrine.[68] Of the
remaining six stones, one, from Manor Water and now in
the Peebles museum, seems to mark the grave of an Irish-
woman,[69] and another, which comes from Overkirkhope in
Ettrick, is of little value for present purposes.[70] The remaining four, which come respectively from Northumberland, Liddesdale, Selkirk and Midlothian, are apparently
the tombstones of civilians. The Northumberland stone,
which was found near the Roman fort at Chesterholm, was
erected to the memory of Brigomaglos.[71] Since the stone
was not in its original position when it was first noticed, it
is not known whether it marked an isolated grave or
whether it formed part of a cemetery. The same is true

[66] *HE* I, I.   [67] *HE* I, 12.
[68] For the latest account of these five stones see R. A. S. Macalister,
Corpus Inscriptionum Celticarum Insularum, I, 493-501.
[69] *Ibid.*, 486-8.
[70] J. Romilly Allen, *The Early Christian Monuments of Scotland*,
pt. 3, 432, fig. 451.
[71] Macalister, *op. cit.*, 475-6.

of the Liddesdale stone to the memory of Carantus the son of Cupitianus, which was found in the bed of Liddel Water.[72] The Midlothian stone, commonly known as the Cat Stane, stands in the parish of Kirkliston, close to the south bank of the Almond and between six and seven miles from Edinburgh.[73] The inscription it bears records that it marks the burial place of Vetta, the son of Victus or Victrix. Edward Lhwyd, describing this monument in about 1700, said that it covered an area of some seven yards in diameter, that it was raised somewhat above the level of the surrounding ground and was encompassed by large stones laid lengthwise. When the area was excavated in 1865 it was found that the monument formed part of a cemetery which was enclosed by a roughly built stone wall, within whose limits no less than fifty stone-lined graves were found. All the graves lay with heads to the west, and no relics of any kind were found with the burials. There can hardly be any doubt that this was a Christian cemetery of the British heroic age, although in the absence of relics it cannot be more precisely dated. The last and most interesting stone of the series comes from the parish of Yarrow in the county of Selkirk.[74] A recent study of this stone by Professor Macalister has shown that the long and in parts obscure inscription which it bears was carved in two stages, and that it represents the epitaphs of two princes who are described as the sons of *Liberalis*. The names of these two princes are read by Professor Macalister as *Nudogenos* and *Dubnogenos*. It was formerly thought that the name *Nodus* or *Nudus* was to be read as the father of the people commemorated in this inscription, and since *liberalis* is the Latin equivalent of the Welsh *hael* it was suggested that this person might be identified with Nudd Hael,[75] a member

[72] *Ibid.*, 491.
[73] *Ibid.*, 486. and the references there cited. See also *Antiquity*, XIX, 208, where O. G. S. Crawford disputes Macalister's reading.
[74] Macalister, *op. cit.*, 491-3.
[75] H. M. and N. K. Chadwick, *The Growth of Literature*, I, 143, and the references there cited.

III

of the Strathclyde family, who is presumed to have lived
in the latter part of the sixth century, but if Professor
Macalister's reading is followed, this identification must be
abandoned. The epithet *hael* was used as a kind of sur-
name by more than one member of the Strathclyde family,
but neither *Nudogenos* nor *Dubnogenos* occurs in any
of the surviving Welsh genealogies which relate to
families located in northern Britain. Excavation in the
neighbourhood of this stone at about the middle of
the nineteenth century suggests that it marked the site of
another British Christian cemetery.[76] None of the
persons named in this small group of inscriptions
has yet been identified, and therefore their evidence,
though valuable in other respects, is of no help chronologically.

One of the characteristics of this age, remarked Gildas,
was fertility in tyrants (by whom he doubtless meant those
who followed the example of Magnus Maximus and rebelled
against the lawful authority, namely Rome). But the final
withdrawal of the means whereby that authority was
asserted, would leave the way open for anyone who was
strong enough to assert his own authority in its place. The
Welsh genealogies, reflecting the process by which the
new political system emerged, record the names of a considerable number of kings who were believed to have ruled
at various times in the fifth and following centuries. These
genealogies can be checked at a sufficient number of points
to suggest that they are reliable at least as far back as the
beginning of the sixth century,[77] but although they contain names in abundance, it is not easy to attach many of
them to particular geographical areas. A glance at the
genealogies of that group of kings who were known collectively as the *Men of the North* will show that all of the
thirteen separate genealogies go back to one of two

[76] PSAS II, 484-9. There are other cemeteries which may belong to
this period, but direct evidence of their date is lacking, see *Arch. Ael.*,
4 S., XXIII, map facing p. 94.
[77] H. M. and N. K. Chadwick, *op. cit.*, I, 151-2.

ancestors, Ceredig Gwledig or Coel Hen.[78] It is certain that the descendants of Ceredig Gwledig were the rulers of the kingdom of Strathclyde and that they had their capital on the rock of Dumbarton near the western end of the Antonine Wall. In the time of Columba the representative of this line was Rodercus, son of Tothail,[79] otherwise known as Rhydderch Hael, who appears in the genealogies in the fifth generation from Ceredig.[80] If Rhydderch was reigning in the second half of the sixth century, it follows that Ceredig will have been reigning in the first half of the fifth century. Patrick's famous *Letter* was addressed to a certain Coroticus who, on the evidence of Muirchu's *Life of St. Patrick*, can be located at Dumbarton.[81] From the fact that Coroticus and Ceredig flourished at the same time, and from the further fact that a descendant of Ceredig's was undoubtedly ruling at Dumbarton in the sixth century, it has been inferred that Ceredig and Coroticus were one and the same person. If this inference is correct, it follows that Ceredig's family was already established at Dumbarton by *c.* 450, and we must therefore look more closely at Patrick's letter in order to see what kind of a kingdom he ruled over.

The occasion of the letter—which was not addressed to Coroticus himself, but to his soldiers—was a marauding expedition which these soldiers had undertaken to Ireland, and in the course of which they had killed or captured a number of Christians who had recently been baptized by Patrick himself.[82] Patrick does not address the soldiers explicitly as Christians, but he leaves no room for doubt that they came from what was nominally a Christian country, because it was the very fact that the raid had been

[78] See the table compiled by Skene, *Four Ancient Books*, I, 168-9.
[79] Adamnan's *Life of Columba*, ed. W. Reeves, bk. I, ch. viii, pp. 123-4.
[80] *Y Cymmrodor*, IX, 172-3, also A. W. Wade-Evans, *Nennius's History of the Britons*, 104-5.
[81] In the heading to Muirchu's *Life of St. Patrick*, Coroticus is called *Coirthech regem Aloo*. For Patrick's *Letter* see N. J. D. White, *Libri Sancti Patricii*, P.R.I.A., xxv, section c, 201-326, 542-52. The references are to this edition.
[82] §§ 2, 3.

made by men who were supposed to be Christians which
made his position among the heathen and newly baptized
in Ireland so difficult. He knew that the fate of the cap-
tives was to be sold on foreign slave markets. He de-
nounced the soldiers as men with whom no Christian should
take food or drink, and as men from whom none should
accept alms, and he urged that the letter should be read as
widely as possible, even in the presence of Coroticus himself. A letter of this kind presupposes the existence of an
organized Christian community which would receive it and
make its contents known, for Patrick particularly asked
that it should be read *coram cunctis plebibus*,[83] and how
did he expect this to be done unless by preachers? For
what purposes would alms be given by soldiers unless for
the maintenance of the church? The abrupt way in which
Patrick turns from rebuking the soldiers to quote the example of the Christian Gauls whose custom it was to redeem
Christians who had been sold into slavery,[84] leads one to
infer that expeditions for the purpose of taking prisoners
who could then be sold in foreign markets were of common
occurrence in Patrick's time. The activities of Coroticus as
a slave trader suggest one source of income which would
enable him to support an army. The existence of that army
calls to mind the curious remark of Gildas that the Romans
left behind them patterns for the making of weapons before
their final departure. As a literal statement of fact it is
interesting, but one would hardly have expected a simple
action of this kind to have passed into current tradition
unless something more important lay behind it, for example
instruction, not so much in the processes of manufacture,
as in the uses of the weapons themselves. The inescapable
fact remains that the Britons, with or without Roman help,
were able to gain a notable success over two of the most
formidable enemies that Roman Britain had ever faced, an
achievement which implies either the formation of British

[83] § 21.
[84] § 14.

III

military organizations under skilled leadership or the weakening of the Picts and Scots by internal troubles. However that may be, it is clear from Patrick's *Letter* that the kingdom over which Ceredig ruled was far from being newly established at the time when that *Letter* was written, i.e. *c.* 450, and that the undertaking which led to its formation had been carried through at some appreciably earlier date.

This line of argument has led us to infer that at least on the western side of northern Britain some kind of political stability had been achieved by *c.* 425, and that the British frontier towards the north then rested on the line of the old Antonine Wall. If this was the case we can the more readily understand the success which attended the missionary and educational activities of Ninian's foundation at Whithorn. It is scarcely to be believed that such work could have been carried out if the conditions of 367 had still been prevalent in the earlier part of the fifth century. Is there any evidence to suggest that the period of the British recovery should be carried still further back, that is into the fourth century? Professor Chadwick drew my attention to a point of considerable interest in the genealogy of Ceredig. The name of Ceredig's father was Cynloyp, which is obscure, but his grandfather and great-grandfather were called respectively Cinhil and Cluim,[85] which are evidently the purely Roman names Quintilius and Clemens. If Ceredig flourished *c.* 450, his great-grandfather will have flourished *c.* 360, and we are immediately led to wonder under what circumstances a powerful native dynasty established at the western end of the Antonine Wall came to claim descent from apparently Romano-British ancestry. At this point we may leave the problem of Dumbarton for a moment in order to consider the situation at the other end of the Antonine Wall.

The counterpart of Dumbarton in the east was *urbs Giudi.* Referring to the two firths, Bede writes—*orientalis*

[85] *Y Cymm.,* IX, 173, also Wade-Evans, *op. cit.,* 104-5.

habet in medio sui urbem Giudi, occidentalis supra se, hoc
est ad dexteram sui, habet urbem Alcluith, quod lingua
eorum signficat petram Cluith.[86] Bede has commonly been
interpreted as meaning that *urbs Giudi* lay on an island in
the Firth of Forth, and the place has therefore been identified with Inchkeith, but, whatever *urbs* may mean in this
context, it is scarcely conceivable that a site for such a
" city " would have been chosen on an island which lay
some four miles offshore in the middle of a tidal estuary.
We know of only one use to which the islands off Britain
were regularly put during this period, and that was to serve
as ecclesiastical sanctuaries. If it has to be supposed that
urbs Giudi was an island stronghold, Cramond Island
would have been a more suitable site. I am not, however,
convinced that this is the right interpretation of Bede. It
seems more likely that in the passage quoted above Bede
was contrasting the position of Alcluith which lay at the
head of the Firth of Clyde, with the position of Giudi which
lay, not out in the middle of the Forth, but half way along
it. If this is the correct interpretation, the site of *urbs
Giudi* should be sought in some suitable position, such as
Cramond itself or perhaps Inveresk, on the southern shore
of the Forth. So far as I know there is no direct evidence
for associating *urbs Giudi* with the kingdom of Manau over
which Cunedda ruled. This latter, however, seems to have
been the counterpart at the eastern end of the Antonine
Wall of Ceredig's kingdom at the western end. Cunedda
himself and a large part of the Votadini over whom he
ruled migrated to north-west Wales, where he founded the
kingdom of Gwynedd, whose ruler in the time of Gildas
was Maelgwn. There will be more to say later about
the date and purpose of this migration, but for the
moment we are concerned with trying to establish the
date at which the kingdom of Manau first came into
being.

According to the Harleian genealogies Cunedda's father

[86] *HE* I, 12.

was called *Aetern*, his grandfather *Patern Pesrut* and his great-grandfather *Tacit*.[87] It has long been recognized that these are Roman names and that the epithet *Pesrut* seems to imply that the man to whom it was given was invested with some kind of Roman authority. The suggestion has been made that the phase of stability which is implied by the establishment of this eastern kingdom and its western counterpart should be equated with the political settlement of Constans in 343,[88] but it is difficult to see how the two kingdoms could have survived intact the great upheaval of 367, unless indeed we are to suppose that the area south of the Antonine Wall was not greatly affected. Moreover, this equation depends on the assumption that Cunedda flourished *c*. 400. Here I must anticipate conclusions by saying that I suspect the generally accepted dating of Cunedda's migration to be erroneous, and that he and Ceredig were approximately contemporary, both flourishing about the middle of the fifth century.

The genealogies show that both Ceredig and Cunedda were believed to be descended from men who bore Roman names. In both cases the Roman nomenclature can be traced as far back as their great-grandfathers, but beyond that it disappears. If Ceredig and Cunedda flourished about the middle of the fifth century, a point which is not in dispute for Ceredig, their great-grandfathers will have flourished somewhat after the middle of the fourth century, that is to say in and after the great troubles of 367. This coincidence suggests a train of thought which has far-reaching consequences, and it will therefore be well to consider how far genealogical material which is not preserved in any manuscript earlier than the twelfth century can legitimately be used to interpret fourth-century history. Genealogies are a characteristic feature of the early literatures of many peoples, and the development of this form of historical record is particularly well-marked among the

---

[87] *Y Cymm*., IX, 170, also Wade-Evans, *op. cit*., 101.
[88] *Northumberland County History*, XV, 113-14.

III

Teutonic, Scandinavian and Celtic peoples.[89]   It has long
been established that the alliterative genealogy, preserved
orally and sometimes in the form of verse,[90] was a means
whereby accurate information could be handed down over
a number of generations which might well cover a period
of several centuries before the genealogies themselves were
first committed to writing.   A case in point is the genealogy
of the Mercian royal family.   This is not now preserved in
any manuscript earlier than the ninth century, but there is
good evidence for thinking that the names Offa and Wer-
mund which represent the eighth and ninth generations
before Penda, are those of historical persons who flourished
on the other side of the North Sea in the second half of the
fourth century.[91]   In this case the genealogy was accurately
preserved in spite of the migration overseas of the family
concerned.   An even longer span is covered by the genealogies of the high kings of Ireland which, in the opinion of
Professor and Mrs. Chadwick, " are more or less trustworthy as far back as the third century, if not further."[92]
On the other hand, it cannot be denied that at certain periods
influences have been at work which tended to corrupt certain genealogies by the addition of spurious elements.   A
good example is provided again by the West-Saxon genealogy which was corrupted by the addition of both Germanic
and Hebrew names with the twofold object of glorifying the
family and lending a Christian colour to its descent.[93]

The most important collection of Welsh genealogies is
contained in MS. Harleian 3859, which seems to have been
written at about the beginning of the twelfth century, but
there is good reason to think that the text of the genealogies,
as also of the *Annales Cambriae* in the same manuscript,

[89] For a discussion of the subject see H. M. and N. K. Chadwick, *op.
cit.*, I, 270-6, to which I am much indebted.
[90] As in the case of part of the West-Saxon genealogy in the preface
to the Parker Chronicle.
[91] The evidence is discussed in detail by H. M. Chadwick, *The Origin
of the English Nation*, 110-36.
[92] *op. cit.*, I, 273.
[93] R. W. Chambers, *Beowulf, An Introduction*, 72-4.

was written *c.* 955, and that even in this form it was not an original work, but was based upon earlier materials.[94]   In the case of the Welsh there was less contact with primitive heathenism and therefore less motive for the introduction of spurious Christian elements, but the other principal motive for genealogical corruption still remained. Since it seems to have been thought that the best way of glorifying a British family was to provide it with a distinguished Roman ancestry, the genealogies of Ceredig and Cunedda might be regarded with suspicion on the very ground that they do contain Roman names. But I doubt if this suspicion would be justified without considering the kind of Roman names they contain. Genealogies which have been corrupted for the purpose of glorifying the family in question do not seem to be difficult to detect. Examples are provided by the families whose descent is traced from Maxim Guletic, i.e. Magnus Maximus, and in one instance through Magnus Maximus back to Helena and Constantine.[95] Another example is a case in which a long list of Roman emperors has been used as a genealogy.[96] The houses of Dumbarton and Manau (later Gwynedd) were among the most famous of all British dynasties. If pedigree makers had been at work, it would have been surprising to find them using such names as Quintilius, Clemens, Aeternus, Paternus and Tacitus when they had available the whole range of Roman emperors from Magnus Maximus back to Augustus himself. We have seen already that the Dumbarton pedigree can be checked by independent sources at points in the fifth and sixth centuries. Maelgwn, who was Cunedda's great-grandson, was given an unenviable prominence by Gildas, and the episode of Cunedda's migration which was so profoundly important for north-west Wales, was another

[94] H. M. and N. K. Chadwick, *op. cit.*, 149-50. The best edition is by E. Phillimore, *Y Cymm.*, IX, 141-83.
[95] Harl. Gen., no. II, *Y Cymm.*, IX, 171, also Wade-Evans, *op. cit.*, 103.
[96] Harl. Gen., no. XVI, *Y Cymm.*, IX, 175-7, also Wade-Evans, *op. cit.*, 107-8.

III

circumstance which makes it likely that the descent of this family would be accurately known. I would not suggest that a case can be proved on the unsupported testimony of the genealogies, but I believe that this testimony may be profitably used as a guide when none better is available. Dr. I. A. Richmond[97] has elsewhere advanced the view that the kingdoms of Strathclyde and Manau may have been Roman foundations representing a deliberate policy of creating buffer states which would serve as zones of influence beyond the frontier proper. The genealogies seem to support this interpretation, but I feel doubtful whether he is right in associating them with the political settlement of Constans in 343. It is unfortunate that there seems to be no method of establishing the dates of Ceredig and Cunedda more precisely. For Ceredig's dates we are dependent on Patrick's *Letter* which was written between 432 and 461, with a check supplied by reckoning backwards from the dates of his successors. The evidence for Cunedda's dates comes from two conflicting sources, one of them being a statement in the *Historia Brittonum* concerning the time of his migration to Wales, and the other being the fact that he was the great-grandfather of Maelgwn whose death is recorded in 548.[98] It would be foolish to maintain that by reckoning backwards at thirty years to a generation from a starting-point which is itself so insecurely established, we can determine accurately the period when the great-grandfathers of these two men lived. There cannot even be any very real confidence that such a calculation would be accurate enough to distinguish between the time of Constans and the time of Theodosius. None the less, unsatisfactory though the evidence is, it seems to point rather to the

[97] *loc. cit.*, n. 88 above.
[98] The passage from the *Hist. Britt.* is discussed further below, p. 34. In the *Ann. Camb.*, where the death of Maelgwn is recorded, dating by the Christian era is not used. The passage of years is marked simply by an abbreviation for *annus*. In correlating these years with the years of the incarnation the editor in the Rolls edition and Phillimore in *Y Cymm.* ed. seem to be one year too early. Cf. the dates adopted by H. M. and N. K. Chadwick, *op. cit.*, I, 148-9.

Theodosian period, partly on chronological grounds and partly because of the difficulty of understanding how the Picts and Scots could have overrun the Hadrianic frontier, as well as most of the province to its rear, without also destroying the states of Manau and Strathclyde, the very purpose of whose establishment was presumably to prevent just such an invasion. The invasion of 367 was the last major undertaking in which the Picts and Scots operated jointly against the British, and so far as we can see the British thereafter remained securely in possession of the whole country between the two Walls until it was conquered from them by the Northumbrians some two and a half centuries later. If we are right in assigning the foundation of Strathclyde and Manau to Theodosius, it would seem that the method adopted to overcome the menace of the Picts and Scots was to carry the war boldly into the enemies' territory and to secure the country thus regained, not by occupying a continuous frontier as in the days of Antoninus Pius, but by setting up two states under Roman direction at each end of the old frontier. To judge from later history this move was completely successful. Was it the introduction to that period which Gildas describes as bringing with it an age so prosperous that none who came after could remember such wealth? And what of the words used by Ammianus about the restoration achieved by Theodosius . . . *recuperatamque provinciam, quae in dicionem concesserat hostium, ita reddiderat statui pristino, ut eodem referente et rectorem haberet legitimum, et Valentia deinde vocaretur arbitrio principis, velut ovantis?*[99] Could there have been any better ground for the celebration of a triumph than the defeat of these old enemies of Roman Britain? It would perhaps be unwise to question the emphatic verdict of such an eminent scholar as R. G. Collingwood,[100] but it is

[99] XXVIII, 3.
[100] R. G. Collingwood and J. N. L. Myres, *Roman Britain and the English Settlements*, 286.

scarcely possible to avoid remarking how strangely apposite are the words of Ammianus to the situation we have been discussing.

Until fresh evidence can be brought to bear, the Roman origin of Strathclyde and Manau must remain largely conjectural. What is certain, however, is that before the middle of the fifth century the two states had turned into powerful British kingdoms. They had, if the expression may be allowed, " gone native." Despite the encroachments of Northumbria and the capture, once by the English[101] and once by the Vikings,[102] of Dumbarton itself, the kingdom of Strathclyde remained one of the most important factors in the politics of northern Britain for another five hundred years. The history of Manau, at least under that name, was shorter, owing to a circumstance to which we have already referred, namely the migration of Cunedda, accompanied as it would seem by many of his people, to north-west Wales. There are two sources of evidence which may be used to determine the date of this migration. The first is a famous passage in the *Historia Brittonum*,[103] which explains how Maelgwn came to rule in Gwynedd by saying that it was because his great-grandfather (*atavus*) Cunedda had come there from the district of Manau Guotodin with eight of his sons 146 years before Maelgwn's reign and had expelled the Scots after inflicting a severe defeat on them. According to the *Annales Cambriae* Maelgwn died in 548. The date of his accession is not known, but since Gildas recognized his pre-eminent position among contemporary British rulers, we may not be far wrong in placing it *c.* 530, and this will place Cunedda's migration *c.* 384. By supposing either that the period of 146 years was meant to be calculated, not from the beginning, but from the end of Maelgwn's reign, a construction which the passage will not readily bear, or that Maelgwn's reign did not begin till *c.* 540, which would make it much shorter than

---

[101] In 756, Symeon of Durham, Rolls ed., II, 40.
[102] In 870, *Annals of Ulster, s.a.* 869.   [103] C. 62.

the words of Gildas seem to suggest, the migration can be made to fall into place as one of the measures taken by Stilicho between 395 and 399 to strengthen a severely threatened frontier district.

The other source of evidence is the fact which is well-established in the genealogies, that Cunedda was Maelgwn's great-grandfather. If, for the sake of achieving round figures, we assume that Maelgwn was fifty-eight when he died, his birth will fall in 490 and the birth of his great-grandfather c. 400. Allow an additional ten years to Maelgwn and Cunedda's birth will fall c. 390. Thus the genealogies point to 390 or a little later for the date of Cunedda's birth. The *Historia Brittonum* points to 390 or a little earlier for the date of his migration. There is therefore a sharp conflict of evidence and the gap is too wide to be spanned by any normal allowance for error which the system of reckoning by thirty years to a generation requires to be made. The conflict becomes all the sharper when we recall that Cunedda was accompanied by eight of his nine sons and is therefore unlikely to have been a man of less than fifty at the time.

We have therefore to decide whether the genealogy or the figure given by the *Historia Brittonum* is likely to provide the more reliable evidence. It is a commonplace that figures very easily become corrupt in the copying of MSS. On the other hand, it is not unknown for a generation to drop out of a genealogy in the same process. To suppose that this has happened at some point between Cunedda and Maelgwn would be a convenient method of reconciling the conflict of evidence—convenient, but in this case inadmissible. In these four generations from Cunedda to Maelgwn we are not dealing with men who are mere names, men known only from the genealogy in which they occur. We know the names not only of the eight sons who went with Cunedda, several of which were long preserved in the names of the places over which they ruled,[104] but also of the other

[104] Sir John Lloyd, *op. cit.*, I, 117-18.

III

son, Typiaun, who was the first-born and who remained
behind in Manau Guotodin, where he died.[105] One of these
eight sons, Enniaun Girt, was the father of Cadwallon the
Longhanded, celebrated in the Triads as leader of one of the
Three Fettered Warbands of the Isle of Britain.[106] Cadwallon the Longhanded was father of Maelgwn. The four
generations are therefore covered with each supported by
other evidence in such a way as to make the possibility
of a lost generation extremely remote.

There is, however, another argument to be taken into
account. The Romans were still in control of North Wales
in 380,[107] and the date supplied by the *Historia Brittonum*
asks us to believe that within four or five years the Scots
had invaded North Wales and become a sufficiently formidable threat to the security of the country to require the
organization of a major campaign to evict them. This is
scarcely credible. It seems unlikely that the settlements
would even begin until some years after the area affected
had passed out of Roman control, presumably by the withdrawal of the garrisons in 383. Welsh tradition which preserved a clear memory of the " Irishmen's huts,"[108] and
which, moreover, ascribed the final expulsion of the Scots
not to Cunedda himself, not even to his sons, but to his
grandson, Cadwallon the Longhanded,[109] is evidence that
the Scottish occupation was not something which lasted
only half a dozen years. On these various grounds we can
scarcely escape the conclusion that the figure given by the
Historia Brittonum, 146 years before the reign of Maelgwn,
is corrupt, that Cunedda belongs to the first half of the fifth
century, and that the migration of the Votadini took place
towards the middle of that century.

The migration of the Votadini seems to have been completely successful in its object of expelling the Scots from

[105] *Y Cymm.*, IX, 182, also Wade-Evans, *op. cit.*, 113-14.
[106] Lloyd, *op. cit.*, I, 120.
[107] *Y Cymm.*, XXXIII, 89-93.
[108] Lloyd, *op. cit.*, I, 111-12.
[109] *Ibid.*, 120.

north-west Wales, but the price which would have to be paid for such success would be to upset the equilibrium established in the north by the Theodosian settlement. We have no means now of estimating the relative strength of the Pictish threat from across the Forth and the Scottish threat in northern Wales, and we can only suppose that the danger of a deep penetration into British territory from the west seemed real enough to justify a move which must have led to a considerable weakening of the northern defences. To have left the eastern end of the old Antonine line completely undefended would have been to invite disaster, and that, no doubt, was why Typiaun, Cunedda's eldest son, was left behind in Manau. The fact that it was Cunedda's eldest son who remained in Manau suggests with some force that Cunedda was aware of the dangers inherent in the move to Wales, and that he thought it necessary to make provision against them. Gildas, it will be recalled, states that after the period of prosperity the threat of invasion was renewed, and that in order to meet this threat the Saxons were called in. Gildas implies, and Bede explicitly states, that the Saxons were at first successful and that the Picts were driven back to the north. Now the arrival of the Saxons and the migration of the Votadini seem to have coincided approximately in point of time, and we may perhaps conjecture that the two events were not unconnected with one another, in other words, that the renewed threat of invasion from the north was due to the weakening of the northern defences which resulted from the migration of the Votadini. The claim that Saxon *foederati* were established somewhere in the north before the middle of the fifth century, and that they fought successfully in the service of the British is a strong one, even when it takes into account only the literary evidence.

The archæological evidence is at present difficult to interpret. It has accumulated piecemeal during the last hundred years in the course of excavations which were conducted by people who were either not qualified to perform such work

38   THE ORIGINS OF NORTHUMBRIA

or who had no proper understanding of the problems involved. Much of the material has been lost completely, and
there is no published *corpus* of what has survived. In all
too many instances, even where the material has survived,
there are no detailed accounts of the circumstances in which
it was found. In these very unsatisfactory conditions the
evidence should perhaps be used rather as a guide in for-
mulating the problems to which further study of the existing remains and the properly conducted excavation of fresh
sites may be expected to provide the answers, than as something from which positive deductions can at present be
made. The evidence in question is virtually confined to
one or other of two areas, the Yorkshire Wolds and the
immediate surroundings of York itself.[110] There seems to
be general agreement among those who are best qualified
to give an opinion that in both of these areas there is some
material which cannot easily be dated later than the fifth
century. For the Wolds it will suffice now to refer to
cremation urns from Sancton[111] and Broughton by Mal-

[110] Relics of the pagan Saxon period have been discovered at several
sites in other parts of Northumbria, but in the aggregate they are too
slight to be of much positive value.

[111] The cremation cemetery lay on high ground about half a mile
north-east of Sancton church. Eight urns, discovered shortly before
1875 and presented to the Ashmolean, are illustrated *Arch.*, xlv, pl.
xxxiii, p. 409, reproduced in *Trans. E. Riding Ant. Soc.*, xvi, pl. iii,
opp. p. 50. A detailed account derived from M. Forster, quoted by
W. Smith, *Old Yorkshire*, 1882, iii, 12-13, refers to the discovery of a
large number of urns, some whole, some fragmentary, and estimates the
cemetery to have covered an area 150 yards by 50 yards. According to
M. Forster this site was distinct from a mixed inhumation-cremation
cemetery somewhat nearer the village. Two more cremation urns discovered in 1892 and 1894, are illustrated in *Trans. E. Riding Ant. Soc.*,
v, 116-17, figs. 1 and 2. T. Shepherd, *ibid.*, xiv, 63, states that the
cremations were laid in rows (as at Heworth, see further below). Another
twenty urns, now in the Hull Museum, are described and illustrated by
T. Shepherd, *ibid.*, xvi, 52-66, pls. iv-xiii. The distinction between the
two separate cemeteries noted by M. Forster is also noted by Baldwin-
Brown, *Arts in Early England*, iv, 803, but not by the Elgees, *Archæ-
ology of Yorkshire*, 179. *VCH*, York, ii, 75-7, notes finds from three
separate sites near Sancton. The situation is extremely confused, but it
is clear that the finds from Sancton cover a long period, and that much
of the material belongs to the sixth century. I am much indebted to
my wife and to the late Miss M. Moulden for undertaking research into
the earliest records relating to this and other pagan Saxon sites in east

ton[112] and to the dwelling site at Elmswell,[113] near Driffield, where the Roman and Anglo-Saxon periods of occupation have been found to merge into one another without any perceptible break. Whether there are any more sites on the Wolds which should be assigned to the fifth century is a matter which must await the proper publication of the whole body of material.

The York area has yielded cremation burials from two, or possibly three, sites within a mile of York Minster, that is to say within a mile from the centre of the legionary fortress. The most important of these is the cemetery at Heworth, which was discovered in the spring of 1878, during the work on the construction of the Foss Islands railway. The fact of its discovery was briefly recorded in contemporary publications.[114] It was not till 1891 that a few more details were published, and it was then stated that forty-two urns had been recovered, but that "a large number" had been destroyed before any notice of their discovery reached the Museum at York.[115] The contents of the urns are stated to have been burnt bones, a pair of bronze tweezers, some glass beads fused by heat, and some buttons. There is no reference to any other objects being found with the urns, which are said to have lain in rows about two feet apart. Some of the urns show marked similarities on the one hand to urns from continental cemeteries[116]

Yorkshire. Their work has shown that behind the apparent tidiness of the standard modern works there is a state of serious confusion. A gazetteer of Anglo-Saxon remains in E. Yorks. on the lines of M. Kitson Clark's gazetteer of the Roman period (*Roman Malton and District Report no. 5*), would be invaluable.

[112] Now in the York Museum, *Archæologia*, XXXVII, 472: Baldwin-Brown, *op. cit.*, IV, 391: *VCH*, York, II, 100. This site is of particular interest because of its proximity to the Roman fort at Malton.

[113] A. L. Congreve, *A Roman and Saxon Site at Elmswell, East Yorks.*, Hull Museum Publications Nos. 193, 198. Also P. Corder, *Excavations at Elmswell, East Yorks.*, H.M.P. No. 207.

[114] *Annual Report of the Council of the Yorkshire Phil. Soc. for 1878*, 8-9. The cemetery was found during the making of a cutting for the railway, *Yorkshire Gazette*, 20 April 1878.

[115] *York Museum Handbook*, 1891, 216.

[116] R. H. Hodgkin, *A History of the Anglo-Saxons*, 1935, I, pl. 29. opp. p. 159.

and on the other to urns from Little Wilbraham[117]
in Cambridgeshire, which in its turn is said to have
yielded some of the earliest types of ordinary Anglo-
Saxon cremation pottery known in England.[118] Some years
earlier, in November 1859, workmen engaged in preparing
a site for some buildings on ground belonging to F. W.
Calvert in the area known as The Mount, about one mile
to the south-west of the Minster in the direction of the
Roman road from York to Tadcaster, discovered an inscribed Roman sarcophagus lying about two feet below the
surface.[119] At the same time and place an unspecified
number of cinerary urns were found " of various, some of
them unusual, forms," together with fragments of Samian
and other pottery.[120] Contemporary reports refer to the
urns and to the sarcophagus in such a way as to imply that
both were believed to be Roman, but some years later six
of the urns were presented to the York Museum by F. W.
Calvert on whose land they had been found, and they had
by then been recognized as Saxon.[121] Unfortunately the
accounts of this discovery are not detailed enough to show
the relation of the Saxon burial urns to the Roman material
which was found at the same time. The Saxons had
evidently used what we know to have been the site of a
large Roman cemetery for their own burials, but there is
no evidence to show whether the cemetery remained in
continuous use or whether the two phases of its occupation
were separated by a considerable interval of time. Other
sources refer to the discovery also in 1859, of five Anglo-
Saxon urns in a garden which is described as lying about
half a mile outside Micklegate Bar. In a paper which was
published nine years after this discovery, and which was
not concerned with York at all, but with Frilford in Berk-

[117] A. Plettke, *Ursprung und Ausbreitung der Angeln und Sachsen*,
Hanover, 1921, taf. 50, 51.
[118] Collingwood and Myres, *op. cit.*, 387.
[119] *Yorkshire Gazette*, 12 Nov. 1859.
[120] Report of a meeting of the *York. Phil. Soc.* printed in the *Yorkshire Gazette*, 10 Dec. 1859.
[121] *York Museum Handbook*, 1875, 134.

shire, George Rolleston remarked of this find : " Several
Roman urns and sarcophagi were found at the same time
and place, the Anglo-Saxons having in this, as in so many
other Roman stations, used the cemeteries of their predecessors."[122] This remark led Baldwin Brown to infer that the
cemetery had been in continuous use from the Roman into
the Anglo-Saxon periods.[123] Some recent writers[124] have
regarded the site on The Mount as being quite distinct from
the site half a mile outside Micklegate Bar. But both finds
are said to have been made in 1859, the descriptions of the
two discoveries are remarkably similar, and The Mount is
in fact about half a mile outside Micklegate Bar. Research
into the earliest accounts of these discoveries suggests rather
strongly that the belief that there were two separate sites
is a misapprehension due to the practice of different writers
using different methods of describing the whereabouts of
one and the same place.

It is a strange circumstance that within a mile from the
centre of a Roman legionary fortress set on low-lying
ground and virtually surrounded by wood or marsh, the
very kind of place where we would not have expected to
find evidence of early Anglo-Saxon settlement, there should
be a large cemetery which bears some indications of being
among the earliest Anglo-Saxon cemeteries, not only in the
north, but also in the whole country. But York was something more than the site of a legionary fortress. It was
also the site of a *colonia* as well as the headquarters of the
Dux Britanniarum, at least as late as 395.[125] It was, in
other words, the most important military centre in Roman
Britain, and as such it had been used more than once as the
main base for Roman campaigns towards the north. Here,
if anywhere in Britain, we might have expected a knowledge
of military affairs to have survived the withdrawal of the
regular Roman forces. How then did it come about that

[122] *Arch.*, 42, pt. 2, 433.
[123] Baldwin-Brown, *op. cit.*, IV, 802.
[124] E.g. F. and H. W. Elgee, *op. cit.*, 179.
[125] C. E. Stevens, *Arch. J.*, XCVII, 141.

York was apparently among the first places in Britain to fall into Anglo-Saxon hands? When we recall that the signal stations on the Yorkshire coast were in occupation about the years 370-395,[126] and that the defences of Malton were repaired about the same time,[127] we may well ask this question not merely of York, but of the East Riding as a whole. It is remarkable that the one area north of Humber which has yielded evidence of intensive Anglo-Saxon settlement during the pagan period should be that very area in which an organized Roman command is known to have survived longest.

If we believe that these settlements were solely the result of an invasion such as that which evidently took place along the rivers debouching into the Wash, we find ourselves faced with a situation which is entirely out of keeping with all the evidence that we have discussed so far. Kent was always exposed to invasion because of the short sea-crossing and East Anglia was hardly less so, but Yorkshire was the very core of the military zone of Roman Britain, and although fortifications would be of little value without properly trained men to defend them, we have seen enough to know that the British in the north made such a good recovery, despite the withdrawal of the Roman armies, that they were able to offer vigorous opposition to invasion from more than one quarter. They kept the Pictish menace under control. They expelled the Scots from northern Wales. They came very near to expelling the English from Bamborough. And even in the reign of Aethelfrith, as it would seem, they were still powerful enough to send an expedition against the English in Yorkshire from as far away as Edinburgh.[128] Yet in the midst of all these achievements they apparently lost control not only of the Wolds but also of York. We have only to accept the testimony of Gildas, Bede and the *Historia Brittonum* that the Saxons first came

[126] Collingwood and Myres, *op. cit.*, 285.
[127] P. Corder, *The Defences of the Roman Fort at Malton*, 68.
[128] See articles summarizing I. Williams' *Caneu Aneirin* by K. Jackson, *Antiquity*, xiii, 25-34, and C. A. Gresham, *Antiquity*, xvi, 237-57.

to the north on the invitation of the Britons, and fought for them against the Picts, and the whole situation immediately becomes intelligible. The cemeteries at Heworth, Sancton and Broughton by Malton, and possibly others, may then be taken to represent the remains, not of Anglo-Saxon invaders, but of Germanic auxiliaries who fought in the service of the Britons and who, as Bede says, were kept supplied with provisions as well as with land on which they could settle in return for their services. The Picts were not a new enemy, and anyone conducting a campaign against them might well be expected to use the base which had served the same purpose for centuries past. If York itself would serve as a military base, the rich corn-growing land on the Wolds would be no less valuable as a source of supply. It may well be that the story of Octha and Ebissa has preserved a confused reminiscence of these early settlements in Yorkshire. The Gildas tradition that the soldiers, becoming discontented with their pay and supplies, suddenly came to a secret agreement with the Picts and revolted against the British provides a most convincing explanation of how it came about that the East Riding fell into English hands so much sooner than any other territory north of the Humber. For reasons which have already been made plain,[129] the acceptance of this interpretation does not in the least necessitate the transfer of Hengest and his men from Kent to Yorkshire.

If the appeal for help which was sent to Aetius in his third consulship has been correctly interpreted, the revolt of the Saxons occurred some time in the years 446-450. It seems likely that they would then be present in the north in considerable numbers, partly because they would not otherwise have been in a position to carry out a successful revolt and partly because their revolt was due, according to Gildas, to the inability of the Britons to keep them supplied with provisions. The *Historia Brittonum* has preserved one scrap of information which may perhaps be connected

[129] Above, pp. 18-19.

with this revolt. The genealogy of the kings of Deira, which is found in the additions to this work, gives the name Soemil as representing the fifth generation in descent from Wodan, and of him it is stated *ipse primus separavit Deur o Birneich*.[130] Soemil in his turn stands five generations before Aelle, who probably died *c*. 600.[131] Soemil will therefore have been born *c*. 400, and will have been active at the time of the Saxon revolt. The dates synchronize. The statement itself is somewhat obscure, but the " separation " from one another of two states bearing British names by a man with a Teutonic name suggests a situation in which one of those states, i.e. Deur, passed under foreign control, a situation not out of keeping with the circumstances of the Saxon revolt. It must, however, be noted that this information about Soemil is not confirmed by any other source, and that the Deiran genealogy preserved in the *Historia Brittonum* is not in agreement with the genealogy found in other sources. The name Soemil is not found at all in the genealogy preserved in the entry for the year 560 (A) of the *Anglo-Saxon Chronicle*. It is found in MSS CCCC 183, BM Vesp. B VI and the *Textus Roffensis*, but it stands seventh in descent from Wodan, instead of fifth as in the *Historia Brittonum*, and furthermore these three texts which are in agreement with one another, differ from the *Historia Brittonum* in the name they give to Soemil's successor. In these circumstances it would be wise to suspend judgement about Soemil's part in the Saxon revolt.

So far as we have been able to detect the main trends in the history of this British heroic age in the north, the evidence suggests with some force that the operations which led to the British recovery were conducted with skill and vigour. There are no less plain indications of some powerful and competent governing authority, probably south of Hadrian's Wall, in the first half of the fifth century. The

---

[130] C. 61.
[131] See below, p. 48.

removal of the greater part of an entire tribe from Lothian
to north Wales can have been no easy task. It demands a
state of affairs in which a single authority controlled the
country across which Cunedda and his people had to pass,
and it suggests a knowledge of Roman imperial ways of
dealing with difficult frontier problems. This latter is also
true of the invitation to the Saxons, for in essence the method
adopted to deal with the Pictish threat in the north was the
same as that adopted to deal with the Scottish threat in Wales.
To call in the help of a foreign people was a dangerous, and
in the event a disastrous, policy, but it was little more than
a development, and one not confined to Britain, of the
Roman practice of the fourth century in the course of which
an increasingly large part of the Roman armies had been
recruited from among the Germanic peoples. If the recovery of the land between the two Walls has been rightly
associated with the Theodosian restoration, there was no
reason why this area should have been seriously affected by
the final withdrawal of the Roman armies. The area of dis-
location would lie south of the Hadrianic frontier. It has
already been remarked that the thirteen genealogies of that
group of kings who were known collectively as *The Men of
the North* go back to one or other of two ancestors, Ceredig
or Coel Hen. We have already dealt with Ceredig, but who
and what was Coel Hen ?

One of the representatives of Coel Hen's family in the
fifth generation was Guenddoleu, who was killed in the
battle of Ardderyd in 574.[132] It seems probable that the
place at which this battle was fought was the same as the
modern Arthuret,[133] a few miles north of Carlisle. Nearby
is the place-name Carwinley and the river name Carwhine-
low. Ekwall suggests[134] that the second and third elements
of Carwinley are English in origin, but is it not possible

[132] *Ann. Cam.*, s.a. 573.
[133] Skene, *Celtic Scotland*, I, 157, also E. Ekwall, *Dict. of English
Place-Names*, s. Arthuret.
[134] *op. cit.*, s. Carwinley.

that both these names derive, as Skene suggested,[135] from Caer Guenddoleu? If these identifications are correct, Guenddoleu will have belonged to the country near the Solway. One of the descendants of Coel Hen in the sixth generation was Cadrod Calchvynydd, the second part of whose name places him with fair certainty at Kelso.[136] Of the four British kings who are recorded in the additions to the *Historia Brittonum*[137] to have fought against Hussa, fifth in succession to Ida of Bernicia, one, namely Rhydderch, was descended from Ceredig, but the other three, Morcant, Gwallaug and Urien, were all descendants of Coel Hen in the fifth generation.[138] In the sixth century therefore Coel Hen's family seem to have been located, broadly speaking, in what is now the Borderland. Guenddoleu, as we have seen, was killed in 574. Morcant, Gwallaug and Urien flourished in the years following Ida's reign, and it is fair to suppose that they were all grown men *c.* 560. Gwrgi and Peredur who represented another branch of Coel Hen's family in the fifth generation, were killed in 581.[139] If this fifth generation was born *c.* 530, Coel Hen himself will have been born *c.* 380, and will accordingly have been in the full vigour of his life when the Roman armies withdrew from Britain.

It has been suggested that Coel Hen's name is preserved in that part of Ayrshire which is called Kyle,[140] and that therefore his family was originally located there, but if the evidence of the genealogies has been correctly interpreted it is not easy to see by what process Coel Hen came to found a dynasty in territory which formed part of the kingdom of Strathclyde, and which lay so close to its capital, nor is it

[135] *op. cit.*, I, 157.
[136] W. J. Watson, *Celtic Place-Names of Scotland*, 343.
[137] C. 63.
[138] W. F. Skene, *Four Ancient Books*, I, 168. For the genealogies of Morcant and Urien in the Harl. MS. see *Y Cymm.*, IX, 173-4. According to the Harl. genealogies Gwallaug belonged to the fourth generation. but a generation seems to be missing from this MS.
[139] *Ann. Camb.*, *s.a.* 580; Skene, *op. cit.*, I, 157.
[140] Watson, *op. cit.*, 127.

easy to see how Coel Hen's descendants came to be in possession of the Borderlands in the sixth century. We should rather have expected the movement which placed Coel Hen's family in these parts to have had its starting point farther south. We have seen that Coel Hen himself was probably a fully-grown man at the time of the withdrawal of the Roman forces. The second element in his name is no more than a by-name (Coel the Old), but it is evident from the genealogies and from other sources that his name contained a third element. In No. X of the Harleian genealogies[141] he is stated to be the son of Guotepauc the son of Tecmant, but there is an intrusive *map* in this genealogy, and Guotepauc is an epithet which belongs properly to Coel Hen himself, making his name Coel (Hen) Guotepauc.[142] Although the descendants of Coel Hen were commonly known as *Coeling*,[143] they were also known as " the sons of Godebawc."[144] Omitting the by-name, Coel Guotepauc seems to be the equivalent of Caelius[?] Voteporix.[145] We seem therefore to have a man bearing a name of Roman formation who was born *c.* 380, and who came to be regarded as the head of a family which by the sixth century embraced several native British dynasties mostly located in northern England and the Borderland. What kind of a man was this likely to be? We think at once of the succession of usurpers set up in the first decade of the fifth century—Marcus, Gratian and Constantine. The first two failed and the third left Britain, but a successful usurpation by a high military official who remained in the area of

[141] *Y Cymm.*, IX, 174.
[142] *Ibid.*, 174, n. 4.
[143] *Y Cymm.*, XXVIII, 208.
[144] *Ibid.*, 213.
[145] The second element of this name is found in Guortepir son of Aircol, Harl. Gen., no. II, the king who is addressed by Gildas and who is thought to be commemorated on the stone from Castell Dwyran (now in Carmarthen Museum), bearing the inscription *memoria voteporigis ·protictoris*, Macalister, *Corp. Insc. Ins. Celt.*, I, 342-3. There may be some element of doubt in the nominative of the name. The form on the inscription must have had a nominative *Voteporix* (*Y Cymm.*, XXVIII, 200, n. I), but the form in the genealogies suggests a nominative *Voteporius*.

his command, and who was able to organize an army out
of the remains left behind after the evacuation, might well
have given Coel Hen just that position which the genealogies assign to him. I do not know of any evidence which
associates Coel Hen directly with York, but if we are looking for the man who was responsible for bringing the
Saxons to the north—and it was here that they came first
according to Gildas—this much at least may be said, that
Coel Hen satisfies several of the conditions which would
be required in such a man—perhaps he satisfies them better
than Vortigern does.

The earliest recorded versions of the Deiran genealogy
contain four names between Soemil and Aelle. They are
uuestorualcna, uuilgils, uuscfrea and yffe,[146] but they are
names only and nothing is known of the men to whom they
belonged. Yffe's successor was Aelle, the first well-
authenticated king of Deira. According to the *Anglo-
Saxon Chronicle*, Aelle ruled from 560 to 588, but neither
of these dates seem to be well-founded. Roger of Wendover
places Aelle's death in 593,[147] and a passage in Bede's *De
Temporum Ratione*[148] implies that he was still alive at the
time of Augustine's mission in 597. The date of the foundation of the kingdom of Bernicia is securely established at
547. It was calculated by Bede from the official lists of
kings and their regnal years which were kept in Northumbria from an early date. It is much more difficult to
see where the Bernicians came from. The virtual absence
of pagan relics from Bernicia, the date at which the kingdom was first established, and the half century of defensive
warfare which followed make it certain that there can have
been no invasion such as occurred in other parts of the
country. We must rather think that the kingdom found
its origin in what was little more than a pirate stronghold
on the rock of Bamborough, the result of a small expedition

---

[146] CCCC 183, f65 a. The names are in the same order in BM Vesp.
B vi, though there are some minor variations in spelling.
[147] *Flor. Hist.*, ed. H. O. Coxe, 1, 96.
[148] C. lxvi, ed. Mommsen, *MGH Auct. Antiquiss.*, xiii, 309.

III

which probably set out from somewhere farther south and reached Bamborough by sea.

We may now summarize the results of this attempt to discern the more important political changes which led ultimately to the establishment of Northumbria. The most serious problem of the latter part of the fourth century, a problem upon whose solution the security of the whole of Britain south of the Forth depended, was to find some means of preventing a recurrence of the disaster of 367. That the problem was effectively solved, there is no reason whatsoever to doubt. There is less certainty about the manner and date of its solution, but so far as the evidence goes it points to a phase of vigorous warfare at the time of the Theodosian restoration, as a result of which the frontier was pushed northwards again to the line on which it had rested in the second century, that is to say to the Antonine Wall. The method of holding this reconquered territory was not to man a continuous frontier, as Lollius Urbicus had done, but to secure its extremities by the creation of two independent states, Strathclyde and Manau, which were at first under Roman control, but which later lost their Roman identity and came to be controlled by men who could indeed claim to be of Romano-British descent, but who were in fact native British kings. On the west the dynasty of Strathclyde continued without a break for many generations, and the kingdom itself remained a power in the politics of northern Britain for the next five centuries. On the east the state of Manau had a shorter history because many of its people, including their ruler Cunedda and eight of his sons, were transferred to north Wales in order to meet a dangerous Scottish threat. There is a conflict of evidence about the date of this migration, but what seems to be the more reliable source of information points to a time about the middle of the fifth century. Cunedda's eldest son remained in Manau, presumably in order to secure the southern side of the Forth against any renewal of Pictish aggression. There is evidence enough to warrant

the conjecture that the Picts did renew their attacks and
that the weakened defences of Manau proved inadequate to
meet them. If this was in fact the case, we can understand
why it became necessary for the British to seek help elsewhere. I see no reason for doubting the testimony of
Gildas, supported as it is by Bede and the *Historia Brittonum*, that the British employed Saxon mercenaries to
help them in their warfare against the Picts in the fifth
century. The archæological evidence is entirely in keeping
with the literary, and it points to the East Riding of Yorkshire, including York itself, as the area in which the Saxons
were settled. The accidental survival of a detailed tradition
about Hengest's invasion of Kent has been allowed to dis-
tort the general picture and to obscure the importance of
this early Saxon settlement in the north. The device of
employing foreign soldiers was at first successful, but after
a short while, not later than 450, the Saxons rebelled and
were able to secure themselves in the possession of York
and of much of the East Riding. By some process of which
we have no detailed record, this nucleus developed into the
kingdom of Deira. About a century later, possibly as an
offshoot from Deira or somewhere farther south, a foothold
was secured at Bamborough. Vigorous British efforts to
dislodge the invaders were unsuccessful and the kingdom
of Bernicia emerged, later to be united with Deira and to
form part of the single kingdom of Northumbria.

No ordinary mortal can expect to be properly qualified
to interpret late Roman, old Welsh, old English and
medieval Latin records, to say nothing of the archæological
evidence. It may therefore be thought presumptuous for
one who cannot claim to be an expert in any of these
branches of learning to have attempted to make use of them
all. Yet without such a synthesis it is certain that the
origins of Northumbria cannot be properly understood.
Much of what I have written must be regarded as conjectural, some may be condemned forthwith as unwarranted
speculation, and there are, of course, many problems upon

which I have not ventured to touch at all. But it has seemed
to me, and I claim no more than this, that the sources,
taken together and not in isolation, do suggest a possible
sequence of events. We have become so accustomed to
regarding this period of history as part of the Dark Ages
that we have perhaps tended to envelop those whom we
study in the darkness through which we ourselves move,
to forget that this was indeed the British Heroic Age. If
we have achieved no more we have perhaps achieved a
better understanding of the background to that passage in
the *Historia Brittonum* which reads :

    *Tunc Talhaern Tataguen in poemate claruit et Neirin, et
Taliessin, et Bluchbard, et Cian, qui vocatur Gueinth
Guaut, simul uno tempore in poemate Britannico claruerunt.*[149]

                       [149] C. 62.

IV

THE NORTHUMBRIANS
AND THEIR SOUTHERN FRONTIER

1. Norðanhymbre.

The Germanic invaders of Britain, wrote Bede in a much-quoted passage in the *Ecclesiastical History*, came from three continental tribes, the Saxons, the Angles and the Jutes. The people of Kent and the Isle of Wight were of Jutish origin, from the Saxons came the East Saxons, the South Saxons and the West Saxons, and from the Angles came the East Angles, the Middle Angles, the Mercians and all the Northumbrians.[1] However great or small may have been the reality of this threefold ethnological division on the European mainland before the invasion of Britain, the testimony alike of Bede himself in other passages of his *History*, as of other early writers, of language and of social customs, suggests rather a twofold division in England, between Jutes on the one hand and a mixed Anglo-Saxon population on the other.[2] Apart from this one passage in Bede's *History*, there is no good evidence for thinking that the so-called Anglian kingdom of Northumbria was ethnologically distinct from the so-called Saxon kingdom of Wessex and we should perhaps be wiser to call them both by the name which they themselves used for the language which they spoke, namely English.[3]

[1] HE I, 15.
[2] See H. M. Chadwick, *The Origin of the English Nation*, 51-84, where the problem is fully discussed.
[3] The term " Anglian " may properly be used of the dialect spoken by the Northumbrians.

THE NORTHUMBRIANS AND THEIR SOUTHERN FRONTIER 99

When Bede wished to designate one or other of the various English kingdoms by name, he almost invariably did so by referring rather to the people of whom it was composed than to the area of land which its inhabitants occupied. Essex he normally called *prouincia Orientalium Saxonum*, but he had no distinct term for Essex itself conceived as a geographical unit. So also with Wessex (*prouincia Occidentalium Saxonum*), East Anglia (*prouincia Orientalium Anglorum*) and the rest. The only exception to this practice was Kent which he commonly called *Cantia*, though he also used *prouincia Cantuariorum*, and the exception here was no doubt due to the adoption by the English of a name which had been current in Roman Britain. In this practice Bede was in keeping with the usage of his age and it was not until a later time that the conception of groups of people regularly gave way to that of defined areas of land. For Northumbria Bede, almost without exception in the *History*, used the term *Nordanhymbri* or *Northanhymbri* usually in the genitive plural dependent on some such word as *prouincia, regnum* or *gens*. It is not without interest, however, to note that on several occasions when he used the term, he added an explanatory gloss, as though to make his meaning plain to those who might not otherwise have understood him. Thus he writes *tota Nordanhymbrorum progenies, id est illarum gentium, quae ad Boream Humbri fluminis inhabitant,*[4] and later, *Aeduini rex Nordanhymbrorum gentis, id est eius, quae ad Borealem Humbrae fluminis inhabitat,*[5] and again, *gens Nordanhymbrorum, hoc est ea natio Anglorum, quae ad Aquilonalem Humbre fluminis plagam habitabat.*[6]

A generation whose ears have recently become attuned to a very large number of foreign place-names in a considerable variety of forms can the more readily appreciate

[4] HE I, 15.
[5] *ib.* II, 5.
[6] *ib.* II, 9.

the difficulty of the problem which must face any author who is writing in a language other than his own, namely how to incorporate vernacular names in his text in such a way as to make both their meaning and their locality plain. The problem was all the greater for Bede because the Latin in which he wrote was the universal literary language of western Europe and it was therefore important that he should make his meaning clear not only to those whose spoken language was English, but also to those who spoke the contemporary languages of, for example, France or the Rhineland. There were some vernacular names, each as *East Seaxe* and *East Engle* which lent themselves readily to translation, without possibility of misunderstanding, by *Orientales Saxones* and *Orientales Angli*, but the vernacular name of his own people which he had to use a great many times, was less easily translated, as the cumbersome length of his own glosses shows. He therefore adopted the course of using the vernacular itself, *Norðanhymbre*, thinly disguised by Latin case endings, but in so doing he seems to have been conscious that there were two points which called for explanation to a reader who might not be familiar with Old English, first the meaning of *norð*, in place of *borealis* or *aquilonalis*, and second the mutation of the root vowel of the river-name Humber owing to the operation of Old English sound laws. There is evidence in other works of Bede that it was only after a period of experiment with other forms that he finally adopted the Latinized vernacular form. In the *History of the Abbots* for example, which was written some fifteen years before the *Ecclesiastical History*, he refers to Northumbria as *Transhumbrana regio*,[7] and again in the chronicle attached to the *De Temporum Ratione* which was written in 725, he writes *Transhumbranae gentis ad aquilonem*.[8] An echo of this earlier usage occurs in the *Ecclesiastical History* in a passage in which he describes Bernicia as *ceteram Transhumbranae*

----

[7] § 4.
[8] ed. Mommsen, M.G.H. XIII, 311.

gentis partem ab Aquilone.[9]   In this passage *Transhum-branae gentis* . . . *ab Aquilone* is patently a translation of *Norðanhymbre*. It is not to be doubted that Bede himself was well aware of the ambiguity of such phrases as *Transhum-brana regio* or *Transhumbrana gens* which would leave a reader not familiar with the geography of northern England in doubt which side of the Humber was meant.   This dis-advantage would be particularly evident to Bede whose home lay north of the Humber, because from his point of view the district which lay across the Humber was Mercia, not Northumbria.

These difficulties were not, of course, peculiar to Bede alone.   In the earliest of all the Northumbrian historical works which relate to the English, the *Anonymous Life of Cuthbert*, the record of events and personalities which form its content is exclusively concerned with Northumbria, and since no occasion for differentiation arose, neither the king-dom nor its people are once mentioned by name.   On the other hand, Eddius, whose *Life of Wilfrid* was written some ten or fifteen years before Bede's *History*, had fre-quent occasion to mention the Northumbrians.   On one occasion he calls a king of Northumbria *regem Aquilon-alium*[10] and on another *regem* . . . *Aquilonensium*,[11] but his normal term for the Northumbrians is *Ultrahum-brenses*, prefixed sometimes by *regio* or *gens*.   It can scarcely be doubted that *Ultrahumbrenses*, like Bede's *Transhumbrana gens*, is a translation of *Norðanhymbre*. *Ultrahumbrenses* would have been less obviously ambigu-ous to Eddius than it would have been to Bede, because, despite his long association with Northumbria, Eddius was a Kentishman by birth and "beyond the Humber" could never have meant anything to him but "north of the Humber."   Notice should certainly be taken of another name which is apparently used of the Northumbrians, in

[9] HE III, 14.
[10] Ch. 43.
[11] Ch. 51.

IV

the *Historia Brittonum*, that is *Saxones Ambronum*[12] or *genus Ambronum*,[13] but it is doubtful whether a great deal of importance can be attached to this form of the name in the context of this particular work. The date of the passages in which it occurs is uncertain and many of the names in other parts of the same work are extremely corrupt. It is at all events much easier to believe that *Ambronum* is a corrupt form deriving ultimately from the river-name Humber than it is to believe that it has any connection with the name of the Frisian island Amrum.[14] That different writers should have reached different solutions to the difficult problem of arraying the vernacular *Norðanhymbre* in a Latin dress is no more than we should have expected. It would indeed have been matter for surprise if they had done otherwise, but it must be remembered that such translations were no more than literary conventions.

Although such terms as *Transhumbrana regio* and *Ultrahumbrenses* are chronologically earlier than Bede's *Nordanhymbri*, there is no evidence for thinking that there was any corresponding change in the vernacular usage. On the contrary *Ultrahumbrenses* represents *Norðanhymbre* as certainly as does Bede's *Nordanhymbri*, and the difference between the two reflects no more than the personal preference of the authors concerned. At the same time there are certain passages, all of them representing works earlier than Bede's *History*, in which the name *Humbrenses*, or something similar, is found. In the letter which was issued by Theodore after the synod of Hatfield in 680 and which, though not preserved independently, is quoted at length by Bede, seemingly from an original document, there is the phrase *Ecgfrido rege Hymbronensium*.[15]

[12] § 57.   [13] § 63.
[14] See Collingwood and Myres, *Roman Britain and the English Settlements*, 412, note 1. The terms used for "Northumbria" by different writers of the seventh and eighth centuries have been collected by J. N. L. Myres, *The Teutonic Settlement of Northern England, History*, n.s., 20, 1935-6, 250 and ff., but while I have made use of his material I do not find it easy to accept his conclusions.
[15] HE IV, 15 (17).

IV

Secondly, a *disciplus Umbrensis* is mentioned in the heading of Theodore's *Penitential*.[16] And thirdly, in the early *Life of Gregory* which was written by a monk of Whitby, the author refers to his own part of the country as *in gente nostra que dicitur Humbrensium*.[17] At first sight these three passages seem to suggest a state of affairs in which the people who lived on either side of the Humber could be described by the single name *Humbrenses*. Such a name might indeed represent a vernacular formation such as *Hymbresætan*, parallel with such formations as *Tomsætan, Wilsætan, Pecsætan and Wreocensætan*.[18] But if such a name was ever widely current it is perhaps odd that we should have no trace of it. There are, however, some grounds for doubting whether the three passages concerned are capable of supporting the conclusions which have been drawn from them. Two of them are connected with Theodore who, so far from being a Northumbrian, was not even an Englishman, and even if we allow that they may not have been written either by Theodore himself or by some foreign clerk in his service, they remain, none the less, Canterbury documents and are therefore not the best evidence for northern English usage. Furthermore, at the time of the synod of Hatfield Ecgfrith was in fact king only of the English north of the Humber. Only two years before he had lost at the battle of the Trent that hegemony over the southern English which had been enjoyed by his three predecessors, Edwin, Oswald and Osuiu, and perhaps for a short time by himself also. Theodore must have been well aware of this defeat, and we should therefore have to convict him of a grave error if he intended *Hymbronenses* to mean "the men of the Humber" rather than the "Northumbrians." But perhaps the most serious doubt, and one which applies also to the passage in the *Life of Gregory*, is the one which arises from the whole course of

[16] Haddan and Stubbs, *Councils and Ecclesiastical Documents*, III, 173.
[17] ed. F. A. Gasquet, ch. 12.
[18] Meaning the men of Tame, Wylye, Peak and Wrekin respectively.

English history in the first seventy years of the seventh century. The conflict between the Northumbrians and the southern English is the one theme which constantly recurs throughout this period, and the history of this conflict can leave us in no doubt that the boundary between the two was already in process of formation as early as the time of Aethelfrith. Are we to suppose that the monk of Whitby was ignoring the fact that this boundary had existed for almost a century before he wrote or shall we believe that the *Humbrenses* were the people who lived where he himself lived, *be norðan Humbre*?

Just as Bede set a fashion which came to be universally adopted in the western world in his reckoning of the passage of years by the use of the dominical system, so also he set a fashion by the adoption in his own writings of the folk-name *Norðanhymbre*. We may indeed say that the place-name Northumberland owes its existence to-day entirely to Bede. *Norðanhymbre* must have been current as a folk-name in the seventh century, but in this form it was in all probability an elliptical version of some such phrase as *seo ðeod ðe be norðan Humbre eardað* (the people who live to the north of the Humber). The use of a river-name or of the name of some other natural feature as a means of indicating a boundary line is by no means uncommon in the *Anglo-Saxon Chronicle*. A striking instance of this usage occurs in the entry for 894 A : *of aelcre byrig be eastan Pedredan ge be westan Sealwuda ge be eastan, ge eac be norþan Temese, 7 be westan Saefern* (from every town to the east of the Parret, and as well to the west as to the east of Selwood, and also to the north of the Thames and to the west of the Severn). Another instance is provided by the entry for 709 A where it is said of Aldhelm, *se wæs be westan Wuda bisc.* (he was bishop to the west of the forest, i.e. Selwood), where the phrase *be westan wuda* is used to designate the diocese of Sherborne. Again, we may note the phrase *al þæt be suþan Humbre wæs* under 827 A where the usage is applied to the Humber itself.

II. *Suðanhymbre*.

It would perhaps be legitimate to infer from the name *Norðanhymbre* the existence of its counterpart, *Suðanhymbre*, but fortunately we are in a position to demonstrate the use of the latter without having to resort to inferences of this kind. The name is recorded four times in the *Anglo-Saxon Chronicle*. Under 449 E, which is derived from Bede, the latter's words *Uoden, de cuius stirpe multarum prouinciarum regium genus orginem duxit*[19] are paraphrased *fram þan Wodne awoc eall ure cynecynn 7 Suðanhymbra eac*. Under 641 E the descriptive epithet *Suðhymbrum* is applied to Penda of Mercia. Similarly under 697 E, the Mercians are styled *Suðanhumbre*, and under 702 D their kingdom is called *Suþanhymbra rice* (E, *Suðhumbra rice*; F, *Suðhymbra rice*) in pointed contrast with *Aldfrið Norþanhymbra cyning* under 705 D. Elsewhere, *Suthymbria* occurs twice in Symeon of Durham's *History of the Kings* in connection with events relating to 1069 and 1122 respectively.[20] It is of interest to note that *Suðanhymbre* occurs only in those MSS. of the *Chronicle* which are descended ultimately from a northern version. Are we to suppose that it represents the usage of the age to which the MSS. themselves belong, namely the eleventh and twelfth centuries, or does it preserve the usage of the years under which it is mentioned, namely the seventh and eighth ?

The first step towards answering this question is to summarize as briefly as possible the relations towards one another of the seven texts which are known jointly as the *Anglo-Saxon Chronicle*.[21] Text A¹ represents a West-Saxon chronicle which, whatever its date and place of origin, was at Winchester in the tenth century and at Canterbury in the

---

[19] HE I, 15.
[20] Rolls Ed. II, 187, 267. See also HE, ed. Plummer, II, 29-30.
[21] The summary which follows is based on A. H. Smith, *The Parker Chronicle*, 3 and ff. In order to save space I have over-simplified the relationships of the various texts to one another.

IV

eleventh. Text A², which was almost totally destroyed in the great fire of 1731, was an eleventh century transcript of A¹. A chronicle which was closely related to A¹ was at some stage sent, it is thought, to Abingdon, where it received various additions. Texts B and C, though they are not identical, may for present purposes be regarded as copies of this now lost Abingdon chronicle. Another copy of the West Saxon original was sent to some northern centre at which various materials were incorporated in it. The original of this northern chronicle has not been preserved, but it is represented by D, a copy of it made probably at Worcester in the eleventh century, and also by E which was compiled at Peterborough in the twelfth century. Although both D and E are of northern ancestry, they do not descend from a common original. F is a post-Conquest bilingual epitome closely related to E's immediate ancestor. It is well known that, covering a period of some seventy years after the point at which Bede's *History* ends (731), the northern ancestors of D and E contained an important series of entries which relate mainly to Northumbrian history and which seem to have the value of almost contemporary record. Did the original northern ancestor, for the period before 731, derive all its material relating to Northumbria from Bede or had it some other source of information upon which to draw? Upon the answer to this question must depend our answer to the other problem, whether *Suðanhymbre* belongs to the age of Symeon or whether Symeon was reviving a usage which belonged to a much earlier period.

Among the entries in the northern version of the *Chronicle* which relate to the early part of the seventh century, there are three which contain additions to or variations from the evidence of Bede. The entry which records the victory of Aethelfrith over Aedan (603 E) is in the main derived from Bede, but it adds that the Scottish army was led to the scene of battle by Hering, son of Hussa, an item which is not recorded in any other source, but

IV

THE NORTHUMBRIANS AND THEIR SOUTHERN FRONTIER 107

which, as commemorating an act of outstanding treachery, might well have been long preserved in folk-memory. Aethelfrith's victory at Chester is recorded by E under 605, some eleven or twelve years too early, but this is no evidence for the use of an independent source, any more than is the figure of 200 as the number of monks slain, against Bede's 1200.[22] Variations of this kind might very easily have occurred in the course of copying. Thirdly, the long entry under 626 E is derived mainly from Bede, except for the remark that, in the course of an expedition against Wessex, Edwin slew five West Saxon kings. This, if it were true, is an item which might well have been suppressed in the southern version of the *Chronicle*, and again tradition seems the likely source. But as we approach the end of the seventh century, there is a notable change in the entries which relate to Northumbria. It will be convenient to extract the entries in question, taking the readings from text E, and compare their information with that supplied by Bede.

685 E ðy ilcan geare man ofsloh Ecgferð cining be norðan sæ 7 mycelne here mid him on xiii kl. Iunii.

In the same year king Ecgfrith was slain to the north of the sea and a great army with him on 20 May.

The entry refers of course to the battle of Nechtanesmere. The day of the month agrees with that given by Bede,[23] whose only indication of the site of the battle is that it was fought in a Pictish province *in angustias inaccessorum montium*. The phrase *be norðan sæ* which must be interpreted as referring to the Firth of Forth, is most striking, partly because of its contrast with Bede's words, suggesting that the author of the entry was not here drawing upon

[22] HE II, 2.
[23] *ib.* IV, 24 (26).

IV

Bede, partly because it demonstrates a northern origin for the entry and partly because it indicates an early date for its composition. The name of the place at which the battle was fought is recorded in the *Annals of Ulster* as *Duin Nechtain*,[24] in the *Historia Brittonum* as *Linn Garan*[25] and in Symeon of Durham as *Nechtanesmere*.[26] If this entry had been a late composition, we would surely have expected its author to have used one or other of these names. That he did not do so suggests that he lived at a time when the English, Bede among them, thought of this battle as the battle in which Ecgfrith was killed rather than as the battle of Nechtanesmere.

697 E   *Her Suðanhymbre ofslogon Ostryðe Æðelredes cwen. Ecgfriðes swuster.*

In this year the people to the south of the Humber slew Osthryth who was Ethelred's queen and Ecgfrith's sister.

Bede records this event in the following words : *Osthryd regina a suis, id est Merciorum, primatibus interemta.*[27] In another connection Bede mentions that Osthryth was the wife of Ethelred and sister of Ecgfrith,[28] but it is of interest to note that he does not mention the death of Osthryth in the body of his *History*. His reference to this latter event is confined to the chronological epitome where it forms one of a small group of annals which have in common that their subject matter is not mentioned in the *History* proper. Plummer thought that Bede's epitome was the source of this entry in the *Chronicle*,[29] but the contrast between *Mercii* and *Suðanhymbre* suggests otherwise. Bede never uses *Suðanhymbre* and we cannot explain the two names as

---

[24] s.a. 685.
[25] § 57.
[26] Rolls Ed. I, 32.
[27] HE v, 24.
[28] *ib*. IV, 19 (21).
[29] Earle and Plummer, *Two Saxon Chronicles*, 2, lxi, note 2.

IV

translations of one another, because both are English words, despite the Latin termination of *Mercii*, and although they refer to the same people, their respective meanings are quite different.

699 E   *Her Pyhtas slogon Berht ealdorman.*

In this year the Picts slew the ealdorman Berht.

Bede's reference to this event is again confined to his chronological epitome. His account varies from the *Chronicle* version in the name of the ealdorman, which he gives as *Berctred*, and in the date, which he gives as 698.[30] These variations would be consistent with independent origins for the two versions, but they are not proof.

705 E   *Her Aldfriŏ Norþanhymbra cining forŏferde on xix K Janr. on Driffelda. þa feng Osred his sunu to rice.*

In this year Aldfrith, king of the Northumbrians, died in Driffield on 14 December. Then Osred his son succeeded to the kingdom.

Bede refers to the death of Aldfrith and to the accession of Osred,[31] but in so doing he mentions neither the place nor the day of Aldfrith's death.

710 E   *þam ilcan geare feoht Beorhtfriŏ ealdorman wiŏ Pyhtas betwix Hæfe 7 Cære.*

In the same year the ealdorman Beorhtfrith fought with the Picts between Avon (?) and Carron (?).

Bede refers to this event, but again only in the chronological epitome under 711, and not in the body of the *History*, in the following terms : *Berctfrid praefectus cum*

[30] HE v, 24.   [31] *ib.* v, 18.

Pictis pugnauit.[32]   It will be noted that he gives no indication of the locality of the battle.   The Irish annals place
it in *campo Manonn*,[33] by which the old kingdom of Manau
is evidently meant, a locality which is in accord with
Skene's suggestion of the rivers Avon and Carron for
Hæfe and *Cære*.[34]

716 E   *Her Osred Norðanhymbra cininga waerð ofslagen
be suðan gemære.*

In this year Osred king of the Northumbrians was
slain to the south of the border.

Bede refers to the death of Osred,[35] but he gives no indication of where it befell.   The most notable point about this
entry is the use of the phrase *be suðan gemære*.   Unfortunately there is not evidence enough to show whether the
northern or southern boundary of Northumbria is meant,[36]
but in this very ambiguity lies the strongest ground for
thinking that this is a contemporary annal.   The use of
the simple, unqualified *be suðan gemære* suggests the work
of an author who lived so close to the event that the possibility of his record appearing ambiguous to later generations
had not occurred to him.

721 E   *Her forðferde se halga biscop Iohs. se wæs biscop
XXXIII geara 7 viii monðas 7 xiii dagas 7 his lic
restað in Beoferlic.*

In this year the holy bishop John died, he was
bishop 33 years and 8 months and 13 days and his
body rests at Beverley.

Bede states only that John was bishop for 33 years, without

[32] *ib.* V, 24.
[33] *Annals of Ulster*, s.a. 710.
[34] W. F. Skene, *Celtic Scotland*, I, 270.
[35] HE V, 22.
[36] See HE, ed. Plummer, II, 336.

IV

the additional details about months and days. He does not
mention Beverley, but says that John was buried in his
monastery *quod dicitur In Silua Derorum*.[37] But these
variations do not necessarily indicate an early date for the
Chronicle entry. Whatever may have been the origin of
the place-name, the form it takes in this passage is not early.
Furthermore the exact details about the length of John's
episcopate are such as might have been found in a list of
bishops by an author writing long after the event.

The results of this analysis may now be summarized.
We have discussed the contents of ten entries relating to
the seventh and early eighth centuries in text E of the
Anglo-Saxon Chronicle. They all relate to events closely
connected with Northumbrian history and they all contain
material either additional to or in variation from the information supplied by Bede. Three of them (603, 605, 626)
relate to the early part of the seventh century, but none of
these three contains information such as might suggest the
keeping of a chronicle in Northumbria at the time to which
the entries themselves refer. The remaining seven cover
the period 685-721. They contain a number of place-names
(*Hæfe, Cære, Driffelda* and *Beoferlic*) which are not mentioned by Bede in his account of the events connected with
them. Such names might have been borrowed by a later
writer from some other source, but two of them *Hæfe* and
Cære are not recorded elsewhere, and we may recall that
in his prose *Life of Cuthbert* Bede not uncommonly omitted
place-names which existed in the *Anonymous Life of Cuthbert* on which this work was based. In particular there are
two phrases, *be norðan sæ* and *be suðan gemære*, which
carry with them a strong suggestion of contemporary usage.
Three of the seven entries (697, 699, 710) record events
which are not mentioned by Bede in the body of his
History, but only in the chronological epitome where they
appear in the form of annals recorded under their respective
years. The wording of these three entries in the *Chronicle*

[37] HE v, 6.

IV

differs sufficiently from the wording in Bede's epitome to suggest that they are not directly dependent on one another.

It is of interest to note that there are, in all, seven entries in Bede's chronological epitome to which he makes no reference in the *History* proper. Three of these seven refer respectively to eclipses of the sun in 538 and 540 and to the accession of Ida in 547. The items relating to the eclipses are such as could have been calculated retrospectively or borrowed from other, not necessarily English, sources. The date of Ida's accession was calculated retrospectively from a list of the Bernician kings. The remaining four entries cover the period 675-725. All of these entries, apart from those which refer to the eclipses, are concerned with events bearing directly on Northumbrian history. The inference seems to be that towards the end of the seventh century an annalistic chronicle, perhaps in the form of entries in Easter tables, was being kept at some Northumbrian centre, perhaps in Jarrow, and that this chronicle was the source of the northern additions to that version of the *Anglo-Saxon Chronicle* from which texts D and E are descended. This chronicle did not terminate with the death of Bede, but was continued, though perhaps with breaks, throughout the eighth century. In the light of this evidence we may feel no small confidence that the name *Suðanhymbre* in the *Chronicle* entries for 641, 697 and 702 represents the usage of the second half of the seventh and the early part of the eighth centuries, and that the people who lived north and south of the Humber were then known respectively as the *Norðanhymbre* and the *Suðanhymbre*. Why did *Suðanhymbre* give way to *Mierce* or, in Bede's Latinized form, *Mercii*?

III. *Mierce.*

The territorial name "Mercia" is formed from an Old English folk-name *Mierce*, which in its turn is a plural formation related to an Old English *mearc*,[38] meaning "boundary" or, as the word has descended into modern English, "march." The name *Mierce* therefore means "the border folk" or "the people of the Marches." Both Eddius and Bede consistently apply a Latinized form of this name, *Mercii*, to the people who lived south of Northumbria and west of Lindsey. The name presupposes the existence of a border whose nature was perhaps not unlike those more famous borders of the later middle ages, the Welsh and Scottish Marches, a border, that is, which formed the dividing line between two hostile groups of people, rather than one formed by natural geographical features alone. It is generally supposed that the border in question was the one which separated the English of the midlands from the Celts of the Welsh kingdoms. We must assume that in the course of their advance westwards across the midlands from the late fifth century onwards, the Mercians would come repeatedly into conflict with Celtic peoples, even though we have no detailed record of such conflict. But it may be questioned whether mere contact with the Welsh would produce conditions in which the name *Mierce* would be likely to arise. If it were so, the name might equally have been used of the West Saxons who were in contact with the Welsh throughout the sixth and seventh centuries as they drove west to Dorset and Devon, and perhaps even more appropriately of the Northumbrians who encountered far more formidable opposition from the Welsh, both of the north and the west, than did either the Mercians or the West Saxons and who in addition came to be near neighbours of both Picts and Scots.

[38] WS *mearc* arises from WG * *mark-* by fronting WG *a* and subsequent fracture before *r*+consonant. *Mierce* seems to arise from a locative form in *-i* with mutated vowel and palatal *c*, see Ekwall, *Dictionary, s.n.* March, also E.P.N.S. *Cambs,* 253. Bülbring, *Altengl. Element.* §§193, 206, and Girvan, *Angelsaksisch Handboek* §92 suppose that in Anglian the diphthong arising from fracture has been smoothed and then raised to *e*, thus *mearc>mærc>merc.* Bede, Moore MS., consistently has *merc-.* On the other hand the fracture of *æ* before *r*+consonant was not carried through consistently in the earliest Northumbrian texts.

Mierce, and the *mearc* to which it is related, seems, however, to imply something more than mere contact. It surely implies the existence of a border which had become more or less stabilized by at least the latter part of the seventh century, and which had been the scene of repeated conflicts between the peoples living on either side of it. It seems, furthermore, to demand a state of affairs in which the people who took their name from it were well known by others than themselves to have been engaged in such conflict. It is, however, a fact that very little is known about the formation of the boundary between the Welsh and the English of the midlands during the seventh century,[39] and such information as there is concerns conflicts between the Welsh and the Northumbrians, rather than between the Welsh and the Mercians. Aethelfrith defeated the Welsh at Chester near the beginning of the century and his successor Edwin conducted campaigns against Gwynedd and Anglesey shortly after. Later, Oswald won a great victory in a battle which was fought, if the identification of *Maserfelth* with Oswestry is correct, not far from the Welsh border, but it was a victory over the Mercians, not over the Welsh. It must be remembered, however, that the evidence for all these engagements comes from Bede and the record of similar struggles between Welsh and Mercians may have been lost simply because there was no Mercian historian to preserve it. We might expect such struggles to have taken place during the reign of Penda, the most powerful of Mercia's rulers in the seventh century, but this the evidence will hardly allow us to do. It was against Northumbria that Penda's efforts were primarily directed, and it was in alliance with the Welshman, Cadwallon, that he came near to victory. The Welsh took part in three major conflicts against the English in the middle part of the seventh century—in Hatfield Chase *c.* 632, at Heavenfield *c.* 634 and at *Winwaed c.* 654—and on each of these three occasions they fought as allies of Penda against the Northumbrians.

[39] Sir John Lloyd, *A History of Wales*, 3rd ed., I, 195.

These are scarcely the conditions in which a boundary between Welsh and Mercians of the kind implied by the term *mearc* can have come into existence. On the other hand there is no evidence to suggest that the alliance between the Welsh and the Mercians continued after Penda's death, and material of another kind[40] indicates that the dividing line between English and Welsh at the end of the seventh century followed much the same course as it did at the end of the eighth. But the real beginning of the Welsh Marches is marked by the construction of Offa's great defensive boundary at the end of the eighth century, that is to say more than a hundred years after the term *Mierce* had come into common use. In the light of this evidence we may perhaps be permitted to wonder whether modern writers have been unconsciously influenced by the later history of the Welsh Marches in accepting without question that this was the border from which the Mercians took their name.

Was there any other boundary from which the Mercians might have been called? Professor Stenton writes :

" The most important fact in the history of the earliest English kingdoms is the clear distinction which was maintained for more than two centuries between the peoples established respectively north and south of the Humber."[41] Among the many passages which might be adduced in support of this statement, there are in particular three in the pages of Bede's *History*. In the first he writes of Aethelbert of Kent that he enlarged his dominions *ad confinium usque Humbrae fluminis maximi, quo meridiani et septentrionales Anglorum populi dirimuntur.*[42] A later passage, in which reference is made to the previous remark on the same subject, describes Aethelbert as lord over all the English races *usque ad terminum Humbrae fluminis.*[43] And finally in a passage which contains a list of those kings who

[40] *ib.* I, 195-7.
[41] *Anglo-Saxon England*, 32.
[42] HE I, 25.
[43] HE II, 3.

held what Bede termed *imperium*, Aethelbert is said to have had authority over *cunctis . . . prouinciis quae Humbrae fluuio et contiguis ei terminis sequestrantur a borealibus.*[44] It will not escape notice that in each of these three passages Bede plainly indicates that the Humber and " the boundaries contiguous to it " marked a dividing line of much greater importance than a mere provincial boundary as between Northumbria on the one hand and Mercia and Lindsey on the other. Lest it might be thought that these three passages, in so far as they relate to the same man, do not in reality reinforce one another, it is perhaps well to remark that other evidence which is both early in date and independent of Bede, confirms Bede's evidence that there was a real distinction between the northern and the southern English in the seventh century.[45] But what did Bede mean by the phrase *contiguis ei terminis*?

Nowadays the name Humber is applied only to the wide estuary below the confluence of the Trent and the Ouse, but there is some evidence which suggests that in earlier times the name was applied to an area which extended a considerable distance to the west of this point. We may note, for example, that Asser could describe York as lying on the north bank of the Humber,[46] though we should perhaps be unwise to attach over much weight to his evidence because there are many rivers in this area, and Asser may not have been very well informed about its geography. More significant is the occurrence in a fourteenth century assize roll of the name *Humbreheued.*[47] The name is now lost, but the place to which it belonged lay within the wapentake of Strafford which embraced the whole of the Don valley. The width of the Humber estuary would combine with its swift-flowing tides to form an effective barrier, once the days of invasion were past, against the movement of hostile armies into northern England by way of Ermine

[44] HE II, 5.
[45] F. M. Stenton, *loc. cit.*
[46] HE, ed. Plummer, II, 30.
[47] E. Ekwall, *English River-Names*, 201.

Street. It is of importance to note that in this way one of the three main routes which had linked north with south in Romano-British times was cut. In the conditions of warfare such as we know them to have been in the seventh century no army could have forced the passage of the Humber to Brough in the face of even moderate opposition.

Westwards from the upper end of the estuary and extending for a considerable distance both north and south of it, there lay a wide expanse of flat marshy land which even now is subject to frequent flooding and which in the seventh century would prove a barrier hardly less effective than the estuary itself. There would be no need to reinforce this natural obstacle with artificial defences. Skirting the southern and western fringe of this tract of marshland, there ran the second of the main Roman roads to the north, the road which branches from Ermine Street a short way to the north of Lincoln and crosses the Trent at Littleborough, the Idle near Austerfield, the Don at Doncaster and the Aire at Castleford. Thence it runs north to a point near Tadcaster where it divides into three branches of which one runs west across the Pennines by Ilkley, a second north to Aldborough and a third north-east to York. Although this road crossed a number of rivers in its course, no one of them would offer an obstacle comparable with the Humber estuary.

The wars between the Northumbrians and the southern English in the seventh century bear ample testimony to the great importance of this road for the security of both sides. The first great trial of strength came c. 616 when Raedwald, king of East Anglia and overlord of the southern English, destroyed Aethelfrith and his army in a battle which was fought *in finibus gentis Merciorum ad orientalem plagam amnis qui uocatur Idlae.*[48] Bede does not name the exact site of the battle, but we can scarcely be mistaken either in supposing that it was fought near the point at

[48] HE II, 12.

which the Roman road crosses the Idle or in believing that the opposing armies had made use of the road as a means of gaining contact. The second great conflict took place seventeen years later, *c.* 633, when Edwin was killed in a battle which was fought *in campo qui uocatur Haethfelth*, that is in Hatfield Chase to the north-east of Doncaster. And again in 655, in another of the great struggles for supremacy between north and south, the Northumbrians defeated Penda at the head of a coalition of the southern English. It is unfortunate that we cannot identify the river *Winwaed* by which the battle was fought, but the indications are that it lay at no great distance from Leeds, and it is therefore probable that the river was one of those which drain into the Humber. To suppose that these battles were no more than struggles for local supremacy would be an error.   Raedwald and Edwin occur fourth and fifth in Bede's list of those who held the *imperium*.   Penda is stated to have led thirty "legions" to the *Winwaed*, and among the many *duces regii* who fell on his side was Aethilheri, king of East Anglia.[49]   The issue at stake was whether a king of the northern English or of the southern English was to enjoy the position conferred upon its holder by the *imperium* and, as we should expect, it was on the borderland between the two that the struggle was waged.   But it was not only in time of war that the Lincoln-Castleford road played its part in early English history.   The road crosses the Trent at Littleborough (*Segelocum*), known to the English as *Tiouulfingacæstir*, and it was here that large numbers of the people of Lindsey were baptized by Paulinus in the presence of Edwin of Northumbria.[50]   A few miles to the north-west the road crosses the Idle close by Austerfield, the scene of a synod which met in 702 to discuss the case of Wilfrid and was attended by Aldfrith of Northumbria, by Wilfrid himself who was then administering the Mercian diocese and was in opposition to Aldfrith, by the

[49] HE III, 24.
[50] HE II, 16.

archbishop of Canterbury and by most of the bishops in the province of Canterbury.[51]

Between the western edge of the marshland, skirted by the Lincoln-Castleford road, and the eastern edge of the Pennines there is a stretch, rather more than fifteen miles wide, of comparatively open country. At its narrowest point it is traversed by the valley of the Don which, after dropping steeply from the hills in a south-easterly direction, turns through a right angle at Sheffield and crosses the open country in a north-easterly direction to Doncaster where it is crossed by the Roman road. A glance at a map will make it plain that this stretch of open country was the one area between the North Sea and the Peak which gave ready access not only northwards to York, but also north-westwards to the Aire Gap which in its turn provided an easy route across the Pennines to north Lancashire and Westmorland. The only natural barrier across it was the Don itself, not a very formidable obstacle at this stage of its course. It is therefore of no small interest to note the existence of a series of defensive works which cross about eleven miles of this open country from a point above the right bank of the Dearne, a little way upstream from its confluence with the Don, to a point above the left bank of the Don north of Sheffield.[52] The works, commonly known as the Roman Ridge or Rig, consist of a bank of loose earth and stones about eight feet high and a ditch some thirty feet wide on its southern side. They are not continuous throughout their length, though from the evidence at present available we cannot say whether this was originally so or not, and over much of their length they are duplicated.[53] To judge from their present state of preservation they must at one time have been a formidable obstacle. We may be certain from the method of construction that, despite its name, this fortification is not Roman, and

[51] Eddius' *Life of Wilfrid*, ed. Colgrave, ch. 46.
[52] See O.S. map *Britain in the Dark Ages*, southern sheet.
[53] V.C.H. *York* II, 55.

although proof can only be supplied by the spade, it is generally held by archæologists to be post-Roman in date. Was it part of the boundaries contiguous to the Humber to which Bede refers? We may note that it runs parallel to the Don and that along the other side of the Don valley runs the lateral Roman road from Doncaster to Templeborough and thence through the Pennines to Brough and Buxton where it joins the road from Littlechester to Manchester. We can see that such a defence work, if it were adequately manned, would have controlled the use of this road and would furthermore have confined a hostile force approaching from the south to the main road north from Doncaster to Castleford and would have prevented any movement towards the Aire Gap except by way of this main road.

From the first half of the tenth century there comes some evidence which suggests that what was believed to be the ancient boundary of Mercia followed a course which, in part at least, did not differ greatly from the existing boundary between Derbyshire and Yorkshire. The brief poem which is recorded in the *Anglo-Saxon Chronicle* under the year 942 and which was written in celebration of the redemption of the Five Boroughs by Edmund, describes the boundary of Mercia as being marked by Humber, *Dor* and *Hwitan wylles geat*. The two latter names are now represented by the villages of Dore and Whitwell,[54] both of which lie in Derbyshire but close to the border with Yorkshire. Both names are purely English formations. At the time of the event celebrated by the poet, Derbyshire was, and had been for a considerable time, part of a Danish confederation, but the spirit of triumphant patriotism by which the poet was evidently inspired would hardly have been justified if the occasion had marked no more than the recovery of boundary marks of comparatively recent formation. The significance of the redemption of the Five Boroughs lay partly in the liberation of a large area of Danish, but Chris-

[54] E. Ekwall, *Dictionary of English Place-Names*, s.n.

tian, territory, from the domination of the heathen Norse rulers of York, but surely it lay also, as the poet himself says, in the recovery of the boundary of Mercia, the boundary which had once separated the southern from the northern English. What other reason could there have been for mentioning Dore and Whitwell so prominently when, so far as we know, they were of importance only in so far as they were boundary marks? The names themselves might be thought to convey the suggestion of a frontier, but we must resist the temptation to interpret *dor* and *geat* ("door" and "gate") as meaning any more than "a pass." They bear this meaning too often in place-names to allow us to suppose that they indicate artificial gateways. When it is observed that Dore lies across the Don, only some six miles beyond the western end of the Roman Ridge, the suggestion that this latter work, at some stage in its history, formed part of Northumbria's southern boundary, becomes a hypothesis which is at least worthy of being put to the proof by the archæologist.

Before turning to consider the course of the boundary between the western edge of the Pennines and the Irish Sea, we may take note of another earthwork which is commonly known as the Grey Ditch and which consists of five stretches of ditch and bank running for some five miles from Mam Tor in north Derbyshire in an east-south-easterly direction towards Bradwell. Unlike the Roman Ridge, its ditch lies on the northern side. A recent detailed survey of this work[55] has yielded circumstantial evidence which comes very near to proof that it is of post-Roman date and has, furthermore, disclosed the existence of a series of trackways which seem to converge on one point as though to suggest a recognized passage through a barrier. Between two of the gaps runs Bathan Gate, the Roman road from Brough to Buxton, that is, a more westerly section of that same road which is overlooked by

[55] *Antiquity*, 1945, XIX, 11-19, B.H.St.J. O'Neil, *Grey Ditch, Bradwell, Derbyshire.*

the Roman Ridge. The Grey Ditch does not cut Bathan Gate but yet flanks it on either side in such a way that the road itself could easily have been cut in time of need. There can be little doubt that this road was the *raison d'être* of the Grey Ditch which lies in upland country of a kind in which defensive works would not have been required unless there had been some recognized passage through it such as a Roman road would supply. Whether or not this too represents part of the boundary between Mercia and Northumbria we cannot say, but its nearest point lies only eight miles from Dore and it seems to belong to a time when the Romano-British communications between north and south were cut, since Bathan Gate, though itself part of a cross-country route, had formerly served as a connecting link between the main eastern and western routes to the north.

It is by no means easy to determine the course which the Northumbrian boundary followed across the plain which separates the western slopes of the Pennines from the Irish Sea. The evidence indeed seems to suggest that it may have fluctuated and that it was never so clearly marked as on the east. Northumbrian influence made itself felt south of the Mersey early in the seventh century with Aethelfrith's victory at Chester between 613 and 616, but Aethelfrith himself was killed soon afterwards near the eastern end of the frontier and we should perhaps be wiser to regard his exploit rather as a successful raid into Welsh territory than as a war of conquest which resulted in the addition of any substantial lands to Northumbria. The easiest route across the Pennines from York, Edwin's capital in Deira, would be through the Aire Gap and the conquest of Elmet which seems to have lain across the entrance to the gap, certainly suggests that the English were exercising pressure in this direction during Edwin's reign. There is, however, an important passage in Eddius' *Life of Wilfrid*[56] whose implications seem to have been

[56] Ch. 17.

THE NORTHUMBRIANS AND THEIR SOUTHERN FRONTIER   123

overlooked by writers on this topic and which suggests that, apart from sporadic raids into Welsh territory, the effective crossing of the Pennines through the Aire Gap may not have been achieved until a considerable time after Edwin's death. The passage occurs in connection with ceremonies attending the dedication of Wilfrid's new church at Ripon between 671 and 678. Standing in front of the altar, Wilfrid read out to the assembled company " a list of the lands which the kings . . . had previously, and on that very day as well, presented to him, with the agreement and over the signatures of the bishops and all the chief men, and also a list of the consecrated places in various parts which the British clergy had deserted when fleeing from the hostile sword wielded by the warriors of our own nation."[57]   The passage continues : *et haec sunt nomina regionum: iuxta Rippel et Ingaedyne et in regione Dunutinga et Incaetlaevum in caeterisque locis.*   It is not clear from this account which were the lands presented on the day of dedication and which were earlier gifts, but none of them can have been made before *c.* 660, the date at which the first monastery at Ripon was built. Of the places which are mentioned by name, *Rippel* is certainly the Ribble, and the identifications which have been suggested[58] for the others are Yeadon, in the west Riding not far from Otley, Dent, near the point at which the boundaries of Yorkshire, Lancashire and Westmorland meet, and Catlow in the parish of Whalley on the Lancashire side of the border with the west Riding. In passing it may be noted that Whalley itself is mentioned in the *Anglo-Saxon Chronicle* under 792 E where it is described as being in Northumbria. Setting aside the other names whose identification cannot be regarded as certain, the reference to *regiones* which lay *iuxta Rippel* suggests that a considerable part of northern Lancashire, but excluding Lancashire north-of-the-sands, passed under the control of Wilfrid at this time. The

---

[57] B. Colgrave's translation.
[58] Colgrave, *op. cit.* 164.

words used by Eddius leave no doubt that the gifts were very extensive and that it was from formal charters confirming the gifts that Wilfrid read out the list of places. We are not likely to be mistaken in seeing here the origin of that process whereby the Ribble became an ecclesiastical frontier separating north Lancashire which owed obedience to York, from south Lancashire which formed part of the Mercian diocese of Lichfield, a frontier which survived till the end of the middle ages and the creation of a new see at Chester by Henry VIII.[59] But the particular interest of the words used by Eddius in describing the occasion lies in their implication that the authority of at least the British church survived in the Ribble area until it yielded before an English invasion which cannot have taken place long before the dedication of the church at Ripon, that is to say, not long before 670. If this is a correct inference, we must suppose that the western boundary of Deira lay on the eastern side of the Pennines until after the middle of the seventh century. The Ribble, however, marks something more than an ecclesiastical boundary. The evidence of place-names shows that it also marks the approximate linguistic boundary between the west midland and Northumbrian dialects of Old English.[60] It may be that the lands between Ribble and Mersey fluctuated between Mercia and Northumbria according as the one or the other was dominant. Certainly Manchester is described as being in Northumbria in what seems to be a contemporary annal in the *Anglo-Saxon Chronicle* under 923 A, but there are no earlier references to Manchester in English sources, and by this date the Scandinavian invasions may have caused alterations to the boundaries of earlier times.

[59] V.C.H. *Lancaster* II, 4-5, but the view expressed there that the land between the Ribble and the Mersey did not become attached to Lichfield until the tenth century is open to question.

[60] E. Ekwall, *The Place-Names of Lancashire*, 228 and ff. It is not easy to reconcile Ekwall's belief, *op. cit.* 232, that Lancashire north of the Ribble was probably conquered by the Northumbrians in the sixth century with the passage quoted above from Eddius.

The evidence which we have considered suggests these conclusions. Literary sources of the late seventh and early eighth centuries contain no evidence which can be interpreted as indicating that at some earlier period of English history the Humber served to unite rather than to divide the people who lived on its opposite sides. On two of the three occasions when the name *Humbrenses*, or something similar is used, it refers to people who in fact lived north of the Humber. But even if this name was more widely used in documents which have not survived, it can never have been more than a literary convention, translating some term such as *Hymbrescætan* of which there is no recorded trace. The people who lived north and south of the Humber knew themselves as *Norðanhymbre* and *Suðanhymbre* respectively. Both of these names were in use in the latter part of the seventh century and probably earlier, but only *Norðanhymbre* has survived, and it owes its survival to its adoption by Bede in his *History* after he, and others, had made unsuccessful attempts to translate it into Latin. *Suðanhymbre*, on the other hand, gave way, again largely under the influence of Bede, to *Mierce*, " the people of the Marches." The most potent of several arguments which suggest that modern writers may have been influenced by the later history of the Welsh March in assuming without question that the Mercians took their name from this March, lies in the fact that in three of the great battles of the seventh century the Welsh were fighting in alliance with the Mercians against the Northumbrians. Although allowance must be made for the lack of Mercian records of the seventh century, all the surviving evidence indicates that the border which separated the southern English from the Northumbrians was of much greater importance in the seventh century than the border between the Mercians and the Welsh. Over much of its course the Northumbrian border was marked by natural features, particularly by the Humber estuary and by the belt of marshland to the west of it. Between the marshland and the Pennines there lay a stretch of open country which, particularly in that it was traversed from north to south by a Roman road, was a source of danger to either side. It was in this zone that the great battles between the northern and southern English were fought. There is some ground for thinking that three of them—Idle, Hatfield Chase and *Winwaed*—came to be enshrined in popular memory by their inclusion in a vernacular poem which dealt with the famous battles of early English history,[61] an anticipation almost of the ballads of Otterburn and Chevy Chase. It may be that this stretch of the frontier was fortified and that the remains of its fortifications are represented by the Roman Ridge. The course which the frontier had followed through the Pennines by Dore and Whitwell was still remembered in the tenth century despite the destruction caused by the Scandinavian invasions. Bede seems to indicate that the boundary was already largely defined by the time of Aethelberht of Kent in the early seventh century, though we ought not to suppose that its course would remain unaffected by the varying fortunes of the opposing sides. On the western side of the Pennines the border was not, so far as our evidence goes, the scene of major conflicts. The Northumbrians made sporadic attacks across the Pennines early in the seventh century, but they seem not to have effected the permanent penetration of the Aire Gap until about 650-670. The evidence of both linguistic and diocesan boundaries suggests that the frontier between the Mercians and the Northumbrians west of the Pennines lay on the Ribble in the latter part of the seventh century. Only a plain statement by an early authority would enable us to say with certainty which of these two borders it was, the Welsh or the Northumbrian, which gave its name to the Mercians, but this at least we may say, that to assume that it was the Welsh is to neglect much evidence to the contrary.

[61] C. E. Wright, *The Cultivation of Saga in Anglo-Saxon England*, 32, referring to a suggestion advanced by R. M. Wilson.

V

THE BOUNDARY BETWEEN BERNICIA
AND DEIRA

A Swedish scholar remarks in a recent study of the Old English material in the eighth century MS. of Bede's *Ecclesiastical History* which is now preserved in the Public Library at Leningrad,[1] that Bede "spent his life at the twin monasteries of Wearmouth and Jarrow on the northern frontier of the ancient kingdom of Deira as defined by a twelfth-century authority."[2] This remark implies that the boundary between Bernicia and Deira on the eastern side of the Pennines lay on the Tyne. It is worth while examining the evidence for this belief partly because the course of the boundary between the two provinces of Northumbria is in itself a matter of importance, partly because there is an additional interest in knowing whether Bede, the greatest of all Northumbrians, lived in Bernicia or in Deira, and partly because the course of the frontier has a bearing upon the division, alleged by some scholars, of the Northumbrian dialect of Old English into North and South Northumbrian in the eighth century.

There is not enough evidence to determine exactly the full extent of Northumbria in Bede's lifetime, and it may indeed be a mistake to suppose that its boundaries were ever clearly defined throughout their whole length. Perhaps the most reliable method of approach to this problem is to consider some of the place-names mentioned by three

[1] MS. Lat. Q.V.I. 18.
[2] O. S. Anderson, *Old English Material in the Leningrad Manuscript of Bede's Ecclesiastical History*, Lund, 1941, 138.

English writers of the late seventh and early eighth centuries, the anonymous Lindisfarne monk who wrote a *Life of Cuthbert* between 699 and 705,[3] Eddius who wrote his *Life of Wilfrid* between c. 710 and c. 720,[4] and Bede himself whose *History* was completed in 731.[5] The Humber estuary forms the most convenient point at which to begin the circuit because there was no other boundary which was so clearly recognized in the whole of England in the early eighth century. The place-names in Yorkshire on or near the coast include *Streanaeshalch* (now generally held to be Whitby) and Hackness, and among those farther inland are the monastery called *Inderauuda* (now Beverley), Goodmanham, Watton, York, Gilling, Ripon, Lastingham and Catterick. In Durham there are Hartlepool, Wearmouth and Jarrow by the sea, and Dalton-le-Dale and Chester-le-Street farther inland. In Northumberland there are Coquet Island, Bamborough, Farne and Lindisfarne by the sea and Hexham inland. Berwickshire yields Coldingham, East Lothian Dunbar and West Lothian Abercorn and Kinneil. The northern end of Northumbria's eastern boundary was marked by the Forth which is described by Bede as a frontier in terms hardly less emphatic than those which he uses of the Humber. It is clear from this selection of names which consists only of those on whose identity there is general agreement and which are culled only from the three authors named above,[6] that there was no part of the coast from Humber to Forth which did not belong to Northumbria in Bede's lifetime. Further, it is equally certain that all the territories which now comprise the littoral counties between these two rivers likewise belonged to Northumbria.

[3] Ed. B. Colgrave, *Two Lives of Saint Cuthbert*, Cambridge, 1940. For the date of the *Anonymous Life*, see *ibid.*, p. 13.
[4] Ed. B. Colgrave, *The Life of Bishop Wilfrid by Eddius Stephanus*, Cambridge, 1927. For the date see *ibid.*, p. x.
[5] Ed. C. Plummer, *Baedae Historia Ecclesiastica Gentis Anglorum*, Oxford, 1896, 2 vols. Hereafter abbreviated as HE where the reference is to the text, and as Plummer's *Bede* where the reference is to Plummer's notes.
[6] In these circumstances it has seemed unnecessary to give references in each instance.

V

Apart from the eastern boundary which everywhere lay on the sea, the southern boundary with Mercia is the one which is most clearly defined. Evidence which has been discussed in the previous volume of these transactions,[7] suggests that it was marked by the wide expanse of marshland at the head of the Humber estuary whence it ran westwards towards the Peak by Whitwell and Dore in northern Derbyshire. These two names are not recorded until the tenth century, but it was then believed that they marked points on Northumbria's southern boundary before the Danish invasions. The early sources yield only one name in Lancashire which can be identified with certainty, the river-name Ribble, but the reference to it is such as to indicate that lands in its neighbourhood belonged to Northumbria in the second half of the seventh century. To this may perhaps be added Whalley which, though not recorded in the earliest sources, is said in the entry in the *Anglo-Saxon Chronicle* for 798 E to have belonged to Northumbria at that time. The early sources yield no names for Westmorland, but in Cumberland there are Carlisle, Derwentwater and St. Herbert's Isle, as well as the rivers Dacre and Derwent. The distribution of names on the western side of the Pennines is naturally somewhat more sparse than on the eastern, but there is little ground in this for thinking that any part of Cumberland or Lancashire north of the Ribble lay outside Northumbria in Bede's lifetime, and these two seem to carry Westmorland with them, despite the lack of place-names in early sources. North of the Solway there are no names in the early English sources for Dumfries or Kirkcudbright, but Bede's reference to Whithorn in Wigtown, even apart from the evidence of the Ruthwell Cross,[8] makes it impossible to believe that the two former counties were not in Northumbria as well as the latter. Apart from those already mentioned, there is only

[7] pp. 98-126.
[8] Ascribed to the first half of the eighth century by B. Dickins and A. S. C. Ross, *The Dream of the Rood*, London, 1934, 6-8.

V

one other modern Scottish county which contains a place-
name mentioned by the early writers as being in Northumbria, namely Roxburgh, which yields Old Melrose, as
well as the rivers Teviot and Leader. The remaining
Scottish counties south of the Firth-Clyde isthmus—Selkirk,
Peebles, Lanark, Ayr and Renfrew—yield no names of
places which can be shown to have belonged to Northumbria
in Bede's lifetime and which can be identified with certainty.
Much of this territory lies above the 1,000 foot contour and
no doubt then, as now, a large part of it was uninhabited,
but there is great difficulty in determining where Northumbria's north-western boundary marched with the Welsh
kingdom of Strathclyde in the early eighth century, and
this is a point on which the Northumbrian sources yield
no evidence.

Northumbria, which was by far the largest of the early
English kingdoms, was divided into two parts, now commonly called Bernicia and Deira. These are convenient
territorial names which were already being used by northern
historians in the twelfth century, but neither of them was
ever used by Eddius or Bede who invariably wrote of the
Bernicii or *Bernici* and the *Deri* or *Deiri*, generally in the
genitive plural dependent on *regnum* or *prouincia*. *Bernicii*
and *Deri* are latinized forms of OE *Bernice* and *Dere* respectively. The derivation of *Bernice* is not certainly
known, but *Dere* is to be connected with a British word
dwfr, " water."[9] Neither of these two names has survived
in any modern place-name, but this is hardly a matter for
surprise since both were regional names such as were not
likely to be adopted as the names of towns or villages. They
would tend to pass naturally out of use, except in the works
of historians, as soon as the districts to which they referred
had ceased to have any living reality. The violent dismemberment of the kingdom of Northumbria which resulted
from the Scandinavian invasions and the consequent
obliteration of many of the old boundaries no doubt helps

[9] *English Place-Name Society*, XIV, 12.

to explain why later historians who might be expected to have had good sources of information, found difficulty in determining the ancient limits of these two provinces. Conflicting views about this matter are given by Reginald of Durham and Richard of Hexham, both of whom wrote in the twelfth century. The former remarks in his *Life of St. Oswald*[10] that Deira formerly reached from Humber to Tyne and Bernicia from Tyne to Forth, but he adds that the land between Tyne and Tees was then a wilderness inhabited only by wild beasts. On the other hand Richard of Hexham[11] writes that in the time of the kings, that is before the Scandinavian invasions, Deira stretched from Humber to Tees, and Bernicia from Tees to Tweed. And thus arises the uncertainty whether Bede belonged to Bernicia or Deira, and whether Wearmouth and Jarrow lay in the diocese of Hexham or York. Richard has undoubtedly made an error, arising from the conditions of his own time, in regarding the Tweed as the northern limit of Bernician, and therefore of Northumbrian, territory before the ninth century. Reginald's remark that what is now the county of Durham was uninhabited in early English times has been held to account for the uncertainty about the division between Bernicia and Deira, but it may be suspected that Reginald's description is no more than a picturesque invention designed to cover his own ignorance. It is true that most of the famous ecclesiastical centres in Durham—Jarrow, Wearmouth, Hartlepool—lie on or near the sea, but it is known that Chester-le-Street was visited by Cuthbert in the seventh century.[12] That he was overtaken by night in some deserted huts not far from there is no evidence of the lack of population. Auckland[13] is only one among a number of places and rivers in the county which contain a Celtic element in their name. Ebchester is

[10] Ed. T. Arnold in the Rolls edition of *Symeon of Durham*, I, 339.
[11] Ed. J. Raine, *Surtees Society Publications*, vol. 44, 2.
[12] B. Colgrave, op. cit., n. 3 above, p. 70.
[13] A. Mawer, *The Place-Names of Northumberland and Durham*, Cambridge, 1920, 7.

traditionally associated with Aebbe of Coldingham.[14] These places are all remote from coastal areas.   Add to these points the widespread distribution in the county of sculptured cross fragments, by no means all of which are as late as the Scandinavian period, as well as the frequency of intercourse between Bernicia and Deira and it becomes difficult to believe that Durham was more sparsely populated during the seventh and eighth centuries than many other parts of Northumbria.

The origin of the division into Bernicia and Deira lies, not in the breaking down of a single unit into lesser parts for purposes of administration, but in the circumstances of the invasions themselves which led to the establishment of two English settlements in widely separated areas north of Humber. Bede knew, or at least recorded, nothing of these origins beyond the fact of Ida's accession, but he was aware that the division was an ancient one—*nam in has duas prouincias gens Nordanhymbrorum antiquitus diuisa erat*[15] —and he was also aware that the royal families which ruled over the two provinces and whose genealogies are preserved independently, were quite distinct from one another in origin, although they came to be united by marriage. First Edwin of Deira and then Oswald of Bernicia were driven into exile during the temporary supremacy of the rival family and for a brief period after the death of Edwin each of the two provinces again had its own king. Edwin's two sons are said to have been killed at the same time as himself, and the writer of some brief notes on Northumbrian history which are attached to the *Historia Brittonum* regarded this disaster as marking the end of the kingdom of Deira. But this was not the case and the truth behind his remark is only that Edwin's own line became extinct. Even though Deira seldom enjoyed any real independence after 633, the evidence is such as to suggest that for much of the seventh

[14] B. Colgrave, op. cit., n. 3 above, 318, and *Bede, His Life, Times and Writings*, ed. A. H. Thompson, Oxford, 1935, 80.
[15] HE, III, 1.

V

century it continued to have its own king who was sometimes opposed to and sometimes allied with the Bernician
ruler of the time.[16]   Osric (633-4),[17] a cousin of Edwin,
succeeded in Deira on Edwin's death.   Bede ascribed to
Oswald (634-42) the credit of reconciling the Bernicians and
Deirans,[18] and there is indeed no evidence of any independent Deiran ruler during Oswald's reign, but during the
earlier part of Osuiu's reign (642-70), Osuini, son of the
Deiran Osric, ruled in Deira until he was murdered at
Osuiu's instigation in 651.   Even after this, Oidilwald (or
Ethelwald), a son of the Bernician Oswald, but related to
the Deirans through his grandmother, reigned in Deira
until his death in 655 in the battle at the *Uinuaed* in which
he fought on Penda's side against his uncle, Osuiu of
Bernicia.   Although this episode seems to have marked the
end of open hostilities between the two families, both Osuiu
and his successor, Ecgfrith, seem to have maintained under-
kings in Deira.   There is no record of any independent
Deiran king after 679, but these episodes show that, even
when the two families were not in open opposition, the
division remained a real one throughout the greater part of
the seventh century.

The boundary between the two provinces is nowhere
defined in the early sources, and again the best method of
approach to the problem is to consider the various places
which are either stated or implied by Bede to have lain in
one or other of the two.   The river Glen in which Paulinus
baptized and the nearby *uilla regia* at Yeavering both lay in
Bernicia.   So also did the unidentified *Maelmin* which was
used by later Northumbrian kings after the abandonment
of Yeavering.[19]   The scene of Cadwallon's death was near
the Rowley Water, then known as *Denisesburna*,[20] and

[16] Plummer's *Bede*, II, 120.
[17] For the chronology of the Northumbrian kings I have followed W.
Levison, *England and the Continent in the Eighth Century*, Oxford,
1946. 272 and ff.
[18] HE, III, 6.
[19] HE, II, 14.
[20] HE, III, 1.

V

since Cadwallon met his death at the hands of the Bernician
Oswald, it may be that the Rowley Water lay in Bernician
territory. This is certainly true of the site of the battle—
Hefenfelth, thought now to be St. Oswald's—which preceded Cadwallon's death, because Bede states that the cross
erected by Oswald before the battle was the first outward
sign of the Christian faith to be set up in Bernicia.[21] The
monks of Hexham were in the habit of making an annual
pilgrimage to the site, and the inference that Hexham, too,
lay in Bernicia is confirmed by other evidence to be discussed below. In the passage in which Bede refers to
Ninian and the monastery at Whithorn he states that this
place also belonged to Bernicia.[22] This passage has a twofold interest for present purposes. First, it carries the
extent of Bernicia across the country to the Irish Sea, that
is to say far beyond the limit of territory which can have
fallen into English hands in the early days of the invasions
and into territory which may not have had a predominantly
English population even in Bede's own time. Secondly, in
his reference to Whithorn, Bede is writing of the contemporary situation. He uses the present tense—*Qui locus, ad
prouinciam Berniciorum pertinens uulgo uocatur Ad Candi-
dam Casam*[23]—and so indicates that in 731 the province of
Bernicia enjoyed an existence as a distinct part of the kingdom of Northumbria, despite the obliteration of the old
dynastic division. *Prouincia Berniciorum* and *prouincia
Deirorum* are, therefore, no archaic terms in Bede's *History*,
but the reflection of administrative divisions of his own day.
Whithorn is the most westerly, St. Oswald's the most
southerly and Yeavering the most northerly point stated
by Bede to have lain in Bernicia. It is, however, reasonable
to suppose that Bernicia reached northwards as far as the
English boundary with the Picts on the Firth of Forth.
 In Deira lay Catterick, the river Swale, the unidentified

[21] HE, III, 2.
[22] HE, III, 4.
[23] *Ibid.*

Campodonum, the old Welsh kingdom of Elmet and the district of *Loidis* from which Leeds takes its name.[24] So also did Beverley which was known to Bede as *Inderauuda*.[25] To these may certainly be added York and Goodmanham. It will be seen that the shortest distance between any two places of which one is known to have been in Bernicia and the other in Deira is the distance between St. Oswald's north of Tyne and Catterick south of Tees, the one river favoured by Reginald and the other by Richard as the boundary between the two provinces. It is, no doubt, from this very obscurity in Bede's direct evidence that the conflict between Reginald and Richard arises. There is, however, other evidence which, though less direct in kind, may yet come near to yielding proof.

The circumstances which led to the murder of Osuini, king of Deira, in 651, are described by Bede in some detail.[26] The affair began with preparations for a pitched battle between the forces of Osuiu and Osuini, and the latter is said to have assembled his forces at a place called *Uilfarœsdun*. This place has not been identified, but its approximate locality can be determined from Bede's remark that it lay about ten miles to the north-west (*contra solstitialem*) of Catterick, which suggests a point of assembly in the triangle between Piercebridge, Greta Bridge and Scotch Corner. Since it is highly improbable that a Deiran king would have ordered his forces to assemble inside hostile territory it may reasonably be supposed that *Uilfarœsdun* lay in Deira. On the other hand it seems no less reasonable to suppose that Osuini would have assembled his forces at a point not far removed from the Bernician frontier. When Osuini saw the strength of the opposing forces, he disbanded his own army and took refuge in the house of one of his earls (*comes Hunwaldus*). but he was betrayed and murdered at *Ingetlingum*. Whether or not this is Gilling near Richmond,

[24] HE, II, 14
[25] HE, V, 2.
[26] HE, III, 14.

V

the place undoubtedly lay in Deira. There is perhaps a hint, but certainly no more, in this passage that the frontier lay on the Tees.

Much more important is the passage in which Bede describes the division of the Northumbrian diocese after the expulsion of Wilfrid in 678.[27] In early times the boundaries of most of the Anglo-Saxon dioceses coincided with the boundaries of the kingdoms to which they belonged. After the synod of Whitby there was a period of some fourteen years during which Northumbria formed a single diocese whose headquarters were at York, but the expulsion of Wilfrid provided an opportunity for putting into operation in Northumbria the policy of increasing the number of bishoprics which had already been carried out by Theodore in other parts of the country. Bosa was accordingly appointed bishop of Deira with his seat at York, and Eata became bishop of Bernicia with a choice of Hexham or Lindisfarne for his seat. Shortly afterwards, Hexham acquired its own bishop, Tunberct, and Eata remained at Lindisfarne. Until at least the beginning of the ninth century, and possibly longer, Bernicia continued to have bishops at both Hexham and Lindisfarne. It may be inferred that these two sees covered the full extent of Bernicia until their number was further increased by the establishment of a third see at Whithorn and a fourth at Abercorn, the latter being intended primarily as a base for work among the Picts.[28] It follows from this that the southern boundary of the see of Hexham, where it marched with York, will have coincided with the boundary between Bernicia and Deira. There seems to be only one direct statement about the boundaries of the see of Hexham. It is given by Richard of Hexham,[29] and since the see had ceased to exist some three centuries before the time at which he was writing, his evidence cannot be regarded as more than a tradition.

[27] HE, IV, 12.
[28] Whithorn survived into the ninth century, but Abercorn became extinct in 685.
[29] Op. cit., n. 11 above, 20.

On the other hand Richard, because he was a Hexham man, is likely to have been as well informed as anyone could be on this matter. He introduces his remarks on the subject as representing the tradition of his own time—*ut autem quidam ferunt*—and goes on to say that the diocese was bounded on the east by the sea, on the south by the Tees, on the west by Wetheral and on the north by the Aln. This statement is not so full as might have been wished, because it leaves some doubt about the course followed by the boundary on the west and in particular suggests that parts of Cumberland which were more than twice as far from Lindisfarne as they were from Hexham, yet belonged to the see of Lindisfarne. But for present purposes the southern boundary, the Tees, is the most important, and Richard's evidence on this point implies that the whole of the county of Durham belonged to the see of Hexham, and therefore that Wearmouth, Jarrow and Hartlepool were in Bernicia, not in Deira. It may well be that Richard's information about the boundaries of the diocese of Hexham was the basis of his belief that the boundary between Bernicia and Deira lay on the Tees. There are several arguments which may be used to test the value of Richard's evidence. The argument from the map is by no means without weight. At the time when the see of Hexham was established, in 678, Northumbria reached as far north as the Forth, and a division of territory which gave to Lindisfarne the whole area from Forth to Aln, more than sixty miles along the coast, and to Hexham only the stretch from Aln to Tyne, less than thirty miles, would have been wholly disproportionate, even if allowance is made for the greater importance of Lindisfarne. Again, Hexham itself lies on the south side of the Tyne, so that a literal interpretation of Reginald's statement that the Tyne was the boundary between Bernicia and Deira would lead to the absurd situation whereby a place in Deira was selected as the seat of what was, on Bede's evidence, a Bernician bishopric. This argument, however, is not so conclusive as it appears to be, because the Tyne is the boundary between the modern Northumberland and Durham only so far as Wylam, whence the line turns southwards to the Derwent. A similar situation might have prevailed in earlier times as between Bernicia and Deira. Thirdly, it may be noted that after his victory at *Uinuaed*, in 655, Osuiu dedicated to the religious life his infant daughter Aelffled, who was received into Hild's monastery at Hartlepool.[30]   For eleven years previously, first under Osuini, himself murdered by Osuiu, and then under Oidilwald who fought against Osuiu at *Uinuaed*, there had been open hostility between Bernicia and Deira. It seems unlikely that in these circumstances Osuiu would have sent his daughter immediately to a Deiran religious house. Within a year or two it became apparent that without Penda's help Deira was no longer able to oppose Bernicia, and once Osuiu was firmly in control of all Northumbrian territory, there would be no obstacle in the way of Hild, and Aelffled with her, moving across the boundary to Whitby.

If, as these points seem to suggest, Richard was correct in thinking that the southern boundary of Bernicia lay on the Tees, it will follow that Jarrow was in the diocese of Hexham, and notice may now be taken of an additional and cogent argument in support of this belief. In the brief account which Bede gives of his own life in the last chapter of his *History*, he states that he was admitted both to the diaconate and to the priesthood by bishop John. These events took place *c.* 691 and *c.* 702 respectively, and although John's connections were mainly with Deira, since he was educated under Hild at Whitby, was translated to York in 705 and later retired to Beverley where he died, he occupied the see of Hexham from 687 to 705. If Jarrow had belonged to Deira it would have been natural for Bede to have received his orders from York, not from Hexham. Furthermore, Bede dedicated most of his theological works to Acca, bishop of Hexham, and several of them were written in direct response to requests from him.[31]   As Plummer

---

[30] HE, III, 24.   [31] Plummer's *Bede*, I, xlix.

V

observed,[32] Bede frequently addresses Acca in terms of the warmest affection and in language wholly appropriate in a priest writing to his bishop. In conclusion it may be said that, although the early literary sources yield no direct evidence, there is a considerable variety of indirect evidence which weights the scales heavily in favour of Richard of Hexham's belief that the boundary between Bernicia and Deira on the eastern side of the Pennines lay on the Tees.

NOTE ON THE DIALECTAL DIVISION..

The division of the Northumbrian dialect of OE into north and south Northumbrian which rests on a small group of texts mainly of the late ninth and tenth centuries, is held to correspond with the political division between Bernicia and Deira (R. Girvan, *Angelsaksisch Handboek*, Haarlem, 1931, § §4 and 5, 3). This is not the place to enter upon a detailed discussion of the antiquity of this dialectal division, but since Anderson (op. cit. note 2 above, 138) seems to find some support in the early MSS. of Bede's *History* for the view, questioned by other scholars (I. Dahl, *Substantival Inflexion in Early Old English Vocalic Stems*, Lund, 1938, 18-21, H. Ström, *Old English Personal Names in Bede's History*, Lund, 1939, 147-8), that the division is as old as Bede's time and that Bede's dialect was predominantly SNb, it is worth while commenting briefly on the evidence on this point of the two oldest MSS. (M written in 737 and L written in 746), both of which are thought to be a fairly faithful reflection of Bede's dialect.

(1) The preservation of OE *æ*, from WG *a*, after *c*, which is characteristic of SNb in later times, is found invariably in both M and L in the place-name element *cæstir* (from Lat. *castra*). It is found also in the personal names *cædmon* and *cælin* (whose WS form is given by Bede as *ceaulin*, HE, II, 5), and it is regular in *cædualla*, though *cead-*, showing the diphthongization of *æ* after *c* which is characteristic of NNb, is found once in M and twice in L. Diphthongization is invariably present in *ceadda*, but there is some evidence for thinking that this is a predominantly Mercian name (E. Ekwall, *The Place-Names of Lancashire*, Manchester, 1922, 29). (2) In the personal-name element deriving from OE *seax*, L invariably shows the SNb form *sex-* (by fracture of *æ* to *ea* and subsequent smoothing) and this form is also regular in M, though there is one

---

[32] *Ibid.*, II, 329.

instance of the NNb *sæx-*. (3) In the treatment of the diphthongs *ea, eo*, SNb forms predominate in both M and L.

The evidence of these three criteria which has been drawn from the material compiled by Ström and Anderson, shows that in both M and L there is a marked predominance of forms corresponding with later SNb, though there is a small admixture of NNb forms. Assuming, as Anderson does, that Bede lived near the northern frontier of Deira and that his dialect was *a priori* SNb, this is what might have been expected, but if the literary evidence has been rightly interpreted, Anderson's assumption rests on a false premise, since Bede lived in Bernicia and some thirty miles from its southern frontier. The occurrence in these two MSS. which ought *a priori* to yield NNb forms, of a heavy predominance of SNb forms suggests that they cannot be used to support the view that the dialectal division is as old as Bede's time, or if it is, that it did not then coincide with the division between Bernicia and Deira. Anderson's view, moreover, forces him to regard the Durham place-names in *chester* which derive from OE *ceastir*—Binchester, Ebchester, Lanchester, Chester-le-Street—as exceptional NNb forms against a SNb background. But in fact in Durham, as in Northumberland, the diphthongized form *ceastir* is the rule, not the exception. The boundary between names in *chester* and names in *caster*, as well as the boundary between *æ* and *ea* after *c* in other place-names, lies on the Tees (*Anglia Beiblatt*, 30, 225, *EPNS*, 1, pt. 2, 15) and thus corresponds with the political boundary indicated by the literary evidence. It is doubtful, however, whether this can be used in support of the literary evidence for the boundary in Bede's time since the earliest MSS. of Bede's *History* invariably have *cæstir* which suggests that the development to *ceaster* in Durham took place later than Bede.

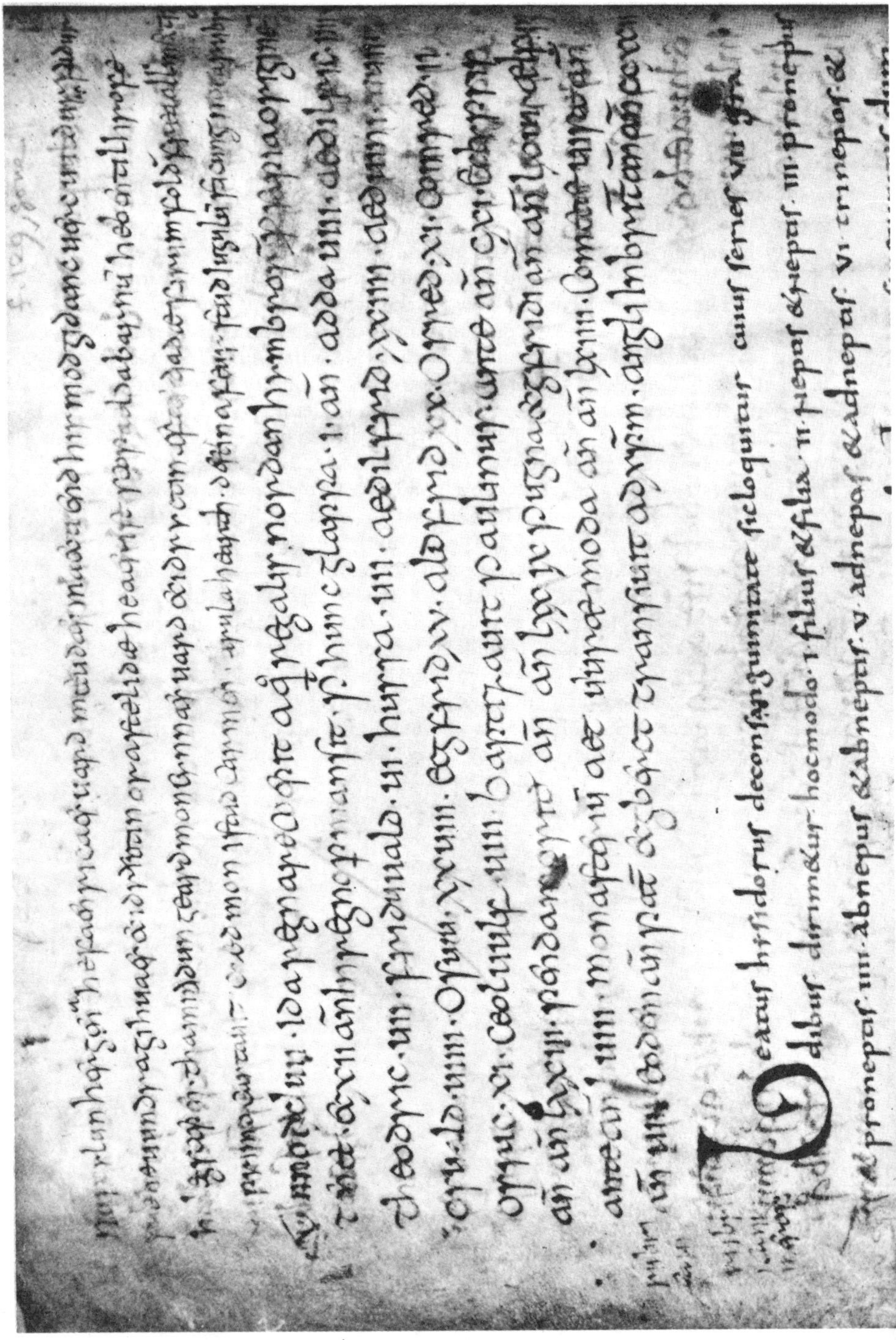

THE *MOORE MEMORANDA* ON NORTHUMBRIAN HISTORY

M. R. James wrote of the Moore MS. of Bede's *Ecclesiastical History*: 'It is not distinguished for beauty of script...nor has it any but the simplest ornament. But it is one of the most important, and, like its author, venerable, books in the country.'[1] The MS. itself contains no certain indications either of the person of the scribe or of the place at which he wrote, but Henry Bradshaw was inclined to think that it might have been written at some Anglo-Saxon centre on the Continent, such as Echternach.[2] Bede's *History* occupies all but one side of 128 folios and the remaining page, folio 128*b*, contains five items of which, it is generally held, the first three were written by the hand which copied the *History* itself and the remaining two by a French hand of the tenth century.[3] The third of these items which consists of some historical memoranda[4] relating to Northumbria, contains internal evidence of the date of its composition and, if the handwriting be the same, it supplies the date of the Moore MS. as a whole. It is written in Latin and amounts only to eight lines,[5] but apart from its bearing on the date of the Moore MS., it has an importance out of all proportion to its length, both as a source of information for which there is now no earlier record and as an example of primitive Northumbrian historiography. It has long been held that the evidence points in general to 737 as the year of its composition, but there have seemed to be various discrepancies which suggest that it might have been written in one or

[1] *Bede, His Life, Times and Writings*, ed. A. H. Thompson (Oxford, 1935), p. 231. See ibid. for a brief history of the MS. which is now in Cambridge University Library, classmark Kk.5.16.

[2] *Palaeographical Society, Facsimiles of Manuscripts and Inscriptions*, 1st ser. II, Pl. 139.

[3] So, by implication, Bradshaw in *Pal. Soc.*, loc. cit., and more explicitly A. H. Smith, *Three Northumbrian Poems* (London, 1933), p. 20, n. 3, and pp. 21–3.

[4] The term 'Memoranda' conveys the most accurate impression of the real nature of this document. The title 'List of Kings' used by Sweet, *Oldest English Texts* (E.E.T.S. 1885), p. 148, is unsatisfactory because it is applicable to only one-half of its contents. It would be inaccurate to call the document a chronicle. Sweet's edition contains two errors, see below, p. 246, nn. 2, 4

[5] F. 128*b*, 5–12.

other of a number of years between 734 and 748.[1] In the text which follows an oblique stroke marks the end of each line in the MS.:

Anno dxluii[2] · ida[3] regnare coepit a quo regalis nordan hymbror*um* *pr*osapia origine*m* / tenet · et xii an*nos* in regno p*er*mansit · P*os*t hunc glappa · i · an*num* · adda uiii · aedilric · iiii · / theodric · uii · friduuald · ui · hussa · uii · aedilfrid · xxiiii · aeduini · xuii : / osuald · uiiii · osuiu · xxuiii · ecgfrid xv · aldfrid xx · osred · xi · coinred · ii / osric · xi · ceoluulf · uiii · baptizauit paulinus · ante an*nos* cxi · eclypsis / an*te* an*nos* lxxiii · penda morit*ur* an*te* an*nos* lxxix pugna ecgfridi an*te* an*nos* lxiii · ælfu*ini* / ante an*nos* luiii[4] · monasteri*um* aet u(i)uræ[5] moda an*te* an*nos* lxiiii · cometae uisae an*te* / an*nos* uiii · eodem an*no* pat*er* ecgberct transiuit ad ch*ris*t*um* · angli in brit*anniam* an*te* an*nos* ccxcii /

Three points about this document immediately catch the eye, first, that much information has been compressed into a very small space, secondly, that only one date is reckoned according to a Year of Grace, and thirdly, that its contents fall naturally into two parts. The first part begins with the statement that Ida, from whom the Northumbrian royal family took its origin, began to reign in 547 and remained on the throne for twelve years. Then follows a list of sixteen names, representing his successors first in the kingdom of Bernicia and then in the kingdom of Northumbria, each name having after it a numeral to indicate the length of the reign in question. The last name in the list is Ceoluulf, the king to whom Bede dedicated his *History*.

[1] See J. Zupitza, 'Über den Hymnus Cädmons', *Zeitschrift für deutsches Alterthum*, XXII (1878), 210–22. See especially 215: 'ganz unbestreitbar ist allerdings das Jahr 737 nicht'.

[2] H. Sweet, *O.E.T.* and *A Second Anglo-Saxon Reader* (Oxford, 1887), p. 89, reads *DCLVII*, but there can be no doubt that *dxluii* is the correct reading. The *d* and *x* are so close together as to suggest that the scribe originally wrote *c* and later corrected this to *x* in fainter ink.

[3] The forms of all the proper names in this document are consistent with the view that it is of the same date as the text of Bede's *History* in the Moore MS. Certain orthographical features which it shares with the Moore text of the *History* and of *Caedmon's Hymn* are in keeping with the view that all three are the work of the same hand, e.g. the variation between *ae* and *æ*, the use of *u* for *w*, the use of *d* to represent *th* and the use of *c* before *t* to represent [x]; see A. H. Smith, op. cit. p. 26.

[4] Sweet, *O.E.T.* p. 148, mistakenly reads *VIII* for *luiii*. This error was corrected in *A Second Anglo-Saxon Reader*, p. 89.

[5] The *i* in *u(i)uræ* is written above the line in the text hand. The early forms of this name show an interchange between *i* and *iu*. The form *u(i)uræ* is in keeping with the form *uiur*- which is consistently used in the Moore MS. of Bede's *History* (IV, 18, 23; V, 21, 24). For forms in -*i*- see E. Ekwall, *English River-Names* (Oxford, 1928), p. 441.

THE *MOORE MEMORANDA* ON NORTHUMBRIAN HISTORY

Bede records (v, 23)[1] that Ceoluulf was the successor of Osric who died 9 May 729,[2] and it is stated in the *Baedae Continuatio*[3] that Ceoluulf turned monk and gave up his throne to Eadberht in 737. The length of Ceoluulf's reign is given correctly as eight years, and it follows that the list of kings will have been completed after his abdication in 737. The omission of the name of his successor, Eadberht, would itself suggest that the list was written before the completion of Eadberht's reign. A moment's reflection will serve to show that the author could have calculated the date 547 from the material which he had in front of him. The sum of the regnal years from Ida to Ceoluulf is 190 and if this total be subtracted from 737, the date 547 is reached.[4] In a calculation of this kind error might arise from a corruption in the regnal years, from reckoning the latter in whole numbers only or from the fact that regnal years seldom if ever coincide with Years of Grace. But the regnal years can be checked against Bede's information as far back as the reign of Edwin, and they contain no sign of corruption. Excepting the date of Ida's accession, the earliest event in Northumbrian history which Bede equates both with a Year of Grace and with a regnal year of a particular king, is the battle of *Degsastan* which he places in 603, being the eleventh year of the reign of Æthelfrith who reigned in all for twenty-four years (1, 34). The dates of the seven kings who preceded Æthelfrith can now be calculated only by using the material contained in the *Moore Memoranda* or its derivatives and working backwards from the earliest fixed point. Bede makes no reference to Ida in the body of his *History*, but in the chronological summary (v, 24) the accession of Ida is recorded under 547 in words identical with those found in the *Memoranda*. There is no doubt that Bede's date was calculated from a similar, but earlier, list of kings, and he himself supplies the evidence for the existence of such a list.

[1] References to Bede in the text are to book and chapter of the *Historia Ecclesiastica*, ed. C. Plummer (Oxford, 1896).

[2] Plummer, op. cit. 1, 349 margin, gives the date as 25 April. In a momentary lapse he has interpreted *VII Id. Mai.* as if it had been *VII Kal. Mai.*

[3] Ed. Plummer, op. cit. 1, 361–3.

[4] In point of fact the compiler probably took the date 547 from Bede, v, 24. The calculation may have been made by Bede himself in the first instance when he adopted the Christian era as a means of reckoning time. The date 547 will have had a special interest for him, but as far as we know neither he nor any other early writer ever correlated the regnal years of the Bernician kings between Ida and Æthelfrith with the Years of Grace. Bede assumed that all these kings reigned consecutively, but the possibility that some of them may have reigned contemporaneously should not be overlooked.

After the death of Edwin on 12 October 633[1] (Bede, II, 20; V, 24) the unity of Northumbria was temporarily lost and the two succeeding kings, Osric of Deira and Eanfrid of Bernicia, abandoned Christianity, but both were killed soon afterwards by Cadwallon. The accession of Oswald restored the unity of Northumbria and re-established Christianity. This brief period of apostasy left a deep impression as well upon Bede as upon others of his age and efforts were made to remove what was felt to be a stain upon the early history of the Church in Northumbria. The method adopted was to omit the names of the two apostates from what were evidently the official lists of the kings. Bede twice refers to this process in words which point unmistakably to the practice of keeping such lists. He writes that until his own day the memory of that unhappy year (*infaustus annus*) was hateful to all men, as well for the apostasy of the English as for the tyranny of the British king:

> Unde cunctis placuit regum tempora computantibus, ut, ablata de medio regum perfidorum memoria, idem annus sequentis regis...regno adsignaretur. [III, 1.]

In a later passage he writes that Oswald reigned nine years

> adnumerato etiam illo, quem et feralis impietas regis Brettonum, et apostasia demens regum Anglorum detestabilem fecerat. Siquidem, ut supra docuimus, unanimo omnium consensu firmatum est, ut nomen et memoria apostatarum de catalogo regum Christianorum prorsus aboleri deberet, neque aliquis regno eorum annus adnotari. [III, 9.]

The result of this decision is reflected in the list of kings given by the *Memoranda*, where it will be seen that Eanfrid, who should have come between Edwin and Oswald, is omitted and that nine years are assigned to Oswald although he reigned only from some date in 634 to 5 August 642. Eanfrid's name is likewise omitted from all the later lists of Northumbrian kings. It must therefore be supposed that a written Northumbrian list existed when Bede was writing his *History*, and no doubt it was from that list that he got his information about Ida. The omission of the names of the two apostates from the official lists is

---

[1] F. M. Stenton, *Anglo-Saxon England* (Oxford, 1943), p. 80, following the view expressed by R. L. Poole, *Studies in Chronology and History* (Oxford, 1934), pp. 38–53, that Bede began his year in September, gives 632 for the date of Edwin's death. W. Levison, *England and the Continent in the Eighth Century* (Oxford, 1946), pp. 265–79, has questioned this view and argued that Bede began his year either at Christmas or at January 1. I have followed Levison throughout but the main thesis of this essay is not affected by the disagreement. With one exception the compiler did not use the Years of Grace and it will be clear from what follows that he was in any case following the current Northumbrian practice in making his chronological calculations

THE *MOORE MEMORANDA* ON NORTHUMBRIAN HISTORY

strongly reminiscent of the Roman custom of *damnatio memoriae*.[1] It is by no means unlikely that Bede and his contemporaries were acquainted with this custom and they may even have had visual testimony of one of its effects, namely the erasure of the names of persons so condemned from public inscriptions.[2]

Except for Edwin, all the kings named in this list were members of the Bernician royal family. No comparable list of the Deiran kings has survived, but the former existence of one can be inferred from Bede's statement that the names of both the apostates were omitted, the Deiran Osric's as well as the Bernician Eanfrid's. It is probable that the entries in the *Anglo-Saxon Chronicle* for the years 560 A, E and 588 A which record the regnal years of the Deiran kings Ælle and Æthelric were derived from a Deiran list. The *Anglo-Saxon Chronicle* also shows acquaintance with the Bernician list in the entry for 716 A, which names the three successive Northumbrian kings, Osred, Coinred and Osric, together with their regnal years. The latter agree with those given in the *Memoranda* except for Osred to whom the *Anglo-Saxon Chronicle* mistakenly assigns seven years instead of eleven. Similar regnal lists are known for Mercia and Wessex.

An alliterative genealogy could be preserved orally for many generations, but a list of kings with their regnal years would very soon become corrupt if its preservation depended solely on memory. It is not possible to say how soon it became the practice to keep these lists in writing, but it would not be wise to assume from Bede's reference to the deletion of the names of the two apostates that written lists were already in existence during Edwin's reign. The chronicle which forms the latter part of Bede's *de Temporibus* (703) consists of little else but lists of generations and of the rulers in the various kingdoms of the ancient world drawn from Isidore. Dating by the Years of Grace is not used, and both in this respect and in the way in which the succession of the Roman emperors is recorded, e.g. *Tiberius ann. xxiii, Claudius ann. xiiii*, the *de Temporibus* provides a very close parallel to the later Anglo-Saxon lists and could have served as a model for them. Similar regnal lists also form a large part of the bigger chronicle at the end of the *de Temporum Ratione* (725). The earliest collection of books brought to Northumbria from the Continent was that assembled by Benedict Biscop who had gathered a substantial library in the course of his visits to Rome already before the foundation of Wearmouth in 674. The mission of Paulinus will have brought some chronological works with it in order to make the calculations which were necessary for the

[1] A point to which my attention has been drawn by Dr I. A. Richmond.
[2] Many such inscriptions are known in northern England. For two examples from Northumberland see *History of Northumberland*, xv (1940), 130, 146 [ed. M. H. Dodds].

249

Church calendar, but the mission itself was short-lived and the relapse which followed shows that the times were not secure enough for the keeping of historical records. But the precedent for the Northumbrian practice was not necessarily Continental. The list of Pictish kings preserved in the Pictish Chronicle[1] provides a very striking parallel to the Northumbrian list and it is perhaps significant that, apart from the regnal lists, the only source which records anything about the early pagan kings of Bernicia seems to have derived its material from Strathclyde.[2]

In later times lists of kings, usually together with royal genealogies and lists of bishops, were widely circulated among the various Anglo-Saxon kingdoms and formed a stock of information which might be drawn upon for the compilation of local chronicles. Although the earliest comprehensive collection of this kind, the ninth-century MS. Vespasian B VI, contains no lists of kings, there are a number of other texts which contain the Northumbrian list and which, from their general agreement, are evidently related, notably the additions to the *Historia Brittonum*,[3] the tenth-century MS. CCCC, 183[4] and the *Textus Roffensis*.[5] The list in the *Historia Brittonum* has been expanded with other material and the forms of its names are often corrupt, but except for the omission of Glappa, Ida's successor, it shows general agreement with the list in the *Moore Memoranda*. The lists in CCCC, 183 and the *Textus Roffensis*, which have been extended for several reigns beyond Ceoluulf, are also in agreement both with each other and with the Moore list, except for one or two small variations in the regnal years which are doubtless due to scribal errors, and for a more serious scribal error in the *Textus Roffensis* which has resulted in the misplacing of eight Northumbrian names and the introduction in their stead of part of a Mercian list and of two genealogies.

In the hands of some of the post-Conquest historians a more serious corruption arose from the identification of two separate kings bearing the same name. The entry for 588 A in the *Anglo-Saxon Chronicle* records the death of Ælle and the accession of Æthelric who is stated to have reigned for five years. Ælle is known to have been king of Deira and it is reasonable to suppose that his successor, Æthelric, was also king of Deira. According to the *Anglo-Saxon Chronicle* he will have reigned 588–93, although there is some reason for thinking that these dates are too early.[6] In the *Moore Memoranda* Aedilric is given

---

[1] Ed. W. F. Skene, *Chronicles of the Picts and Scots* (Edinburgh, 1867), pp. 3–10.
[2] H. M. and N. K. Chadwick, *The Growth of Literature*, I, 155–7 (Cambridge, 1932).
[3] *M.G.H. Auct. Antiq.* XIII (Berlin, 1898), 206.   [4] F. 65b.
[5] F. 102a and b.   [6] See below, p. 251, n. 1.

THE *MOORE MEMORANDA* ON NORTHUMBRIAN HISTORY

as the name of the fourth king of Bernicia and according to the data supplied by the *Memoranda* he will have reigned 568–72. In order to identify the Bernician Aedilric (568–72) with the Deiran Æthelric (588–93 according to the A.S.C.) the list of Northumbrian kings has been re-arranged in some texts in order to bring the Bernician Æthelric to the right date, that is to say, by making him the predecessor of Æthelfrith. The corrupt list is found in Florence of Worcester who explains the reference to Æthelric as king of Deira by stating that he had expelled the young heir Edwin from the kingdom of Deira and himself ruled the two kingdoms together.[1] The union of Bernicia and Deira at such an early date is against historical probability and Florence is refuted by the earlier lists. The corrupt order is also found in the *de primo Saxonum Adventu*,[2] but Symeon has preserved the better tradition.[3] Bede does not mention any of the six kings who are stated to have ruled between Ida and Æthelfrith. Some historical notes which seem to have originated in Strathclyde and which were incorporated in the *Historia Brittonum* record one or two details of the wars fought by various British kings against Theodric and Hussa.

The second half of the document consists of the barest possible record, no more than would serve as an aid to the memory, of nine historical events of which all except three were of direct importance for the early history of Northumbria. The three exceptions comprise references to an eclipse, to the appearance of comets and to the arrival of the English in Britain. This part of the document is of almost unique interest among Anglo-Saxon historical records in its method of recording the date at which these various events occurred. This same scribe, as it seems, had filled all but one side of 128 folios with the text of Bede's *History* which itself contained a large number of dates reckoned according to the Year of Grace, but when he came to write these historical notes on the last page he rejected Bede's method and used his own. The method he used—perhaps because it gave him a more vivid sense of the passage of time—was to record the number of years which had passed

[1] *Chronicon ex Chronicis*, ed. B. Thorpe (London, 1848), I, 268. F. M. Stenton, op. cit. p. 75, writes: 'Ælle, the first recorded king of Deira, is only a name, and there was an ancient tradition that on his death in 588, Æthelric of Bernicia, acquired his kingdom.' The corruption of the regnal lists in order to identify two separate kings seems to be the most likely origin of this tradition. The history of Deira is very obscure at this period and it is doubtful whether the date 588 which is given by the Parker Chronicle as the year of Ælle's death is reliable. Bede, *de Temporum Ratione*, implies that Ælle was still alive at the time of Augustine's arrival in 597, cap. lxvi, ed. T. Mommsen, *M.G.H. Auct. Antiq.* XIII (Berlin, 1898), 309.
[2] Ed. T. Arnold, Rolls ed. of Symeon of Durham, II, 365–84.   [3] Rolls ed. II, 14.

between the time at which each particular event had occurred and the time at which he himself was writing. The obvious weakness of this system is that any document in which it was employed would be valid only for the year in which it was written. With the passage of each year, every numeral in such a document would have to be altered in order to keep it up to date, and if the year in which the scribe wrote was forgotten or could not otherwise be calculated, it might well become altogether useless as a basis from which to reckon the absolute chronology of the events recorded. In the present instance there is no such danger because the dates calculated by Bede according to the Years of Grace supply a check at almost every point. A compilation of this kind might serve as a useful source of information, but it could never form the starting point of any other historical record without a radical alteration of its form. It was, in other words, still-born and not a living thing. The Leningrad MS. of Bede's *History* shows traces of a similar system of retrospective reckoning.[1] In the margins of the pages which contain the chronological summary (folio 159 *a*, *b*) a series of small Roman numerals written in the same hand as the text and standing opposite the Years of Grace can be discerned. The marginal numerals decrease as the Years of Grace increase and, except in one instance, the sum of the two equals 746 which is evidently the date of the MS. itself. The Leningrad MS. shows the scribe once again, as it were, translating the new method of dating into a form which he could more easily understand.

The nine recorded events may now be considered individually and it will be assumed throughout as a working hypothesis that the scribe made his calculations from the year of Ceoluulf's abdication, namely 737.

1. 'baptizauit Paulinus ante annos cxi.' Bede (II, 9) records that Paulinus was consecrated bishop about 21 July 625 and that Edwin's daughter, Eanfled, was baptized by him at Pentecost in the following year. In the chronological summary (V, 24) he records more precisely that Eanfled was baptized on the eve of Pentecost, 7 June 626:—111+626=737.

2. 'eclypsis ante annos lxxiii.' Bede (III, 27) records an eclipse of the sun at about the tenth hour of the third day of May 664. He refers to it again in the chronological summary, but he there gives only the year in which it occurred. The real date[2] of the eclipse was 1 May 664:—73+664=737.

---

[1] See Olga Dobiache-Rojdestvensky, 'Un Manuscrit de Bede à Leningrad' (*Speculum*, III, 314–21). This important MS. was not known to Plummer.

[2] J. Fr. Schroeter, *Spezieller Kanon der zentralen Sonnen- und Mondfinsternisse* (Kristiania, 1923), 19. For the reasons which made this eclipse particularly memorable see Plummer's note on *H.E.* III, 27.

3. 'Penda moritur ante annos lxxix.' Bede is not precise about the manner and time of Penda's death, but he implies that he was killed in or soon after the battle at the *Uinuaed* (III, 24). He states that almost all the leaders on Penda's side were killed in this battle, but the only one he mentions by name is Æthelhere, brother of Anna king of the East Angles. After describing the battle, he records Oswy's gift of various estates to the Church as a thank-offering and he then relates that Oswy brought the war to an end *in regione Loidis* on 15 November in the thirteenth year of his reign. A further paragraph is devoted to the succession of bishops in Mercia and at the end of this paragraph Bede adds that Oswy held authority over the Mercians for three years after the death of Penda. This is the only reference to the death of Penda in the chapter. It is not quite clear whether Bede regarded the conclusion of the war *in regione Loidis* as an event distinct from the battle at the *Uinuaed*, but the naming of the precise day on which the war was brought to an end rather suggests that he was not distinguishing between two separate occasions, but was only defining the area in which the battle had been fought. On the other hand, if Penda was killed in the battle at the *Uinuaed* it is rather strange that Bede should not have said so. He mentions the death of the East Anglian Æthelhere, but the death of Penda would be an event of much greater significance for Northumbria. Bede states that Paulinus died on 10 October 644 in the second year of Oswy's reign (III, 14). If 10 October 644 fell in Oswy's second year, 10 October in his thirteenth year will have fallen in 655. The battle at the *Uinuaed* was fought on 15 November following, that is 15 November 655. Bede does not give the Year of Grace in which the battle was fought in the body of his *History*, but he entered Penda's death under 655 in the chronological summary. The *Moore Memoranda* place Penda's death 79 years before:—79+ 655= 734, and the working hypothesis seems to break down, but the matter should be examined more closely. After Penda's death, Mercia was governed by Oswy of Northumbria who gave what Bede called the kingdom of the southern Mercians to Peada, Penda's son. Peada was subsequently murdered and in 658 the Mercians broke away from Oswy's rule and Wulfhere became their king (III, 24). It follows that there was no king of all Mercia between 655 and 658. The death of one of Northumbria's greatest enemies would be an event of considerable importance to a Northumbrian chronicler, and if there were available a list of the Mercian kings with their regnal years, similar to the Northumbrian list, one would expect him to have drawn upon it. A fragment of such a list is found in CCCC, 183[1] and in the *Textus Roffensis*,[2]

[1] F. 66a.   [2] F. 102a, b.

but it begins only with Penda himself. This fragmentary Mercian list assigns twenty-one years to Penda, thus apparently making him succeed in 634, whereas the *Anglo-Saxon Chronicle* assigns him thirty years and makes him succeed in 626. It is clear from this evidence that the material relating to the length of Penda's reign was defective, perhaps because of Bede's lack of precision about the date of his death, and bearing in mind the period of three years following Penda's death during which the Mercians were subject to Northumbria, it may well be that the compiler of the *Moore Memoranda*, or his informant, thought that Wulfhere, who became the next king of all Mercia in 658, was the immediate successor of Penda and that he accordingly supposed Penda to have died in the year of Wulfhere's accession. The three alternatives which must be taken into account are that the working hypothesis breaks down, that the scribe has been led into error by defective sources of information, or that Penda died in 658. The third alternative can be rejected because it is refuted by Bede (v, 24), but the other two may be allowed to stand until the six remaining items of the *Memoranda* have been examined.

4. 'pugna Ecgfridi ante annos lxiii.' It has generally been assumed that this item refers to the battle of Nechtansmere in 685.[1] The sum of 63 and 685 gives 748 and it has accordingly been suggested that this was the year in which the *Memoranda* were written, but this is plainly an error. Eddius (c. 20) records a campaign in which Ecgfrith of Northumbria defeated a coalition of the southern English which was led by Wulfhere of Mercia and, although he does not mention either the time or the place at which the battle was fought, he represents it as a decisive victory for the Northumbrians. Bede (iv, 12) makes only a passing reference to this campaign in connection with the province of Lindsey which came under Northumbrian control as a result of it, and writing of the year 678 he describes it as having been fought *nuperrime*. The campaign cannot have taken place earlier than 670, the year of Ecgfrith's accession or later than the end of 674, the year of Wulfhere's death. Ecgfrith is known to have been present at the council of Hertford on 24 September 672 and he can hardly have been there if he was engaged in a war with Mercia.[2] The campaign might have been fought before the council was held, but for the moment it will continue to be assumed that the scribe was writing in 737 and that he believed Ecgfrith's campaign against Wulfhere to have been

---

[1] So A. H. Smith, op. cit. p. 21, following Zupitza, op. cit. p. 215.

[2] See *The Life of Bishop Wilfrid by Eddius Stephanus*, ed. B. Colgrave (Cambridge, 1927) p. 166. Colgrave dates the council 673. On the reasons for preferring 672 see W. Levison op. cit. pp. 266–7.

fought sixty-three years previously, that is in 674. If the assumption proves to be correct, the *Memoranda* will be found to supply a date which was not known to, or at least not used by, Bede, and it will show that Eddius has not exaggerated the importance of the campaign.

5. 'Ælfuini ante annos luiii.' Bede (IV, 21) records that Ælfuini, the brother of Ecgfrith king of Northumbria, was killed in the battle of the Trent which was fought in the ninth year of Ecgfrith's reign. Ecgfrith's predecessor on the Northumbrian throne, Oswy, died in all probability on 15 February 670, so that Ecgfrith's ninth year will have run from 15 February 678 to 14 February 679.[1] In the chronological summary Bede places Ælfuini's death under 679:—58+679= 737.

6. 'monasterium aet U(i)uræ moda ante annos lxiiii.' According to Bede's *Historia Abbatum* (c. 4), which at the point in question draws upon the anonymous *Vita Ceolfridi* (c. 7), the monastery at Wearmouth was founded in 674 in the second Indiction and the fourth year of Ecgfrith:—64+674= 738. But the hypothesis does not necessarily break down. Ecgfrith's predecessor died probably on 15 February 670 and Ecgfrith's fourth year will accordingly have ended on 14 February 674. It would therefore have been quite legitimate to regard 673 as the fourth year of Ecgfrith. The day of the month on which Wearmouth was founded has not been recorded, and we can only say that it must have been after the change in the number of the Indiction in September 673 and before 15 February 674, the beginning of Ecgfrith's fifth year. The evidence of the *Moore Memoranda*, if it can be pressed so far, rather suggests what is in itself more likely, namely that the foundation took place in the autumn of 673, rather than in the first weeks of 674. If this was indeed the case, Bede's date, 674 in the second Indiction and the fourth year of Ecgfrith, could be explained by the supposition that, in omitting the day of the month on which the monastery was founded and in equating the fourth year of Ecgfrith with 674, he overlooked the fact that the number of the Indiction changed almost four months earlier than the Year of Grace.[2]

7. 'cometae uisae ante annos uiii.' Two comets are recorded by Bede

---

[1] Levison, op. cit. p. 271, argues that in synchronizing regnal years with Years of Grace it was Bede's custom to regard the whole of that Year of Grace in which a king died as his last regnal year and to reckon the next Year of Grace as the first regnal year of the succeeding king. Thus he equated Ecgfrith's ninth year with 679 in spite of the fact that more than three-quarters of that ninth regnal year fell in 678.

[2] For other instances where Bede may have fallen into this minor error see Levison, op. cit. p. 267.

(v, 23) to have appeared in January 729. He refers to them again in the chronological summary under the same year:—8+729=737.

8. 'eodem anno pater Ecgberct transiuit ad Christum.'[1] Bede (v, 22) records the death of Ecgberct on 24 April 729:—8+729=737.

9. 'Angli in Britanniam ante annos ccxcii':—737—292=445. There can be no doubt that the scribe was here drawing upon the same tradition as that used by Bede, if not actually upon Bede himself. In I, 23, Bede refers to the accession of the emperor Maurice in 582 and adds that the fourteenth year of his reign was about the one hundred and fiftieth since the arrival of the English. This would place the latter *c.* 445. In II, 14, he states that 627 was about the one hundred and eightieth year since the arrival of the English, and finally, in what forms the last sentence of his *History* proper (v, 23), he describes 731 as being about the two hundred and eighty-fifth year since their arrival. When it is remembered that Bede was always careful to qualify these dates with *circiter*, it will be seen that there is no discrepancy between Bede and the *Memoranda* and that this item supplies no reason for thinking that the author of the latter was not working from 737.

It is now plain that the working hypothesis has been abundantly justified. The evidence of Bede shows beyond any doubt that in six of the nine items (1, 2, 5, 7, 8, 9), the author of the *Memoranda* made his calculations from 737. In item 9 the point which required confirmation was not whether the scribe was correct in placing the arrival of the English in 445, but whether he had correctly reported current Northumbrian tradition on this matter. Of the three remaining items, judgement was suspended on item 3 until the whole document had been examined, but it is now clear that the second of the two alternatives left open, namely that the scribe has fallen into error through the defectiveness of his sources, must be accepted. The problem raised by item 4 was not the solution of a discrepancy between the *Memoranda* and other sources, but whether the former showed sufficient signs of accuracy as a whole to justify the acceptance from it of a date which is not given either by Bede or by Eddius. It has now proved possible to convict the author of only one error and it has been shown how he may have come to fall into that error. It may therefore be stated with confidence that the year of Ecgfrith's campaign against Wulfhere was 674. Finally it was seen that item 6 implied the date 673 for the foundation of the monastery at Wearmouth, whereas Bede states that it was founded in 674. Reasons have already been advanced for thinking that

[1] It was this Ecgberct who converted the monks of Iona to the Roman practices (*H.E.* v, 22), a fact which explains the interest with which Bede followed his career.

THE *MOORE MEMORANDA* ON NORTHUMBRIAN HISTORY

this discrepancy ought not to throw any doubt on the belief that the compiler was reckoning from 737. It is scarcely credible that a scribe would make his calculations for a document of this kind from any other year than that in which he was himself writing, and therefore the only remaining source of doubt about the date of the Moore MS. as a whole is whether or not the hand which wrote the *Memoranda* is the same as the hand which wrote the *History*. Wherever the Moore MS. was written, and at the moment this is only matter for conjecture, it cannot be doubted that its author was a Northumbrian, and his reference to the date of the foundation of Wearmouth suggests that he may have been a monk there. He records the accession of Ida in words identical with those used by Bede in his chronological summary and he may well have borrowed them from there. The list of kings was no doubt taken from a Northumbrian regnal list of the kind to which Bede refers. It is more difficult to say what was the source of the rest of his material. Six of the nine items recorded in the second part of the document may have been drawn from Bede's *History*, but the variations from Bede in the remaining three suggest that all this material was drawn from the common stock of information out of which Bede compiled his *History*. Some of the events recorded, notably the first arrival of the English and the eclipse of the sun in May 664, had already been noted by Bede in the chronicle which forms the latter part of his *de Temporibus*, but there is no general correspondence between this latter, either in its short form or in its expanded form in the *de Temporum Ratione*, and the *Moore Memoranda*. The view has lately been expressed[1] that the mass of fixed dates which form the core of Bede's *History* may have been derived from annals which were originally recorded in Easter tables. It is known that Dionysian tables were used in England during the seventh century as a convenient place on which important historical events might be briefly recorded, and we may think it not unlikely that some such table was the source from which the compiler of the *Memoranda* drew the material for the second half of his work.

Emmanuel College,
Cambridge

[1] C. W. Jones, *Bedae Opera de Temporibus* (Cambridge, Mass. 1943), p. 121.

BIBLIOGRAPHY

The standard edition of the Latin text of the *History* is *Baedae historia ecclesiastica Anglorum*, ed. C. PLUMMER, 2 vols. (Oxford 1896). THOMAS STAPLETON'S Elizabethan translation, revised by J. E. KING, is found in the two volume edition of the *History* in the Loeb Classical Library (London 1930). Other translations are by J. STEVENS revised by J. A. GILES (Everyman Library) and L. SHERLEY-PRICE (Penguin Classics). A new edition with translation is being prepared by R. A. B. MYNORS and B. COLGRAVE and will be published in Nelson's Medieval Classics series.

For one of the eighth century manuscripts in facsimile see *The Leningrad Bede*, ed. O. ARNGART, *Early English Manuscripts in Facsimile*, vol. 2. (Copenhagen 1952). A facsimile of the Moore manuscript in the same series is now being prepared.

Among other works which may be found helpful are the following:—

CHAMBERS, R. W., *Bede* (Annual lecture on a master mind). *Proceedings of the British Academy*, vol. 22, pp. 129-56 (1936).

DUCKETT, E. S., *Anglo-Saxon Saints and Scholars* (New York, 1947).

HUNTER BLAIR, P., "The *Moore Memoranda* on Northumbrian History", in *The Early Cultures of North-West Europe*, ed. C. FOX and B. DICKINS (Cambridge, 1950).

LAISTNER, M. L. W. and KING, H. H., *A Hand-List of Bede Manuscripts* (Cornell University Press, 1943).

LAISTNER, M. L. W., *Thought and Letters in Western Europe* (revised ed. 1957).

LAISTNER, M. L. W., *The Intellectual Heritage of the Early Middle Ages* (Cornell University Press, 1957).

LOWE, E. A., *Codices Latini Antiquiores, a palaeographical guide to Latin Manuscripts prior to the ninth century*, vol. II (London, 1935).

LOWE, E. A., "An Autograph of the Venerable Bede?", *Revue Bénédictine*, t. LXVIII (1958), pp. 200-202.

LOWE, E. A., "A Key to Bede's Scriptorium, Some Observations on the Leningrad Manuscript of the '*Historia Ecclesiastica Gentis Anglorum*'", *Scriptorium*, vol. XII (1958), pp. 182-190.

LEVISON, W., *England and the Continent in the Eighth Century* (Oxford, 1950).

SCHAPIRO, M., "The Decoration of the Leningrad Manuscript of Bede", *Scriptorium*, vol. XII (1958), pp. 191-207.

VII

Bede's *Ecclesiastical History of the English Nation* and its Importance Today

THERE ARE MANY WHO FIND, as they read more deeply in Bede's works, that they grow no less in their affection for the whole man himself than in admiration for his intellect, and as one looks around this church which was dedicated to St. Paul twelve hundred and seventy four years ago this day, it is not easy, and perhaps there are some who may think it not even desirable, to avoid some stirring of the emotions, some faint beating of the heart. Those of us in particular who look upon ourselves as fellow Northumbrians with Bede, will surely find as we read and read again the *Ecclesiastical History of the English Nation* that here is a book whose author's rightful claim upon us is for something more than mere admiration. It is a book which has been described by a distinguished scholar, whose detailed knowledge of Bede's works entitles him to speak with authority, as being by universal consent "the supreme example of Bede's genius".[1]

The quality which still seems to speak to us more clearly than any other from the pages of Bede's writings is that of their author's humility, the humility of a scholar whose knowledge is deep enough to have revealed to him how much more he has yet to learn. For this reason it may be that Bede would have deprecated a description of the *History* as being the work of a genius, even though we may believe that he would have been human enough to have been pleased. What he himself may have thought of its qualities and defects is a matter about which we may speculate if we wish, but we move to surer ground in believing that he did himself regard the *History* as marking in a special way the climax of all his scholarly endeavours.

Much of the last chapter of the *History* consists of a long list of the earlier works which he had written, a list preceded by a few biographical details marking what had seemed to him to be the milestones of his earthly journey – his birth, his early education at the hands first of Benedict Biscop and then of Ceolfrith, his ordination as deacon in his nineteenth year and as priest in his thirtieth. Then came the long quiet years within the monastery during which, amid the observance of the monastic rule and the daily charge of singing in the church, he had been able to indulge, to the inestimable benefit of posterity, his delight in learning, in teaching or in writing. This last chapter, with its sense of retrospection and completion, marks something more than the end of a work. It is surely Bede's own recognition that now, a man of sixty or thereabouts, he had

[1] M. L. W. LAISTNER, *The Intellectual Heritage of the Early Middle Ages*, Cornell University Press, 1957, p. 99.

reached the climax, though not quite the end, of his intellectual achievements. That he should have foreseen in this way the undisputed judgement of posterity is in itself a striking illustration of his powers of historical insight.

The title by which we know the work is that which Bede himself used in the prefatory letter of dedication addressed to Ceoluulf, king of Northumbria – *Historia Gentis Anglorum Ecclesiastica* – and again, with a slight but not insignificant variation, in the closing chapter where he refers to it as the *Historia Ecclesiastica Brittaniarum, et maxime Gentis Anglorum*. We are not left in any doubt that Bede regarded his work as being specifically an ecclesiastical history concerned primarily with the English, but concerned also with other peoples occupying a country which, in a past still very near to Bede's age, had formed the British provinces of the Roman Empire. There is no occasion for surprise in finding that Bede's conception of ecclesiastical history embraced matters which nowadays, when dockets and pigeon holes are held in high esteem, might be regarded rather as political or military or even social history. Nevertheless we owe it to Bede to suppose that he chose his title with the scholarly care which he devoted to the rest of the work and that he would not include matters which were irrelevant to his theme. Although we may regret that he did not tell us whether *Beowulf* was ever recited at the court of Northumbrian kings, we may not charge it as a fault in what is so clearly stated by its author to be an *Historia Ecclesiastica*.

The work is divided into five books of varying, but not markedly disproportionate length, although the first of the five which begins with Julius Caesar's invasion of Britain and ends with Aethelfrith's victory at *Degsastan* in 603, spans six and a half centuries, in comparison with the hundred and thirty years covered by the remaining four books together. An account of the early contacts between Rome and Britain in the days of Julius Caesar and Claudius leads easily enough through the legendary story of the conversion of Lucius, king of Britain, the persecutions of Diocletian, the martyrdom of St. Alban, the rise of the Pelagian heresy and the coming of the Saxons, to a renewal of the lost contact with Rome by the arrival of Augustine and his fellow missionaries in Thanet in 597. There follows an account of the early years of missionary activity in south-eastern England and of some of the difficulties with which Augustine was faced, more particularly in his relations with the British clergy, and the book closes with a short account of the situation in the still pagan kingdom of Northumbria. The change from the building of a monastery at Canterbury (described in *I, 33*) to the victory of the pagan Northumbrian Aethelfrith at *Degsastan* (described in *I, 34*) demonstrates by its very abruptness Bede's ability to see how events which were far removed from one another geographically and isolated from one another in their nature, had nevertheless a close relationship in time.

The broad sweep of the first book gives place to a more detailed approach in the second whose compass is no more than the twenty seven years from the death of Pope Gregory in 605 to the death of

Edwin, the first Christian king of Northumbria, in 632. Its content is fairly divided between the fortunes, good and ill, of the Roman mission in the south-east of the country and a new venture which brought Paulinus to baptise in the Swale near Catterick and in the Glen near Yeavering. The death of Edwin in the battle at Hatfield was followed by the almost total destruction of this first Christian church in Northumbria and its significance seems no less great to us now than it did to Bede when he made it the subject of the last chapter in his second book. The dominant theme of the third book which opens with the *infaustus annus* of the two apostate Northumbrian kings and ends about thirty five years later, shortly before the arrival of archbishop Theodore at Canterbury, is the establishment of missionaries of the Columban church in Northumbria at the invitation of Oswald and their subsequent permeation of much of the midland and eastern parts of England. In addition to Oswald and his old enemy, Penda of Mercia, we read in this third book of Aidan at Lindisfarne, of Fursey in East Anglia, of Finan in the midlands and of Cedd among the East Saxons. But in Bede's eyes, if we may judge by the length of the chapter which he devoted to it, the great Easter controversy and the decisions reached at the Synod of Whitby seemed the most important topic of the age.

At about the time of the Synod of Whitby the country suffered from a severe visitation of the plague and when Theodore reached Canterbury in 669, it was to find a church disorganised almost as much by the loss of its leaders through sudden death, as by dissension over the Easter problem. Much of the fourth book which covers a bare twenty years ending with the death of Cuthbert in 687, is concerned with the measures taken by Theodore to give order, good government and sound learning to a church which was greatly in need of all three. Among those who are prominent in its pages are the abbesses Hild of Whitby and Audrey of Ely, as well as Cuthbert himself and Wilfrid. All four of these were living in Bede's childhood and Wilfrid indeed did not die until Bede was approaching the age of forty. It is, however, in the fifth and last book which extends from 687 till 731 that Bede was writing the ecclesiastical history of the times through which he had himself lived. Near the end of this book he wrote of the reigning Northumbrian king, that Ceoluulf to whom the *History* itself is dedicated, that the beginning and course of his reign had been filled with so many and such great disturbances that it could not yet be known what ought to be written about them.

Roger of Wendover claimed that Bede began to write the *History* in 725. He may have done so but there is no independent evidence to support Roger's claim and it seems probable that his date arises from confusion between the *History* and one of Bede's works on chronology, the *de Temporum Ratione*, which is known to belong to the year 725. There is better evidence, provided by the *History* itself, for the date at which it was completed. In one passage (*V, 11*) Bede refers to Willibrord, one of the many Northumbrians who were active as missionaries on the continent, as being still alive and in the thirty sixth year of his episcopacy at the time when Bede was

5

writing. What seems likely to be the best authority, a marginal note
on Willibrord's *Calendar*, perhaps written in his own hand, places
his consecration in 695 and Bede adds that it fell on St. Cecilia's
day which is in November. It follows that this part of the *History*
was written before November 731.

Near the end of the fourth book, in a chapter devoted to a
general survey of the country, Bede writes of "the state of the whole
of Britain at this present time, that is in about the 285th year since
the coming of the English to Britain and in the year of the Incarnation of our Lord 731". Elsewhere in the same chapter there is
recorded the death of an archbishop of Canterbury on 13 January
731 and the consecration of his successor on 10 June of the same
year. These passages show that the narrative of the *History* was
continued to about midsummer of 731 and suggest that the work
as a whole was completed between midsummer and late autumn of
that year. There are, however, some indications of a revision which
made it possible to include a reference to an event which took place
in Gaul in 732. Unfortunately the reference to this event (*V, 23*),
the defeat of the Moslems by Charles Martel in the battle of Tours
in October 732, is oblique rather than explicit, but even if we accept
it there is no trace of any reference to other events which are known
to have occurred after June 731.

Those who ask why Bede wrote the *History* are likely to reach
different answers as the question itself is differently interpreted. One
answer is that he did so at the instigation of his contemporary
Albinus, abbot of St. Augustine's monastery in Canterbury. There
is no evidence that Albinus ever visited Jarrow and we do not know
that Bede ever travelled further south than York, but the two
exchanged gifts and letters, and it is in one of these last that Bede
refers to the part played by Albinus as initiator of the work. Again
in the *Preface* he writes that it was the exhortations of this same
Albinus which chiefly encouraged him to undertake the book. A
second answer might be, though we lack similar documentary evidence for it, that the exhortations of Albinus amounted only to
helpful encouragement towards the execution of a decision which is
likely to have come slowly to maturity over the years and whose
outcome may seem to us to represent the rich harvest which almost
inevitably followed from Bede's earlier labours in the fields of
grammar, chronology, natural science, hagiography and biblical
exegesis.

A third answer is one towards which Bede himself helps us
when we recall that the chief delights of his life had lain in learning,
teaching and writing. The *Ecclesiastical History* serves all three of
these ends and if we turn again to its *Preface* we shall find a clear
statement of the kind of teaching which Bede thought would benefit
those who read the work or listened to it as it was being read aloud
to them. Commending Ceoluulf for the zeal which he had shown
in his endeavours to become acquainted with the deeds of famous
men of the past, especially those of the English race, Bede continues
– "If history tells good things about good men, the attentive listener

6

is encouraged to imitate what is good; but if it relates evil things about wicked men nonetheless the devout and godly listener or reader, shunning that which is hurtful and perverted, is the more earnestly kindled to pursue those things which he knows to be good and worthy in the sight of God". There could be no clearer statement that Bede's major purpose in writing this work was to hold up the mirror of the past as a guide to Christian action and morality in the present.

A work which begins with the times of Julius Caesar and ends with the author's own age will necessarily be based on widely differing sorts of materials. Bede himself divided these materials into three categories, deriving them *ex litteris antiquorum uel ex traditione maiorum uel ex mea . . . cognitione* (*V*, *24*). The writings of the ancients were well represented in the library at Jarrow and here Bede would find at hand the works which he needed for the earlier part of his narrative. Apart from lesser extracts taken from a variety of scattered sources, he used three principal authorities for that part of his first Book which extends from Julius Caesar to the times of Augustine, the *History* of Orosius, the *de Excidio et Conquestu Brittaniae* of Gildas and the *Vita Germani* of Constantius. He frequently quotes at length from these three sources, and in noting that he does so without acknowledgment, we must note also that in this respect he was following the custom of his age.

Yet even for these more remote times there were points of detail on which he was able to add interesting information. Orosius was his main source for his account of Caesar's invasion but it may have been one of his Canterbury informants who told him that the lead-cased wooden stakes with which the Britons had sought to impede the Romans in their crossing of the Thames, were still to be seen standing, thick as a man's thigh, fixed and immovable in the river bed (*I*, *2*). Archaeologists might nowadays wish to make a different interpretation of Bede's evidence on this point. They have long since been able to demonstrate that his account of the history of the Roman Walls is untenable, yet we may recall that this account has been described as "the first complete Mural theory, with a reasoned account of the Vallum, the Stone Wall and the Scottish Turf Wall", showing a level of historical thought which was not reached again in this connection for eight and a half centuries.[1] That Bede took a lively interest in antiquities is evident from his descriptions of the inscribed monument, perhaps a rune stone, which commemorated Horsa in Kent (*I*, *15*), of the wooden tomb fashioned like a small house and placed over the grave of Chad (*IV*, *3*) and of the wooden church built by Finan at Lindisfarne (*III*, *25*). In these and other passages we may observe Bede's skill in heightening the interest of his narrative by the addition of relevant detail.

Written sources formed the basis of much that he wrote about the progress of the church in Kent and the adjacent parts of south-

[1] R. G. COLLINGWOOD, "Hadrian's Wall: A History of the Problem", *Journal of Roman Studies*, XI (1921), p. 47.

eastern England, but these were sources of a different kind from those which he had used in the earliest parts of the *History*. For this later period there was no work comparable with the *History* of Orosius or the work of Gildas, and Bede had to compile his own narrative from the materials which were sent to him. His chief helper in this respect was Albinus who examined both the written records and the traditional accounts that were accessible to him in Canterbury and then sent north to Bede, either in writing or by word of mouth, whatever he thought might be of interest. His messenger was Nothhelm, then a priest of the church of London, who later went to Rome and with the permission of Pope Gregory II searched the archives for letters which might be relevant to Bede's purpose. In such ways letters of the popes, sometimes given in summary form, but often at full length, formal records such as the decrees of the synod of Hertford in 672 and the account of the council of Hatfield in 680, together with a series of Canterbury annals, enabled Bede to write a well-documented account.

One of the documents given in full by Bede and purporting to contain the replies of Pope Gregory to a number of questions put by Augustine (*I, 27*) was regarded with evident suspicion at about the time of Bede's death in 735. In that year Boniface wrote to Nothhelm who had then become archbishop of Canterbury, asking him if he would cause "an enquiry to be made with the most scrupulous care whether or not that document has been proved to be by the aforenamed father, Saint Gregory. For the registrars say that it is not to be found in the archives of the Roman church among other documents of the aforesaid pope".[1] Unhappily we do not know what was the outcome of Nothhelm's enquiry, but even if Bede may have been the victim of a forger in respect of this one document, there can be no doubt about the general veracity of his account as a whole.

Although Albinus was Bede's chief helper in supplying him with information, there were those who were able, either by writing to him or directly by word of mouth, to inform him of events in other parts of the country. Such were Daniel, bishop of the West Saxons, Cyneberht, bishop of Lindsey, and the monks of Lastingham who were able to tell him of the deeds of Chad and Cedd among the Mercians and the East Saxons. Touching his account of the ecclesiastical history of Northumbria, he has this to say in the *Preface* – "I did not learn it from any one authority, but by the faithful testimony of innumerable witnesses who might know or remember the same; besides what I had of my own knowledge".

The chronological framework for his Northumbrian narrative rested in part upon the regnal lists which are known to have been kept in his day, and perhaps long before his day, in Northumbria and which contained the names of kings in due order together with information about the length of each king's reign. In addition to these he was able to use lists of bishops of similar construction, as

[1] Trans. from E. EMERTON, *The Letters of Saint Boniface*, Columbia University Press, 1940, pp. 62-3.

well as Northumbrian annals in which items of particular importance had been recorded. We can identify some of the written sources which he used to clothe this framework, such, for example, as the papal letters written to Edwin and his wife, and the *Life of Cuthbert* which Bede himself had written using the earlier anonymous Lindisfarne *Life* as his principal source. It is, however, the material which he derived *ex traditione majorum* which lies at the very heart of his account of the early church in Northumbria.

Those who think that the more fully documented account of the church in Kent makes better history than the early traditions about the church in Northumbria would do well to recall that documents are no less easy to forge than traditions, and sometimes more worth the forging. Paulinus first came to Northumbria less than fifty years before Bede was born and it seems a safe presumption that Bede's grandfather was alive at the time. The span of years from Edwin's baptism to Bede's ordination to the priesthood is a short one and when even an account of the personal appearance of Paulinus could be preserved till Bede's age in what is self-evidently a reliable tradition, we need not doubt the essential truth of much that Bede recorded *ex traditione majorum*. Bede learnt about the tall, stooping figure of Paulinus, with his black hair, thin face and hooked nose, from the abbot of a monastery in Lincolnshire who himself had learnt it from an old man who had himself been baptised by Paulinus in the Trent at midday (*II, 16*).

Bede was able to draw upon the memories of his elders in such ways as these for events in the life of Edwin which, as much because of the manner of their telling as for their historical importance, are now among the most widely known parts of the *History* – the chapters which tell of Edwin's exile at the court of an East Anglian king, of the debate among the Northumbrian councillors about Christianity, of the destruction of the heathen temple at Goodmanham and of the attempt upon Edwin's life by an assassin sent from Wessex. The heathen temple at Goodmanham has not yet been located, but aerial photography and subsequent excavation have revealed the royal palace at Yeavering, lying on a spur of ground overlooking the Glen in whose waters Bede tells us many Northumbrians were baptised.

The excavations at Yeavering have shown us how much there is behind Bede's brief reference to the *uilla regia* which lay there in Edwin's time, and the archaeological evidence which they have yielded provides striking confirmation of his accuracy in such a matter of historical detail. There is, however, another aspect of the *History* which may prove a difficulty to those of its readers who pass from a *Preface*, written in a form not inappropriate to a work of twentieth century historical scholarship, to read in the very first chapter of the first book that the scrapings of leaves of books brought from Ireland had proved an effective cure for snake bite. The miraculous holds a very large place in the *History* and the modern reader, unfamiliar with the background against which it is written, is likely to find some difficulty in reconciling the miraculous

9

and the historical elements. Miracles are attributed not only to such persons as Alban and Germanus, but also, and in abundant measure, to those who lived nearer Bede's own times, such as Oswald, Aidan, Hild, Cuthbert and John of Beverley. Some were taken from written sources, such as the *Life of Cuthbert* and others from men whose credibility as reliable witnesses is heavily stressed by Bede.

This difficulty is one which will lessen with a growing acquaintance with medieval literature as a whole, until a stage is reached at which we may say, in the words of a scholar who has devoted much of his life to the study of hagiography, that "if there were none of these strange and incredible tales in Bede's History we should have had every reason for astonishment. The only cause for surprise . . . is that there are not more of them".[1] Throughout the middle ages popular opinion expected, and even demanded, that miracles should be performed by a saint and his relics, and in recording what was popularly believed Bede was not only serving the didactic ends of his *History* – relating good deeds of good men – but also faithfully fulfilling what he believed to be the true function of a historian. Much of his third book consists of miracles attributed to Oswald and Aidan. At the end of the series, he tells us that he has written these things about Aidan, not as commending his errors in the observance of Easter which indeed he greatly detested, but as a true historian relating in simple fashion the things which were done by him or through him (*III, 17*). This phrase *verax historicus* echoes a phrase which we find at the end of the Preface – "I humbly beg the reader if he finds anything in these books that I have written which is other than truthful, he will not blame me who have laboured zealously, as the true law of history requires – *quod uera lex historiae est* – to transmit in simple fashion those things which I have collected from common report for the instruction of posterity".

As a theologian Bede reflects in his commentaries the contemporary theological belief that the days of the miraculous, necessary in the earliest times of the church, were now largely past. As a biographer he wrote, in the *Historia Abbatum*, an objective, factual account of the lives of the abbots of Wearmouth and Jarrow wholly free of all trace of the miraculous. But as a historian he could not omit the miraculous from the *Ecclesiastical History*, because to have done so would have been to present a picture of the early English church gravely distorted by the absence from it of any reflection of a major element in the popular belief of the times.

Nowadays the author of a work of scholarship will commonly send a copy of his work to some person whom he regards as competent to criticise it and make suggestions for its improvement before it is published. When the work has been returned he may then write a preface in which he will explain the purpose which it is intended to serve and express his thanks to those who have helped him. This is precisely what Bede did when the *History* had reached the stage at which it was almost ready to be published. So far as

[1] B. COLGRAVE, "Bede's Miracle Stories", in *Bede: His Life, Times and Writings*, ed. A. HAMILTON THOMPSON, Oxford 1935, p. 201.

we know the first copy of the work to leave Jarrow was one sent to Ceoluulf, king of Northumbria. Ceoluulf succeeded to his kingdom in 729 and two years later, in a plot whose details have not been recorded for us, he was seized and compelled by force to receive the monastic tonsure. Later in the same year he was restored to the throne but in 737, two years after Bede's death, he abdicated and entered the monastery of Lindisfarne where he spent the remaining twenty seven years of his life as a monk.

Ceoluulf's name is found in the list of benefactors of Lindisfarne in the *Liber Vitae* and Durham tradition attributed to him the gift to Lindisfarne of extensive lands in the northern part of Northumbria. Ceoluulf's interest, not only in the church itself, but also in the past history of the English race, for which Bede particularly commends him, would enable him to season his royal patronage of letters with a degree of well-informed and scholarly opinion which has not always been shown by royal patrons, and which was evidently valued by Bede. After the first draft had been returned to Jarrow with, as we may think, Ceoluulf's comments, a revised copy was made at Jarrow and was then sent to Ceoluulf, not for him to keep, but as an exemplar *ad transscribendum* so that with his own copy by him Ceoluulf would then be able to study the work at leisure. We do not know where Ceoluulf had the Jarrow exemplar copied. It may have been done by scribes of the royal household or perhaps at Lindisfarne. We have one other piece of direct evidence relating to the early circulation of the *History*. In the letter from Bede to Albinus to which reference has already been made, Bede writes of having sent him a copy of the *History* as soon as he had been able to complete it. As with the copy sent to Ceoluulf, so the copy sent by Bede to Albinus was not a gift from Jarrow to remain permanently at Canterbury, but an exemplar lent *ad transscribendum*. In this way the library of St. Augustine's at Canterbury became possessed of a copy of the *History* in or about 732, and no doubt the work was similarly lent to other monasteries for copying, to York, for example, whose bishop, Egbert, made archbishop in 735, looked upon Bede as his master and teacher, and perhaps also to Hexham, although misfortune had lately befallen its bishop, Acca, Bede's close personal friend.

The number of surviving manuscripts of the *History* is more than one hundred and fifty, a figure which is proof enough of the popularity of the work throughout western Europe in the middle ages. When we recall how many of the monastic libraries of England were destroyed during the Viking attacks, we may realise that even this large figure must fall very far short of the total number of copies that were made. A number of them belong to the eighth century and of these early manuscripts there are three which have a particular claim upon our interest, for all three are thought to be Northumbrian books. One of these three which is commonly known as "C" (British Museum MS Cotton Tiberius C. ii) has the nearly contemporary addition of the word *nostro* above the passage *patre et antistite cudberchto* and this reference to Cuthbert as "our" bishop is strongly suggestive of a Lindisfarne origin for the book. The second of the three, called "L" after its present home in Leningrad, has been rediscovered in recent times. Although it has never yet been used by an editor, it has now been reproduced in facsimile and the more it is studied, the plainer it becomes that "L" can now be claimed as the best surviving witness of the text of the *History*. There are some who think that it may also be the oldest. Moreover Professor E. A. Lowe has lately asked whether the words *Beda Famulus Christi Indignus* which form the last line of the colophon on f. 161 may not in fact be Bede's own autograph. He asks the question but cautiously refrains from answering it. If this is indeed Bede's own autograph, then MS L cannot be later than 735, the year of Bede's death. It is difficult to see how proof can ever be reached for this exciting possibility, but it does now seem certain that "L" was written here in Jarrow.

Thirdly there is "M", so called from its having belonged at one time to John Moore, bishop of Ely. For more than two centuries "M" has been looked upon as the chief of the many MSS of the *History*, for its text as well as for its antiquity, and even if, as seems likely, there is now a rival which may push it into second place on grounds of quality, as well perhaps as of antiquity, it remains nevertheless one of the outstanding books of English origin to have come down to us from the middle ages. Moreover, like "L", it is I believe, a Jarrow book. It will be published in facsimile later this year and perhaps it may be of some interest to follow its history so far as the evidence allows.

The Moore manuscript was not written before 734, a fact to which some evidence contained on the recto of its last complete leaf bears witness. The verso of this same leaf has on its upper half some material which relates to several items of Northumbrian history and which was almost certainly written in the year 737. We cannot, however, be sure whether these last items were added in 737 to a copy of the *History* which had been written in 734 or 735, or whether the manuscript as a whole belongs to 737. The point would not be of any particular importance if it were not that Bede himself died in 735. Those of us who have the good fortune to handle this venerable book may wonder as we turn its well-preserved leaves whether those pages too were ever turned by the hand of Bede himself.

It is a plain unornamented book, with none of the luxury of the Lindisfarne Gospels, and it is written in a Northumbrian minuscule of an austere beauty which seems suited to its scholarly content, but which yields plain signs that its scribe, though skilled in his craft, was writing in some haste. He was very apt to leave words out, though most of his omissions were made good by a contemporary correcting hand, and he was at great pains not to waste any space. The result of his labours is a workmanlike, serviceable manuscript which, though in some respects not so good as the Leningrad text, has hitherto served as the basis of all printed editions of the *Ecclesiastical History* since that of John and George Smith published in 1722. The eighth century was a time of great activity by Anglo-Saxon, and expecially Northumbrian, missionaries on the European mainland, and many letters have survived to bear witness to the part played by English scribes, including those of Wearmouth and Jarrow, in supplying copies of books for the libraries of new monastic foundations abroad. Several of these letters ask in particular for the works of Bede and it seems very likely that it was in response to some such request that the Moore manuscript left Jarrow and found its way to France. We do not know exactly when it went or where it found its new home, but it was certainly in France by the tenth century and probably by the ninth, as we can see from a variety of additions made to it in the hand of a scribe writing a Caroline minuscule. Moreover, in France it became the parent of a large family of continental manuscripts of the *History*.

The manuscript remained in France throughout the middle ages, as we may learn from a marginal addition in a French hand of the fifteenth century indicating that at that time it belonged to the library of St. Julian's cathedral at Le Mans. At the time of the Treaty of Ryswick in 1697 it passed, together with many other manuscripts, into the hands of a Scot called Alexander Cunningham who later sold his purchases to John Moore, at that time bishop of Norwich. In this way the manuscript whose name is taken from John Moore, returned to the land of its origin after an exile lasting something more than eight hundred years. William Nicholson, bishop of Carlisle, dined with John Moore on 19 January 1702 and he recorded in his diary that on this occasion he had seen the manuscript in Moore's library. Moore was translated to Ely in 1707 and after his death in 1714 his library was purchased by George I who presented it to the university of Cambridge in 1715. Since that date the Moore Bede has remained one of the most valuable possessions of that library.

The *Ecclesiastical History* continued to be widely read and copied throughout the middle ages. About forty of the surviving manuscripts belong to the fourteenth or fifteenth centuries. It was first translated into English – Old English as we should now call it – in the time of Alfred the Great. The Latin text was already in print before 1500 and in the sixteenth century editions were published at Strasbourg, Antwerp, Louvain, Paris and Heidelberg. The first modern English translation was the work of Thomas Stapleton who was renouned as one of the most learned men of his time and as a skilful controversialist in the Roman Catholic interest. His translation was published at Antwerp in 1565 and in a prefatory letter addressed to Queen Elizabeth, Stapleton wrote: –

"In this history it shall appeare in what faith your noble Realme was christened, and hath almost these thousand yeres continewed: to the glory of God, the enriching of the crowne, and great welth and quiet of the realme. In this history your highness shall see in how many and weighty pointes the pretended refourmers of the church in your Grace's dominions have departed from the patern of that sounde and catholike

13

faith planted first among Englishemen by holy S. Augustine our Apostle".

The first English edition of the Latin text was prepared by Abraham Wheloc and published at Cambridge in 1643, this work also containing the *editio princeps* of the Old English version. The first critical edition of the *History* was the work of John and George Smith. John Smith, a Westmorland man by birth, held curacies in different parts of the county of Durham and thereafter became a prebendary of Durham cathedral and rector of Bishopwearmouth where he rebuilt the rectory and restored the chancel of the church. He spent much of his time at Cambridge working on the Moore manuscript of the *History*, but he died in 1715 before the work was finished. His son, George, who was born in Durham and buried in the churchyard of St. Oswald's, carried the work to completion with great success, although he was only twenty two at the time of his father's death. The new edition was published in a fine folio volume at Cambridge in 1722. The next great advance was the notable edition of Charles Plummer which was published at Oxford in 1896 and to which all students of the *History* are greatly indebted. Before very long we hope to see the new edition which is now being prepared by Professor Mynors and Bertram Colgrave who will be the first editors to use the fine eighth century Leningrad manuscript of the work.

The *Ecclesiastical History* has now been read for more than twelve centuries and therein lies proof enough of the living qualities of this great work. There are some who approach it as professional historians, analysing, dissecting, criticising, but still finding in it the major source of information about the conversion of the English to Christianity and about the fortunes of the earliest English church. There are others who may read it for the stories which its author has to tell, whether in his own lucid and simple Latin, in Thomas Stapleton's vigorous Elizabethan prose or in a modern English translation. And there are others who may still read it remembering Bede's own hope that his account of things said and done in the past might encourage men to imitate the good and to shun the evil. Whoever the reader may be, he can rest assured that as he grows in knowledge about the *Ecclesiastical History* itself, about its venerable author and about the world in which he lived and wrote, so also will he grow in admiration for this great achievement. The words which Boniface wrote in a letter to the archbishop of York ten years after Bede's death need but little adaptation to fit them to the circumstances of this present day.

"I beg you also to have copied and sent to me some of the works of the lector Bede whom, as we learn, divine grace has endowed with spiritual understanding and allowed to shine forth in your country, so that we too may profit by the light of that torch which the Lord has granted to you".

VIII

The Bernicians and their Northern Frontier

MATERIALS

The purpose of this study is to examine some of the evidence for the early history of the most northerly of the English settlements in Britain, to trace the gradual extension of English rule northwards from the coast of Northumberland across the south-eastern lowlands of Scotland and to determine the stages which led to the stabilisation of the frontier on the Forth in the early years of the eighth century. Since these topics will be approached primarily from the English point of view, it is necessary to make a short inquiry into the beginnings of Northumbrian historiography.[1]

There is no evidence that the English knew the Latin alphabet at the time of their invasion of Britain. The two principal sources from which they could later have learnt it were the Celtic and Roman churches, and although the form of script used in Northumbria in the eighth century[2] proves that Northumbrian scholarship owed much to the Celtic, and particularly the Irish, church, the beginnings of Northumbrian historiography certainly owed something to Rome as well as to the Irish.[3] If Bede's account of the

---

[1] Some use will also be made of the Pictish records which have recently been examined by H. M. Chadwick, *Early Scotland* (Cambridge, 1949), 1–37, and of the Irish annals whose high value for the seventh and eighth centuries has long been recognised. Much of the written evidence of Welsh origin demands further study before its authenticity and value can be established, e.g. the poems attributed to Taliesin and the legends of Kentigern, Merlin and Leudonus. See, however, pp. 84 ff. above. Further work is also needed before the relevant place-name evidence can be used. A. Mawer's *The Place-Names of Northumberland and Durham* (Cambridge, 1920) needs revising. A general survey of the Celtic place-names of south-eastern Scotland has been made by W. J. Watson, *History of the Celtic Place-Names of Scotland* (Edinburgh, 1926), 126–54, and there is a recent comprehensive survey of *The Place-Names of West Lothian* (Edinburgh, 1941) by A. Macdonald. The volume of English archaeological material of the pagan period is so small as to be almost negligible and the material culture of the native population concerned is almost unknown.

[2] E. A. Lowe, *Codices Latini Antiquiores*, II (Oxford, 1935), x.

[3] It is impossible to determine the relative strength of the various influences

conversion of the Northumbrians is correct, it may be supposed that the first books to reach the English in the north were such service books as Paulinus needed on his visit to Yorkshire in 626,[1] but the mission of Paulinus was short-lived and is unlikely to have had any lasting results in the encouragement of writing among the Northumbrians, unless through the agency of James the Deacon who remained near Catterick after Paulinus himself had fled from the pagan reaction which followed Edwin's death.[2] It is well, however, to remember that by 626 the Bernicians had been in contact with the northern Welsh for nearly sixty years (the Deirans perhaps for very much longer) and that the Welsh themselves claimed credit for the baptism of many of the Northumbrians.[3] To assume from Bede's silence on the point that the Welsh church played no part in the conversion of the Northumbrians would be unwise, since Bede himself was strongly prejudiced in matters concerning the Celtic and Roman churches and he lost no opportunity of belittling the Welsh church in particular.[4] There seems, however, to be no direct evidence that the influence of the Celtic church was strongly felt among the English of Northumbria until 635 when Lindisfarne became the headquarters of a mission from Iona after Oswald's victory over Cadwallon.[5] Oswald himself had previously spent some years in exile among the Scots and had learnt to speak their language well enough to be able to act as interpreter for Aidan in Northumbria.[6] From Bede's account[7] it is clear that Scottish monks settled in Northumbrian territory in considerable numbers during Oswald's reign and that Lindisfarne was only one of several

which met in Northumbria in the seventh century. C. W. Jones (*Bedae Opera de Temporibus*, Cambridge, Mass., 1943, 105–13) has recently demonstrated the importance of Irish influence on Northumbrian scholarship, especially in computistical works. Although there can be no quarrel with his belief that Northumbrian scholarship owed little to the Augustinian mission, he seems to underestimate the strength of Mediterranean influence after the synod of Whitby.

[1] *Historia Ecclesiastica*, ed. C. Plummer (Oxford, 1896), II, ix. All references to the text of Bede's *Historia Ecclesiastica*, hereafter cited as *HE.*, are by book and chapter to this edition.

[2] *HE.* II, xx.

[3] *Historia Brittonum*, cap. 63.

[4] As a particular instance it may be noted that, despite Bede's remarks to the contrary, the 19-year Easter cycle was well known in the Welsh church (H. M. and N. K. Chadwick, *The Growth of Literature*, I (Cambridge, 1932), 147, n. 1).

[5] *HE.* III, iii.

[6] *Ibid.*

[7] *Ibid.*

THE BERNICIANS AND THEIR NORTHERN FRONTIER

monastic centres which they established.[1] They are said to have instructed both young and old in the studies and observance of monastic discipline and no doubt the Latin alphabet came to be more widely known in Northumbria as a result of this teaching. The conflict between the Celtic and the Roman churches had important consequences for the growth of historiography in Northumbria, partly because neither side could argue its case without some understanding of complex problems of chronology and partly because the adherence of the Northumbrian church to Rome led to fresh contacts with Mediterranean scholarship. Soon after the synod of Whitby (664),[2] Benedict Biscop began the first of several journeys to Rome during which he acquired a quantity of books for the libraries at Monkwearmouth and Jarrow, and in these libraries lay the materials from which Bede gained his learning.

It is probable that the oldest surviving written record from Northumbria which can be dated with confidence, is the inscribed stone slab commemorating the dedication of Benedict Biscop's church at Jarrow on the 9th of the Kalends of May in the 15th year of the reign of king Ecgfrið and the 4th year of abbot Ceolfrið.[3] The date corresponds to 24 April 685 (about four weeks before Ecgfrið's death at Dunnichen Moss), but it is of interest to note that the method of identifying the year is by reference to the regnal year of the reigning king and not to the year of the Incarnation.

[1] Bede is much less hostile to the Scottish and Pictish churches than to the Welsh church, and he is therefore a more trustworthy witness in his evidence about the former. It seems likely that his attitude would be affected partly by the undeniably large part played by the Scots in the conversion of the Northumbrians and partly by the Pictish mission sent by Nechtan IV to Ceolfrið, abbot of Monkwearmouth and Jarrow, during his own lifetime. See below, p. 172.

[2] In the chronology of Northumbrian history in the seventh century I have consistently followed the views of W. Levison, *England and the Continent in the Eighth Century* (Oxford, 1946), 265–79. F. M. Stenton, *Anglo-Saxon England* (1947), prefers 663.

[3] *Archaeologia Aeliana*, n.s., x (1885), 199, and XXII (1900), 34; also Æ. Hübner, *Inscriptiones Brittaniae Christianae* (Berlin, 1876), 71. For a note on the chronology involved see W. Levison, *op. cit.* 273, n. 2. Before 1782 the stone was built into the north side of the nave of St Paul's church. It is now in the west wall of the tower, over the arch leading from the nave into the chancel. The elaborateness of the inscription, which compares favourably both in content and technique with most other surviving examples of Anglo-Saxon epigraphy, might be taken to imply the existence of other kinds of written record at Jarrow at this date. Benedict Biscop is known to have employed Gaulish stone-masons on his church at Monkwearmouth (*Historia Abbatum*, cap. 5), but the occurrence of some insular forms on the Jarrow stone suggests native workmanship.

Some of the other inscribed stones from Jarrow, Lindisfarne, Hartlepool and elsewhere may also belong to near the end of the seventh or the beginning of the eighth century, but their inscriptions which are sometimes in runes and sometimes in Roman lettering, are not sufficiently detailed to allow exact dating except in one or two instances.[1]

Excluding memorial inscriptions, Northumbrian scholars had begun to make five different kinds of written historical record by the time of Bede's death in 735, and at least four different centres— Lindisfarne, the twin foundations of Monkwearmouth and Jarrow, Ripon and Whitby—are known to have been concerned in their compilation.[2]

(1) *Genealogies.* These are a form of record which can be regarded as being of Germanic origin since they owed nothing to recent Mediterranean or Celtic influence except their conversion from oral into written records. The Northumbrian genealogies are not now preserved in any document earlier than the ninth century,[3] but the earliest surviving version contains internal evidence that its compiler had used older written material, and that in particular his information about the Bernician kings was derived from a source which had been put into writing during or soon after the reign of Ecgfrið (670–85).[4]

(2) *Regnal lists.* These consist of lists of kings together with the number of years each king was believed to have reigned. The earliest surviving regnal list for Northumbria is contained in the Moore MS. of Bede's *History* and was compiled in 737, but it was not the first of its kind to be kept in Northumbria.[5] Such lists may have been inspired by lists of consuls and emperors such as were kept in the Mediterranean world and were used by Bede in the chronicles attached to his works on chronology (*de Temporibus* 703

---

[1] G. Baldwin-Brown, *The Arts in Early England*, v (London, 1921), 58–70, *Archaeologia*, LXXIV (1923–4), 258–66 and LXXXIX (1943), 40–6.

[2] It is probable that other monastic centres in Northumbria were similarly engaged, notably York, Hexham, Hartlepool and Melrose, but nothing now survives which can certainly be attributed to any of these houses at so early a date.

[3] B.M. Cotton MS. Vespasian B 6, ed. H. Sweet, *The Oldest English Texts* (London, 1885), 169–70.

[4] R. W. Chambers, *Beowulf, An Introduction* (Cambridge, 1921), 196.

[5] P. Hunter Blair, 'The Moore Memoranda on Northumbrian History', in *The Early Cultures of North-West Europe*, ed. Sir Cyril Fox and B. Dickins (Cambridge, 1950), 245–57.

THE BERNICIANS AND THEIR NORTHERN FRONTIER

and *de Temporum Ratione* 725), but the practice of keeping lists of this kind is a common form of primitive historiography. The regnal lists were of the first importance to Bede because they enabled him to calculate the dates of events according to the years of the Christian era long after the occurrence of the events themselves. Indeed these lists formed the principal basis for Bede's chronology of Northumbrian history in the sixth and probably most of the seventh century.[1] Regnal lists could be expanded into a more detailed kind of historical record by the addition of notices of events other than the mere length of a king's reign. The so-called Pictish Chronicle is an example of such an expanded list.[2]

(3) *Annals.* The principal differences between the annals and the regnal lists are that the former were concerned with events other than the mere succession of kings and that the Christian era formed the basis of their chronology from the first. Bede's *History* (731) was the first major work of English origin in which this era was consistently used, but traces of its use in Northumbria at an earlier date for purposes of annalistic record can still be found. After the synod of Whitby the nineteen-year cycle which had been advocated by Victorius of Aquitaine, came into use in Northumbria as the normal means of calculating the date of Easter.[3] The first of the eight columns into which the Easter tables based on this cycle were divided, contained the number of the year according to the Christian era and in Northumbria, as previously in other parts of Europe, it was observed that by making an entry in the appropriate position in the margin of such a table it was possible to secure a lasting record not only of a given event, but also of the particular year in which that event occurred.[4] With the separation of these entries and their dates from the Easter tables there was born the annalistic chronicle based on the Christian era. The proof of this practice lies in the survival of copies of the great paschal table of 532 years which were taken to the Continent by Northumbrian missionaries in the eighth century and which contain a number of

[1] Bede almost invariably refers both to the year of the Christian era and to the regnal year when giving the date of particular events in the *History*. There are no dates in the *Anonymous Life of Cuthbert* (between 699 and 705), but some are found in Eddius' *Life of Wilfrid*.

[2] Ed. W. F. Skene, *Chronicles of the Picts and Scots* (Edinburgh, 1867), 3–10. See M. O. Anderson's articles in *Scottish Historical Review*, XXVIII (1949), 108–118, XXIX (1950), 13–22.

[3] C. W. Jones, *op. cit.* 103–4.

[4] R. L. Poole, *Chronicles and Annals* (Oxford, 1926), 26.

entries relating to Northumbria.[1] These, together with some others relating to Kent, served as the foundation for a considerable number of continental chronicles. It is not now possible to determine either when or where the practice of making entries of this kind first began in Northumbria. It has been noticed that the dedication slab from Jarrow (685) uses the regnal year and this usage no doubt represents the normal practice of the time, but Easter tables had certainly been constructed in Northumbria before 703 since Bede gave instructions for their compilation in the *de Temporibus* which was written in that year. Among the Northumbrian material which may derive from entries in Easter tables are one or two entries relating to the latter part of the seventh century in the *Anglo-Saxon Chronicle*, one or two entries in the chronological summary at the end of Bede's *History*[2] and also some of the items in the Moore MS. *Memoranda*.

(4) *Hagiography.* The writing of saints' *Lives* was the earliest form of what may properly be called literary composition in Northumbria and the practice had become fairly widespread before Bede's death. There now exist copies of four early *Lives* which were written in different Northumbrian monasteries: (*a*) The *Anonymous Life of Cuthbert* which was written at Lindisfarne between 699 and 705[3] and which served as the basis of Bede's works on the same subject; (*b*) the *Life of Wilfrid* which was written at Ripon by Eddius Stephanus within a few years of 715;[4] (*c*) an *Anonymous Life of Ceolfrið* written at Monkwearmouth or Jarrow after the death of Ceolfrið in 716, but probably before 735;[5] (*d*) an *Anonymous Life of Gregory* written by a monk of Whitby probably before 731.[6]

---

[1] P. Lehmann, *Fuldaer Studien, Sitzungsb. der Bayer. Akad. der Wissenschaften*, Phil.-Philol. Klasse (München, 1925), 37–46.

[2] For these two groups of material see *Archaeologia Aeliana*, 4th ser., XXVI (1948), 107–12.

[3] Ed. with translation, B. Colgrave, *Two Lives of St Cuthbert* (Cambridge, 1940). For the date see *ibid.* 13.

[4] Ed. with translation, B. Colgrave, *Eddius Stephanus' Life of Wilfrid* (Cambridge, 1927). For the date see *ibid.* x–xi.

[5] Ed. under the title *Historia Abbatum auctore Anonymo*, C. Plummer, *Venerabilis Baedae Opera Historica* (Oxford, 1896), I, 388–404. Translated D. S. Boutflower, *Life of Ceolfrid, Abbot of Wearmouth and Jarrow* (Sunderland, 1912). For the date see Boutflower, 45–6.

[6] Part of the text was edited by P. Ewald, *Die älteste Biographie Gregors I* in *Historische Aufsätze dem Andenken an Georg Waitz Gewidmet* (Hannover, 1886), 17–54, also by C. Plummer, *op. cit.* II, 389–91. For a complete text see F. A. Gasquet, *A Life of Pope St Gregory the Great* (Westminster, 1904). Part of the

To these four may be added Bede's *Historia Abbatum*[1] which is mainly biographical. It is self-evident that this group of material is chiefly of value for the ecclesiastical history of Northumbria in the seventh century. Cuthbert and Wilfrid were both born *c.* 634 and Ceolfrið *c.* 642, and their biographers therefore had no occasion to go back to the beginnings of Northumbrian history. The Whitby *Life of Gregory* makes one or two references to southern Northumbria before the conversion.

(5) *Narrative history.* The supreme, and indeed the only, example of this kind of record is Bede's *History.* Any attempt to assess the value of this work in its entirety would be wholly out of place here, but it is relevant to consider what may be its worth for events earlier than *c.* 650. Bede was born *c.* 670 and he finished the *History* in 731. He could therefore have drawn extensively upon the knowledge of contemporary witnesses as far back as *c.* 690 or a little earlier, and at second-hand upon the memories of their elders as far back as the middle of the century or again a little earlier. For most of the events which had occurred before *c.* 650 he must have relied upon tradition which had either remained wholly oral or which had found its way into writing at a date which can hardly have been much earlier than *c.* 685, except of course where he was able to draw information from documents of foreign origin. Among this written material may be placed the genealogies, the regnal lists and the material from Easter tables. The value of unwritten traditional material in Bede's environment is likely to have been greatest where matters ecclesiastical were concerned. Perhaps the most striking instance in the *History* is the passage in which Bede describes the appearance of Paulinus—'tall of stature, a little stooping, his hair black, his nose slender and aquiline, his aspect both venerable and majestic',[2] information which Bede had from a priest called Deda who had learnt it from a very old man who had himself been baptised by Paulinus. Here, at third-hand, oral tradition which is plainly authentic, carries back to 628, but even so there is a gap of some eighty years between the age of Paulinus and the age of Ida, Bernicia's first king. Although there is no reason to suppose that this gap could not have been spanned in Bede's time—

text with translation is in the *Downside Review*, XXIII, new series, IV (1904), 15–29. A complete translation is given by C. W. Jones in *Saints' Lives and Chronicles in Early England* (Cornell Univ. Press, 1947), 97–121. For evidence of date see Plummer, I, 389.

[1] Ed. Plummer, I, 364–87.   [2] *HE.* II, 16.

VIII

THE BERNICIANS AND THEIR NORTHERN FRONTIER

Beowulf and *The Lives of the Two Offas* are sufficiently striking examples of the tenacity of folk memory[1]—it is a fact that, with the possible exception of events connected with Æðelfrið, no vestige of any native English tradition relating to the pagan period of Northumbrian history has survived.[2] It is hardly to be supposed that no such traditions existed, since Alcuin would then have had no occasion to rebuke the monks of Lindisfarne for listening to the old stories rather than to the works of the Christian fathers,[3] but so long as the main purpose of those who knew how to write was the furtherance of Christianity, there was little likelihood that these stories would be preserved except by oral tradition. Yet if stories of pagan times were not usually thought fit matter to be preserved in writing, the history of the church itself provided a new outlet for the native gift of story-telling, and it was from this source that Bede drew most of his material for the history of Northumbria in the first half of the seventh century. In particular his account of the reign of Edwin was derived almost entirely from stories or sagas which had evolved round the person of this first Christian king of Northumbria.[4]

[1] For the historical elements in these two works, see R. W. Chambers, *op. cit.* 1–40, and H. M. Chadwick, *The Origin of the English Nation* (Cambridge, 1924), 111–36.

[2] The stories of Coifi, the Deiran high-priest (*HE*. II, 13), and of the Deiran slave-boys in the market at Rome (*HE*. II, 1) owe their survival to their connection with the conversion.

[3] The passage is quoted by C. E. Wright, *The Cultivation of Saga in Anglo-Saxon England* (Edinburgh, 1939), 20–1.

[4] Cf. Wright, 73. Since they are not historical works in the sense intended here, I have excluded from this survey such works as the *Lindisfarne Gospels* and St Willibrord's *Calendar* which are regarded by E. A. Lowe as the earliest surviving Northumbrian MSS. which can be dated with confidence (*op. cit.* xiii). If Lowe is correct in accepting the authenticity of Aldred's note on the origin of the Lindisfarne Gospels and in supposing that they were written before Eadfrið became bishop of Lindisfarne, i.e. before 698, we must assume a standard of draughtsmanship in Northumbria at this date far higher than might otherwise have been inferred. For an attempt to demonstrate on artistic grounds that the gospel fragments now preserved in the Durham MSS. A. II. 10, C. III. 13 and C. III. 20, are as old as the middle of the seventh century see *Acta Archaeologica*, XVIII (1947), 162–71, but the case is not proven, nor is it certain that the work was written in Northumbria. R. A. B. Mynors (*Durham Cathedral Manuscripts*, Oxford, 1939, 17) places these fragments in the seventh or eighth century. For a recent and detailed analysis of most of the Northumbrian works mentioned in this brief survey reference should be made to C. W. Jones', *Saints' Lives and Chronicles in Early England* (Cornell Univ. Press, 1947).

THE PAGAN PERIOD

Bede states in the chronological summary which forms the last chapter of his *History*, though not in the body of the work itself, that Ida to whom the Northumbrian royal family traced its origin, began to reign in 547 and that his reign lasted twelve years. The same statement is found verbatim in the Moore MS. *Memoranda* and no doubt these two items, if not directly related, are at least dependent on a common original. The preceding inquiry into early Northumbrian historiography reveals the means which would permit the calculation of the date of an event which had occurred over a hundred years before the English of Northumbria had begun to keep written records, and also enables some estimate of the accuracy of this date to be formed. The method would be to add together the regnal years of all the Bernician kings and to subtract the total so reached from the year of the Christian era in which the calculation was made. If it is supposed, for example, that the calculation was made in 729, the year of Ceoluulf's accession, the sum of the regnal years would be 182 and the difference between these two figures would give the date 547. The sum of the regnal years can now be reckoned only from the material contained in the Moore *Memoranda* which was written two years after Bede's death, but it is clear from Bede's own remarks that a similar body of material was available to him. The same method could be used for calculating the date according to the Christian era of any event which was believed from written record or from popular tradition to have occurred in a particular year of a particular king's reign. If indeed, as seems very probable, the older system of chronology had been by reference to regnal years, Bede or some other would have had to make a similar calculation for many of the events whose date he recorded. This, however, need not detract from the value of his dates provided that the evidence upon which the calculations were made was adequate. The accuracy of his conclusion in the case of Ida's accession rests upon the validity of two presumptions, first that the numerals denoting the regnal years were free from error, and this there is no means of checking, and second that all the kings in question ruled in regular succession to one another. This is known to have been so from the time of Æðelfrið onwards, but there is no evidence to show whether the presumption is valid for his seven predecessors. Bede, however, believed that it was so and his belief

VIII

must be accepted. Therefore, even if the date for Ida's accession cannot be regarded as having the value of contemporary evidence, it may none the less be accepted as likely to be correct within a year or two. According to the genealogy preserved in MS. Vespasian B 6 Ida's descent was as follows:

ida eopping. eoppa oesing. oesa eðilberhting. eðilberht angengeoting. angengeot alusing. alusa ingibranding. ingibrand wegbranding. wegbrand bernicing. beornic beldaeging. beldaeg wodning. uoden frealafing.[1]

Excepting the kings of Essex,[2] all the Anglo-Saxon royal families whose genealogies have been preserved, traced their descent from Woden, and the Wessex kings also traced their descent from the same son of Woden, though it is doubtful whether any significance should be attached to this fact.[3] The only obviously fictitious element in this genealogy is *beornic* who may be regarded as the eponym of Bernicia, but it may also be noted that the earlier generations lack the vowel alliteration which is remarkably persistent in the later history of the dynasty. Since none of Ida's supposed ancestors has yet been identified with any known historical person, the authenticity of the genealogy cannot be established, neither can it be made to yield any clue to Ida's place of origin. It has been argued that the English inhabitants of Lindisfarne were colonists from north Lincolnshire. The first element in Bede's adjective *Lindisfarnensis* which he uses of Lindisfarne, is the same as the first element in the name which he applies to the people of Lindsey, namely *gens Lindisfarorum*, but it is open to question whether this is adequate ground for postulating that the inhabitants of Lindisfarne came from Lindsey.[4]

---

[1] H. Sweet, *Oldest English Texts*, 170.
[2] *Ibid.* 179, and H. M. Chadwick, *Studies on Anglo-Saxon Institutions* (Cambridge, 1905), 275-7.
[3] P. K. Johnstone (*Antiquity* XX, 1946, 31-7) argues that Cerdic of Wessex was connected with northern Britain, but his argument is not convincing.
[4] This interpretation is advanced by E. Ekwall (*Dictionary of English Place-Names*, 3rd ed. Oxford, 1947, s.v. Lindisfarne) and endorsed by Max Förster (*Der Flussname Themse und seine Sippe*, 165-7, *Sitzungsb. d. bayer. Akad. d. Wiss., Philo-Hist. Abteilung*, 1941, 1, München; I am indebted to Professor Jackson for drawing my attention to this work). Förster interprets OE *Lindesfarona ēa* as 'Insel der Lindsey-Fahrer', although the parallels which he quotes, *Hallands-fari, Sjālands-fari*, etc., are not strictly analogous. He quotes Symeon

THE BERNICIANS AND THEIR NORTHERN FRONTIER

The scene of the attack which led to the foundation of Bernicia is not known to be recorded in any source of either English or Celtic origin, but Bede believed that rather less than a century after the beginning of Ida's reign the Bernician capital lay at Bamborough on the coast of Northumberland, where a massive outcrop of rock offered an almost impregnable front to the land. This place, which was known to Bede as *ciuitas* or *urbs regia*, was thought by him to have taken its name from a queen called Bebba, but he does not say who was the husband of this queen and attempts by later writers to identify him show some variation.[1] The association of Ida and his successors in the sixth century with Bamborough and its neighbourhood rests upon two authorities, the *Anglo-Saxon Chronicle* and the *Historia Brittonum*. The original form of the relevant entry in text A of the *Chronicle* was no more than a translation of the corresponding entry in Bede's chronological summary, as may readily be seen when the two entries are placed side by side:

Anno DXLVII, Ida regnare coepit, a quo regalis Nordanhymbrorum prosapia originem tenet, et XII annis in regno permansit (*HE* v, xxiv).

Her Ida feng to rice, þonon Norþanhymbra cynecyn onwoc (and rixode xii gear, —D).

In its original form, therefore, text A provides no evidence for associating Ida with Bamborough, but in the northern version of

of Durham's evidence (ed. T. Arnold, Rolls Series, I, 51 and II, 54) that Lindisfarne took its name from a stream called *Lindis* which ran into the sea from the mainland opposite the island, but dismisses it because no stream of that name is otherwise recorded in the area. It appears to be the fact that OBr. **lind-on*, 'water', is present in both the names Lindisfarne and Lindsey, as well in the names of the places as in those of the people who lived there, but the hypothesis that the one is derived from the other seems to demand more solid evidence. It is much easier to believe that what Symeon took to be a river-name was in reality the old name of the tidal waters between Lindisfarne and the mainland, and that the name refers not to the people who travelled to or from Lindsey, but to the people who came or went across the waters.

[1] *HE.* III, vi, xii, xvi, xvii, and Plummer's note II, 141. Bede mentions the name twice, once in the ablative *Bebba* and once in the genitive *Bebbae* where the terminations may be presumed to be Latin, though *Bebbae* corresponds with an uninflected archaic OE. nominative, see H. Ström, *Old English Personal Names in Bede's History* (Lund, 1939), 64, 142. See also the statement in *The Three Northern Counties of England*, ed. C. Headlam (Gateshead, 1939), 19, that Bebba, Shada, Brada and Grogga are the names of crags on the Great Whin Sill, though the writer gives no evidence for the antiquity of these names.

VIII

the *Chronicle*, represented by texts D and E, the following additional information is found:

and he (Ida) timbrode Bebbanburh, seo wæs ærost mid hegge betyned, and ðæræfter mid wealle.[1]

This additional information was subsequently inserted in text A in a late hand,[2] and it therefore has no independent value in this text. Its value in texts D and E is that of a tradition whose existing MS. evidence is not older than the eleventh century. As for its content, it may be remarked that anyone who had read Bede's *History* might have inferred the existence of a stockade at Bamborough in the seventh century from the account of Penda's attempt to destroy the place by fire.[3] On the other hand it seems very unlikely, from what is known of Anglo-Saxon methods of fortification, that there would ever have been stone fortifications at Bamborough during the Anglo-Saxon period. It would therefore be unwise to give much weight to the evidence of the *Anglo-Saxon Chronicle* on these points.

The relevant passages in the *Historia Brittonum* are as follows:

Ida filius Eobba tenuit regiones in sinistrali parte Brittanniae, id est Umbri maris, et regnavit annis duodecim, et unxit Dinguayrdi Guurth Berneich (cap. 61).

Eadfered Flesaurs...dedit uxori suae Dinguoaroy quae vocatur Bebbab, et de nomine suae uxoris suscepit nomen, id est Bebbanburth (cap. 63).[4]

The equation in the second of these two passages of the place which was called after Bebba with *Dinguoaroy* is of considerable interest since it appears to give the Celtic name of Bamborough,[5] but it may

---

[1] The text is from D, ed. E. Classen and F. E. Harmer, *An Anglo-Saxon Chronicle* (Manchester, 1926), 8. The version in E differs only in its orthography. F has no independent value for this purpose.
[2] See R. Flower and H. Smith, *The Parker Chronicle and Laws*, E.E.T.S., facsimile edition (London, 1941), fo. 6a.
[3] *HE*. III, xvi.
[4] Ed. T. Mommsen, *MGH*. Auct. Antiq. XIII (Berlin, 1898), 205–6.
[5] See K. Meyer, *Fianaigecht, Royal Irish Academy, Todd Lecture Series*, XVI (1910), xiii, and W. J. Watson, *Celtic Place-Names of Scotland* (Edinburgh, 1926), 132. Meyer quotes the title of a now lost Irish tale about an Irish expedition against the English—*Slúagad Fiachnai maic Baítáin co Dún nGúaire i Saxanaib*, 'The hosting of Fiachna son of Baítán to *Dún Gúairi* in the land of the Saxons'. Baítán was not, as Meyer suggests, Baítán mac Cairill, but Baítán the high-king.

THE BERNICIANS AND THEIR NORTHERN FRONTIER

be noted that the passage refers to Æðelfrið (*Eadfered Flesaurs*), not to Ida, and that not all authorities are agreed that Bebba was Æðelfrið's wife. The evidence of the first passage is hardly more satisfactory because of the obscurity of the phrase *unxit Dinguayrdi Guurth Berneich* which is interpreted in one group of MSS. of the *Historia Brittonum* as meaning that Ida joined Bernicia to Deira. Nevertheless the tradition represented by these passages appears to be at least as old as the beginning of the ninth century and it is therefore not wholly without value. The evidence of the *Anglo-Saxon Chronicle* and the *Historia Brittonum* does not, however, yield ground for any confident advance beyond Bede's belief that Bamborough was a stronghold of the Bernician kings in the first half of the seventh century.[1]

According to the data in the Moore *Memoranda*, seven kings reigned in Bernicia before Æðelfrið, the last of the pagans. The list is as follows:

1.	Ida	12 years	(547–59)
2.	Glappa	1 year	(559–60)
3.	Adda	8 years	(560–68)
4.	Aedilric	4 years	(568–72)
5.	Theodric	7 years	(572–79)
6.	Friduuald	6 years	(579–85)
7.	Hussa	7 years	(585–92)

---

[1] A small, poorly-equipped cemetery of the Anglo-Saxon, but not necessarily pagan, period lay on the coast at Howick Heugh, a few miles south of Bamborough (*Arch. Ael.* 4th ser., xvi, 120–8). It is the only adequately recorded example of its kind north of Tyne. There is some slight evidence of other cemeteries at Hepple and near Milfield (*ibid.* 128). Anglo-Saxon brooches, singly or in pairs, have been found at Whitehill, near Tynemouth (Baldwin-Brown, *op. cit.* IV, 810), Benwell (*Arch. Ael.* 4th ser., xiii, 117–21), Corstopitum (Baldwin-Brown, IV, 811) and Birdoswald (*ibid.*). Additional material of the Anglo-Saxon period has been recovered during recent work at *Corstopitum* (unpublished). There is a well-known 'hanging-bowl' from Capheaton (*Arch. Ael.* 4th ser., viii, 328–38). None of these finds is necessarily earlier than the seventh century. Other finds from Northumberland which are possibly, but not certainly, of the Anglo-Saxon period are recorded from Barrasford (*Arch. Ael.* n.s., vii, 14), Hepple, Sweethope, Lowick (B.M. Registers, 2080–90) and Tosson (*Proc. Soc. Ant. Scot.* IV, 61). The entire body of this material from Northumberland would be scarcely equivalent to the contents of six well-furnished graves from, for example, the Cambridge region. So far as I am aware no burials which are certainly of the pagan period are recorded from Scotland. See Baldwin-Brown, IV, 812 and *Proc. Soc. Ant. Scot.* XLIX, 332 for some alleged Anglo-Saxon material from Dalmeny Park on the Firth of Forth and Buchan in Aberdeenshire, but the evidence is not satisfactory in either case.

THE BERNICIANS AND THEIR NORTHERN FRONTIER

So far as is known no early authority ever calculated the dates of these seven reigns according to the years of the Christian era,[1] a calculation which can now be made only from the figures contained in the regnal lists in the manner already demonstrated for the date of Ida's accession. Since it is not to be supposed that each of these seven kings ruled an exact whole number of years, the dates of their reigns should not be regarded as more than approximately accurate. In some later authorities the order of these kings was altered so as to identify *Aedilric* with another king of the same name who is alleged to have ruled in Deira at a slightly later date. The names of nos. 4, 5 and 6 are compound forms of normal Germanic type. Some, if not all, of the remaining four appear to be hypocoristic forms. According to the genealogies Ida was the father of *Aedilric* and *Aedilric* the father of *Æðelfrið*. According to the *Historia Brittonum*, cap. 63, *Adda* also was a son of Ida, and in view of the alliteration of the names this may well have been so. Nothing is known of the descent of the remaining four—*Glappa*, *Theodric*, *Friduuald* and *Hussa*—but it will be seen that their names alliterate neither among themselves nor with the others, as though to suggest that more than one family may have been involved.

Apart from his brief reference to Ida, Bede does not mention any of these seven kings, and there seems to be only one source, the additions to the *Historia Brittonum*, which refers to any events connected with their history. The framework of these sections of the *Historia Brittonum* consists of genealogies and regnal lists which relate to various English kingdoms and which seem to be derived ultimately from an English document.[2] To this framework there have been added a small number of historical notes which relate primarily to Bernicia and to a lesser extent to Deira and Mercia. It is evident from the use of Welsh names for some of the battles of the seventh century, e.g. *Meicen* for Bede's *Haethfelth*[3] and *Gueith Linn Garan* for the *Nechtanesmere* of later writers, as also from the use of *ciues* for the Welsh and *hostes* for the English, that

---

[1] The dates are so calculated in the *Annales Lindisfarnenses* but W. Levison, *op. cit.* 114, held these to be a Durham compilation of the twelfth century, though he did not live to fulfil his hope, expressed *ibid.* n. 4, of proving his belief. One of the points which he might have made is that these annals rearrange the pagan kings in a manner characteristic of later authorities.

[2] H. M. and N. K. Chadwick, *Growth of Literature*, I, 155.

[3] Mrs Bromwich informs me that she has reason to suspect that the equation of *Meicen* with *Haethfelth* is incorrect.

these historical notes are of Welsh, and probably north Welsh, origin, but they seem not to have reached their present form until about the beginning of the ninth century. Their particular interest lies in the synchronisms which they seem to establish between certain of the native rulers and two of the pagan kings of Bernicia, and in their association of the opposing English and Welsh sides with an identifiable locality. *Dutigirn* is said to have fought against the English during the *floruit* of a number of famous Welsh bards, including Taliesin, and four other Welsh rulers, *Urbgen, Riderch hen, Guallauc* and *Morcant*, are said to have fought against *Hussa*. It is said further of *Urbgen* that he and his sons fought against *Deodric* and that during a period of warfare in which the advantage was held at one time by the enemy and at another by the people (*ciues*), *Urbgen* besieged the enemy for three days and three nights in an island called *Metcaud*, but was himself killed at the instigation of *Morcant* who was jealous of *Urbgen's* success in leading the attack. Nothing else is known of *Dutigern* or of the locality to which he belonged. *Urbgen* is to be identified with Urien, ruler of Rheged,[1] and *Riderch hen* can be recognised as the *Rodercus* who is mentioned by Adamnan[2] as contemporary with Columba and who was king of Strathclyde, fifth in succession from Ceredig. *Guallauc*[3] and *Morcant* have not been securely associated with any particular locality, but the genealogies of both are found among those families who comprise *The Men of the North*.[4] The two English kings *Deodric* (Theodric 572–79) and *Hussa* (585–92) appear in the Moore *Memoranda* regnal list as fifth and seventh in succession to Ida. A later passage in the *Historia Brittonum* refers to *Metcaud* as the island in which Cuthbert died and so establishes the equation with Lindisfarne or its neighbouring islands.[5]

These passages suggest that some thirty years after the establishment of Ida's kingdom, the English invaders had made little or no progress inland and had even come near to total expulsion at one time. It is, however, difficult to feel entirely confident that the two

[1] For some evidence of the extent of Rheged see H. M. Chadwick, *Early Scotland*, 144, 160.

[2] *Life of St Columba*, I, viii, ed. W. Reeves (Edinburgh, 1874), 123.

[3] See p. 84, n. 1 above.   [4] H. M. Chadwick, *Early Scotland*, 143–4.

[5] Cuthbert died in his hermitage on Farne and his body was subsequently brought to Lindisfarne, *Anon. Vit. Cuth.* IV, xiii and *Bed. Vit. Cuth.* xxxix, xl, ed. B. Colgrave, *Two Lives of Saint Cuthbert* (Cambridge, 1940), 130–1, 282–9. But the point need not weigh against the identification of *Metcaud* with Lindisfarne. Cf. *Annals of Tigernach s.a.* [630] *Inis Metgoit*.

groups of material, the English and the Welsh, have been accurately synchronised. For example the *Historia Brittonum* alleges[1] that the people of Kent were converted during the reign of Friðwald of Bernicia, but according to the data in the Moore regnal list Friðwald reigned 579–85, whereas it is known that Kent was not converted till 597. The reference to Taliesin and the other Welsh bards, to the treacherous killing of Urien and to the siege of Lindisfarne point to Welsh heroic poetry rather than to an annalistic chronicle as the source of the Welsh material (cf. p. 91 above) and the synchronisms may rest upon no more than the guesswork of a compiler who was attempting to conflate material from two unrelated sources. It would therefore be wise to treat the chronological implications of these passages with some reserve.[2]

Æðelfrið whose name follows that of Hussa in the regnal lists, is the first of the Bernician kings about whose reign English sources record anything more than its mere length. The Moore list and Bede himself both assign him twenty-four years, and from these data, as well as from Bede's equation of his eleventh regnal year with the first year of the emperor Phocas and with the year A.D. 603,[3] it can be reckoned that he ruled *c.* 593–616. The *Historia Brittonum*[4] adds that for the second twelve years of his reign he was king of Deira as well as Bernicia, from which, in conjunction with some independent evidence relating to the expulsion of Edwin, it seems probable that he conquered Deira *c.* 605, but no details of the conquest are known. Bede records three incidents relating to Æðelfrið —a victory over the Scots at *Degsastan* in 603,[5] a victory over the Welsh near Chester at a date which is not specified, but which seems to have been between 612 and 615,[6] and his defeat and death at the hands of Rædwald, king of East Anglia and protector of the exiled

[1] Cap. 63.
[2] The twelfth-century Glasgow legends which tell of Kentigern and Merlin (Lailoken), and of the latter's death at Drumelzier on the Tweed contain no hint of the presence of English nearby. At the time to which these legends refer, namely the latter part of the sixth century, Drumelzier is said to have belonged to a prince called Meldred. They have been discussed by H. M. and N. K. Chadwick, *op. cit.* I, 108–13 who find some features which point to their antiquity. [3] *HE.* I, xxxiv. [4] Cap. 63. [5] *HE.* I, xxxiv.
[6] *Ibid.* II, ii. Bede's treatment of this incident affords a striking instance of his hostility to the Welsh church. He interrupts his account of Augustine's mission in order to insert the story of the Welsh defeat at Chester which he interprets as the fulfilment of Augustine's prophecy that misfortunes would befall the Welsh (*gens perfida*) because of their refusal to cooperate with the Roman mission. For the date of the battle see Plummer's note on this passage (II, 76–7).

THE BERNICIANS AND THEIR NORTHERN FRONTIER

Edwin, in a battle near the Idle on the frontier between Northumbria and Mercia in 616.[1] In addition to these particular details, Bede also records what has the appearance of being a popular tradition about Æðelfriŏ, namely that he conquered more British territory than did any other English king and that in some parts of these conquered territories the British were exterminated and their lands occupied by the English, while in others the British were made to pay tribute.[2] Æðelfriŏ is likewise mentioned in Welsh tradition,[3] but no doubt the evil repute which he gained among the Welsh was largely due to the slaughter of the Welsh monks in the battle at Chester. It is evident, therefore, that the popular belief among both the English and the Welsh was that Æðelfriŏ was the man responsible for transforming what had been little more than a few scattered strongholds on the coast into a powerful kingdom of wide territorial extent. The murder of Urien of Rheged, and the conflict of opposing Welsh forces at the battle of Arthuret,[4] near Netherby (c. 573), suggest that the inability of the Welsh to sustain a combined opposition was among the factors contributing to the Welsh defeat, but there is not enough evidence to trace the course of events in any detail.

A Welsh elegiac poem, the *Gododdin*,[5] which is ascribed to the bard Aneirin, seems to tell part of the story of an unsuccessful Welsh attempt to form a major coalition against the English invaders, possibly during Æðelfriŏ's reign. The poem is now preserved only in a single MS. of the thirteenth century, but Welsh scholars believe that, although it contains some later material, most of the poem is a genuine composition of the sixth century. The poem is in the form of an elegy on the British warriors who were killed during an expedition to a place called *Catraeth*. One of the leaders of this expedition is represented as a chieftain ruling at Edinburgh (or possibly Carriden) who assembled a war-band from

[1] *Ibid.* II, xii.
[2] *Ibid.* I, xxxiv. The valleys of Aln, Breamish, Till and Tweed are likely to have been the first areas to be affected by an English advance inland from the coast. The place-names Edlingham, Whittingham, Eglingham, Ellingham and Chillingham point to a concentrated early settlement. The greatest distance between any two of these places is only a little over ten miles.
[3] Plummer's notes on *HE.* I, xxxiv (II, 64, 66). Cf. p. 85 above.
[4] A. O. Anderson, *Early Sources of Scottish History*, I (Edinburgh, 1922), 73–4. This work, to which I am greatly indebted, is cited hereafter as *ESSH*.
[5] The following account is based on articles by K. Jackson, *Antiquity*, XIII (1939), 25–34, and C. A. Gresham, *ibid.* XVI (1942), 237–57, summarising I. Williams' *Canu Aneirin* (Cardiff, 1938). See also pp. 88 ff. above.

VIII

among his people, the *Gododdin*, that is the inhabitants of the kingdom of Manau Guotodin which lay near the head of the Firth of Forth, and led them against the English invaders. The expedition ended in the complete annihilation of the Welsh forces, and it seems to be generally agreed among Welsh scholars[1] that *Catraeth*, the scene of the disaster, is to be identified with Catterick. There is no direct evidence of date, but on the one hand there is no mention of Urien of Rheged, and on the other it may be doubted whether the *Gododdin* would have been in a position to venture so far south after Æðelfrið's victory over the Scots in 603. This cannot be regarded as by any means satisfactory evidence, especially as the exact date of Urien's death is not known, but the suggestion of a date in the closing years of the sixth century is at least in accord with other evidence for the *floruit* of Cynon, son of Clydno, who is said to have been the sole Welsh survivor of the battle and who is the only one of the many persons mentioned in the poem who can be identified with certainty from other sources.

It is impossible with so little information to assess the results of the Welsh defeat at *Catraeth* with any confidence, but so far as the evidence goes, this was perhaps the last occasion on which the north Welsh took the initiative with their countrymen of Yorkshire, Lancashire and north Wales in a joint attack against the English, and in view of the obvious strategic importance of Catterick, it is likely that the English victory marked an important step in the process which led eventually to the complete isolation of the north Welsh. The English themselves seem never again to have been in any danger of expulsion from the territories which they had occupied between Humber and Tweed, and when next they are found in conflict with external enemies, these enemies were, in the north, the Scots of Dalriada led by Aedan, and in the south the Welsh of Wales led by Cadwallon and allied with the English of Mercia led by Penda.

The kingdom of Dalriada which comprised territories on the mainland and among the islands to the north and west of Strathclyde, was probably founded soon after the middle of the fifth century.[2] The original settlement seems to have been on a com-

---

[1] K. Jackson and I. Williams, *loc. cit.*; also H. M. and N. K. Chadwick, *op. cit.* I, 164–5 and n. 2. Cf. also p. 88, n. 2 above.

[2] H. M. Chadwick, *Early Scotland*, 121–3, argues for a date some forty years earlier than that favoured by W. F. Skene, *Celtic Scotland* (Edinburgh, 1876), I, 139–40, and A. O. Anderson, *ESSH.*, I, 1–2.

paratively small scale and it may well have been established as a deliberate stroke of Welsh policy designed to interrupt the main Pictish sea route down the west coast of Scotland.[1] This at least was the result of the settlement, whether by accident or design. In about 574,[2] that is approximately when Rhydderch of Strathclyde and Urien of Rheged are said to have been besieging the English in Lindisfarne, Aedan, son of Gabran, became king of Dalriada and soon afterwards he began to extend his influence towards the east. Irish sources record a victory won by Aedan in the battle of *Mano* (*cath Manand*), c. 583.[3] It is uncertain whether *Mano* here means Manau Guotodin or the Isle of Man, but Chadwick[4] favoured the former. About fifteen years later Aedan is said to have been defeated in Circinn (i.e. Angus, formerly Forfar),[5] the Pictish province between Tay and Dee in which lies Dunnichen Moss, the scene of Ecgfriŏ's defeat in 685. Adamnan's *Life of Columba*[6] records a victory won by Aedan over the *Miathi*, perhaps the same as the *Maeatae* who were located north of the Antonine Wall in Roman times. The date of the battle cannot be determined except within the limits of c. 574, the time of Aedan's accession, and 597, the year of Columba's death. There is much uncertainty about these campaigns, but the evidence suggests that, for a time, Aedan was able to secure control over part of the southern Pictish territories. His activities in the frontier district separating the Welsh of Manau Guotodin[7] from the southern Picts would be likely to facilitate the advance of the English northwards to the Forth and it was perhaps in this way that they came into conflict with Aedan at *Degsastan* in 603.

Bede is the principal source of information about the battle at *Degsastan*,[8] the earliest event in Northumbrian history, apart from the foundation of Bernicia, which he thought fit to record. It was fought, he writes, between Aedan, king of the Scots who lived in Britain, and Æŏelfriŏ, supported by his brother Theodbald, *in loco celeberrimo, qui dicitur Degsastan, id est Degsa lapis*. That part of the

---

[1] Chadwick, *Early Scotland*, xxi.

[2] *ESSH*. I, 125–6. [3] *Ibid*. I, 89.

[4] *Early Scotland*, 124; but Anderson takes *Mano* to be the Isle of Man, *ESSH*, I, 89–90.

[5] *ESSH*. I, 118. [6] I, viii, quoted *ESSH*. I, 96.

[7] There is a Welsh tradition (preserved in the *De Situ Brecheniauc*) that Aedan's mother was a Welsh princess called Luan who may possibly have been connected with Manau Guotodin, W. F. Skene, *op. cit*. I, 160–1 and n. 79.

[8] *HE*. I, xxxiv.

Northumbrian army which was commanded by Theodbald was wholly destroyed and Theodbald himself was killed. Nevertheless, Æðelfrið's victory was complete. The battle was fought in the year A.D. 603 which was the eleventh year of Æðelfrið's reign and the first of the emperor Phocas. The source of Bede's information cannot be traced in any work of either English or Celtic origin. His reference to the battlefield as *locus celeberrimus* suggests that stories about it were still current in his own day, but his precision about the date seems to hint that he used something more than oral tradition. In the *Anglo-Saxon Chronicle* the most detailed account is found in texts D and E. This account is mostly derived from Bede, but it adds one item of information which is not found in any other source, namely *Hering Hussan sunu lædde þone here ðider*. Hussa is probably identical with the king of that name who appears in the seventh place in the list of kings in the Moore *Memoranda*. Hering is not otherwise known in early sources.[1] Unfortunately it is not clear whether the passage is to be interpreted as meaning that Hering led the Northumbrian army to *Degsastan* or whether he played the traitor by acting as guide to the Scots. In the ninth century and later the word *here* is almost invariably used in the *Anglo-Saxon Chronicle* of a foreign army, but it does not occur often enough in the earlier parts of this work to allow its precise meaning to be established. The Irish annals record the defeat of Aedan by the Saxons in a battle in which Eanfrið, brother of Æðelfrið, is said to have been killed by Maelumai, son of Baítán, but the entry does not say where the battle was fought and it is doubtful whether its contents can be trusted.[2] English sources show no acquaintance with a brother of Æðelfrið called Eanfrið. Æðelfrið had a son of that name, but he was still alive some thirty years after *Degsastan*.[3] The death of Maelumai, son of Baítán, is recorded in the *Annals of Ulster* under the year 600 (i.e. 601).[4] It is possible that a contingent from northern Ireland may have fought on Aedan's side at *Degsastan*.

Fordun gives a detailed account of the battle, but his accounts of other events in this period of English history are so full of fiction

---

[1] John of Eversden, the thirteenth-century continuator of Florence of Worcester, writes *Hyring fuit primus rex qui regnavit post Britannos in Northumbria* (Florence of Worcester's *Chronicon*, ed. B. Thorpe, London, 1848, II, 250). The statement is too late to be of any value.

[2] *ESSH*. I, 123.   [3] *HE*. III, i.

[4] For the identity of Baítán, cf. p. 148, n. 5 above.

that no trust can be placed in him. There does not seem to be any evidence that the northern Welsh were directly engaged.[1] Despite the care with which Bede recorded the name of the battlefield, it has so far proved impossible to locate the site. The only clues to its general whereabouts are to be found in Bede's indication that the initiative was taken by Aedan who felt himself driven to action because of the rapid encroachment of the English upon Welsh territory, and in the apparent attempt made by Aedan earlier in his reign to secure control of the kingdom of the southern Picts.[2] The battle at *Degsastan* apart, there is no good evidence of

[1] In his note on *HE*. I, xxxiv, Plummer (II, 66) refers cautiously to 'the tradition preserved by Fordun, iii, 30, that Aedan was allied with the Britons under a king Malgo (Maelgwn)' and thus seems to imply that the Britons may have fought on Aedan's side at *Degsastan*, but Plummer's reference to Fordun is incorrect. There is no reference to Malgo in Fordun iii, 30, but there is a reference to him in iii, 28 (ed. W. F. Skene, 114). This latter chapter, however, does not refer to *Degsastan*, but to Aedan's alleged victory over *Cenlinus* (Ceaulin) at *Fethanlege*. Needless to say Fordun's account is wholly fictitious. The silence of both the *Historia Brittonum* and the *Annales Cambriae* suggest rather that the Welsh did not play any active part at *Degsastan*.

[2] No useful purpose would be served by tabulating here the many attempts which have been made to identify the site of *Degsastan*, but since so many writers have supposed the place to be Dawston in Roxburghshire, the grounds for this supposition must be examined. So far as I am aware, the first of the modern writers to suggest an identification was Edmund Gibson who wrote 'parum dubito quin sit idem qui hodie Dauston in agro Cumberland' (*Chronicon Saxonicum*, Oxford, 1692, *Nominum Locorum Explicatio*, 23). In 1722 John Smith stated that the site was unknown, but he referred both to Gibson's suggestion and to a suggestion by a bishop of Carlisle who proposed 'Dawston juxta Jedbrough' (*Beda Historiae Ecclesiasticae*, Cambridge, 1722, 74). Professor Dickins suggests to me that the bishop in question was probably William Nicolson (1702–18). Sharon Turner supposed the site to be Dawston near Jedbrough (*History of the Anglo-Saxons*, 1799, I, 263), as also did G. Chalmers (*Caledonia*, 1807, I, 253 n. s). In all these writers, however, the identification was no more than a guess wholly unsupported by evidence. W. F. Skene (*Celtic Scotland*, Edinburgh, 1876, I, 162–3) seemed to find corroborative evidence in the visible remains of the earthwork known as the Catrail which are found near Dawston and which he interpreted as the boundary between the Northumbrian English and the Strathclyde Welsh at the time of the battle. Even accepting Skene's interpretation of the Catrail, and it is of doubtful validity, this is no evidence for identifying *Degsastan* with Dawston. Among more recent writers who have accepted Dawston with varying degrees of hesitation are C. Plummer (*Baedae Opera Historica*, Oxford, 1896, I, 66), T. Hodgkin (*History of England to 1066*, London, 1906, 134), C. Oman (*England Before the Norman Conquest*, 7th ed., London, 1929, 251) and R. H. Hodgkin (*History of the Anglo-Saxons*, 1st ed., Oxford, 1935, I, 197). But there was still no evidence beyond the repeated assertions of successive generations of historians. Some uneasiness was felt, however, by those who knew that OE. *Degsastan* would normally produce not Dawston, but Daystone, as was pointed out by F. M. Stenton (*Anglo-Saxon*

THE BERNICIANS AND THEIR NORTHERN FRONTIER

any major conflict in which the Northumbrians were engaged in south-eastern Scotland until shortly before Ecgfriờ's defeat at Dunnichen Moss in 685 and if one might hazard a conjecture, it would be that *Degsastan* was fought between Scots and English for the eventual control of all the old Welsh territories which lay between Tweed and Forth. The defeat of Aedan in 603 seems to have created the conditions which allowed the English frontier to be pushed northwards towards the old Antonine line. Thenceforth the Scots were eliminated from the claimants to supremacy in northern Britain until after the union with the Picts and the weakening of Northumbria by the Scandinavian invasions of the ninth century. Bede was fully aware of the significance of Aedan's defeat and he appraised its consequences in these words:

Neque ex eo tempore quisquam regum Scottorum in Brittania aduersus gentem Anglorum usque ad hanc diem in proelium uenire audebat.[1]

England, Oxford, 1943, 77 n. 2). Owing to the circumstances of the time, it was not till some years after the publication of this latter work that M. Förster's detailed examination of the name became available in this country (M. Förster, *Der Flussname Themse und seine Sippe*, 796–811). Förster argues that the place-name embodies a British personal name and that it existed in two parallel forms meaning respectively 'the stone of Dagān' and 'the stone of *Dagissu'. He supposes that Bede's informant knew the latter of these two forms which he Anglicised to *Dægisanstan and that this developed normally: *Dæigisanstan> *Degisanstan > Degsastan. On the other hand the English who settled in the neighbourhood of the battlefield adopted the parallel form with *Dagan* which developed through OE. *Daga(n)stan to Dawstane (Dawson). In this way Förster seeks to show that OE. *Degsastan* can be related to the modern Dawston or Dawstane. But while thus seeming to remove a difficulty in the way of the identification, Förster himself advances no evidence for making the identification in the first place. The modern name Dawston or Dawstane is applied to a small burn and to a stretch of the neighbouring fell which is called Dawston Rigg. The burn is one of several burns or sikes which rise on Saughtree Fell. It has an independent existence of no more than two miles when it joins Liddel Water about three miles below the latter's source. To anyone acquainted with this wild and barren fell country, Förster's picture of English invaders settling here and adopting a place-name from the defeated British will not be convincing. For all that has been written about the site of *Degsastan*, no advance has been made beyond the position of John Smith in 1722: 'hic locus, Bedae seculo tam celebris, hodie ignotus est.'

[1] *HE.* I, xxxiv.

THE BERNICIANS AND THEIR NORTHERN FRONTIER

THE EARLY CHRISTIAN PERIOD

Nothing further is known of Æðelfrið's activities in the north after his victory at *Degsastan*. His conquest of Deira *c*. 605,[1] his defeat of the Welsh at Chester shortly before 615[2] and his own death near the Mercian frontier in 616[3] suggest that much of the second half of his reign was spent in attempting to secure the control of territories towards the south and west of Northumbria, and perhaps also in organising the frontier against Mercia.[4] Bede's account of the reign of his successor, Edwin (617–33), is considerably more detailed, but it consists mainly of a variety of traditional material relating to the conversion of the Northumbrians. In his military operations, Edwin was primarily engaged, as might have been expected in a representative of the Deiran dynasty, in attempting to extend English authority westwards from the East Riding of Yorkshire, and nothing is known of his presence in northern Northumbria beyond a brief visit to a *uilla regia* in Bernicia at a place which Bede calls *Adgefrin*.[5] The site of this *uilla* has never been located, but its name is preserved in Yevering Bell,[6] the north-eastern bastion of the Cheviots overlooking the valley of the Glen in which Paulinus is said to have baptised large numbers of Bernicians.[7]

The most important consequences of Edwin's reign for the situation in the north lay in the temporary expulsion of the

[1] Above, p. 152.   [2] *HE*. II, ii.   [3] *Ibid*. xii.

[4] For a discussion of some evidence bearing on the course of this frontier see *Arch. Ael.*, 4th ser., XXVI (1948), 112–26.

[5] *HE*. II, xiv. See, however, M. Förster, *Anglia*, LXIV (1940), 106–16, who regards Edwin as the probable conqueror of Edinburgh and seeks to derive the name from OE *Eadwines-burh*. But many others have denied this derivation (see the refs. cited *ibid*. 106) and on historical grounds a connection with Edwin of Northumbria seems unlikely. OE. *Éadwine* is not an uncommon name.

[6] A. H. A. Hogg has drawn attention to an earthwork at Old Yevering which invites investigation, *Antiquity*, XXIII (1949), 211–14. An aerial photograph taken by Dr St Joseph has revealed some extremely interesting ground markings. Some preliminary excavations began in the spring of 1953.

[7] A well at Holystone in Northumberland is marked by a modern stone cross bearing an inscription which records that it marks the site at which Paulinus baptised many Bernicians. Lest a false tradition should be perpetuated, it is worth recording that the association of Paulinus with Holystone rests solely upon a canting translation of a false reading from Bede. The latter states (*HE*. II, xiv) that Edwin was baptised at York *in ecclesia Petri apostoli*. This passage has been misread as *in ecclesia sancti Petri* and translated 'in the church of Holystone', with Bede's reference to York silently suppressed.

Bernician dynasty which led not only to the establishment of friendly relations between the English and the Scots, but also to the first recorded contact between the English and the Picts. Bede tells of a considerable exodus of the Bernician nobility at this time,[1] and among those who took refuge with the Picts and Scots were the three sons of Æðelfrið who subsequently ruled in Northumbria, Eanfrið, Oswald and Osuiu. A less trustworthy source states that their sister Æbbe, who later became abbess of Coldingham, was also among the exiles.[2] According to both Pictish and Irish sources, Talargan king of the Picts who died in 657, was the son of a man variously called *Anfrait, Anfrith, Enfret*, etc.[3] This name undoubtedly represents OE. Eanfrið and it is very probable that the man in question was Eanfrið, son of Æðelfrið, who returned to Northumbria in 633 and was killed in 634. He had been converted during his period of exile, but later apostasised. If the identification is correct, it must be supposed that he had married a Pictish princess during the period 617–33. His son, Talargan, presumably inherited the Pictish kingdom through his mother according to the principal of matrilinear succession prevalent among the Picts. In this way the Bernician kings not only became related to the Pictish line, but may well have come to suppose, since matrilinear succession was not practised among the English, that they had some claim to the Pictish kingdom itself. There is also some evidence to show that Eanfrið had a daughter by his Pictish wife and that she married a king of Strathclyde.[4] The relationship is shown in the following table:

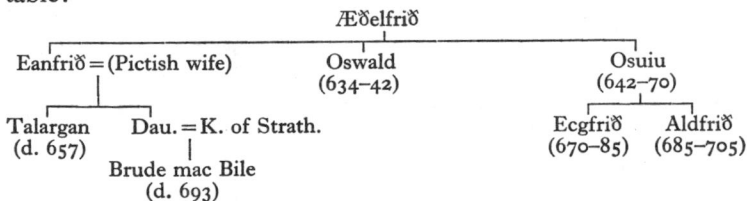

Æðelfrið

Eanfrið = (Pictish wife)	Oswald (634–42)	Osuiu (642–70)
Talargan (d. 657) Dau. = K. of Strath.		Ecgfrið (670–85) Aldfrið (685–705)
Brude mac Bile (d. 693)		

Ecgfrið was thus first cousin to Talargan and first cousin once removed to Brude mac Bile by whom he was defeated at Dunnichen Moss.

The restoration of Æðelfrið's sons was followed in its turn by a considerable influx of Scottish monks into Northumbria, with

[1] *HE.* III, i.
[2] *ESSH.* I, 142.
[3] *Ibid.* I, cxxiv, 172, 176.
[4] *ESSH.* I, 193.

THE BERNICIANS AND THEIR NORTHERN FRONTIER

profound consequences for almost every aspect of Northumbrian history.[1] The monastery at Lindisfarne became the main centre of Scottish ecclesiastical activity in Northumbria, but according to Bede it was only one of a number of similar foundations. Oswald (634–42) who succeeded to the kingdom after Eanfriŏ had reigned only for a single year, is stated to have exercised dominion over both Scots and Picts,[2] although nothing is known either of the means by which this dominion was acquired or of the way in which it was exercised. Since the Picts do not seem to have held any substantial territories south of the Forth at this time, the implication of Bede's evidence on this point is that Northumbrian authority had not only reached but also crossed the Forth before Oswald's death in 642. But Bede's evidence seems to be not wholly consistent on this point since he remarks in his list of kings who held the *imperium*[3] that the extent of Oswald's kingdom was the same as that of his predecessor Edwin, and in this list Osuiu is the first of the Northumbrian kings who is expressly stated to have exercised authority over the Picts and Scots. Nevertheless, it is perhaps significant that Oswald's reign coincided with the reign of Domnall Brecc, king of Dalriada *c.* 629–42, during which the Scots lost the control over southern Pictish territory which they seem to have held ever since the time of Aedan, son of Gabran. Domnall Brecc was himself killed by Owen, king of Strathclyde, in the valley of the upper Carron in Stirlingshire. The manner of his death which became celebrated in Welsh poetry (cf. p. 89) was among the last episodes in the history of the northern Welsh of which report became current in Wales.[4]

Both Wilfrid and Cuthbert grew to manhood during Osuiu's reign and the material assembled by their biographers presents a slightly more detailed picture than can be discerned in the earlier years of the century. Cuthbert, who was born within a year or two of 634, spent part of his childhood with a foster-mother who bore an English name—Kenswiŏ—and who lived in an English village called *Hruringaham*.[5] This village has never been identified, but it is unlikely that it lay very far from Melrose or from the hills above Leader Water where Cuthbert later worked as a shepherd.[6] In or soon after 651 he entered Melrose which was then ruled by an

---

[1] See above, p. 138–9.   [2] *HE.* iii, vi.   [3] *HE.* ii, v.
[4] H. M. Chadwick, *Early Scotland*, 126; *ESSH.* i, 161, 166–7.
[5] *Anon. Vit. Cuth.* ii, vii, *Bed. Vit. Cuth.* xiv, ed. Colgrave 90 and 200.
[6] *Anon. Vit. Cuth.* i, v, ed. Colgrave 68.

THE BERNICIANS AND THEIR NORTHERN FRONTIER

English abbot and while he was a member of this community he preached in Teviotdale[1] and visited Æbbe[2] in her monastery at Coldingham. There is no direct evidence for the date at which this monastery was founded. Early sources first mention it in connection with Æbbe herself, but there is a tradition that it had been founded by Aidan who died in 651.[3] These scenes from Cuthbert's early life suggest that by the middle of the seventh century the territories which now comprise the shires of Berwick and Roxburgh and which are bounded on the north by the Lammermuirs and on the west by Ettrick Forest, were firmly in English hands. The degree of security implied by the existence of monastic communities at Coldingham and Melrose lends some support to Bede's evidence that the English frontier had in fact reached the Forth during Oswald's reign. It might well be a mistake, however, to suppose that the advance of this frontier involved the overcoming of any substantial opposition. The way had been prepared on the one hand by the flight of Æðelfriδ's sons to the north during Edwin's reign and on the other by the return flow of Scottish immigrants to Northumbria during Oswald's reign. The territories of south-eastern Scotland which were thus absorbed into Northumbria had previously been Welsh, but the sources contain none but the most obscure hint of any conflict with the English in which the Welsh of this area were engaged during the seventh century.

After the murder of Urien of Rheged, Welsh opposition to the expansion of Northumbria came primarily from the south-west rather than from the north. Æðelfriδ had penetrated as far as

[1] *Anon. Vit. Cuth.* II, v, ed. Colgrave 84. It is not known when the monastery at Melrose was founded. There is a tradition of uncertain value that Moluoc, i.e. Lugaid of Lismore, who died *c.* 592, had been a monk there, *ESSH.* I, 19.

[2] *Anon. Vit. Cuth.* II, 3, *Bed. Vit. Cuth.* x, ed. Colgrave 80 and 188.

[3] B. Colgrave, *op. cit.* 318 and *Bede, His Life Times and Writings*, ed. A. H. Thompson (Oxford, 1935), 79. Bede mentions the place three times by the name *Coludi urbs* (Bede, *Vit. Cuth.* x; *HE.* IV, xvii and xxiii). The OE form occurs in the *Anon. Vit. Cuth.* II, ii, ed. Colgrave 80, as *Colodesbyrig*, and in Eddius, *Vit. Wilf.* ch. xxxix, ed. Colgrave 78, as *Colodaesburg*. The correlation of *urbs* with OE. *burg* is interesting. Elsewhere Bede regularly uses *urbs* of an inhabited stronghold, e.g. *urbs Alcluith* (*HE.* I, xii), *urbs Giudi* (*ibid.*), and *urbs regia* for Bamborough (*HE.* III, vi, xvi). Cf. also *urbs Inbroninis* (Eddius, xxxvi, ed. Colgrave 72) which as the scene of Wilfrid's imprisonment must have been fortified. The implication seems to be that *Coludi urbs*, the site of Æbbe's monastery, had had an earlier history as a fortified stronghold. O. G. S.Crawford (*Antiquity*, VIII, 1934, 202–3) draws attention to surviving remnants of fortifications and suggests that the site is mentioned by the name *Caer Golud* in a poem in the *Book of Taliesin*.

Chester before 615[1] and Edwin too was active in this area. Bede represents Cadwallon, king of Gwynedd, as the prime mover, and Penda as his subsidiary ally, in the events which led to Edwin's death at *Haethfelth* in 633.[2] It was also Cadwallon who defeated and killed both Eanfrið of Bernicia and Osric of Deira,[3] and who was himself defeated by Oswald at *Hefenfelth* in 634.[4] The evidence of the *Historia Brittonum*[5] shows that the Welsh were themselves aware of the circumstances which had brought the kingdom of Gwynedd into existence and it may have been no accident that it was a king of Gwynedd who took such vigorous action against the English invaders then overrunning precisely that territory, i.e. Manau Guotodin, which had once belonged to his own ancestors. Bede does not mention Welsh participation in the battle at *Maserfelth* in 642 in which Oswald was killed,[6] but it is recorded in the *Annales Cambriae* under the name *bellum Cocboy*,[7] and if the identification of the site with Oswestry is correct, it seems probable that the Welsh would be concerned. After the death of Cadwallon, the leadership of the opposition to the Northumbrians fell to Penda, but there is more than a hint that Penda acted to the end in collaboration with the Welsh.

Penda is said to have been killed in 655 and the circumstances which resulted in his death are recorded in two independent accounts which are at variance with one another and are not easily reconcilable. Bede's account,[8] the earlier of the two, records that Osuiu, troubled by Penda's repeated attacks against Northumbria, attempted to buy peace from him by offering as a price *innumera et majora, quam credi potest, ornamenta regia uel donaria.* The bribe was refused and a battle in which very large forces were engaged, was fought near the river *Uinuaed.* After recording various gifts made by Osuiu to the church as thankofferings, Bede adds that the war was brought to an end in the district of *Loidis*, and he is usually interpreted as implying that Penda had been killed in the battle at the *Uinuaed.*[9] The river itself has not been identified, but it is held

---

[1] *HE.* II, ii. [2] *HE.* II, xx. [3] *HE.* III, i. [4] *HE.* III, ii.
[5] Cap. 62. [6] *HE.* III, ix. [7] *S.a.* [644]. [8] *HE.* III, xxiv.
[9] Bede's evidence on this point is curiously obscure. At the end of the chapter in which he describes the battle at the *Uinuaed*, he refers twice to events occurring so many years after Penda's death but without any previous statement that Penda had been killed. If Bede knew that he had been killed at the *Uinuaed*, it is difficult to believe that he would not have said so. Cf. the evidence of the *Annales Cambriae* below, p. 165, n. 1.

that the modern *Leeds* derives from *Loidis*,[1] and on the assumption that Bede's reference to *regio Loidis* was merely intended to give a general indication of the area in which the *Uinuaed* lay and not to suggest that the completion of the war was a subsequent event distinct from the battle itself, it may be supposed that the *Uinuaed* was one of the many rivers which flow into the Humber. Bede's account gives no indication that there were any Welsh participants in the battle, nor does it suggest that the event had any but an indirect bearing upon the situation in the north of Northumbria.

The second account of these events is contained in the *Historia Brittonum*. Mommsen's text of the passage reads as follows:[2]

et ipse [*sc.* Osguid] occidit Pantha in campo Gai et nunc facta est strages Gai campi et reges Brittonum interfecti sunt, qui exierant cum rege Pantha in expeditione usque ad urbem quae vocatur Iudeu. tunc reddidit Osguid omnes divitias quae erant cum eo in urbe, usque in manu Pendae et Penda distribuit ea regibus Brittonum, id est Atbret Iudeu. solus autem Catgabail rex Guenedotae regionis cum exercitu suo evasit de nocte consurgens, quapropter vocatus est Catgabail Cat guommed.

There is no disagreement about the identities of the three persons mentioned in this passage. *Pantha, Osguid* and *Catgabail, rex Guenedotae regionis*, represent respectively Penda of Mercia, Osuiu of Northumbria and Cadafael of Gwynedd. There are, however, considerable difficulties about both the identification of the place-names and the interpretation of the passage as a whole. *Campus Gai* which is also the name given to the battle in the *Annales Cambriae*, is unknown. It is tempting to associate *urbs quae vocatur Iudeu* with *urbs Giudi* which according to Bede lay halfway along the Firth of Forth.[3] Both these names may perhaps be associated with the Ravenna cosmographer's *Evidensca* and this latter may be Inveresk, but there is no certainty.[4] The word *manu* is interpreted as a proper name by A. O. Anderson[5] who takes it to refer to the kingdom of Manau and translates—'then Osuiu rendered all the riches that were with him in the town, as far as Manau, to Penda; and Penda distributed them to the kings of the Britons; that is

---

[1] Ledsham and Ledstone are also said to contain the same element as appears in *Loidis*, Ekwall, *op. cit.* s.n., and F. T. Wainwright, *Trans. Hist. Soc. Lancs. Chesh.* XCIII (1941), 8 n. 2.
[2] *MGH.* Auct. Ant. XIII, 208.   [3] *HE.* I, xii.
[4] I. A. Richmond and O. G. S. Crawford, 'The British Section of the Ravenna Cosmography', *Archaeologia*, XCIII (1949), 34.
[5] *ESSH.* I, 15–16.

THE BERNICIANS AND THEIR NORTHERN FRONTIER

"the restitution of Iudeu"'. If this interpretation of *manu* is correct, there is further ground for associating *urbs Iudeu* with *urbs Giudi* since, from Bede's description of its locality, the latter evidently lay in Manau. The assertion that the Welsh were intimately concerned with these events can be safely accepted, and it will be further observed that both the accounts refer to Osuiu's attempt to buy peace from Penda; but it seems to be impossible to reconcile the suggestion that Penda had penetrated as far north as Lothian with the identification of Bede's locality for the battle at the *Uinuaed* near Northumbria's southern frontier.[1] It seems probable that the second part of the passage in the *Historia Brittonum* is to be regarded as explanatory of the first. A rational interpretation of the passage would be that Osuiu, driven to extremities by a deep Mercian penetration of Northumbria, had raised money in order to buy off Penda and that Penda had subsequently redistributed this money in order to secure Welsh allies for a further attack against Osuiu; but in default of further evidence, it does not seem possible to establish the course of events precisely. The only point which is clear beyond dispute is that the defeat of Penda removed all threat of danger to Northumbria from Mercia and that Northumbrian supremacy remained unchallenged for many years to come.

While Cuthbert was a monk at Melrose, that is between 651 and 664, he is said to have undertaken a journey to the Picts. Both the identity and the locality of the people whom he is alleged to have visited on this journey have long been matter for discussion and although no solution of the problem can be offered here, one or two points about the incident are worth considering. Previous commentators have concentrated their attention on the version of the story which is given by Bede, seeming to suppose that his account is necessarily more authoritative than the account given by the Lindisfarne writer, despite the fact that the latter is the earlier and was itself Bede's source. The relevant passage in the Lindisfarne life opens as follows:[2]

Alio quoque tempore de eodem monasterio quod dicitur Mailros, cum duobus fratribus pergens et nauigans ad terram Pictorum, ubi dicitur Niuduera regio prospere peruenerunt.

[1] It may be, of course, that the two events were distinct episodes within a more prolonged campaign. The *Annales Cambriae* place the death of Penda in the year following *strages Gai campi*.   [2] II, iv, ed. B. Colgrave, 82–5.

The account goes on to relate that the travellers, who had set out soon after Christmas, were stormbound for some days on a deserted part of the coast and that their food began to run short. Three pieces of dolphin's flesh were provided in answer to their prayers, enough to feed them for three days, and on the fourth day they were able to come safely to port. The interest of the Lindisfarne monk in this story lies solely in the miraculous provision of food. He gives no answers to the questions which his own narrative might prompt in the mind of a reader whose interest lay in the journey itself rather than in the circumstances attendant upon it. Why did Cuthbert wish to visit the Picts in the middle of winter? It is said that his objective lay in Pictish territory, but was *Niuduera regio* itself that objective or was it merely an involuntary stopping-place on the way? Did Cuthbert and his companions go forward after the storm had abated or were they already on their way home at the time? Either because of his inability to express himself clearly or, perhaps more probably, because of his concentration on the miraculous element to the exclusion of all else, the Lindisfarne monk gives the answer to none of these questions. The most that can be extracted from his account is that Cuthbert and his companions were storm-bound in an area which the author believed to be called *Niuduera regio* and which lay somewhere on the coast between Melrose and an objective across the Pictish frontier. There is no evidence to show which side of that frontier *Niuduera regio* lay nor whether it was visited on the outward or the homeward journey.

Bede's version of the story begins as follows:

Quodam etenim tempore pergens de suo monasterio pro necessitate causae accidentis ad terram Pictorum qui Niduari uocantur, nauigando peruenit.[1]

And he goes on to say that because Cuthbert and his companions had expected to return soon they had taken no food with them, but bad weather forced them to remain longer than they had intended. After the storm and the miraculous provision of food, they returned to their own country. The most remarkable feature of Bede's account is that, without adding any fresh facts, it yet answers all but one of the questions raised by the other. Bede states plainly that the *Niduari* were Picts and that the travellers returned home after the storm, and he implies no less plainly that it was among the *Niduari*

---

[1] XI, ed. B. Colgrave, 192–5.

that Cuthbert's business lay. Nothing could well be less ambiguous, but had Bede really any more information about the journey than the anonymous writer? It is beyond doubt that the *Anonymous Life* was the main source of Bede's *Life* and although instances of verbal identity between the two sources are comparatively rare, the correspondence of the anonymous author's *pergens et nauigans*... *peruenerunt*, by which he seems to indicate that part of the journey was made by land and part by sea, with Bede's *pergens*...*nauigando peruenit* is worth noting. There are, however, two small points which suggest that the *Anonymous Life* was indeed Bede's only source of information about this particular incident. The anonymous writer introduces his story with the phrase *alio quoque tempore* and then plunges directly into the narrative without anything to indicate the reason of Cuthbert's journey. Bede seems to have been conscious of this omission, as any historian would be, but there can be no doubt that if he had known the reason he would have given it, instead of being content with the somewhat lame phrase *pro necessitate causae accidentis* which in itself amounts to a confession of ignorance. The second point is that the anonymous author states that he learnt the story from one of the monks who accompanied Cuthbert—*nomine Tydi qui presbyter est adhuc uiuens*—a point which Bede gives only in paraphrase with the omission of the name. It was Bede's normal practice to give his authority for information which he had received orally from some living person, but not for information derived from written works. The suspicion is difficult to avoid that Bede, finding before him an account which raised more questions than it answered, allowed himself the liberty of removing its ambiguities and so editing it as to leave a straightforward narrative of a kind which would satisfy an orderly mind. In this light Bede's statement that the *Niduari* were Picts means only that he thought that the anonymous writer meant to say that they were Picts.

Various writers have sought to place the *Niduari* in Galloway and to connect their name with the Galloway Nith or with the *Nouantae* or with both.[1] Although there is some evidence to suggest that there may have been some Picts in Galloway,[2] Bede seems not to

---

[1] E.g. W. F. Skene, *Celtic Scotland*, I, 132–4, n. 19; M. Förster, *Englische Studien*, LVI (1922), 109–16; *Anglia*, LIX (1935), 296–8.
[2] The problem is discussed by W. J. Watson, *op. cit.* 174–9, and A. O. Anderson, *Scottish Historical Review*, XXVII (1948), 25–47.

have known of any south of the Forth-Clyde isthmus. There is, however, another cogent objection to this theory, namely that Cuthbert's journey which began from Melrose, was made partly by sea. This difficulty has not, of course, been overlooked by earlier writers, but the method of escape from it, by postulating a sea passage across or down the Solway, is unconvincing, and it may be suspected that if there had not been a river Nith in Galloway, no writer would ever have thought of looking for *Niuduera regio* anywhere else than near the east coast of Scotland. Bede himself knew of only one frontier line between Northumbrians and Picts—the Firth of Forth[1]—and there must remain a strong presumption that this was the general direction of Cuthbert's journey. If this presumption is correct it must be supposed that, whether or not Cuthbert reached Pictish territory, the Lindisfarne writer believed that the Picts whom he intended to visit were either on friendly terms with the Northumbrians or subject to English rule at the time.[2]

[1] *HE.* IV, xxiv.

[2] Any further attempt to solve this difficult problem should take account of the following points. (1) Although a form *Nuid-*, for which there is no MS. evidence, would make it easier to establish a connection with a lost river-name Nith or Nidd, there is some evidence that *-iu-*, as well as *-ui-*, was used as an OE. orthographic variation for the *-y-* from which the *-i-* in a modern Nith could develop; A. H. Smith, *Three Northumbrian Poems* (London, 1933), 30, para. 8 *c*. Any connection with OE. *nīud-* may be dismissed because of the meaning of the word; cf. *niudlicae* 'eagerly', *Leiden Riddle*, l. 14, ed. A. H. Smith, *op. cit.* 46. Levison's suggestion, *Antiquity*, XIV (1940), 289, of a connection with OE. *neoðe-*, *niðe-* 'down', meaning Lower or Southern Picts, is unconvincing. (2) The second element of *Niuduera* is the gen. plur. of OE. *wer* 'man', cf. *Sweordwerum* in *Widsith*, ed. Fr. Klaeber, *Beowulf* (New York, 1928), 270, l. 62, and such compounds as *folcweras, leodweras, portweras*, J. Bosworth and T. N. Toller, *An Anglo-Saxon Dictionary*, with *Supplement* (*s.v.*). The second element of *Niduari* is a latinised nom. plur. from OE. *ware*, normally found as a plural, but deriving from a sing. *waru*, cf. *Meanware*, E. Ekwall, *English River-Names* (Oxford, 1928), 288, *Limenwaru*, *ibid.* 244 and many other instances. (3) *Regio* is used in the *Anon. Vit. Cuth.* as the term for a unit of local government in Northumbria, cf. *regio Kintis* (IV, 3), *regio Ahse* (IV, 5). Other writers of the time use the word in this sense for other parts of England. That this is the sense intended in the present context is evident from the phrase *ubi dicitur Niuduera regio* where the last two words are inseparable and together form a district name in which *regio* is to be regarded as translating some vernacular term similar in meaning to OE. *scir*. Does this use of the terms *-weras, -ware* and *regio* suggest that the place was not in Pictish territory at all, but was a frontier district in Northumbria? And is it possible that *Niud-* which the Lindisfarne monk learnt by word of mouth and not from a written document, is a corrupt form of Bede's *Giudi*? Cf. the forms *mur nGiudan* (=Firth of Forth), W. J. Watson, *Celtic Place-Names of Scotland* (Edinburgh, 1926) 209 n. 2, and *muir nGiudan*,

THE BERNICIANS AND THEIR NORTHERN FRONTIER

Whatever the relations between the Picts and the Northumbrians during the reigns of the sons of Æðelfrið, it is clear that the two peoples were not on friendly terms at the beginning of Ecgfrið's reign. Eddius[1] gives a vivid description of an unsuccessful attempt by the Picts to free themselves from English rule early in this reign, though he does not mention either the scene of the engagement or its exact date. There is a reference in the Irish annals[2] to the expulsion of Drust from the kingdom of the Picts under the year 672, but it is not clear whether this was a consequence of Ecgfrið's victory over the Picts or of the circumstances which led to the accession of Brude mac Bile, Ecgfrið's cousin and opponent at Dunnichen Moss. A later entry in the Irish annals, s.a. 676,[3] refers enigmatically to the drowning of many Picts in *Land-Abae*, an incident which may be compared with the statement by Eddius that two rivers were filled with Pictish corpses on the occasion of Ecgfrið's victory. In consequence of their defeat, the Picts, that is presumably the southern Picts, are said to have remained subject to English rule until 685.

There can be no doubt that by the beginning of Ecgfrið's reign the whole of eastern Scotland south of the Firth of Forth was securely in English hands and that the kingdom of Manau had ceased to exist. In or soon after 680 the monastery at Abercorn, the date of whose foundation is not known, became the episcopal seat of Trumuini who, despite the fact that Abercorn itself lay in English territory, is described by Bede as bishop *ad prouinciam Pictorum*.[4] The Picts had of course long been Christian, but at this date they still observed Celtic forms and no doubt their conversion to orthodox ways was among the purposes for which this see was established. When Wilfrid returned to England in 680 after visiting Rome, the case which he stated before a Northumbrian synod was rejected and Wilfrid himself imprisoned at first in a place called *Inbroninis*[5] which has not been identified, but subsequently at Dunbar where he was placed under the care of a *praefectus* called Tydlin.[6] The choice of such a place for the imprisonment of a man in Wilfrid's position may be regarded as a sure indication that both

A. O. Anderson, *ESSH*, I, 127, where the combination *nG* may have yielded a sound for which the OE. alphabet had no exact phonetic equivalent, but which could have been approximately represented by *n*.

[1] xix, ed. Colgrave, 40–3.   [2] *ESSH*. I, 181.
[3] *Ibid.* I, 183.   [4] *HE*. IV, xii.
[5] Eddius, xxxvi, ed. Colgrave 72.   [6] *Ibid.* xxxviii, ed. Colgrave 76.

the place and its neighbourhood were then securely in English hands. The title *praefectus* by which Tydlin of Dunbar was known to Eddius, is comparatively common in early sources and it not infrequently represents OE. *gerefa* or *ealdorman*. It is to be traced in Kent and Wessex as well as in Northumbria; but the evidence suggests that the status of this official may have varied widely in different parts of the country and that in Northumbria in particular he was a man whose prominence is sometimes better conveyed by the title 'earl' than 'reeve'.[1] The analogy of the southern evidence which is rather more detailed than the northern, suggests that the seat of a Northumbrian *praefectus* in the seventh century probably served as the administrative centre of the surrounding district. If this is correct, Tydlin's territory may be supposed to have covered most of the area between the Lammermuirs and the Firth of Forth. There is, however, some evidence to suggest that Dunbar was not the only, nor even the most important, centre of local government near the northern frontier of Northumbria at this time.

Eddius records that in his victory over the Picts at the beginning of his reign Ecgfriỗ was assisted 'by his brave sub-king Beornhaeth'.[2] About twelve years later, Ecgfriỗ sent an expedition to invade Ireland under the leadership of Berct, styled *dux* by Bede[3] and *ealdorman* by the *Anglo-Saxon Chronicle*.[4] In the following year Ecgfriỗ was himself killed at Dunnichen Moss. In 698 Bede[5] records the death of one *Berctred dux regius* in battle against the Picts. The *Anglo-Saxon Chronicle*[6] calls him *Berht ealdorman* and Irish sources make him the son of Beornhaeth.[7] It seems probable that the man who was killed in 698 and who is variously called *Berctred* or *Berht* is the same as the man who invaded Ireland in 684. In 711 a third man with a similar name, *Berctfrid*, fought a successful battle against the Picts seemingly in the Carse of Falkirk.[8] This man, styled *praefectus* by Bede and *ealdorman* by the *Anglo-Saxon Chronicle* is known to have been a person of considerable importance in Northumbria. He took a prominent part in the synod by the river Nidd at which the archbishop of Canterbury presided and which led to the restoration to Wilfrid of his churches at Ripon

[1] H. M. Chadwick, *Studies on Anglo-Saxon Institutions* (Cambridge, 1905), 228 ff., 260.
[2] Cap. xix—*cum Beornheth audaci subregulo.* Ed. Colgrave, 42.
[3] *HE.* IV, xxiv.   [4] 684 E.   [5] *HE.* V, xxiv.   [6] 699 E.
[7] *ESSH.* I, 206.
[8] *HE.* V, xxiv, *ASC.* 710 E. Cf. also *ESSH.* I, 213.

VIII

and Hexham. Berctfrid's part in the synod is described in some detail by Eddius who calls him in one passage *secundus a rege princeps* and in another *regis princeps*.[1]

These scattered references yield the names of three Northumbrian officials, Beornhaeth who assisted Ecgfrið in a successful campaign against the Picts, Berct or Berctred, thought by Irish sources to be his son, who led an expedition against Ireland in 684 and was killed fighting against the Picts in 698, and Berctfrid who defeated the Picts in 711. These men are variously styled *dux, praefectus, princeps* and *ealdorman*, and two of them were of such particular eminence that they could be called the one *subregulus* and the other *secundus a rege princeps*. These facts point strongly to the existence in the late seventh and early eighth centuries of an important Northumbrian office whose holder was primarily responsible for the defence of the northern frontier against the Picts.

The peace and prosperity of a large part of Britain depended on the adequate defence of its northern frontier against the Picts and Scots. The disaster of 367, the absence after the Roman withdrawal of any substantial professional army and the rearrangement of ethnological boundaries caused by the Scottish and English invasions alike dictated that this frontier should rest on the Forth-Clyde line. It is probable that the migration of the *Votadini* to Wales in the fifth century, the defeat of the Scots in the beginning of the sixth century and the establishment of friendly relations with the Picts and Scots when the sons of Æðelfrið were exiled during the early part of the seventh century facilitated the advance of the English towards the Firth of Forth and so enabled them to secure control of Pictish territory beyond the Forth. A Pictish rebellion against Northumbrian domination early in Ecgfrið's reign was successfully crushed, but Ecgfrið's fatal expedition into Forfar in 685[2]—an expedition which is reminiscent of the campaigns of Agricola and Severus against the same potential threat—demonstrated the need for securing the frontier on a defensible line. The evidence relating to the campaigns of the Northumbrians against the Picts during the next twenty-five years suggests that this frontier was marked approximately by the line of the Antonine Wall. What was the base from which these campaigns were

[1] Cap. lx, ed. Colgrave, 130–1.
[2] For an excellent account of the battle see F. T. Wainwright, ' Nechtanesmere ', *Antiquity* (1948), 82–97.

171

VIII

THE BERNICIANS AND THEIR NORTHERN FRONTIER

conducted? It can hardly have been Dunbar which lay too far to the east. The only alternative seems to be *urbs Giudi* to which Bede refers[1] in such a way as to suggest that it seemed to him to be a place hardly less important than *urbs Alcluith*, the British stronghold at the western end of the frontier.

Berctfrid's victory in 711 is the last recorded incident in the frontier warfare against the Picts which had been waged intermittently since at least the accession of Ecgfriŏ forty years earlier. It was followed by an abrupt change in the relations between Picts and Northumbrians for which the church was mainly responsible. In 706 Nechtan IV succeeded to the Pictish throne[2] and at some date which was certainly after 709 and probably after 711, he sent envoys to Ceolfriŏ, abbot of Monkwearmouth and Jarrow, to ask for advice on the right method of keeping Easter and on various other matters of ecclesiastical ritual. He asked also that craftsmen should be sent him to build a stone church *iuxta morem Romanorum* which he promised to dedicate to St Peter. The envoys returned to Nechtan and took with them a long letter expounding the Easter problem in all its complexity. After the letter had reached Nechtan, he ordered that the old Easter tables should be destroyed and that the new ones brought from Northumbria should be copied and distributed throughout all the provinces of the Picts. The friendly relations which were established between the Northumbrians and the Picts in this way seem to have remained undisturbed for many years. Describing the situation on Northumbria's northern frontier in 731, Bede wrote:[3]

Pictorum quoque natio tempore hoc et foedus pacis cum gente habet Anglorum, et catholicae pacis ac ueritatis cum uniuersali ecclesia particeps existere gaudet. Scotti, qui Brittaniam incolunt, suis contenti finibus nil contra gentem Anglorum insidiarum moliuntur aut fraudium.

[1] *HE.* i, xii.
[2] *Ibid.* v, xxi. The embassy can hardly have been sent before Berctfriŏ's victory over the Picts which Bede places in 711.
[3] *HE.* v, xxiii.

Some Observations on
the 'Historia Regum' Attributed to
Symeon of Durham

Historia Regum is the handy title given to an important northern
English compilation which had been attributed to Symeon of
Durham before the end of the twelfth century. The attribution rests
on no sure foundation, but this is not of great consequence since the
value of its content for English history before the Norman Conquest depends more upon the accuracy with which it has recorded
earlier material, now lost, than upon any original contribution
made to it by a twelfth-century writer. Apart from a greatly
abbreviated version now to be found in Paris,[1] the work survives in
but a single manuscript which formed part of Matthew Parker's
bequest to the library of Corpus Christi College, Cambridge, where
it bears the number 139.
    Now consisting of a single volume of ii + 180 folios, the book was
formerly two separate volumes with the division falling between
fos. 165 and 166. Fos. i–ii consist of preliminary matter which
includes a fifteenth-century sketch of the Virgin and Child, a list of
contents of similar date, and references to the works of Gennadius,
Jerome, Eusebius and Dexter, son of Pagatianus. Fos. 166–80,
which contain a copy of the *Historia Brittonum* and of a *Life of
Gildas*, have no organic connection with fos. 1–165 and no further
account will be taken either of them or of the preliminary matter
on fos. i–ii. Fos. 1–165 form a book of twenty gatherings written in
double columns. The gatherings are numbered in the lower margin
on the last page of each, save for the twentieth which now contains
only four leaves. A note on the upper margin of fo. 165 v reads *hic
desunt septem folia*. The purpose of the study which follows is twofold, first to see whether this book contains sufficient internal evidence to show the place and date at which it was written, and

---

[1] Paris, Bib. Nat. MS. nouv. acq. lat. 692.

second, to look more closely at item 7, the *Historia Regum* attributed to Symeon of Durham, in order to discover what can be learnt about the different elements which have gone to its making.[1]

1. THE CONTENT OF MANUSCRIPT C.C.C.C. 139, fos.1–165

In the list of items which follows account is taken of evidence which may help to show where and when the manuscript was written.[2]

(1) Fos. 1r–16v, a *Universal History* (*historia omnimoda*). On fo. 16 there is a list of popes ending with Calixtus II, 1119–24.

(2) Fos. 17r–35v, extracts from the *Chronicon* of Regino of Prum.

(3) Fos. 36r–46r, Richard of Hexham's *de gestis regis Stephani et de bello Standardii*.[3] The *incipit* ascribes the work to Richard who was elected prior of Hexham in 1141 and formally confirmed in office in 1142. He was still in office in 1154, but was dead by 1167.[4] Against the background of the major events which he describes— the death of Henry I and the accession of Stephen, the battle of the

---

[1] I am deeply indebted to the Master and Fellows of Corpus Christi College, Cambridge, particularly to the librarian, not only for giving me such ready access to the manuscript, but also for allowing it to be deposited at the University Library, Cambridge, so that it could be seen beside U.L.C. MS. Ff. 1. 27. I am also grateful for permission given to reproduce the photographs which appear facing p. 117 (Plate 1), taken by the University Library's photographer.

[2] The contents have been listed in modern times by J. Hodgson Hinde, *Symeonis Dunelmensis Opera et Collectanea*, Publications of the Surtees Society, vol. LI (1868), pp. lxvii–lxxiii, and by M. R. James, *A Descriptive Catalogue of the Manuscripts of Corpus Christi College, Cambridge* (1912), I, 317–23. The MS. was never paginated in the red chalk familiar from many of the Parker MSS., and remains still without any complete pagination. My folio references are consistently one less than those given by Hodgson Hinde because he ignored fo. i, which is covered with paper on the recto, and reckoned fo. ii as fo. 1. The first leaf of each gathering from 1 to XI inclusive now bears a pencilled foliation number in a modern hand. There is no such number on the first leaf of XII (fo. 93r). The numbering is resumed on the first leaf of XIII, but the number written is 103 when it ought to have been 101, and from here to the end of the book the pencilled foliation numbers are consistently in error, being two ahead of the correct number. Since the same error occurs in M. R. James's account of the MS. it seems probable that it was he who added the pencilled numbers. Thus my folio numbers agree with his as far as the *incipit* on fo. 51v, but with the *explicit* on fo. 129v they become consistently two less. Though the error is a trivial one which can easily be set right on the MS. itself, it seems important to record it lest subsequent comparison of the MS. with the catalogue might suggest the loss of two leaves from the thirteenth gathering.

[3] Ed. J. Raine, *The Priory of Hexham*, Publications of the Surtees Society, vol. XLIV (1864), I, 63–106, also R. Howlett, *Chronicles of Stephen, Henry II and Richard I*, Rolls Series, vol. III (1886), 137–78.

[4] For biographical details see J. Raine, *op. cit.* pp. cxlii–cxliv.

OBSERVATIONS ON THE 'HISTORIA REGUM'

Standard, the visit of the papal legate Alberic and the terms of the treaty between Stephen and David—the work contains internal evidence which amply confirms its Hexham origin. It ends with events of 1139.

(4) Fos. 46r–48v, a chronicle from Adam to the emperor Henry V. Most of this work consists of little more than a reckoning of the passage of years from the beginning of the world. From 718 it expands into a brief chronicle of Frankish affairs. Thereafter follow some entries which relate to English, and predominantly Northumbrian, events of the seventh century, but these entries have no independent value.

(5) Fos. 48v–50r, a letter to Hugh, dean of York, *de archiepiscopis eboraci*. The *incipit* attributes the letter to Symeon, called monk of the church of St Cuthbert of Durham, and Symeon refers to himself in the first person in the body of the letter.[1] The content of the work, which has little historical value, consists for the most part of a briefly annotated list of the archbishops of York. After Oswald (972–92) only the list of names is given. The last three in the list are William Fitzherbert, Henry Murdac and Roger of Bishop's Bridge. Roger held the archbishopric from 1154 till his death in 1181.[2] In another manuscript of this work[3] the list of archbishops ends with Thurstan who was in office 1119–40.[4] Raine[5] states that the recipient of the letter was Hugh, dean of York 1130–2, but there was an earlier Hugh who held the same office 1090–1119. Symeon is believed to have been alive in 1104 and 1126, but the dates of his birth and death have not been recorded.[6] Just as the Corpus manuscript seems to represent a later recension than that which is found in the fifteenth-century Cottonian manuscript, so also the Cottonian manuscript may reflect a recension later than that which may have existed in a manuscript no longer surviving. Certainly it would be unwise to argue from this letter that Symeon was still alive in 1130, though he well may have been.

[1] Ed. J. Raine, *The Historians of the Church of York and its Archbishops*, Rolls Series, II (1886), 252–8.
[2] *Handbook of British Chronology*, ed. F. M. Powicke, Roy. Hist. Soc. (1939), p. 177.
[3] British Museum MS. Cotton Titus A XIX, attributed by J. Raine, *Historians of the Church of York*, II, xvi, to the fifteenth century.
[4] *Handbook of British Chronology*, p. 177.
[5] *Loc. cit.*
[6] H. S. Offler, *Medieval Historians of Durham*, Inaugural Lecture at Durham (1958), 6–8.

IX

There is one other major point of distinction between the two manuscripts of the letter. The Cottonian text has this to say of Archbishop Wulfhere at the time of the Danish attack on York—

Inter has strages remotius se agebat apud Hatyngham episcopus.[1]

The Corpus manuscript reads—

Inter has strages remotius se agebat episcopus Wlferius apud addingeham in occidentali parte eboraci in ualle que uocatur hweruerdale. super ripam fluminis hwerf inter oteleiam et castellum de scipctun (*sic* MS., Raine reads *Scipetun*).[2]

Raine states[3] that this additional passage is an interlineation in the Corpus Christi manuscript, but this is not the case. The text of the letter in this manuscript is written in a single hand throughout and has no interlineations or marginal additions. The reference to the local topography of western Yorkshire should be noted.

(6) Fos. 50r–51v, a tract *de obsessione Dunelmi et de probitate Ucthredi comitis*.[4] This short, but historically valuable, work is mainly concerned with the history of several estates which were given by Aldhun, bishop of Durham 995–1018, as his daughter's dowry on her marriage to Uhtred, earl of Northumbria. Its narrative spans the eleventh century as far as 1073, but seems to stop short of the death of Waltheof, earl of Northumbria, in 1076.[5] It was probably written at Durham late in the eleventh century. A sixteenth-century addition to the *incipit* attributes the work to Symeon, but there is no other evidence to support this attribution.

(7) Fos. 51v–129v, the *Historia Regum*. This work, which occupies nearly half the book, is enclosed within an elaborate *incipit* and a slightly less elaborate *explicit*. Both will be examined in detail below with the other evidence bearing upon the date, composition and origin of the work as a whole.

(8) Fos. 129v–147r, the continuation of Symeon's *Historia Regum* by John, prior of Hexham, entitled *historia Johannis prioris haugustaldensis ecclesie. xxv. annorum*.[6] The continuation covers the years 1130–53, but in this the only known manuscript the regularity

---

[1] Raine's text.   [2] C.C.C.C. MS. 139, fo. 50v, col. i.
[3] *Op. cit.* p. 255 n. 1.
[4] Ed. T. Arnold, *Symeonis Monachi Opera Omnia*, Rolls Series (1882), I, 215–20. Arnold's edition of Symeon's works is cited hereafter as T. Arnold, *Symeon*.
[5] F. S. Scott, 'Earl Waltheof of Northumbria', *Archaeologia Æliana*, 4th series, XXX (1952), 150.
[6] Ed. J. Raine, *Hexham*, I, 107–72, and T. Arnold, *Symeon*, II, 284–332.

IX

OBSERVATIONS ON THE 'HISTORIA REGUM'

of the annals is interrupted in the middle of the entry for 1138 (fo. 132r) by a number of items derived from other authors. These intrusive items are listed below as items (9)–(12). Prior John's continuation is resumed on fo. 138r and the work proceeds without further interruption until its end in 1153.

(9) Fo. 132r, rubric erased. Prior John's account of the battle of the Standard ends at fo. 132r, col. 2, line 20. The next three lines formerly contained a rubric which was later erased[1] and in the central part of the erasure there is now a rough sketch of a comet. Following the erased rubric there is an entry which begins—

Anno. M.C.XXXIII. stella cometis. . . .

There follows an account of the burning of London and of a variety of natural phenomena. Raine, who seems to have regarded the placing of the entry at this point as a mere error of copying, transferred it to the appropriate year in his edition of Prior John's work and he remarked that the whole passage had been borrowed by the continuator of Florence of Worcester.[2] It seems certain, however, that the entry formed no part of Prior John's work as he himself left it. The borrowing has surely been the other way and the passage is rather to be regarded as a late insertion into Prior John's work borrowed from Florence of Worcester's continuator.[3]

(10) Fo. 132v, an account of the battle of the Standard composed by Serlo in 72 lines of verse.[4] Born in 1109 and educated at York, Serlo went to Fountains in 1138, the year in which the battle was fought. In 1147 he went to help in the foundation of Kirkstall where he is thought to have died c. 1207 after dictating, when almost a hundred years old, an account of the origin and early history of Fountains.[5]

---

[1] Traces of the red ink can still be seen but they seem to have been overlooked by M. R. James as well as by the editors of Prior John's *Continuation*. My enumeration of items is accordingly ahead of James's from this point.

[2] J. Raine, *Hexham*, I, 110 note *j*.

[3] Both Raine and Arnold overlooked the erased rubric and Arnold gives no hint that the whole passage from § 7 on p. 295 to the bottom of p. 296 in his edition of Symeon's *Historia Regum* is found verbatim, save for one or two minor changes in the continuation of Florence of Worcester, ed. B. Thorpe, *Florentii Wigorniensis Monachi Chronicon ex Chronicis* (1848–9), II, 93–4.

[4] Ed. J. Raine, *Lawrence of Durham*, Surtees Society Publications, LXX (1880), 74–6.

[5] For biographical details see *Dict. Nat. Biog.*, also D. Knowles, *The Monastic Order in England* (1949), pp. 232–3.

67

OBSERVATIONS ON THE 'HISTORIA REGUM'

(11) Fo. 133r, v, an account of the defeat and death of Somer-led.[1] The work consists of 80 lines of doggerel Latin verse, usually with both internal and end rhyme. According to its last couplet, it was composed in honour of St Kentigern by a man called William who is thought to have been a clerk at Glasgow and who claims that he was an eyewitness of the events which he describes. The poem gives an account of an attack which was led by Somerled against Glasgow in 1164 and which is well documented in contemporary Scottish and Irish sources.[2]

(12) Fos. 133v–138r, a tract on the battle of the Standard written by Ailred of Rievaulx.[3] The exact date of its composition is uncertain, but the evidence points to the period 1155–7.[4]

(13) Fos. 147r–149v, the story, written by Ailred of Rievaulx, of the erring nun of Watton, a Gilbertine house in Yorkshire.[5] The nun is said to have been comforted by Henry Murdac, archbishop of York, who appeared to her in a vision after his death. The story must therefore be later than 1153 and a likely approximation would be c. 1160.[6]

(14) Fos. 150r–152v, an account of the foundation and fortunes of St Mary's abbey at York.

(15) Fo. 152v, a very brief item which includes a reference, in elaborate chronological terms, to the foundation of Fountains in 1132.

(16) Fos. 153r–158r, a letter, written by Thurstan, archbishop of York 1119–40, to William of Corbeil, archbishop of Canterbury 1123–36, about the exodus of monks from St Mary's, York, which led to the foundation of the Cistercian house at Fountains in 1132.[7] There are several other manuscripts of this valuable and contemporary account.[8]

(17–20) Fos. 158r–161v, four brief extracts from the *Gesta*

---

[1] Ed. W. F. Skene, *The Historians of Scotland*, I, Fordun (1871), 449–51; J. Raine, *Lawrence of Durham*, pp. 78–80, and T. Arnold, *Symeon*, II, 386–8.
[2] A. O. Anderson, *Early Sources of Scottish History* (1922), II, 254–8. My items 10 and 11 correspond with James's 9 and 9a.
[3] Ed. R. Howlett, *Chronicles of the Reigns of Stephen, Henry II and Richard I*, III (1886), 181–99.
[4] F. M. Powicke, *The Life of Ailred of Rievaulx* (1950), pp. xcvii and xcix.
[5] Migne, *Pat. Lat.* 195, coll. 789–96.
[6] F. M. Powicke, *op. cit.* pp. lxxxi–lxxxii.
[7] Ed. J. R. Walbran, *Memorials of Fountains Abbey*, Publications of the Surtees Society, vol. XLII (Durham, 1863), I, 11–29.
[8] *Ibid.* p. 11 n. 1.

OBSERVATIONS ON THE 'HISTORIA REGUM'

Regum of William of Malmesbury: (*a*) *De uita et conversacione Gereberti pape*,[1] (*b*) *Visio Karoli imperatoris*,[2] (*c*) *Visio Sancti Maurilii*,[3] (*d*) *De anulo statue commendato*.[4] (21) Fo. 162r, a fragment of Northumbrian saga telling of the relations of Ælla who was ruling in Northumbria at the time of the Danish attack on York in 867, with the wife of Ærnulf, a merchant of York. This is a variant of the well-known story of Beorn Butsecarl.[5]

(22) Fo. 165r–v, a brief item *de eo quod eboracensis ecclesia nullum dominium super scottos habere debet*.

(23) Fo. 165v, a brief item in which a clerk interrogates the spirit of Malcolm appearing to him in a vision. The Malcolm in question is Malcolm IV of Scotland who died in 1165.[6]

This list of items speaks plainly enough the answer to one of the two problems to which answer is needed, namely the approximate date at which the manuscript was written. The latest episodes of which its compilers show knowledge are the death of Somerled in 1164 (item 11) and the death of Malcolm IV of Scotland in 1165 (item 23). The item recording the death of Somerled is interpolated into the midst of Prior John's *Continuation* of the *Historia Regum* and it follows that not only Prior John's work (item 8) and the other interpolated items (9, 10, 12), but also all the other items to the end of the book (items 13–23) were written in the form in which we find them in this manuscript not earlier than 1164. The list of archbishops in Symeon's letter (item 5) to Hugh, dean of York, ends with Roger of Bishop's Bridge who was in office 1154–81 and there is a fair presumption, wanting evidence to the contrary, that Roger was still in office when this version of the letter was written. It will be shown below[7] that the rubrics which mark the beginning (fo. 51v) and end (fo. 129v) of the *Historia Regum* were not composed before 1164. It will also be shown[8] that the entry in the *Historia*

---

[1] W. Stubbs, *Willelmi Malmesbiriensis Monachi de Gestis Regum Anglorum*, Rolls Series (1887–9), I, 193–201.
[2] *Ibid.* I, 112–13.   [3] *Ibid.* II, 327–8.
[4] *Ibid.* I, 256.
[5] For the text of this version see T. D. Hardy and C. T. Martin, *Gaimar, Lestorie des Engles*, Rolls Series (1888), I, 328–38. For Gaimar's own version see *ibid.* I, 104–17. See also C. E. Wright, *The Cultivation of Saga in Anglo-Saxon England* (1939), 73, 77, 107–15.
[6] W. F. Skene, *Fordun*, p. 452; J. Raine, *Lawrence of Durham*, pp. 81–2; and A. O. Anderson, *Early Sources of Scottish History*, II, 262.
[7] See below, pp. 77–8.   [8] See below, pp. 110–11.

OBSERVATIONS ON THE 'HISTORIA REGUM'

Regum for 1074 contains a list of the abbots at York and Whitby, the York list ending with a reference to Clement *qui et in praesenti* and the Whitby list with Richard *qui nunc superest*. Clement's predecessor at York, Severinus, died in 1161 and Clement himself in 1184.[1] Richard of Whitby succeeded Benedict in 1148 and died in 1175.[2] There seems to be little room for doubt that the book as a whole was compiled in the second half of the twelfth century and perhaps *c.* 1170 will seem a likely approximation.

The list of contents speaks no less plainly of the northern origin of the book, with its works written by, or attributed to, Symeon of Durham, Richard of Hexham, John of Hexham, Serlo of Kirkstall and Ailred of Rievaulx. Hexham in particular has been claimed as its home,[3] but there are difficulties in the way of accepting a Hexham attribution for the book as a whole, despite strong indications of Hexham interest.

The two entries in the *Historia Regum* which record respectively the death of Acca in 740 and the death of Alchmund in 781 have been embroidered by the addition of long passages of Hexham interest and relating to translations of the relics of these two bishops.[4] In the case of Acca the translation is described as having taken place more than 300 years after his death (i.e. after 1040) and in the case of Alchmund the translation is placed more than 250 years after his death (i.e. after 1030).

Saving perhaps its foundation in 1112, the outstanding event in the domestic history of the Augustinian house at Hexham during the twelfth century was the ceremonial translation of the relics of the early bishops of Hexham in 1155. Ailred's *de Sanctis Ecclesiae Haugustaldensis*,[5] thought to be based on a sermon preached by him at Hexham on this occasion, contains an account of the translation of the relics of four of the eighth-century bishops of Hexham —Acca (d. 740), Frithuberht (d. 766), Alchmund (d. 781) and Tilberht (d. 789). Ailred himself was not in any doubt that the translations of 1155 about which he wrote in his *de Sanctis* were wholly distinct from the translations recorded in the *Historia Regum*, for he added to his own account of Alchmund's translation in 1155 an account of the earlier translation in terms which show a large mea-

[1] *V.C.H. York*, III (1913), 111.   [2] *Ibid.* p. 104.
[3] M. R. James, *Catalogue*, I, 323, also F. M. Powicke, *Life of Ailred of Rievaulx*, p. xcv.
[4] The entries are discussed in greater detail below, pp. 87–90.
[5] J. Raine, *Hexham*, I, 173–203.

OBSERVATIONS ON THE 'HISTORIA REGUM'

sure of verbal identity with the *Historia Regum*.[1] If the author of the Acca and Alchmund interpolations in the *Historia Regum* had been aware of the translations of 1155, it seems likely that he would have made use of the additional material about Acca and Alchmund and also that he would have adorned the obits of Frithuberht and Tilberht in a similar way. Yet nowhere in the whole book is there any hint of an awareness of the Hexham translations of 1155. This must surely seem a difficulty to anyone wishing to claim that the book was written at Hexham *c.* 1170–80 when many witnesses of the events of 1155 would still be living.

A second difficulty about the Hexham attribution arises from the manner in which Prior John's *Continuation* of the *Historia Regum* is laid before the reader. Its narrative is not presented as a continuous whole, but is divided into two parts which are separated from one another by four interpolated items (numbered 9–12 above). The break occurs after Prior John's description of the battle of the Standard in 1138, and two of the four interpolated items, the accounts of the same event by Serlo (item 10) and by Ailred (item 12), although interrupting the flow of Prior John's narrative, are at least immediately relevant. So much cannot be said of the other two interpolated items, the account of the comet and subsequent phenomena of the year 1133 (item 9) and the account of Somerled's death in 1164 (item 11). Little is known about the details of Prior John's life, but it is thought that he became prior of Hexham *c.* 1160 and it is known that he was still prior in 1189.[2] The Hexham case must therefore meet the difficulty of explaining how a Hexham scribe came to present in this mutilated form a work written by a man who at that very time was holding office as prior of Hexham itself.

These are both negative arguments and both rest on the claim which cannot be regarded as more than a probability, that the book was written *c.* 1170. Even so they seem to weaken considerably the case for Hexham authorship, and this case may seem to become untenable against positive arguments which point strongly to a different part of northern England. The extracts from Regino of Prum (item 2), the works of Richard and John of Hexham (items 3 and 8) and the *Historia Regum* (item 7) account for approximately three-fourths of the content of the whole book, but these are works which, though striking a dominantly northern note, are yet con-

---

[1] *de Sanctis*, chap. XII.   [2] J. Raine, *Hexham*, pp. clii–cliii.

cerned with matters of much more than merely local interest. Very different are the last eleven items (13–23), which are contained in the last nineteen folios (fos. 147r–165v).

Setting aside the four extracts from William of Malmesbury (items 17–20), the remaining seven items concern the story of a nun of Watton in the East Riding written by Ailred of Rievaulx (item 13), St Mary's abbey, York (item 14), the foundation of Fountains abbey (item 15), preliminaries leading to the foundation of Fountains abbey (item 16), the wife of a merchant of York (item 21), the relations between the church of York and the Scots (item 22) and finally a clerk's vision of Malcolm IV (item 23). It is the last, and only the last, of these seven items which yields no signs of a particular local interest. All the rest are directly concerned either with York or with Yorkshire, and it is surely these small items, the miscellanea filling up the remaining pages of the book after the major items had been copied into it, that give the better indication of where the book was written.

Keeping in mind the pronounced Yorkshire interest among the miscellanea in the latter part of the book, it may be recalled that the earlier part contains no fewer than four separate accounts of the battle of the Standard which was fought near Northallerton (items 3, 8, 10 and 12), that Symeon's letter to Hugh, dean of York (item 5), is distinguished from the Cottonian manuscript of the same work in part by the additional detail which it gives about the topography of the West Riding, and that what seems to represent the latest addition to the *Historia Regum* consists of references to the contemporary abbots of York and Whitby. It may fairly be said that the whole body of internal evidence points clearly in one direction, and it may be claimed that the weight of the evidence is sufficient to establish that the book came, not from Hexham, but from the scriptorium of a Yorkshire house. Although the list of items will not of itself allow the book to be more exactly located, there seem to be one or two pointers. Despite the concern of several items with York itself, a York origin would be difficult to reconcile with the inclusion of item 22 which is devoted to a statement of the reasons why the church of York had no right to exercise supremacy over the Scots. On the other hand, there seem to be one or two positive hints of connections with a Cistercian house. Rievaulx, the home of Ailred who wrote items 12 and 13, was the first Cistercian foundation in Yorkshire, and as one thinks of Ailred, so one thinks of his close connections with Hexham (items 3 and 8) and with Scotland (item 11). In item 13 the Cistercian archbishop of York, Henry Murdac, is portrayed in a markedly favourable light, and the Cistercian interest is again apparent in the two items relating to Fountains (items 15 and 16).

A survey of the content of the book, without taking any other factors into account, suggests a Yorkshire origin in general and perhaps a Cistercian house in particular. It was long ago observed by others[1] that this manuscript might be connected in some way with another of the manuscripts which at one time belonged to Matthew Parker and which is now housed partly in the University Library, Cambridge, and partly in the library of Corpus Christi College, Cambridge, its two parts being respectively U.L.C. MS. Ff. 1. 27 and C.C.C.C. MS. 66. These two manuscripts between them contain two books of which one comes from Bury St Edmunds and the other from St Mary's Abbey at Sawley in Yorkshire, but the two books have been so split that part of the Bury book and part of the Sawley book are in Ff. 1. 27 and the remainder of both are in C.C.C.C. 66.[2] We are here concerned only with the Sawley book which consists of U.L.C. MS. Ff. 1. 27, pp. 1-40, 73-252 and C.C.C.C. MS. 66, pp. 1-114. The attribution of the book to Sawley rests upon the note *liber Sancte Marie de Salleia* at the top of p. 2 of C.C.C.C. MS. 66 in a hand attributed by Ker to the twelfth or thirteenth century.[3]

MS. Ff. 1. 27 includes the *de Excidio* of Gildas (pp. 1-14), the *Historia Brittonum* (pp. 14-40), Bede's *de Temporibus* (pp. 73-116), Symeon's *Historia Dunelmensis Ecclesiae* (pp. 122-86), the *Historia de Sancto Cuthberto* (pp. 195-202), Æthelwulf's *de Abbatibus* (pp. 203-14) and Richard's *de Moderno et Antiquo Statu (Haugustaldensis) Ecclesiae* (pp. 221-36). Among minor items are a list of estates alleged to have been given to St Cuthbert by Ecgfrith, king of Northumbria (p. 186), a list of relics preserved in the church at Durham (p. 194) and the Old English verses *de Situ Dunelmi* (p. 202). Thus the Sawley book, like C.C.C.C. MS. 139, is a miscellaneous collection of works showing a strong antiquarian in-

[1] J. Hodgson Hinde, *Symeonis...opera*, p. lxxi, and Th. Mommsen, *M.G.H., Auct. Antiquiss.* XIII (Berlin, 1898), 124.
[2] See M. R. James, *Catalogue*, I, 137-44 for the content of C.C.C.C. MS. 66, and p. 145 for the original contents of the two Bury and Sawley manuscripts.
[3] N. R. Ker, *Catalogue of Manuscripts containing Anglo-Saxon* (1957), p. 12.

terest in the history of the ancient kingdom of Northumbria and more particularly in the history of St Cuthbert's see. Indeed these two volumes between them contain a large part of the surviving material relating to the history of Northumbria between the death of Bede and the Norman Conquest. Although two such volumes might have been compiled independently at different centres, the coincidence of content between the two is striking and no doubt this was the main ground that inclined Mommsen to the belief that C.C.C.C. MS. 139 was a Sawley book, a belief which was rejected by James in favour of Hexham. Sawley, lying in the extreme west of the West Riding of Yorkshire close by the Ribble and not to be confused with Sawley near Ripon, was a Cistercian house founded in 1147/8 by monks from Newminster which was itself a daughter house of Fountains. It thus meets the conditions suggested by the content of MS. 139 for a Yorkshire, and probably Cistercian, origin for the book, and such an origin would explain the local topographical interest in the West Riding shown in item 5.[1]

The argument that C.C.C.C. MS. 139 comes from the same scriptorium as the Sawley parts of U.L.C. MS. Ff. 1. 27 and C.C.C.C. MS. 66, and therefore must itself be a Sawley book, does not rest solely on the common antiquarian interest which the two books show in the past history of Northumbria. The Sawley text of Symeon's *Historia Dunelmensis Ecclesiae* takes third place in order of date and importance behind the Durham Cosins MS. V. II. 6 and the British Museum Cotton MS. Faustina A v and is itself followed in fourth place by the Phillips MS. which has recently been restored to Durham, its original home.[2] One of the ways in which the Sawley text of the *Historia* differs from all the other known manuscripts of the work is in the terms in which it refers to the author, Symeon, in the rubrics. The *incipit* to the *Preface* reads thus:

Incipit prefatio reuerendi symeonis | monachi et precentoris ecclesie sancti Cuth|berti Dunelmi. in historia de exordio christia|nitatis et religionis tocius northumbrie. | de fide et origine sancti oswaldi regis . et | martiris . et de predicatione sancti aidani . | episcopi . |[3]

---

[1] See above, p. 66.
[2] J. Conway Davies, 'A Recovered Manuscript of Symeon of Durham', *Durham University Journal*, vol. XLIV, new series vol. XIII (1951), 22–8.
[3] U.L.C. MS. Ff. 1. 27, p. 123, col. 1.

OBSERVATIONS ON THE 'HISTORIA REGUM'

The *incipit* to the *Historia* itself reads:

Incipit historia | sancte et suavis me|morie simeonis | monachi sancti cuth|berti Dunelmi . de exordio christianita|tis et religionis tocius | northumbrie . et de exortu | et processu lindisfarnensis siue dunelmensis | ecclesie |[1]

No such detail is found in the *explicit* which reads simply:

explicit historia simeonis[2]

The terms of these rubrics may be compared with the rubrics marking the beginning and end of the *Historia Regum* in C.C.C.C. MS. 139. The *incipit* reads:

Incipit historia sancte et suauis memorie | Symeonis monachi et precentoris | ecclesie sancti Cuthberti Dunelmi de regibus | anglorum et dacorum et creberrimis bellis . ra|pinis . et incendiis eorum . post obitum uenerabilis Bede presbyteri fere usque ad obitum | regis primi Henrici filii Willelmi nothi | qui angliam adquisiuit . id est . ccc. | .xxix. annorum .et. iiii mensium. |[3]

The *explicit* reads:

Explicit historia suauis et sancte | memorie Symeonis monachi et | precentoris ecclesie sancti Cuthberti Dunelmi . annorum .cccc. xxix. et mensium quattuor. |[4]

The words *historia sancte et suauis memorie Symeonis* occur both in the *incipit* to the *Historia Dunelmensis Ecclesiae* and in the *incipit* to the *Historia Regum,* and also, save for the transposition of *sancte* and *suauis,* in the *explicit* to the *Historia Regum.* The words *Symeonis monachi et precentoris ecclesie sancti Cuthberti Dunelmi* occur three times—once in the *incipit* to the *Preface* of the *Historia Dunelmensis Ecclesiae,* a second time in the *incipit* to the *Historia* itself and a third time in the *explicit* to the *Historia Regum.* The *incipit* to the *Preface* calls Symeon *precentor* and so also do both the *incipit* and the *explicit* to the *Historia Regum.* Nowhere else save in these two manuscripts is this title given to Symeon. There seems to be no room for doubt that all these rubrics were composed by the same person, and we shall not be surprised to find that they are

[1] U.L.C. MS. Ff. l. 27, p. 131, col. 1.
[2] *Ibid.* p. 186, col. 2.
[3] The *incipit* is on fo. 51 v and occupies lines 29–37 of col. 2, that is to say the bottom of the column. Most of the column, that is lines 12–28, is blank. The top of the column, lines 1–11, is occupied by the previous item. For comment on the placing of this *incipit* see below, p. 77.
[4] Fo. 129v, col. 2.

all in the same handwriting (see plate I, facing page 117).[1] It seems certain that Mommsen was right and that C.C.C.C. MS. 139 is a Sawley book.

2. AN ANALYSIS OF ITEM 7 IN MANUSCRIPT C.C.C.C. 139

Item 7 is the material which lies between the two elaborate rubrics of which the *incipit* is found on fo. 51 v and the *explicit* on fo. 129 v. Although it is a convenience, established by the usage of several generations of scholars, to call this material the *Historia Regum*, this title does not occur either in the rubrics or in the body of the material itself, and care must be taken lest a mere convenience of terminology may seem to impose upon the material to which it refers a unity of substance and form which that material is very far from possessing. The ascription of it all to a named author, Symeon of Durham, creates additional need for care, and it would perhaps be well to accept as a point of departure that the so-called *Historia Regum* is a miscellaneous collection of material, some of it in narrative and some of it in annalistic form, some of it derived from known sources, some of it from lost sources, and some of it original, but all of it having an artificial unity imposed upon it from the fact that it is found consecutively in one book written at Sawley in the second half of the twelfth century and defined by rubrics professing to mark its beginning and end.

The contents of the work will be examined under the following heads:

The Rubrics.
(1) The Kentish Legends.
(2) The Early Northumbrian Kings.
(3) Material derived mainly from Bede.
(4) A Chronicle from 732 to 802.
(5) A Chronicle from 849 to 887, derived mainly from Asser.
(6) A Chronicle from 888 to 957.
(7) Extracts from William of Malmesbury.

[1] J. Hodgson Hinde (*Symeonis...Opera*, I, lxxi) thought that the hand that wrote the *Historia Regum* in C.C.C.C. MS. 139 also wrote the *Historia Dunelmensis Ecclesiae* and several other items in U.L.C. MS. Ff. 1. 27. This could only be determined by a detailed palaeographical examination of both MSS. After placing the rubrics side by side and studying them carefully I am convinced of the identity of hand, but am not competent to give an opinion on the wider question.

OBSERVATIONS ON THE 'HISTORIA REGUM'

(8) A Chronicle from 848 to 1118, derived mainly from Florence of Worcester.

(9) A Chronicle from 1119 to 1129.

The Rubrics

The *incipit* occupies the last eight lines of the second column of fo. 51 v. The first eleven lines of this column are occupied by the previous item and the remainder of the column (ll. 12–28) is blank. The corresponding *explicit* is found at fo. 129 v, col. 2.[1] The *incipit* ought to mark the beginning of a history running from or soon after 735, the year of Bede's death, but in fact it is followed immediately at the head of fo. 52 r by a second rubric[2] and by a variety of material which extends over eighteen pages of the manuscript (fos. 52 r–60 v) and which all relates to times before the death of Bede. The inference to be drawn from this fact, and also from the position of the rubric on the page, is either that the rubricator was ill-informed about the content of the work whose beginning his rubric was intended to mark, or else, and perhaps the alternatives are not exclusive, that when he came to add the rubric after the work itself had been copied, he found that no space had been left at the right place and he therefore wrote it in the nearest convenient blank space, which happened to be at the bottom of fo. 51 v.

The *explicit* on fo. 129 v follows the entry for 1129 and is itself followed by the *incipit* which marks the beginning of Prior John's *Continuation* from 1130. The *incipit* to the *Historia Regum* defines it as a work extending 'after the death of the venerable Bede, priest, almost as far as the death of King Henry I, son of William the Bastard who conquered England, that is 429 years and 4 months'. The *explicit* repeats exactly the length of the work in years and months, but without reference to the death of either Bede or Henry I. The reference to Henry as the first king of that name will at once suggest that this rubric was not composed until after the accession of Henry II in 1154. The *explicit* follows the entry for 1129, six years before the death of Henry I, and there can be no doubt that it is to this year 1129 that the phrase *fere usque ad obitum regis primi Henrici* refers, but the interval between the death of Bede (735) and the year 1129 is not 429 years and 4 months as the

---

[1] For the text of both rubrics see above, p. 75.
[2] See below, p. 78.

rubric states. If we subtract 429 from 1129 we reach the date 700 which has no particular significance for the *Historia Regum*, nor do we reach any more significant date by subtracting 429 from 1153, the year in which Prior John's *Continuation* ends. The alternative, and seemingly most natural, course is to add 429 years and 4 months to the date of Bede's death, and this will give September 1164, a date far beyond the point to which the current of the *Historia Regum* reaches. Yet this date has a clear significance, not so much for item 7 itself, the *Historia Regum*, as for the whole book of which it forms a part. We have seen that the latest events to which this book refers are the death of Somerled in 1164 (item 11) and the death of Malcolm IV of Scotland in 1165 (item 23). The reasonable conclusion is that September 1164 marks the date by which the copying of the *Historia Regum* at Sawley had been completed and the rubrics themselves written.

The rubricator thus distinguished, in a somewhat muddled way, between two dates—1129, the year at which Symeon's work was believed to have ended, and 1164, the year in which the Sawley copy was completed. A similar distinction can be observed within the *Historia Regum* itself. The entry for the year 1072 which contains a list of the earls of Northumbria ends *hodieque rex Henricus Northymbriam in sua tenet manu*. The context shows that the reference is to Henry I, although *primus* is not here used to qualify *Henricus* as it is in the *incipit*. This passage is appropriate to a work which continued no further than 1129, that is, in the words of the *incipit*, almost as far as the death of Henry. Part of the entry for 1074 shows by its reference to the contemporary abbots of York and Whitby that it is appropriate to a date between 1161 and 1175.[1]

(1) The Kentish Legends

The *incipit* of the *Historia Regum* at the bottom of fo. 51v is immediately followed at the head of fo. 52r by a second rubric which reads:

Incipit passio sanctorum Ethelberti atque Ethelredi regie stirpis puerorum.

The matter to which this rubric refers runs from fo. 52r to fo. 54v (pp. 3–13 of Arnold's text) and its earlier part, which relates to the kings of Kent from Æthelberht to Egbert (d. 673), is derived almost

---

[1] See above, p. 70.

IX

OBSERVATIONS ON THE 'HISTORIA REGUM'

wholly from Bede.[1] The remaining and greater part tells of the martyrdom of Æthelberht and Æthelræd, two Kentish princes who were murdered by Thunur, an evil counsellor of their cousin Egbert, the reigning king of Kent, of Egbert's gift of land in Thanet, in atonement for his failure to prevent the crime, to Eormenbeorg/Domneva, sister of the murdered princes, and of the foundation on this land of a religious house of which Eormenbeorg became abbess, to be followed later by her daughter Mildred.

The *passio* of the two Kentish princes forms part of a widespread group of legends which relate historically to the second half of the seventh century, geographically to Minster-in-Thanet and Canterbury, and personally to Eormenbeorg/Domneva and her daughter Mildred. The legends are found in greater or less detail in two Old English sources, *Þa halgan on Angelcynne*, which Liebermann believed to have been composed shortly before 1000,[2] and a now fragmentary *Life of St Mildred* which is preserved in an eleventh-century manuscript.[3] The latter is closely related to the first part of the former and sometimes agrees verbally with it. There is a brief reference to the *passio* in a Canterbury addition to the entry for 640 in the A text of the *Anglo-Saxon Chronicle*. The legends are also recounted in a Latin *Life of St Mildred* written by Goscelin of Canterbury late in the eleventh century,[4] as well as in the works of various historians writing in the twelfth and thirteenth centuries. This considerable body of material would require detailed study before any sure conclusions could be reached about the growth and distribution of the legends and the relations of the different versions to one another. Meanwhile note may be taken of some points relevant to two problems—the date at which the legends became current in the north and the reason for their inclusion in the *Historia Regum*.

According to the version found in the *Historia Regum*, Deusdedit, archbishop of Canterbury, was present at the meeting summoned by King Egbert after the murder of the two princes had

---

[1] *H.E.* II, 5 and III, 8. The amount derived from Bede is much greater than is shown in Arnold's text.
[2] F. Liebermann, *Die Heiligen Englands* (Hannover, 1889), p. iv. For Liebermann's texts of *Þa halgan* and comparative material, see *ibid.* pp. 1–19.
[3] Ed. O. Cockayne, *Leechdoms, Wortcunning and Starcraft of Early England*, Rolls Series (1866), III, 422–9. See also N. R. Ker, *Catalogue*, pp. 172–3.
[4] T. D. Hardy, *Descriptive Catalogue of Materials relating to the History of Great Britain and Ireland*, Rolls Series (1862), I, pt. i, 376–9.

79

been discovered. Deusdedit, however, died in 664 on the same day as Eorconberht, Egbert's predecessor on the Kentish throne,[1] and it follows that Deusdedit cannot have been archbishop when Egbert was king. The Old English *Life of St Mildred* agrees with the *Historia Regum* in this error, but Goscelin, presumably drawing upon additional information about the dates of the Kentish kings and of the archbishops which would be available to him in Canterbury, removed the name of Deusdedit and substituted that of Theodore. Secondly, the *Historia Regum* mentions Eastry as the first and Wakering as the second burial place of the two princes, but it makes no reference to the translation of their relics to Ramsey in 991.[2] The form of the place-name—*Easterige*—preserves the archaic element **gē* which is no longer recognisable as such in the forms of the name current after the Norman Conquest.[3] Thirdly, the version of the legends told in the *Historia Regum* refers to no detail later than the death of Mildred, who is said to have been buried in a church dedicated to the Virgin Mary. It contains no reference to the claim to the possession of the relics which was advanced by Goscelin on behalf of St Augustine's or to the counter-claim made by the canons of St Gregory's, Canterbury.[4] Fourthly, the *Historia Regum* agrees with the Old English *Life* of St Mildred in making Eormenbeorg and Domneva[5] alternative names of the same person, while Goscelin, in his *Life* of the saint, makes them two sisters. It seems clear from these four points that the *passio* reached the north in a form untouched by Goscelin of Canterbury who is thought to have been at work on his *Life* of St Mildred in the last decade of the eleventh century,[6] and in this respect it belongs to an earlier rather than a later stage in the growth of the legends as a whole. The archaic form of the place-name *Easterige* and the absence of any reference to the removal of the relics of the two princes to Ramsey in 991 may further suggest that an antique text lies behind the Northumbrian version. What-

[1] Bede, *H.E.* IV, I.

[2] Liebermann, *op. cit.* p. 13. The relics were still claimed by Ramsey in 1192 when they were placed in shrines. W. H. Hart and P. A. Lyons, *Cartularium Monasterii de Rameseia*, Rolls Series (1893), III, 177.

[3] J. K. Wallenberg, *Kentish Place-Names* (Uppsala Universitets Årsskrift, 1931), p. 73.

[4] W. Levison, *England and the Continent in the Eighth Century* (Oxford, 1946), p. 199 n. 1.

[5] The name is a conflation of *domina* and O.E. *Ēafe*.

[6] T. D. Hardy, *Catalogue*, I, i, 379.

ever its form and whatever its date, no reader of the *Historia Regum* can be left in any doubt that it was largely rewritten by an editor who delighted in conceits of syntax, the use of uncommon words and the most bombastic language which his ingenuity could devise.

It is not easy to see why this Kentish material was included in a work which was primarily concerned with northern affairs and which, according to the rubric, referred only to the times after the death of Bede. A guess, unsupported by any evidence, might be that at some stage Eormenbeorg of Minster-in-Thanet was confused with the lady of the same name who became the second wife of Ecgfrith, king of Northumbria, and who likewise became an abbess, though not in the south. Yet the version of the legends found in the *Historia Regum* gives no hint of any such confusion and it may be that a passage in the fragmentary Old English *Life* of St Mildred will suggest a more likely explanation.

Eormenbeorg was married to Merewalh, one of the rulers of the *Magonsætan* whose lands lay in northern Herefordshire and southern Shropshire.[1] There were three daughters of the marriage, all of whom came to be recognised as saints. Mildburh, the eldest of the three, built a nunnery at Wenlock of which she became abbess. She is thought to have died *c.* 722 and she was buried in her own nunnery. Mildred (O.E. Mildðryð), the second, became abbess of Minster-in-Thanet in succession to her mother. She enjoyed a widespread cult after her death and is the most prominent figure in the legends associated with Minster. The youngest of the three was called Mildgyth. The first part of *Þa halgan on Angelcynne* gives a considerable amount of information about Mildred,[2] and the second part records that Mildburh's relics were at Wenlock,[3] but neither part records anything beyond the name of the youngest, Mildgyth. There seems to be only one source which records anything about Mildgyth beyond her parentage, namely the O.E. *Life of St Mildred* in which it is said:

Sce mildgyð resteð on norðembran, þær wæron hire mihta oft gecyðede 7 get sindon.
St Mildgyð lies in Northumbria where her miraculous powers were often exhibited and still are.[4]

[1] F. M. Stenton, *Anglo-Saxon England*, 2nd ed. (1947), pp. 46–7.
[2] Liebermann, *op. cit.* pp. 3–5.
[3] *Ibid.* p. 11.　　　　[4] O. Cockayne, *op. cit.* pp. 424–5.

OBSERVATIONS ON THE 'HISTORIA REGUM'

The phrase 7 *get sindon* may be no more than a stock remark and should not necessarily be interpreted as meaning that the particular whereabouts of the relics in Northumbria were known at the time of writing. Both the date and the historical value of the *Life of St Mildred* have yet to be established, but it is certainly a compilation of southern origin and it seems very unlikely that a southern hagiographer would admit that the bones of one member of a family so distinguished for its saintliness, and of southern connections, were in Northumbria unless he believed that that was in fact the case. Yet unhappily there seems to be no evidence to show either the date at which the relics were translated to the north or the place in Northumbria at which they were kept. Even so the presence of Mildgyth's relics in Northumbria provides a possible reason for the inclusion of the Kentish legends in a Northumbrian compilation.

(2) *The Early Northumbrian Kings*

The transition from the Kentish *passio* to the material which follows is achieved somewhat awkwardly by the following passage on fo. 54v:

In exordio huius operis genealogiam regum cantuariorum strictim prælibauimus, nunc northanhymbrorum libet demonstrare ut ad eorum tempora ualeamus peruenire, de quibus non est narratum post obitum reuerentissimi sacerdotis Bedæ.[1]

The material to which this introductory sentence refers consists basically of a list of the Northumbrian kings from Ida to Ceoluulf with their regnal years. The source of this information is undoubtedly a regnal list such as has been preserved in a variety of texts, but the bare bones have been clothed in that same kind of bombastic phraseology that characterises the Kentish *Passio*, and further adorned with two suitably adapted passages from Boethius's *de*

[1] This same passage, with the exception of the words *cantuariorum strictim prælibauimus, nunc* marks the beginning of Roger of Howden's *Chronicle*. Arnold, *Symeon*, II, xiii, held these four words to be an interpolation into a sentence whose earlier form is preserved by Roger of Howden. It is, of course, equally possible that the change has been the other way and that the four words were omitted from Roger's *Chronicle* because that work did not include the Kentish *passio*. I have deliberately limited the scope of this present study to the *Historia Regum* itself. Stubbs's preface to his edition of Roger of Howden, *Chronica Magistri Rogeri de Houedene*, Rolls Series (1858), is of the first importance for its discussion of the relationship of the *Historia Regum* to other works of the twelfth and thirteenth centuries.

OBSERVATIONS ON THE 'HISTORIA REGUM'

Consolatione Philosophiæ. The oldest and most authoritative of the regnal lists dates from 737 and forms part of the *Moore Memoranda* on fo. 128v of the Moore manuscript of Bede's *History*.[1] The Northumbrian list is also found on fo. 65v of C.C.C.C. MS. 183, the book which contains a copy of Bede's prose *Life of St Cuthbert* believed to have been presented by Æthelstan to St Cuthbert's see at Chester-le-Street in the tenth century.[2] The order in which the eight pagan rulers of Bernicia from Ida to Æthelfrith are given in the *Historia Regum* agrees exactly with the order found in the Moore Manuscript and in C.C.C.C. MS. 183 and there are no more than slight variations in the numbers of the regnal years. In three other and later sources, Florence of Worcester[3] and the two north country tracts entitled respectively *Libellus de Primo Saxonum Adventu*[4] and *Series Regum Northymbrensium*[5] there are marked differences not merely in the regnal years but also in the order of the kings themselves. It is clear that the *Historia Regum* follows the older and more authoritative tradition.

(3) *Material derived mainly from Bede*

The content of most of fos. 55r–57r, corresponding with pp. 15–22 of Arnold's text, is derived verbatim, or occasionally in paraphrase, from Bede's *Historia Abbatum*, with two or three intrusive passages marked by the ornate style characteristic of the preceding parts of the *Historia Regum*. The eight known manuscripts of the *Historia Abbatum*[6] were divided by Plummer into two clearly defined groups[7] of which one comprises the tenth-century British Museum MS. Harley 3020, designated H_1, and what Plummer took to be a twelfth-century transcript of it, Bodleian MS. Digby 112, designated Δ. These two form the H-text which was that adopted by Plummer. The remaining six manuscripts form a separate group and in most cases where they differ from the H-text they agree among themselves.

---

[1] *Early English Manuscripts in Facsimile*, vol. 9, *The Moore Bede*, ed. P. Hunter Blair (1959), fo. 128v.
[2] N. Ker, *Catalogue*, pp. 64–5.   [3] Ed. B. Thorpe, I, 268.
[4] Ed. T. Arnold, *Symeon*, II, 374.
[5] *Ibid.* II, 390.
[6] M. L. W. Laistner, *A Hand-List of Bede Manuscripts* (Cornell, 1943), pp. 112–13.
[7] C. Plummer, *Bedæ Opera Historica* (Oxford, 1896), I, cxxxii–cxxxviii.

OBSERVATIONS ON THE 'HISTORIA REGUM'

Since the *Historia Regum* only uses extracts from the *Historia Abbatum* full and detailed comparison between the different texts is not possible at every point, but there is enough common ground to allow significant conclusions to be drawn about the affinities of that version of the *Historia Abbatum* which is found in the *Historia Regum*. Plummer drew attention to three peculiarities which distinguish the H_1 and Δ text from the other group—the readings *militans* for *militare*, *leuam* for *aquilonem* and *nomine* for *regimine*—and in all three instances the *Historia Regum* agrees with H_1, thus leaving no room for doubt that its source was an H-text.[1] Plummer also noted certain minor differences between H_1 and Δ, but he could only find one instance of importance in which Δ shows a reading in agreement with the other group. In § 7 of the *Historia Abbatum*[2] H_1 has the meaningless *quia bene se ac fructuose ordinatum esse conspexit*, but Δ and the other six manuscripts read *donasse* for *ordinatum esse*. Plummer thought that this might have been an independent correction made by the scribe of Δ and that perhaps the original reading was *ordinasse*. The corresponding passage in the *Historia Regum* reads *quia bene ac fructuose ordinatam conspexit*[3] which in its context gives good sense, though sense rather different from that given by the reading found in Δ and the other six manuscripts which agree with Δ. The *Historia Regum* is here closer to H_1 than to Δ, and it seems possible that it may even have preserved the correct reading.

The extracts from the *Historia Abbatum* are followed by a poem of twelve lines upon times and seasons, with an additional couplet in which the verses are attributed to the authorship of Bede. The poem is introduced with an expression of the writer's wish to say something about Bede himself and with a reference to a work of Bede's which he calls *de annalibus, hoc est, de rebus singulorum annorum*. The poem was certainly not composed by Bede, though evidence of its wide popularity suggests that he is likely to have been familiar with it in one form or another. It is preserved in the form found in the *Historia Regum* in a number of manuscripts ranging from the ninth to the twelfth century, most of them continental and the oldest being a ninth-century Reichenau

---

[1] The references to Arnold's text of the *Historia Regum* are p. 16, l. 5; p. 17, l. 1; p. 18, l. 30. For the corresponding passages in Plummer's text of the *Historia Abbatum* see p. 365, l. 3; p. 368, l. 2; p. 372, l. 1.

[2] Plummer, *op. cit.* p. 370, l. 11.

[3] Arnold's text, p. 17, ll. 12–13.

OBSERVATIONS ON THE 'HISTORIA REGUM'

manuscript.[1] An earlier, but slightly different version of the poem
is found in the *Versus Sancti Columbani ad Sethum*, thought to
have been composed *c.* 610.[2] In this version are found lines 2–9,
11 and 12 of the version found in the *Historia Regum*, but
Columbanus was not their author any more than Bede. Six of
the twelve lines in the *Historia Regum* version go back beyond
Columbanus to the *Satisfactio* of Dracontius.[3] Some of the lines
may go back even beyond Dracontius since Jerome, in his commentary on Ezekiel i. 7, refers to a poem *ver, æstas, autumnus,
hiems et mensis et annus*.[4]

The short poem on times and seasons is followed by a much
longer poem under the rubric *lamentatio bede presbyteri* (fo. 57r,
col. 1). There seems to be no doubt that this poem, otherwise
known as *de Die Iudicii*, was written by Bede himself. In Migne's
text[5] the poem ends with a nine-line *Precatio ad Deum*, which was
shown by Manitius[6] to be derived from Eugenius of Toledo, but
the text in the *Historia Regum* lacks this *Precatio* and in its place
has five other lines, the last of which contains a reference to Acca.
Laistner noted that the copy found in the Manchester MS. Rylands
116, of the tenth or eleventh century from Trier, likewise lacks the
Precatio and quotes the first four of the five additional lines found
in the *Historia Regum*, understandably omitting the invocation of
Acca in the fifth, since continental readers 'would have no interest
in a Northumbrian bishop of Bede's day'.[7] It is not easy to under-

[1] Karlsruhe Landesbibliothek Aug. 167, fo. 13, see A. Riese, *Anthologia Latina*
(Leipzig, 1906), I, ii, no. 676, pp. 151–2. This MS., which dates 836–48, also
contains Bede's *H.E.* v, 24, his *de Natura Rerum*, his *de Temporibus* and his *de
Temporum Ratione*; see Laistner, *Hand-List*, pp. 110, 140, 145 and 149. The
reference in the *Historia Regum* to Bede's *de annalibus, hoc est, de rebus singulorum
annorum* is perhaps to the chronicle which forms c. lxvi of the *de Temporum
Ratione*, and it is significant that the poem and the *de Temporum Ratione* should
be associated with one another in this early manuscript.
[2] Ed. W. Grundlach, *M.G.H., Epist.* III (Berlin, 1892), 185, ll. 63–71.
[3] Ed. F. Vollmer, *M.G.H., Auct. Antiquiss.* XIV (Berlin, 1905), 114–29. The six
lines of the *Historia Regum* version are lines 3, 4, 5, 6, 8 and 12, and they correspond respectively with lines 219, 247, 249, 251, 259 and 253 of the *Satisfactio*. It
will be noted that only odd-numbered lines are borrowed, that is to say only the
hexameters from the elegiac couplets in which the *Satisfactio* is written.
[4] A. Riese, *loc. cit.* p. 152 note.   [5] *Patrologia Latina*, 94, coll. 633–8.
[6] M. Manitius, *Geschichte der lateinischen Literatur des Mittelalters* (Munich,
1911), I, 86.
[7] M. L. W. Laistner, *Hand-List*, pp. 126–7. Laistner lists thirty-six MSS. of
the *de Die Iudicii*, and while it would be of great interest to establish the place of
the *Historia Regum* text in the general textual tradition of the poem, the task
would be too big an undertaking for the scope of this present study.

stand why the compiler of the *Historia Regum* thought the *de Die Iudicii* to be relevant to his purpose at this, or indeed at any other, part of his work, though there may perhaps be a pointer, if his reference to what he calls *de annalibus* has been rightly interpreted as being to the chronicle which forms chap. LXVI of the *de Temporum Ratione*, in the fact that chap. LXX of the *de Temporum Ratione* is concerned with the same topic and is entitled *de Die Iudicii*.

The remainder of the Bedan material is derived chiefly from *H.E.* V, 23, Bede's account of the state of Britain in 731, and to a smaller extent from *H.E.* V, 24, with Bede's account of his life and works. Apart from the fact, of no great significance, that the events of 731 are wrongly attributed to 732, there are only two points in this material which call for comment. The death of Berctwald, archbishop of Canterbury, is placed *die V Iduum Ianuariarum*. This reading is characteristic of C-type manuscripts of the *History*, in contrast with the M-type reading which omits V.[1] Secondly, the writer states that if anyone wishes to know more about what Bede did *legat capitulum XXV historiæ Anglorum gentis*. In most manuscripts of the *History* Bede's chronological summary and his account of his life and works form a single and final chapter, that is, V, 24, but in the Durham MS. B II 35 (Plummer's MS. D), and in other manuscripts dependent on it, the account of his life and works forms a separate chapter, that is, V, 25. The Durham manuscript is of the late eleventh century and of the C type, being closely akin to C itself.[2]

(4) *A Chronicle from 732 to 802*

The entry for the year 732 marks the beginning of a chronicle which, apart from some minor interruptions and irregularities, retains an annalistic form throughout the remainder of the *Historia Regum*. The entries from 732 to 802 (55 in all, with 16 blank years) have long been recognised as providing a source of high value for the history of Northumbria in the eighth century, a value which is enhanced by the scarcity of other records for this period. The distribution of the sixteen years for which there is no entry is more or less even, but there is a marked contrast between the very short

[1] C. Plummer, *op. cit.* I, 349 note 13.
[2] R. A. B. Mynors, *Durham Cathedral Manuscripts*, no. 47; M. L. W. Laistner, *Hand-List*, p. 96; C. Plummer, *op. cit.* I, cv and 356.

OBSERVATIONS ON THE 'HISTORIA REGUM'

entries from 732 to *c*. 750 and the much longer and more detailed entries from *c*. 750 to 802. Although there can be no doubt that this part of the *Historia Regum* has preserved what is basically an eighth-century chronicle, there can equally be no doubt that this chronicle has been modified and subjected to interpolations by more than one writer of later date. Several passages reveal an editor or a scribe copying from a source and making minor modifications as he does so—*refert historia uel cronica huius patriæ* (740), *quidam referunt...nos uero dicimus* (745), *ueluti declarat subsequens sermo scriptoris* (774), *quid gestum sit dcclxxix sequens declarabit sermo* (778), *ut sequens demonstrabit articulus* (779).

(*a*) *The Acca and Alchmund interpolations*

At two points, 740 and 781, the annals are interrupted by long passages which concern the relics of two of the Hexham bishops, Acca and Alchmund, and which are undoubtedly interpolations. The Acca interpolation, under the year 740, records that Acca died on 20 October and was buried outside the east end of the church at Hexham, where his tomb was marked by two sculptured stone crosses, of which one bore an inscription. More than 300 years later—*post annos plusquam ccc depositionis suae*—when his remains were translated, his vestments were found to be preserved as new in the tomb and on his breast was a small wooden altar bearing a dedicatory inscription. There follow a number of miracle stories designed partly to show that all Acca's bones were at Hexham and partly to demonstrate the miraculous powers of the saint himself.

The first story tells of a Hexham monk called Aldred of whom it is said that he was brought up in the house of his brother who was a priest at Hexham before that place had been given by Thomas II, archbishop of York, to the canons regular who still served there. Aldred's brother wished to separate the bones of Acca from the dust of his body. While he was preparing to do this, it happened that Aldred found himself alone with the relics and the thought entered his mind that even a very distinguished church would consider itself greatly honoured to possess a single bone of so great a saint. He therefore tried to steal one bone in order that he might give it to another church, but his efforts were thwarted by divine intervention. The other stories tell of cures effected by Acca's relics and of an occasion on which Acca and the saints of Hexham saved the church from being destroyed by Malcolm, king of Scots. The story was well-known by common report, says the writer, but it was well to commit it to writing lest it should be forgotten through the lapse of time.

The Alchmund interpolation under 781 is similar in character though shorter. Alchmund, it is said, was buried near Acca and his remains were translated more than 250 years later. The story of this translation relates that Alchmund himself appeared in a vision to a certain man of Hexham telling him to go to Alfred, son of Westweor, a priest of the church of Durham, and bid him remove Alchmund's remains to a more honourable position in the church of Hexham. Alfred went to Hexham and preparations for the translation were made. There was not time to complete the work in a day and the relics were therefore placed in a side aisle for the night, whence they were to be moved to a more prominent position on the morrow. Alfred, the Durham priest, stole one of Alchmund's finger bones with the intention of giving it to the church of Durham. When the morrow came all attempts to move the relics proved in vain. During the following night Alchmund again appeared in a vision to the same man as before, showing him one of his hands, from which a bone of the middle finger was missing, and demanding that restitution should be made. The vision was made known to all the brethren the next day, Alfred confessed his crime and restored the missing bone, whereupon the translation of the relics was completed without further difficulty.

A *terminus post quem* for the composition of the Acca interpolation is supplied by the reference to the gift of Hexham to the canons regular by Thomas II, archbishop of York, an event which occurred in 1113, and there are several other chronological pointers. Acca's translation is dated after 1050, Alchmund's after 1030. Aldred's brother, unnamed in the story, can be identified with Eilaf, priest of Hexham who died in 1138 and who was the father of Ailred of Rievaulx, and the Malcolm, king of Scots, whose vain attempt to destroy Hexham was in danger of being forgotten through lapse of time, was Malcolm Canmore (1058–93). Although the Alchmund interpolation contains no evidence which proves that it could not have been written before the twelfth century, there can be no real doubt that it was written at the same time and for the same purpose as the Acca interpolation. The clue to that purpose lies in the activities of Alfred, son of Westweor, as they are described by Symeon in the *Historia Dunelmensis Ecclesiae*.

OBSERVATIONS ON THE 'HISTORIA REGUM'

Symeon devoted a whole chapter to Alfred, a zealous collector of relics, whose greatest triumph was to secure the bones of Bede for Durham.[1] He had been commanded in a vision, says Symeon, to visit the sites of the ancient monasteries and churches of Northumbria, and as he did so, he excavated the relics of many saints, leaving them above ground to be venerated by the people, but bringing a portion of them to Durham to be placed by the body of Cuthbert. Among the saints whose relics were thus recovered Symeon names two anchorites, a king, two abbesses and two bishops —Acca and Alchmund of Hexham. Comparison of Symeon's chapter in the *Historia Dunelmensis Ecclesiae* on the activities of Alfred, son of Westweor, with the Acca and Alchmund interpolations in the *Historia Regum* leaves little room for doubt that the prime purpose of the latter was to refute Symeon's claim in the former that Durham possessed some of the relics of the two Hexham bishops. Even a very distinguished church (*etiam praecelsa quaelibet ecclesia*), Aldred is made to say, would think itself highly honoured at possessing but a single one of Acca's bones. The reference is surely to Durham, but Aldred failed to secure even that single bone. Similarly with the Alchmund interpolation—there is a ready admission that Alfred, the Durham priest, did indeed visit Hexham to secure relics, as Symeon claimed, but a detailed demonstration of his utter failure to secure even one finger bone.

All this is surely the work of a skilful Hexham propagandist seeking to show that the discoveries made when the two Hexham bishops were translated in the eleventh century reflected no less honour upon the church at Hexham than did the discoveries attending the translation of Cuthbert in 1104 upon the church at Durham. Acca's vestments were no less well preserved than Cuthbert's, and if there was a portable altar in the tomb of Cuthbert, so also there was one in Acca's.[2] If, at the time when these interpolations were made, the *Historia Regum* was already associated with Symeon's name, they become all the more effective as propaganda through being inserted in the work of the most notable Durham historian of the time. The date of the insertion must lie after 1113, when the Augustinian canons first went to Hexham, and probably

---

[1] *Historia Dunelmensis Ecclesiae*, III, 7. Ed. T. Arnold, *Symeon*, II, 87–90.

[2] In the light of this strong propagandist element in the Acca interpolation, how much trust can be put in what is said about the two stone crosses which are said to have marked Acca's tomb?

before 1155 when there was a further great translation of Hexham relics, including those of Frithuberht and Tilberht.[1] Arnold assumed that these interpolations were made at Hexham by a Hexham writer, but this assumption does not seem to be a necessary one. It has been noted above[2] that the Corpus Christi book, of which the *Historia Regum* forms item 7, contains two pieces written by Ailred of Rievaulx, items 12 and 13. Were the Acca and Alchmund interpolations also written by Ailred, whose father was a Hexham priest, whose family was prominent in the neighbourhood of both Hexham and Durham and whose works include the *de Sanctis Ecclesiae Haugustaldensis*? Whether this be so or not, they are written in a simple, lucid style which offers the strongest contrast with the turgid bombast characteristic of some earlier parts of the *Historia Regum*.

(b) *Other secondary material*

Parts of the entries for 732–4 are found in certain eighth-century manuscripts of Bede's *History* as an appendix to the *History* proper. Two small points of detail may be noticed. In manuscript M of the *History* the eclipse of the sun in 733 is dated *xviiii Kl. Sept.*, whereas manuscript C has *xviii Kl. Sept.* In the same entry where M reads *scuto*, C reads *sicut*. The *Historia Regum* follows the M reading at both places, yet we are not bound to suppose that these annals were derived from a manuscript of the *History* at all since they are likely to have had an independent existence. The *Historia Regum* entries for these years do in fact include some material not found in any manuscript of the *History*.

The entry recording the death of Tatwine, archbishop of Canterbury, in 734, is followed by the names of his eight predecessors. As with the early Northumbrian kings, a mere list of names of the archbishops has been expanded with a quantity of uninformative verbiage whose style shows plainly enough that it proceeds from the same hand that worked upon the Kentish *Passio* and the Northumbrian regnal list.

The notice of the death of Ceolwulf, king of Northumbria, in the entry for 764 is followed by the opening lines of Bede's *Preface* to his *History*. Where the received text of the *History* reads *nunc ad transscribendum ac plenius ex tempore meditandum retransmitto*, the *Historia Regum* has the unintelligible *meditaturum* for the correct

---

[1] See above, pp. 70–1.   [2] P. 68.

meditandum. In all the manuscripts of Bede's *History* known to
Plummer he found the reading *meditaturum* in only one, the eighth-
century British Museum MS. Cotton Tiberius CII.[1]

The description of Lindisfarne under the year 793 draws upon
Bede's *de Natura Rerum*, Aldhelm and Boethius. There are also
two short passages which recur in Symeon's *Historia Dunelmensis
Ecclesiae*, but there is nothing to show which way the borrowing has
been. Other annals contain brief quotations from Pliny's *Natural
History* (752) and Boethius's *de Consolatione Philosophiae* (779, 799,
801, 802).

(*c*) *Episcopal succession*

In the chronicle which remains after setting aside late interpolations and secondary matter, many of the entries are concerned with
episcopal succession. Including Canterbury there were thirteen
dioceses in the southern province of the church in England in 735,
and there is some reference here to the episcopal succession at all
but two of them, Winchester and Dunwich. The succession of archbishops at Canterbury is complete from the death of Tatwine in
734 to the election of Æthelheard in 791, save that there is no
reference to the death of Cuthbert, whose appointment is recorded
in 740, or to the appointment of his successor, Breguwine, whose
death is recorded in 765. The omission of these two events is probably due to the editorial manipulation of the annals for 759, 760 and
761, since some of the events for these three years have been run
together into a single entry. For Rochester, London, Elmham,
Selsey, Sherborne, Hereford and Worcester, it appears to be the
case that all changes in the episcopal succession which are known
to have occurred in the period 732–45 are recorded, though not in
any detail. With the exception of the death of Hathuberht, bishop
of London, in 801, there is no reference to the succession at any of
these seven dioceses after 745. It seems as if the necessary information had ceased reaching the north after this date.

The information about the midland sees is fuller, but not complete. Two bishops of Leicester are named, Totta (for Torhthelm,
737, 764) and Eadberht (764), but there is no reference to Eadberht's
death. The succession is complete for Lindsey as far as the death of
Ceolwulf in 796, but the Lichfield succession does not go beyond

---

[1] He found it as an alternative reading in the fourteenth-century Oxford MS.
Bodleian 712. See Plummer, *Bede*, I, cxiv.

the appointment of Cuthfrith in 765. In the four Northumbrian sees the succession is complete for York and Hexham. Four of the eight entries concerning the York succession relate the events in question to the day of the month, and six of the thirteen entries referring to the Hexham bishops do likewise. The record is complete for Whithorn save for the lack of any reference to the death of Pectwine in 735 and the appointment of his successor Frithuwald, but one event in the succession, the death of Pectwine (776) is related to the day of the month. The Lindisfarne succession is complete only as far as the resignation (780) and death (783) of Cynewulf. The record of the appointment of Hygebald (781) is a marginal addition not in the text hand. No event in the Lindisfarne succession is dated to the day of the month. In addition to the bishops in England, there is record of a succession of three English bishops at the see of Mayo in Ireland (768, 773, 786). This succession does not seem to be recorded in any other chronicle of English origin.

Several entries refer to ecclesiastics other than bishops. Five abbots are named in association with particular monasteries—Wulfhæth of Beverley (773), Botwine (786), Alberht (786) and Sigred (787), all of Ripon, and Edwine of Gainford (801). There is also record of the deaths of five abbots whose monasteries are not named—Herebald (745), Frehelm (764), Sibald (771), Swithulf (772) and Ebbi (775). Abbot Osbald who died in 799 is said to have been buried in the church of York. In addition the death is noticed of two anchorites, Balthere (756) and Etha (767), and of two men who are styled *lector*, Egric (771) and Colchu (794).

(d) *Regnal succession*

Except in the case of Northumbria, the amount of information given about regnal succession is much less than that given about episcopal succession. The complex history of the Northumbrian dynasty is traced in close detail, but for the rest of the country this kind of information is no more than incidental. There are two references to regnal succession in East Anglia (737, 749), two to Wessex (739, 786), one to Mercia (796) and two to the Pictish kings (761, 775).

(e) *Information about continental affairs*

Pauli was the first to realise to the full the importance of the series of entries in this part of the *Historia Regum* relating to continental affairs.[1] The entries number twelve in all, beginning with the death of Boniface in 754 and ending with the coronation of Charlemagne in Rome in 800, and in respect both of their content and of their chronology they are of high value. Continental sources differ between 754 and 755 for the date of the martyrdom of Boniface, but Levison pronounced in favour of Tangl's view that 754, the date given by the *Historia Regum*, is the correct one.[2] The second of this series of entries records the consecration of Aluberht in York as bishop of the Old Saxons (767). The next five relate to Frankish affairs. They record the death of Pepin (768), the death of Carloman and the accession of his brother Charlemagne to the whole kingdom of which he had previously held only half (771), Charlemagne's first expedition against the Saxons (772), the destruction of the Lombard kingdom through Charlemagne's capture of Pavia and the Lombard king Desiderius (774), and Charlemagne's campaign against the Saxons in which he captured the Eresburg and the Sigiburg and recovered *prouincia Bohweri* (775). The remaining five entries in the series concern the Adoptionist controversy (792), the death of Pope Adrian (794, the correct date being 25 December 795), Charlemagne's victory over the Avars (795), the maltreatment of Pope Leo III (799) and finally the visit of Charlemagne to Rome in 800.

As Pauli showed there is only one demonstrable error in the chronology of these entries, namely the placing of Adrian's death in 794 instead of 795, and this could well have arisen through different usages for the beginning of the year. The entries themselves are in some instances (notably 775, 795, 800) remarkably detailed and informative, and they are certainly to be regarded as primary sources of information, not merely as derivatives of continental annals. The light which Levison was able to throw on the very close relations which existed between England and the continent in the eighth century makes it appear less a matter of surprise now than it did to Pauli some ninety years ago that a Northumbrian chronicle should contain information of this kind. Northumbrian churchmen played a dominant part in the English mission to the continent in the eighth century and these

[1] R. Pauli, 'Karl der Grosse in northumbrischen Annalen', *Forschungen zur Deutschen Geschichte*, Zwölfter Band (1872), pp. 139–66.
[2] W. Levison, *England and the Continent in the Eighth Century* (1946), p. 90 n. 2.

OBSERVATIONS ON THE 'HISTORIA REGUM'

continental entries are a reflection of the close interest which the Northumbrian church would take in the progress of continental affairs.[1]

(f) *Chronology*

There are thirty-four events in these annals whose dates are recorded to the day of the month on which they occurred. Two of these thirty-four refer to continental happenings, the death of a pope (794) and the visit of Charlemagne to Rome (800). A third refers to the death of Tatwine, archbishop of Canterbury (734). The remaining thirty-one refer to episodes in Northumbrian history. The proportion of these events is markedly higher in the later stages of the chronicle than in the earlier. In the period 732–58 there are entries for twenty of the years concerned, but only seven events are dated to the day of the month. In the period 792–801 there are entries for each of the ten years concerned and fourteen events are dated to the day of the month, as many as five of them in the year 796 alone.

There are twelve entries which themselves yield evidence enabling some check to be made of their chronological accuracy:

(1) 732—*die x kl septembris v feria* (Thursday, 23 August). In 732, 23 August fell on a Saturday, but since 732 was a leap year, 23 August fell on a Thursday in 731. There is therefore an error here, but it does not consist in the faulty correlation of the date of the month with the day of the week. The fault is in the misplacing of all the events recorded in this annal under 732 instead of 731. There are four such events and since the other three of them can all be shown on independent evidence to have occurred in 731, it is reasonable to suppose that the fourth (that is the event assigned to Thursday, 23 August) likewise belongs to 731.

(2) 733, an eclipse of the sun *xix kl septembris circa horam diei terciam* (14 August). This eclipse is correctly dated.[2]

(3) 734, an eclipse of the moon *ii kl februarii circa galli cantum* (31 January about cockcrow). This is correct as to the year and the hour, but the day of the month is one week late. The eclipse was on

---

[1] W. Stubbs, *Roger of Howden*, I, xxix n. 2 thought that Alcuin might have been concerned in the transmission of information, but there are likely to have been many others in a position to secure and transmit to Northumbria information of the kind recorded in these entries.

[2] J. Fr. Schroeter, *Spezieller Kanon der zentralen Sonnen- und Mondfinsternisse* (Kristiania, 1923), p. 85.

OBSERVATIONS ON THE 'HISTORIA REGUM'

24 January and the period of totality was 02.24 to 04.02.[1] If for *ii kl* the reading were *ix kl*, an easy corruption, the date would be correct in all respects.

(4) 734, the ordination of Frithuberht to the bishopric of Hexham *die vi idus septembris* (8 September). This date marks the feast of the Nativity of the Virgin Mary and is therefore a likely one for the ceremony in question.

(5) 740—*die x kl Jan feria vii* (Saturday, 23 December). In 740, 23 December was a Friday. If the year was reckoned to begin in September, 740 corresponds with 739 when 23 December was a Wednesday. Perhaps *feria vii* is a corruption of *feria iiii*.

(6) 741—*ix kl mai. feria i* (Sunday, 23 April). In 741, 23 April was in fact a Sunday.

(7) 752—*pridie kl augusti* (31 July), an eclipse of the moon. This is correctly dated.[2]

(8) 756—*viii kl decembris* (24 November), an eclipse of the moon. This entry is of particular interest because of the period of the year at which the eclipse took place. There was only one total eclipse of the moon in 756 and it occurred on 18 May, but there was a total eclipse on 23 November in 755. The eclipse began at 16.53 and ended at 20.31.[3] If the writer reckoned the day to begin at sunset of the previous evening, he was correct in dating the eclipse to 24 November, and if, moreover, he reckoned his year to begin in September, he was equally correct in calling the year 756.

(9) Under 759, but referring to 761—*bellum v iii id augusti in quo cecidit oswine post triduum prima feria* (6 August). In 761, 6 August fell on a Thursday and the statement that Oswine was killed on a Sunday after three days accords with the day of the month on which the battle is said to have begun.

(10) 796—*v kl aprilis...inter gallicinium et auroram* (28 March between cockcrow and dawn), an eclipse of the moon. This is correct as to year, day and hour. The period of totality was 05.40 to 06.18.[4]

(11) 796—*x v iii k septembris die dominica* (Sunday, 15 August), the election of Eanbald as archbishop of York. In 796, 15 August was a Monday, but it was a Saturday in 795. It is possible that a minim has been lost and that for *xviii* we should read *xviiii* which would yield Sunday, 14 August.

[1] J. F. Schroeter, *op. cit.* p. 182.
[2] *Ibid.* p. 184.
[3] *Ibid.* p. 184.
[4] *Ibid.* p. 188.

(12) 797—*vi id septembris* (8 September), the confirmation of Eanbald as archbishop of York. In 797, 8 September was a Friday, but it was also the feast of the Nativity of the Virgin Mary.

Of these twelve items the entries relating to the five eclipses are the most valuable for the evidence they provide of chronological accuracy. Three of the five are correctly dated in all respects (733, 752, 796), a fourth is correct if it is assumed that the year was held to begin in September and the fifth is correct as to year and month, but one week out as to the day of the month. When it is recalled that all these eclipses occurred in the eighth century, that the manuscript as we have it is of the late twelfth century, that the entries concerned must have been copied many times and that numerals are very liable to become corrupted in the course of copying, the impression must be that the degree of chronological accuracy achieved is remarkably high. The remaining items are less conclusive, but they tend only to confirm the impression of accuracy. The evidence relating to the eclipse of 756 suggests that the annalist reckoned the beginning of his year from September, and this will account for discrepancies between the *Historia Regum* and texts D and E of the *Anglo-Saxon Chronicle* in the dates of certain events which occurred between the beginning of September and the end of December. The death of Pectwine on 19 September is placed in 777 by the *Historia Regum*, but in 776 by D and E—similarly with the burning of Bearn on 24 December, placed in 780 by the *Historia Regum* and in 779 by D and E, and with the death of Alchmund on 7 September, placed in 781 by the *Historia Regum* and in 780 by D and E. It seems safe to suppose that in other instances, where D and E date events one year earlier than the *Historia Regum*, the discrepancy is likewise due to the use by the two sources of different starting-points for the year.

(g) *Points of style*

Comment has been made on the inflated phraseology which is characteristic of the style used in the writing of the Kentish *Passio*, the list of early Northumbrian kings and the list of the early archbishops of Canterbury. In one particular respect this feature is also characteristic of the annals which run from 732 to 802. These entries refer more than eighty times to the death of individuals and in doing so they make use of some fifty different expressions. The short conventional expressions on the one hand—*obiit, interiit,*

OBSERVATIONS ON THE 'HISTORIA REGUM'

defunctus est, mortuus est, interemptus est, interfectus est—contrast
with a wide variety of bombastic circumlocutions on the other,
such as *uectigal morti egrediens et pergens ad eum qui mortuus uitam
perpetuam concedit* (775), *ergastulum huius laboriosæ uitæ deseruit
mercedem iubelei anni percipiendo* (786), *ex rapidis flatibus huius
sæculi spiritum emisit ad superos eternæ felicitatis iubilos* (787).
Although some of the shorter, conventional expressions are used
several times in these annals, there is no instance of any of the
elaborate circumlocutions, of which there are some twenty-five in
all, being used more than once. Moreover, there is only one
instance in which one and the same term for death is used twice in
the same annal, and in this particular year (796) the writer had
occasion to refer to death six times. It is evident that a determined
attempt has been made to achieve literary effect and to depart from
the monotony of an annalistic chronicle recording isolated events.
This peculiarity is by no means confined to the later years of the
chronicle but is characteristic of the whole series of annals from
732 to 802.

Another feature of the style of these annals is the use of three
verbs placed in immediate succession to one another. There are
eight examples of this trick distributed more or less evenly through
the annals—*captus, attonsus et remissus est* (732), *tenuit, amisit,
perdidit* (758), *occiditur, sepelitur, obliuiscitur* (775), *uallatus, comfor-
tatus, glorificatus* (775), *subrogatur, consecratur eleuaturque* (781),
quassauit, perdidit, contriuit (794), *adorat, ditat, exornat* (800), *con-
seruaret, regeret ac defenderet* (800). In the previous section of the
Historia Regum there is found *fundauit, perfecit, rexit* in a passage
quoted from Bede's *Historia Abbatum*[1] and *dat, tollit minuitque*
occurs in the eleventh line of the poem on times and seasons.[2] Two
other instances which occur in section 5 will be noticed below.[3]
Alcuin used the device in his poem *de sanctis Eboracis*.[4]

Pauli commented on the lavish use of superlatives in the annals
relating to continental events. Carloman is called *famosissimus*, and
Charlemagne *rex inuictissimus, bellicosissimus, fortissimus, benignissi-
mus* and *armipotens imperator*. A number of other phrases recall the
same inflated phrasing which characterises not only the other annals

[1] T. Arnold, *Symeon*, II, 21.   [2] *Ibid.* II, 23.
[3] See below, p. 103.
[4] Line 1450—*docuit, nutriuit, amauit*, but the words seem to be borrowed from
an earlier source, see W. Levison, *England and the Continent in the Eighth Century*,
p. 150 n. 6.

in the period 731–802, but also the earlier parts of the *Historia Regum*, such as *manu ualida* (772, 795), *inedicibilia* (775, 788), *bellicosis suae maiestatis uiris* (772), *bellica uirtute et regali maiestate* (800).

(*h*) *Place of origin*

There is no direct internal evidence to show where these annals were written. The strong ecclesiastical interest is no more than might be expected in a chronicle of this period, but perhaps the detailed information given about the successive Northumbrian kings may be held to suggest a source in close touch with the main centre of government. There are two entries which seem to give a hint of the geographical viewpoint of their author, those which refer respectively to the expulsion of Alhred in 774 and of Osbald in 796. Alhred, after what seems to have been a formal deposition from the throne, is said to have departed with a few companions first to Bamburgh and then to Kenneth, king of the Picts. Osbald, after being deserted, put to flight and expelled from the kingdom, then withdrew, accompanied by a few companions, to Lindisfarne, whence he took ship to the king of the Picts. The account of Osbald's flight is followed immediately by a reference to the enthronement of his successor at the altar of St Paul in St Peter's church at York. In both these instances the words used by the annalist are those of a man who looked upon the two exiled rulers as going away from the place at which he was writing, not coming towards it. There are other entries which refer to Bamburgh and Lindisfarne (750, 793) in some detail, yet a Lindisfarne annalist is not likely to have written in this way of his own immediate neighbourhood. Moreover, as we have seen, the information given about the episcopal succession at Lindisfarne is imperfect. Other places mentioned in these annals that now lie in the county of Northumberland are Corbridge (786), Hexham (788) and Tynemouth (792). *Scythlescester iuxta murum* (788) probably refers to a place in Northumberland (perhaps Chesters), and so also may *Bartun*, modern Barton, and *Wduforda*, modern Woodford (797), but the identity of these two places is not certain. There are references to two places in the county of Durham—Sockburn (796) and Gainford (801)—though both of them lie close to the Tees. It is probable that the *monasterium ad ostium Doni* (794) refers to Jarrow.

In Yorkshire there are references to Catterick (762, 769, 792), Ripon (786, 787, 790), Beverley (773), Crayke (767) and Doncaster

OBSERVATIONS ON THE 'HISTORIA REGUM'

(764). There are many references to York itself—the burning of the minster at York on Sunday, 23 April 741, further damage to York by fire in 764, the location of Crayke as lying ten miles from York (767), the death in York of Eadbert, once king and then cleric, on 20 August 768, the forcible tonsuring of King Osred in York in 790, the abduction of the sons of Ælfwold from the principal church in York in 791, the death in York of Æthelheard, once ealdorman then cleric, on 1 August 794, the death in York of Alric, once ealdorman then cleric, shortly before 28 March 796, the coronation of Eardwulf at the altar of St Paul in the church of St Peter at York on 26 May 796, and the burial of Archbishop Eanbald in the same church in the same year, and finally the burial of Osbald, successively *dux, patricius, rex* and *abbas*, in the church at York in 799.

These entries, and particularly the detail into which some of them enter, make it seem very probable that the annals in which they occur were compiled if not in York itself, at least in some monastery not very far away from York. On the other hand, it might be argued that a predominance of entries referring to York is no more than should be expected since York was both the civil and ecclesiastical capital of the kingdom of Northumbria at this date. Moreover, there are a number of unidentified place-names whose identification might well alter the picture. These names are: *methil wongtune* (758),[1] *winchanheale* (765, cf. *pincahala* at 787 where, as at 765, the place-name is in an oblique case preceded by the preposition *in*, and *pincanhalth* 798);[2] *seletune* (780, the form being governed by the preposition *in*); *wlfeswelle* (781); *scythlescester iuxta murum* (788, presumably in Northumberland and near the Roman Wall); *hearrahalch* (790); *wonwaldremere* (791, governed by *in*); *aynburg* (792); *ætlæte* (796);[3] *cettingaham* (800).

(5) *A Chronicle from 849 to 887*

Regarded chronologically the entry for 802 belongs to the previous section of the *Historia Regum* (the chronicle from 732 to 802), since there is a gap of nearly half a century before the next entry, which is for the year 849. In content, however, the entry for 802 marks a

---

[1] Both Hodgson Hinde and Arnold misread *methil* as *mechil*.
[2] The confusion between the initial *w* and *p* is the common confusion between *p* and O.E. *wynn*. The old identification with Finchale is not now accepted. Arnold's reading *Wincanheale* is mistaken.
[3] Hodgson Hinde's reading *Etclete* is undoubtedly mistaken.

sharp break with the preceding annals. The Northumbrian interest ceases abruptly with the entry for 801 and is replaced in 802 by an exclusively West Saxon interest—the death of Brihtric, king of Wessex, and the succession of Egbert, the story of Eadburga, Brihtric's wife, her treatment at the hands of Charlemagne and her death in Pavia. Much of the story of Eadburga is identical with the version of the story told by Asser in his *Life of Alfred*.[1]

The entries from 849 to 887 are normally introduced with the formula *anno dominicæ incarnationis...nativitatis autem Elfredi...* in place of the simple *anno* of the previous section. There are no entries for the years 850, 856–9, 861–3, 865, 878 and 885. Both in the introductory formula and in the years for which there are no entries the *Historia Regum* corresponds with the annals which formed the framework of Asser's *Life of Alfred*, save in one or two minor details. The *Historia Regum* places under 852 information which Asser has under 851, and under 877 information which Asser has under 878. Under 854, a year for which Asser has no entry, the *Historia Regum* records that Archbishop Wulfhere (of York) received the pallium and that Eardwulf became bishop of Lindisfarne.

The relationship of this part of the *Historia Regum* to Asser presents an extremely difficult, and in the end perhaps insoluble, problem because of the now complete lack of manuscript authority for Asser's work. There is record of only one manuscript, the Cottonian MS. Otho A XII, thought to have been of about the year 1000, and it was burnt in the fire of 1731. Stevenson thought that this very manuscript was itself the source for this section of the *Historia Regum*, basing his belief on the existence of some half-dozen errors which were common to Otho A XII and the *Historia Regum*,[2] but he was well aware of the difficulties of reaching a sure conclusion because of the omission from the *Historia Regum* of whole chapters of Asser and the paraphrasing of others. Yet there are some points which suggest that Stevenson may have been mistaken.

There are six passages involving place-names where the *Historia Regum* differs from the presumed readings of Otho A XII. In chap. 49 Asser refers to Exeter *qui dicitur Saxonice Exanceastre, Britannice autem Cairuuisc, Latine quoque civitas in orientali ripa fluminis Uuisc sita est.* Plainly there has been an omission after *civitas* and

---

[1] W. H. Stevenson, *Asser's Life of King Alfred* (Oxford, 1904), chaps. 14–15.
[2] *Ibid.* xlviii–xlix.

OBSERVATIONS ON THE 'HISTORIA REGUM'

Florence of Worcester,[1] here drawing upon Asser, supplies *Exae* after *civitas*, but the *Historia Regum* reads *ciuitas aquarum* (*s.a.* 876). But *aquarum* is added, suggesting that there was indeed a word missing in the exemplar. In chap. 55 Asser describes the whereabouts of Ecgberht's Stone as being in the eastern part of the forest *qui dicitur Seluudu, Latine autem sylva magna, Britannice Coit Maur*. The *Historia Regum* (*s.a.* 877) here reads *qui anglice eloquio dicitur Mucelpudu, Latine uero magna silua, Britannice more Coitmapur*. Arnold here read *mucel purlu*, but there is no doubt that the manuscript reading is *mucel pudu*, nor is there any doubt that it should be amended to *mucel wudu*, the O.E. *wynn* having been confused, as it so often was, with the Roman *p*. The same confusion has given rise to the reading *mapur* for *mawur*. The use of *Mucel Wudu*, the Great Forest, in place of Asser's *Seluudu*, Selwood, is very striking. The wood is twice called by some form of the name Selwood in the *Anglo-Saxon Chronicle* (878, 894), and once it is called simply The Forest (*wudu*, 709). The *Historia Regum* here seems to have preserved a local south-west English usage, a reading for whose presence in a Northumbrian chronicle it is very difficult to account except on the supposition that it was present in the compiler's source.

The other four passages show the presence in the *Historia Regum* of an idiomatic usage which does not occur in the corresponding places in Asser. Where the text of Asser reads *Sandwic* (chap. 6, l. 3), *Cippanhamme* (chap. 9, l. 12), *Rædigam* (chap. 35, l. 5) and *Æscesdun* (chap. 37, l. 3), the *Historia Regum* has *etsandwic* (852), *etcippanhama* (853), *etredingum* (871) and *etscesdun* (871). In each case the *Historia Regum* has preserved the familiar Old English usage of the locative preposition *æt* before a place-name. In Latin works O.E. *æt* or *on* was sometimes translated by Latin *in* or *ad*, as in Bede's *in Gyruum, in Hrypum, ad Gefrin*. An example of the use of *æt* in the previous section of the *Historia Regum* is found in the unidentified *ætlæte* (796). The *æt*-formula was not used in the lost Otho A XII, and unless we are to imagine a copyist deliberately introducing into his work an outmoded formula which was not present in his source, we can but suppose that it got into the *Historia Regum* from a source which at least was not Otho A XII.

Arguments based on the absence from the *Historia Regum* of passages occurring in Asser are dangerous, yet there are some

[1] Ed. B. Thorpe, I, 93.

101

points of detail which should not be overlooked. Stevenson (p. 155) commented on the use by Asser of the word *paga* with a meaning virtually equivalent to O.E. *scīr*, for example *Summurtunensis pagae comes* (chap. 12), *in paga quae dicitur Lindesig* (chap. 45), *omnes accolae Summurtunensis pagae et Wiltunensis, omnes accolae Hamtunensis pagae* (chap. 55). This term in this sense seems not to occur in Latin annals of English origin except where there is dependence on Asser, and Stevenson thought that its occurrence in Asser might be due to Frankish influence. Apart from the examples quoted above there are other instances of a similar use of the word in chaps. 1, 5, 12, 35, 42 and 53 of Asser's work. Although the word *paga* is used in the corresponding passages in Florence of Worcester where he was drawing upon Asser, and also in the later section of the *Historia Regum* (section 8, see below, pp. 107 ff.) which draws upon Asser, but only indirectly through Florence of Worcester, it is never found in the present section of the *Historia Regum*.

In chap. 1 Asser states that Alfred was born *in villa regia, quae dicitur Uuanating, in illa paga, quae nominatur Berrocscire; quae paga taliter vocatur a Berroc silva, ubi buxus abundantissime nascitur.* The corresponding passage in the *Historia Regum* (*s.a.* 849) reads *in regali villa quae ab Anglis Wanetinge appellatur* with no reference to the location of Wantage in Berkshire or to the etymology of the name Berkshire. In chap. 3 Asser refers to the pagans wintering *in insula, quae vocatur Sceapieg, quod interpretatur 'insula ovium'; quae sita est in Tamesi flumine inter East-Seaxum et Cantuarios, sed ad Cantiam propior est quam ad East-Seaxum.* In the corresponding passage the *Historia Regum* (*s.a.* 851) reads *in insula quae vocatur Scepige, id est insula ovium* without any reference to the geographical position of the island. In chap. 5 Asser has *in Suthrie, quae paga sita est in meridiana Tamesis fluminis ripa ab occidentali parte Cantiae*, but in the corresponding passage the *Historia Regum* (*s.a.* 851) has simply *ad suhtrige* without any reference to its geographical situation. Is the absence of the term *paga* from this section of the *Historia Regum*, as also of the passages of geographical description, simply due to the whim of a copyist or editor, or does it suggest the use of a different source? The evidence is perhaps sufficient to raise doubts about the rightness of Stevenson's view that the lost Cottonian MS. Otho A xii was the source of this section of the *Historia Regum*.

OBSERVATIONS ON THE 'HISTORIA REGUM'

In the whole section there are only three entries which are of particularly Northumbrian interest and which are not dependent in some way upon Asser. These three record the receipt of a pallium by Wulfhere, archbishop of York, and the succession of Eardulf to the bishopric of Lindisfarne (854), the flight of Bishop Eardwulf and Abbot Eadred from Lindisfarne with the body of Cuthbert (875) and the appearance of Cuthbert in a vision to Alfred (877).

Whereas section 4 of the *Historia Regum* is original and almost wholly of Northumbrian interest in its content, section 5 is secondary and almost wholly West Saxon. In this respect the contrast between the two parts of the work could scarcely be sharper, yet there can be little doubt that both sections proceed in their present form from the same editorial hand, as the following points will show:

(i) Again and again where the compiler departs from the literal text of his source, he breaks into that florid, bombastic style of writing which characterises the earlier parts of the work. In particular we find a continuing delight in elaborate expressions for the recording of death. Under 871 the death of Ethelred of Wessex is thus recorded—

...plenus etate et perfectus in bonitate, post perpetrationem insignium bellorum, future vite et perpetui regni felicitatem coepit videre, cum rege seculorum in terra viventium.

Similar language is used of the death of Burgred in 874 and of Pope Marinus in 884.

(ii) Comment has been made above on the frequent use in section 4 of three consecutive verbs. In section 5 may be noted *cepit, occidit, subdiditque* (853) and *turbati sunt, admirati sunt, commoti sunt* (871). There is a somewhat similar usage in the entry for 869—*debacchans et insaniens, occidens et pergens*. None of these occurs in Asser.

(iii) Section 5 contains further instances of attempts to avoid the monotony of the annalistic form by the use of phrasing tending towards the narrative. Thus the entry for 869 opens with the standard—

anno dccclxix, aetatis uero Elfredi xxi...

but for the following year we find—

sequenti uero anno, dum solis jubar mundi perlustraret orbes, et annus aduenisset dccclxx ab incarnatione domini tunc refulsit tempus quo Elfred rex vicesimum primum habuit annum.

OBSERVATIONS ON THE 'HISTORIA REGUM'

All this is sheer bombast. In the entry for 882 is the phrase *quid deinde gestum sit referre libet*... which may be compared with the similar phrase in the entry for 799 (section 4) *quid gestum sit eodem anno, referre libet*. The closing words of the entry for 849 (section 5)—

His sic praelibatis jam pro posse susceptum exequamur negotium suscepti operis...

may be compared with the phrase which links section 1 (the Kentish Legends) with section 2 (Early Northumbrian Kings)—

In exordio huius operis genealogiam regum Cantuariorum strictim praelibavimus, etc.

(iv) There are certain verbal parallelisms between sections 4 and 5. Compare the following from 871 (section 5)—

Sciebant pro certo ipsi principes populorum beatas fore res publicas, si eas vel studiosi sapientie regerent, vel si earum rectores studere sapientie contigisset (Boethius, *de Cons. Phil.* I, 4).

with the following from 800 (section 4)—

Intellexit beatas fore res publicas, si eas vel studiosi sapientie regerent, vel si earum rectores studere sapientie contigisset.

Compare also *Romuleas adire sedes coepit* from 855 (section 5) with *Romuleae urbis moenia ingreditur* from 800 (section 4). The word *inedicibilis* seems to have been a particular favourite of the compiler. In section 4 may be noted *inedicibilibus* (775), *inedicibilia* (788), *inedicibilem* (793), *inedicibiliter* (798) and in section 5 *inedicibilis* (853) and *inedicibilia* (877). *Inedicibilia* also occurs in section 1.[1]

(v) Quotations from Boethius have been noted in sections 2 and 4. Boethius is also quoted in section 5 under 868, 871 and 887. The formula *anno dominicae incarnationis* was used by Asser only as far as 887 (chap. 84), the remainder of his work (chaps. 85–106) being written wholly in narrative form. The *Historia Regum* follows the same arrangement. Although the compiler abbreviates or paraphrases his source considerably, his dependence upon Asser is here much greater than Arnold's text of the *Historia Regum* suggests.[2]

(6) *A Chronicle from 888 to 957*

Excluding the marginal entry misplaced under 891, there are entries for 33 of the 70 years covered by this section of the *Historia*

---

[1] Arnold's *Symeon*, II, 13, line 8.
[2] All the material in large type on pp. 89–91 of Arnold's edition as far as the entry for 888 is dependent on Asser, chaps. 91–2, 98–101, much of it verbatim.

OBSERVATIONS ON THE 'HISTORIA REGUM'

Regum. The span of time is much the same as that covered by the annals of section 4 (732–801), but whereas those occupy more than 35 pages in Arnold's edition (of which the Acca and Alchmund interpolations account for about 9), this series occupies a little less than 4 pages. In matters of content, accuracy, outlook and style the annals for 888–957 are in striking contrast with the earlier series. The ecclesiastical interest is very slight, with only two references to the archiepiscopal succession at York (892, 900) and two to the bishops of St Cuthbert's see (899, 925), but perhaps this is largely a reflection of the state of the church in Northumbria at this time. The detailed interest shown by the earlier annals in matters purely Northumbrian is replaced by an interest which, although still recognisably Northumbrian, is much more national in outlook, again perhaps reflecting changed conditions.

The succession of the kings of England is fully recorded from the death of Alfred to the accession of Edgar, and a considerable number of the entries are concerned solely with their activities. Although there are some annals of primarily southern interest (888, 890, 894), a strong northern interest is reflected in a series of entries relating to the Norse kings who ruled at York during the first half of the tenth century, as also in the accounts of Athelstan's invasion of Scotland in 934, of the battle at *Wendun* (*Brunanburh*) in 937, and of several other items in the history of northern England and southern Scotland. Much of this material is valuable, yet the annals as a whole seem to have suffered in point of accuracy from careless compilers or careless copyists. The death of Edward the Elder is dated 923 instead of 924 and that of Edmund 948 instead of 946. Eadwig is wrongly called *Eadwinus* twice (955, 957) and his death is wrongly dated. Guthrum is mistakenly called *rex Northanhymbrorum* (890), the mistake evidently arising from a mis-translation of the O.E. *se norþerna cyning* which is found in all texts of the *Anglo-Saxon Chronicle* (890). The entry recording that Athelstan ordered his brother Edwin to be drowned in the sea (933) is in sharp conflict with what is recorded of Edwin's death in the *Gesta abbatum S. Bertini*,[1] and the end of the Northumbrian monarchy appears to be dated two years too early to 952 instead of 954. There are no references to any eclipses nor are there any events dated to the day of the month.

The individual entries are written with an economy of words

[1] D. Whitelock, *English Historical Documents*, c. 500–1042, p. 318.

and a simplicity of style which provides a striking contrast with the preceding parts of the *Historia Regum*. Nowhere do they show any trace of those stylistic features which have been found to be characteristic of sections 1–5. Although the northern interest of the annals is strong enough to make a Northumbrian origin seem probable, there is not sufficient detail to allow them to be ascribed to any particular locality within Northumbria. Several of the entries evidently derive from a copy of the *Anglo-Saxon Chronicle* and their general air of impersonality may suggest that they have been culled from a common stock of information parts of which may well have been available in slightly varying form and with slightly varying emphasis at more than one centre where records were being kept. The last entry in the series, that for 957, after recording the death of Edgar, refers to his successors Edward the Martyr, Ethelred the Unready and Edward the Confessor, so that it cannot have taken its present form earlier than the accession of Edward in 1042.

(7) *Extracts from William of Malmesbury*

Thus far the *Historia Regum*, though composed of materials varying in kind and in historical value, has maintained a more or less regular chronological sequence from the times of the earliest Northumbrian kings as far as the middle of the tenth century, but after the entry for 957 there comes a change more abrupt than any that has been previously noted. The reader is first prepared for a recapitulation of what has already been said of King Alfred by the following sentence on fo. 76r, col. 1:

Sequitur recapitulatio superiorum de rege elfredo. Deinde successio regum per ordinem, qui et qualiter ad regnum peruenerunt anglorum.

But no such *recapitulatio* follows. Instead there is a rubric:

De historia Willelmi Malmesbirie.

The remainder of fo. 76r and the greater part of fo. 76v contain extracts from the *Gesta Regum* of William of Malmesbury relating to portents seen by Edgar and their interpretation by his mother, to a prophetic vision of the happiness of Edward the Confessor's reign, to the portent of female twins which some interpreted as signifying the union of England and Normandy, and finally to a vision seen by Edward the Confessor on his deathbed of the forthcoming conquest of England. The insertion at this point of the *Historia*

Regum of these seemingly irrelevant extracts from William of Malmesbury may perhaps have been suggested by the references to Edgar and Edward the Confessor in the annal for 957, and certainly they would have seemed less out of place had they preceded rather than followed the sentence *sequitur recapitulatio*, etc. It will be recalled that items 17–20 of the Corpus Christi book consist of extracts from the same work.

(8) *A Chronicle from 848 to 1118*

The last entry in section 6 is for the year 957, but the first entry for section 8 is for the year 848, so that there are two parallel accounts for the period between these two dates. The sentence *sequitur recapitulatio* was evidently intended as an explanatory comment on the interruption of the normal chronological sequence at this point, but it has been moved from its appropriate place by the insertion of the extracts from William of Malmesbury. Almost the whole of this section of the *Historia Regum* from 848 to 1119 is derived from Florence of Worcester and is therefore of only slight value as a primary source. The only available edition of Florence of Worcester's *Chronicon* is wholly inadequate as a basis upon which to examine the exact relationship of this section of the *Historia Regum* to its principal source, yet something can be done towards determining the relationship of the two overlapping sections of the *Historia Regum* not only towards one another, but also towards Asser on the one hand and Florence of Worcester on the other.

Florence himself made extensive use of Asser, but, as Stevenson pointed out,[1] he took great liberties with the text, transposing large sections of it to suit the convenience of his own plan. If we compare the text of the *Historia Regum* with the text of Florence of Worcester at points where Florence's text is itself dependent upon Asser, we find that in this section the *Historia Regum* invariably follows Florence in his rearrangement of Asser. Two examples will suffice to demonstrate the point. After copying under the year 871 Asser's account of Alfred's family and of his patronage of the arts, drawn from Asser, chaps. 75–6, Florence turned back to Asser, chap. 42 in order to extract from it Asser's account of the battle of Wilton. At the corresponding passage in the *Historia Regum* Florence's rearrangement of Asser is followed precisely although

[1] W. H. Stevenson, *Asser's Life of King Alfred*, pp. lvi–lvii.

OBSERVATIONS ON THE 'HISTORIA REGUM'

the whole is compressed into a much shorter space. In 872 Florence recorded the consecration of Wærferth, bishop of Worcester, and he followed this item, which he had derived from some source other than Asser, by quoting the greater part of Asser, chaps. 77–8. He then turned back to Asser, chaps. 45–6, from which he derived his material for the next two years. The same arrangement is found in the corresponding passage in the *Historia Regum*, though again with considerable abbreviation. The opening lines of the *Historia Regum* entry for 872 derive from Florence where he is not dependent upon Asser and are immediately followed by Florence's quotation from Asser, chap. 77. There can thus be no doubt that the borrowing into the *Historia Regum* has been made indirectly through Florence and not directly from Asser himself.

There are many other passages in which the *Historia Regum* can be shown to follow Florence in his rearrangements of Asser's text.

There are also numerous passages in this section of the *Historia Regum* which follow Florence in minor verbal alterations of Asser's text. Three examples will suffice:

(i) Asser, chap. 11—filium suum Aelfredum iterum....
     Flor. and *HR*, 855.—filiumque suum Aelfredum, quem plus ceteris dilexit, iterum....
(ii) Asser, chap. 30—et Aelfred fratrem dirigunt....
     Flor. and *HR*, 868.—et ad fratrem eius Aelfredum dirigunt....
(iii) Asser, chap. 35—in loco qui dicitur Englafeld obviavit....
     Flor. and *HR*, 871.—in loco qui Anglice Englafeld, Latine Anglorum campus, dicitur obviavit....

Many other instances could be quoted.

On the other hand there are certain passages in this section of the *Historia Regum* which contain material found in Asser, but not in Florence. It may have been these passages which suggested to Stubbs, in the introduction to his edition of Roger of Howden,[1] that this part of the *Historia Regum* showed signs that its compiler had made independent use of Asser. The entry for 848 consists mainly of the genealogy of Alfred which is found in Asser, chap. 1, and there are several details in which it follows Florence in slight modifications of Asser's text, thereby showing derivation from Asser through Florence. But Asser's text contains a ten-line quotation from the *Carmen Paschale* of Sedulius. These lines do not occur in Florence's version of the genealogy, yet the first three of the ten do

---

[1] *Chronica Rogeri de Hoveden*, ed. W. S. Stubbs, Rolls Series, I, xxx.

occur in the version given by the *Historia Regum*. It might be assumed that the *Historia Regum* had here been making direct use of Asser, but for the fact that the same three lines also occur under the year 848 in section 5 of the *Historia Regum*, that is to say in the first of the two parallel sets of entries. The quotation from Sedulius is evidence that section 8 of the *Historia Regum* (the chronicle from 848 to 1119) has been influenced by section 5 (the chronicle from 849 to 887), not that section 8 has made direct use of Asser. Another example of the same process is found in the entry in the *Historia Regum* for 866 (section 8). The first part of the entry for this year is derived through Florence from Asser, chap. 21, but the remainder consists of an account of Alfred's childhood, including the famous story of the book of poetry which he learnt by heart. This account is not given by Florence, but the whole passage is found verbatim under 866 in section 5 of the *Historia Regum*. There can be no doubt that the passage in section 8 of the *Historia Regum* is derived from the corresponding passage in section 5, because the story as told in section 5 is in some parts verbally identical with Asser and in some parts not, but the story as told in section 8 is verbally identical throughout with the version in section 5. The relationship of the *Historia Regum* towards Asser may be summarised thus:

(i) Section 5 of the *Historia Regum* (849–87) appears to be derived direct from a text of Asser.

(ii) Section 8 of the *Historia Regum* (848–1119) draws upon Asser indirectly through Florence of Worcester.

(iii) There is some material in section 8 of the *Historia Regum* which is found in Asser, but not in Florence, but wherever this occurs the same material is found in section 5 of the *Historia Regum* whence it has been borrowed into section 8.

Setting aside all that is derived from Florence of Worcester there remain within the period 848–1069 some twenty-five entries which relate to northern affairs and a very small number (898, 906, 941, 994) which refer to Rollo and Richard of Normandy. About ten of these twenty-five northern entries refer to the activities of English and Norse rulers in Northumbria, a few of them being duplicates of entries under the corresponding years in sections 5 and 6, and the remainder are of ecclesiastical interest. Among these last there are four entries relating to the archiepiscopal succession at York, but three of them (854, 892, 900) correspond with entries in section 6.

The remaining one (873) refers to the restoration of Wulfhere to his archbishopric from which he had previously fled before the Danes. After 900 and as far as 1060 changes in the York succession are only recorded in so far as they are also recorded by Florence of Worcester from whom they were derived. In other words there is no hint of any local interest emanating from York itself. The remaining ecclesiastical entries all relate to St Cuthbert's see whether at Lindisfarne, Chester-le-Street or Durham. Some of the entries relating to St Cuthbert's bishops in section 8 correspond with similar, though not identical, entries in sections 5 and 6, but at two places the material in section 8 is markedly different from that found in section 5. Both record the appointment of Eardwulf to Lindisfarne in 854, but section 8 adds a detailed list of the possessions of the see of St Cuthbert. Again both sections record the establishment of St Cuthbert's see at Chester-le-Street in 883, but section 8 adds details about rights of sanctuary at St Cuthbert's shrine and about the gift to his see of all lands between Tyne and Tees.

Whereas information about the succession at York for most of the tenth and eleventh centuries is derived second-hand from Florence, the succession of Durham bishops is not always, or even normally, dependent on Florence, but has been derived from an independent, presumably Durham, source, as may be seen from the entries relating to Aldred in 968, Aldhun in 1018, Eadmund in 1020 and 1042, Edred in 1042 and Egelric in 1043. In the light of this evidence there can be no doubt that these northern interpolations were the work of a Durham writer, and that therefore section 8 as a whole can be confidently regarded as a Durham work without taking into account the authenticity of the rubrics ascribing the *Historia Regum* to Symeon himself.

Although Florence of Worcester continues to be the principal source for this part of the *Historia Regum*, the entries for the later part of the eleventh century contain an increasing amount of original matter relating to northern affairs, the change being marked by the long and detailed entries for 1069 and 1070. Three of these original northern entries contain passages yielding evidence which bears upon the construction of this section of the *Historia Regum*.

Under 1074 an account of the restoration of monastic life to Northumbria includes references to Clement and Richard as being the present abbots of York and Whitby respectively. These passages, as we have seen, are likely to have taken their existing form between 1161 and 1175, most probably in 1164, the year in which, it has been argued, the rubrics were compiled.[1] Under 1072 there is an account of the successive earls of Northumbria from the time of Eric, the last of the Northumbrian kings, until the time of Henry I who is described as holding the earldom *hodie*. This passage we have seen to be appropriate to a work which ended in 1129.[2] Thirdly, under the year 1070 in the midst of an account of Malcolm Canmore's invasion of England there is a reference to Gospatric *qui ut supradictum est* purchased the earldom of Northumbria from William I. The words *ut supradictum est* are inappropriate at this point because at no previous place in the *Historia Regum* has there been any reference to his purchase of the earldom. There is, however, a reference to this transaction in the list of Northumbrian earls in the entry for 1072. The reasonable inference, made by Arnold, is that some part of the text has been shifted and that at some stage the list of earls now placed under 1072 formerly held a place before 1070. Arnold suggested 952 as being a likely place because the list would then follow appropriately on the statement under that year that henceforth the province of Northumbria was administered by earls, and partly because the list is in fact found under 952 in Roger of Howden's *Chronica*.[3]

(9) *A Chronicle from 1119 to 1129*

This part of the *Historia Regum* is, with the exception of a small number of passages derived from Eadmer, an original authority of high value. It is certainly of northern origin, but, apart from the rubrics ascribing the whole of the *Historia Regum* to Symeon, there is no evidence to show who wrote it.

The *Historia Regum* ends with the entry for 1129 on fo. 129v. There follows the *explicit* and then the next item—John of Hexham's *Continuation* for the years 1130–53.

It is the last two of the nine sections into which the *Historia Regum* has been analysed that present the least difficulty, the chronicle from 849 to 1119 and the chronicle from 1119 to 1129. These two combine to form a history of England from the

[1] See above, p. 78.   [2] See above, p. 78.
[3] See Arnold's *Symeon*, II, 196–7 note. I do not agree with Arnold in thinking that the 'blundering interpolator', as he calls the person supposedly responsible for misplacing the list of earls, was the Hexham writer, since I do not believe that Arnold's Hexham writer ever existed.

birth of Alfred until shortly before the death of Henry I, the distinction between the two being that, whereas the first and much the greater part is almost wholly derived from Florence of Worcester, the second is all but wholly original. The additions made to the text of Florence in the first part are primarily concerned with the bishops and lands of St Cuthbert, and the annals from 1119 to 1129 reflect a predominantly northern interest. Judged solely upon internal evidence, there can scarcely be any doubt that the combined sections 8 and 9 running from 848 to 1129 are a twelfth-century Durham compilation. Symeon of Durham is known to have been alive in 1104 and also in 1126, and there is a presumption that the scribe at Sawley who composed the rubrics attributing the entire *Historia Regum* to Symeon had at least some ground for associating the two with one another. There seems to be a fair case for regarding the additional northern material inserted into Florence's work and the writing of the entries for 1119–29 as being the contribution of Symeon himself. It is possible, though not certainly known, that the interruption of the work after the end of the entry for 1129 was due to Symeon's death in or soon after 1130.

If the combined sections 8 and 9, the chronicle from 848 to 1129, can be accepted as being the work, mostly derived but partly original, of Symeon himself, is it then possible to determine whether this work underwent any changes during the thirty-five years between the last entry supposedly written by Symeon and the date which has been argued for the making of the Sawley copy, namely 1164? Since Symeon merely copied Florence until well on into the eleventh century, some may wonder why he did not begin where Florence began, namely at 450, instead of at 848 as the Sawley copy suggests that he began. Perhaps he did, but this problem seems beyond solution. There are three other ways in which it seems probable that Symeon's work was altered after it had left his hands. First is the addition of a name or names to the lists of the abbots of York and Whitby in the entry for 1074 so as to bring them up to date. This alteration, which will have been made between 1161 and 1175, can confidently be attributed to Sawley. Next there is the apparent removal of the list of Northumbrian earls from some part of the work earlier than 1070 to the year 1072 where it now stands. And finally there is the insertion into those parts of the work where Symeon's source, Florence, was itself dependent on Asser, of some passages from Asser which had not been used by Florence, but which were derived from section 5 of the *Historia Regum*. These last two alterations might, like the first, have been made at Sawley, but we cannot be so sure because there is no means of determining the date at which they were made. Moreover, we do not know whether Symeon's work reached Sawley direct from Durham or whether it came in a roundabout way, perhaps from Newminster, the mother house of Sawley, or perhaps from Fountains, the mother house of Newminster.

Symeon's history, if sections 8 and 9 may be so called, is preceded by some extracts from William of Malmesbury. The *Gesta Regum*, from which the extracts are taken, was finished in 1125, so that it would have been chronologically possible for Symeon to have read and used the work. On the other hand it has been seen that four other extracts from the *Gesta Regum* of William of Malmesbury occur in a later part of the Sawley book, forming items 17–20 on fos. 158r–161v. Moreover, it has also been noticed that the Sawley copyist maltreated John of Hexham's *Historia* (item 8) by inserting into its midst four short items (items 9–12) of which two (items 9 and 11) are wholly without relevance to the matter in hand. For these reasons it seems better to regard the extracts from William of Malmesbury which form section 7 as being the work of the Sawley scribe, rather than to look upon them as part of Symeon's *History*, to which they do not belong either chronologically or in respect of their subject-matter.

There remain sections 1–6, a strangely assorted collection of material, some of it northern in its interest, some Kentish and some West Saxon, some of it derived from known sources, some of it not now to be found elsewhere. Superficially these sections are linked chronologically in so far as they are in general sequence, although there are some breaks and interruptions. The chronological links appear to be strongest between section 4 (732–802), section 5 (849–87) and section 6 (888–957), but this chronological bond is partly illusory and there is in fact a sharp and real break of a different kind between sections 5 and 6. Frequent comment has been made on the stylistic peculiarities which characterise the early parts of the *Historia Regum*. Section 6 is wholly free from all these peculiarities, displaying an economy of words which offers the strongest contrast with the verbosity of all that precedes it. It is difficult to believe that the author of the bombastic circumlocutions was also the author of the entries for 901, 902, 914 and 919 which contain respectively four, three, seven and four words each. Two further points about section 6 call for comment, first that it contains several demonstrable errors and second that its entry for 957 did not reach its present form until after the accession of Edward the Confessor. If section 6 had stood wholly in isolation it might well have been judged to be a compilation of the eleventh century or later, preserving some valuable information derived, but not always without error, from one or more lost sources which were probably northern in origin.

Style is perhaps an uncertain touchstone, yet close study of sections 1–5 of the *Historia Regum* can hardly fail to leave a strong conviction that it is the style in which they are written that forms the real bond between them, that, in other words, all these five sections bear the imprint of one and the same writer. This style is characterised by ornate and flowery language which is particularly noticeable in the circumlocutions used for the simple *obiit, defunctus est*, etc. A brief, but characteristic, passage from each of the five sections may help to demonstrate the point:

Section 1—the Kentish Legends:

Unde, regni monarchia sollertissime pro sibi illato posse disposita, vocante sequi enim inter omnia fecerat justi remuneratoris clemencia, carnalibus privatur, et ad ardua ætheris cum sanctis regnaturus sustollitur.[1]

Section 2—the Early Northumbrian Kings:

Is secreta inferni visitans Theoderico imperia deriliquid qui bis binis annis regnum tenens, regnum simul perdidit et vitam.[2]

Section 3—material from Bede:

...celestia regna petiuit ut duo diademata capiti imponeret secundum nominis sui palmam, hoc est Easter et Wine, uerum pascha ipse inclitus percipiendo, quod est uerum epinicion.[3]

Section 4—chronicle from 732 to 802:

...qui in domino deo confisus ad montem virtutum secundum nominis sui palmam transmigrauit victoriosus.[4]

Section 5—chronicle from 849 to 887, from Asser:

His temporibus fideliter glorioseque regimine rexit ecclesiam Christi Plegmundus archiepiscopus, qui venerandus vir sapientie fructibus renidebat, præditus bis binis columpnis, justitiæ, videlicet, prudentiæ, temperantiæ, fortitudinis.[5]

---

[1] Arnold's *Symeon*, II, 4.   [2] *Ibid.* II, 14.
[3] *Ibid.* II, 19. The first three words are Bede's. The rest is added.
[4] *Ibid.* II, 31.   [5] *Ibid.* II, 88.

Comment has been made above on other points which suggest the work of a single editorial hand—the device of using three successive verbs of which there are two instances in section 3, eight in section 4 and two in section 5, the quotations from Boethius which occur in sections 2, 4 and 5, the use of the word *inedicibilis* which has been noted once in section 1, four times in section 4 and twice in section 5, as well as occasional verbal parallelisms between one section and another.

All these points touching the style in which the material has been presented seem to bind sections 1–5 into a unit and at the same time to distinguish them from the remainder of the *Historia Regum*. There are, however, two passages within sections 1–5 which are demonstrably late and which reveal none of the peculiarities shared by the material in which they are embedded, although both are long enough to provide a fair test. The two passages, both of them in section 4, are the Acca and Alchmund interpolations under 740 and 781 respectively. The simple, lucid style in which they are written is in striking contrast to the flowery language of the material within which they are embedded. These interpolations, it has been argued, were written after 1113 and probably before 1155 by someone who was seeking to support Hexham against claims advanced by Symeon on behalf of Durham in his *Historia Dunelmensis Ecclesiae*. There is no reason for supposing that they were written at Hexham and good reason for thinking that they were not written at Durham. Since it is inconceivable that the Acca and Alchmund interpolations, and these alone, could have escaped the stylistic adornments marking the rest of sections 1–5, we may fairly suppose that sections 1–5 already formed a single unit before the Acca and Alchmund interpolations were made. This at least enables it to be said that it was not the Sawley scribe who was responsible for joining these sections together. Those who are familiar with the style of the *Historia Dunelmensis Ecclesiae* will be equally sure that it was not Symeon of Durham. It is indeed impossible to find any parallel to this kind of writing among the northern English historians who were at work in the twelfth century.

Let us look again at the points which have emerged from the analysis of sections 1–5, particularly with regard to their sources. In section 1 (the Kentish Legends) there is no reference to the translation of the relics of the murdered princes in 991 nor any indication of the influence of Goscelin of Canterbury. The place-name

Easterige retains a form no longer current in the eleventh century. In section 2 the list of Northumbrian kings agrees with the eighth-century list in the Moore Manuscript of Bede against the corrupt order found in Florence of Worcester and Northumbrian lists of the twelfth century. In section 3 the readings of the extracts from the *Historia Abbatum* generally agree with the tenth-century H_1 text, but where H_1 has the meaningless *quia bene se ac fructuose ordinatum esse conspexit*, we find *quia bene ac fructuose ordinatam conspexit* which is not found in any other manuscript of the *Historia Abbatum*, but which is convincing enough to suggest that it may well be the original reading. Section 3 also preserves what seems certainly to be the original ending of Bede's *de Die Iudicii* in contrast with those manuscripts of the work which have an ending borrowed from Eugenius of Toledo. In section 4 the annals from 732 to 802 show a remarkable degree of accuracy wherever they can be tested, especially in their chronology. The reading *meditaturum* for *meditandum* in the entry for 764 finds its only known parallel in the eighth-century British Museum MS. Cotton Tiberius C. ii. In section 5, the text of Asser which was used contained what seems to be a local south-west English usage *Mucel Uudu* for Selwood and also used the *æt*-formula in place-names. These several points suggest that, in addition to the stylistic characteristics which sections 1–5 share with one another, there is another feature which they have in common, namely their dependence upon sources of good quality and their use, wherever appropriate tests can be made, of earlier rather than later versions of those sources. Saving the Acca and Alchmund interpolations which are undoubtedly late insertions, there is no point in the whole of these five sections where it is possible to show the use of a source, or of a particular manuscript of a source, of a date later than *c.* 900, the date by which a copy of Asser's *Life of Alfred* could have reached the north.[1]

It will never be possible to unravel completely the different stages which have gone to the making of C.C.C.C. MS. 139. There is good evidence for believing the manuscript to have been written at Sawley in the West Riding of Yorkshire during the second half of the twelfth century, probably *c.* 1165–70, and for regarding it as one of two Sawley books which bear witness to a strong interest in

---

[1] It is implied in chap. 91 of the *Life* that Asser was writing in 893. The work ends in a way which suggests that it was left unfinished.

the past history of Northumbria and more particularly in the see of St Cuthbert. The second of these two books is now divided between U.L.C. MS. Ff. 1. 27 and C.C.C.C. MS. 66. The attribution of item 7 in C.C.C.C. MS. 139, the *Historia Regum*, to Symeon of Durham rests upon two rubrics which were compiled at Sawley probably in 1164 by an author who does not inspire great confidence in his knowledge or accuracy. Analysis of this item suggests that it falls into three divisions. The last division consists of a chronicle from 848 to 1129, being almost wholly derived from Florence of Worcester as far as 1119, but original from 1119 to 1129. This division shows clear evidence of Durham interest and there is a reasonable presumption that it was the work of Symeon of Durham in its original parts. The middle division, a brief chronicle from 888 to 957, may well be an eleventh-century compilation drawn from a variety of sources. Although it is not always accurate, it contains some valuable information about the Norse rulers of York and it is certainly of northern origin even though it cannot be more exactly located. There is ground for thinking that at some stage in its development this division had appended to it a list of the earls of Northumbria as far as the time of Henry I.

The first division is a miscellany whose identifiable sources include a Kentish *Passio*, a Northumbrian regnal list, some of the works of Bede and a copy of Asser's *Life of Alfred*. In addition it contains a valuable series of Northumbrian annals. These very diverse elements are held together by two bonds, first by the use of accurate and seemingly early versions of their identifiable sources, and second by common characteristics in the style of their Latin. Two passages, the Acca and Alchmund interpolations, which disclose a Hexham interest, though not necessarily a Hexham origin, were added to this division in the twelfth century. Saving these two interpolations, the division as a whole does not reveal the use of any sources later than the beginning of the tenth century. Its most important element, the annals from 732 to 802, probably originated near York.

Thus far the unravelling process rests upon reasonably sound evidence, but it is difficult to go further without tending towards inadequately supported conjecture. In particular the date of what has been called here the first division of the *Historia Regum* offers a tantalising problem which may perhaps have to remain without proven solution. To have shown, if indeed it has been shown, that

IX

none of its sources is later than *c.* 900, is not to have proved that the division itself is an early tenth-century compilation. In the end judgement will perhaps rest upon opinions about its latinity and here one looks for parallels neither to the lucidity of Bede's Latin nor to the simple style used by the northern historians of the twelfth and thirteenth centuries. One is reminded rather of a passage in which William of Malmesbury wrote about the characteristics of a certain tenth-century book in which he found a panegyric in praise of Athelstan

in quo scriptor cum difficultate materiae luctabatur, judicium animi sui non valens pro voto proferre. Cujus hic verba compendio subjicerem, nisi quia ultra opinionem in laudibus principis vagatur, eo dicendi genere quod suffultum rex facundiae Romanae Tullius in rhetoricis appellat.[1]

Particularly in the Kentish *Passio*, where the narrative form gave greater scope, there is an echo of some of those outrageous convolutions of verbosity that distinguish the Latin charters of the time of Athelstan.[2]

ADDENDUM

When this article was already in page-proof, I learnt from Mr Richard Vaughan, librarian of Corpus Christi College, Cambridge, that the application by him and Professor C. R. Cheney of ultra-violet light to the first page of Corpus Christi College MS. 139 plainly revealed the former presence of the Sawley *ex libris*, subsequently erased and not now visible to the naked eye.

[1] *Gesta Regum*, Rolls Series, I, 144.
[2] Professor Whitelock kindly read this article in proof and I am indebted to her for a number of helpful comments.

(a)

(b)

(c)

I. (a) the *Historia Regum*, C.C.C.C. MS. 139, fo. 51 v.   (b) and (c) the *Historia Dunelmensis Ecclesiae*, U.L.C. MS. Ff. 1. 27, pp. 123 and 131.

X

THE HISTORICAL WRITINGS OF BEDE

Bede was born c. 671, about 260 years after the end of the Roman occupation of Britain, and about 225 years after what came to be regarded as the year in which the English first came to Britain. He died on 25 May 735, aged about 64. At the end of the *Historia Ecclesiastica Gentis Anglorum* he records that he had spent the whole of his life from the age of seven within the walls of the monastery at Wearmouth and Jarrow. Although the two places were physically separated from one another by a few miles, he regarded them as comprising only one single monastery dedicated to St. Peter and St. Paul. He writes that « amid the observance of monastic discipline and the daily charge of singing in the church, my delight has always been in learning, teaching or writing »[1]. We do not know the exact date of his earliest piece of writing, but it was about or soon after the year 700, and between that date and his death he wrote in all a total of some 60 volumes. When we read his works we must not forget that he was born, passed his whole life and died close to what had once been the uttermost north-western limit of the Roman Empire. He would have agreed with William of Malmesbury who described his birthplace as lying on the furthest shore of an island which some called *alter orbis*, because it was so remote that not many geographers had

(1) *Historia Ecclesiastica*, ed. C. PLUMMER, 1896, V, 24.

discovered its existence [2]. Many years before Bede's birth, Gregory the Great, in a letter to Eulogius, bishop of Alexandria, described the English as a people who lived in a corner of the world and who until recently had put their trust in sticks and stones [3]. Bede was well aware himself of his remoteness from the centres of antiquity and in one of his commentaries he asked his readers not to complain because he had written so much about what he had learnt from ancient authors about trees and herbs. He had not done so out of conceit, but there was no other way for those who lived in a remote island of the Ocean far outside the world to learn about what happened in Arabia, India, Judaea and Egypt, except through the writings of those who had been there [4]. When we read Bede's works we must always remember that Bede's birthright was not the birthright of classical antiquity, not even the *Romanitas* of Gaul, but the birthright of pagan barbarism which he inherited from his father and grandfather.

Those inclined to take a strict view might argue that out of the total of some 60 volumes only one, the *Historia Ecclesiastica Gentis Anglorum*, whose narrative runs to midsummer of 731 and which probably received some revision in 732, can be regarded as a work of history. Yet it would be an excessively narrow view which rejected as not being historical works, the *Historia Abbatum*, the prose *Vita Sancti Cuthberti* and the chronicles at the end of his two works concerned primarily with chronology – the *de Temporibus* of 703 and the *de Temporum Ratione* of 725. There are indeed passages in his exegetical works which are relevant to an appreciation of his historical interests.

(2) *Gesta Regum*, ed. W. STUBBS, *Rolls Series* 1887-9, I, 62-3.
(3) *Ep.*, ed. P. EWALD and L. HARTMANN, *Mon. Ger. Hist.*, VIII, 29.
(4) *In Cant. Cant.*, ed. MIGNE, *Pat. Lat.*, 91, 1077.

Scholars of an earlier age were mostly content to regard Bede as « the father of English learning » and to treat what he tells us about the history of the English in Britain with the veneration which some may think it still deserves. The current fashion is to dissect the completed work in an attempt to evaluate the different materials of which the *Historia Ecclesiastica* is composed and to determine the way in which these materials reached Jarrow. It is a measure of Bede's originality, in an age when historical writing was at a low ebb, that he foresaw that others with minds as critical as his own would want to know with what authority, and for what purpose, he wrote the *Historia*. Prompted by his sense of historical foresight and his regard for historical authority he answered both questions in the long *Preface* to the *Historia*, showing incidentally a more generous recognition of his debt to others than some modern historians are wont to do. Even on his deathbed his concern was for accuracy. Engaged in translating extracts from the works of Isidore of Seville, he wrote: « I do not want my children to read what is false or to labour at this in vain after my death ». This was not a disparaging reference to the unreliability of Isidore, but the expression of a concern lest the pupils of his school at Jarrow might be misled by faulty translations [5].

Bede is currently enjoying what is called in popular jargon a bad press. His skill and accuracy as a chronologist have been attacked. He has been accused of distorting history by a display of prejudice against the Celtic, and particularly the Welsh, church. He has been represent-

---

(5) I agree with J. FONTAINE, *Isidore de Seville, Traité de la Nature*, 79, n. 1, in interpreting the passage in this way, rather than with C. W. JONES, *Bedae Opera de Temporibus*, p. 131, who thought that Bede's concern was lest his pupils might find *mendacium* in Isidore's works.

ed as the dupe of a forger. He has been regarded as treating northern English folk-tales as though they were a reliable source of information about events occurring in distant Rome. Finally, he has been accused of committing that greatest of crimes in a historian – the suppression of evidence which does not accord with a preconceived historical theory. These several charges amount to an assault on Bede's intellectual honesty.

It would be a sad reflection on the work of modern historians who have access to material, written as well as archaeological, which was unknown to Bede, if they were unable to point to the probability of error committed by him in some details. Yet if we know a little that Bede did not know, we do well to remember how much he knew that we can never know. It is unquestionably our duty to be no less critical of Bede's writings than he was himself in his attitude towards his own sources. He, too, was charged with heresy in his own day. Yet ought we not to make our critical approach with at least something of the intellectual humility which his writings reveal as one of Bede's endearing characteristics ? We can still take to heart the rebuke which he administered to himself and to others in one of the homilies which reflect the mature thought of his later years:-

« When we notice, while we are talking, that some of the less learned brethren cannot understand those mysteries of the Scriptures which we have not always known, but which we have gradually learnt to know with God's help, we are apt to be immediately puffed up. We despise them and boast about our learning as if it were uniquely profound and as if there were not a great many others much more learned than ourselves. We who do not like to be despised by those more learned than ourselves, delight in despising, or even ridiculing, those who are less learned than us » [6].

(6) *Bedae Opera Homiletica*, I, 19, ed. D. HURST, *C.C.S.L.* CXXII, 138.

In the very first paragraph of the *Preface* to the *Historia*, addressed to his king, Bede set forth in plain terms his own view of the purpose which this *Historia* was intended to serve. He believed that if history related good things of good men, the attentive hearer would be incited to imitate what was good, and that if it recounted evil things of wicked men, the godly hearer or reader would nevertheless shun what was wrong and become the more eager to do what he knew to be good and worthy of God. And at the end of this same *Preface* he begged his readers that if, in what he had written, they were to find anything set down otherwise than in accordance with truth, they would not impute it to him who, according to the true law of history – *quod vera lex historiae est* – had laboured sincerely to commit to writing for the instruction of posterity such things as he had been able to gather from common report.

Bede wrote, then, *ad instructionem posteritatis*, and the instruction which he left for posterity was not in order that it might be better informed about the course of the Anglo-Saxon invasions of Britain, but that, reading about the way in which those invaders had abandoned heathenism and embraced the only true faith, they might themselves be moved to a more Godly way of life.

We ought not to view Bede's historical writings in complete isolation from his other writings, since all were devoted to the same end, and we can find the phrase *vera lex historiae* in his commentary on St. Luke's Gospel. Commenting on Luke 2, 33, *et erat pater ejus et mater mirantes super his quae dicebantur de illo*, Bede remarks that the evangelist does not call Joseph the father of the Saviour because he was so in very truth, but because it was believed by all that he was so. In calling Joseph the father of Christ, Bede continues, the evangelist was not denying

202

the virginity of Mary but expressing the belief of common people which is the true law of history – *opinionem vulgi exprimens, quae vera historiae lex est* [7]. There is a distinction here between revealed truth and what was held to be true among common people, but of course the phrase *vera historiae lex* is not original in Bede. He would find it in a work of Jerome's which we know that he used, the tract *Adversus Helvidium*. Jerome writes that save for Joseph, Elisabeth and Mary herself, everyone thought that Jesus was the son of Mary, « so much so that even the Evangelists, voicing the opinion of the common people which is the true law of history – *opinionem vulgi exprimentes, quae vera historiae lex est* – said that he was the father of the Saviour » [8]. Bede had good precedent for adopting the view that it was the function of history to record what ordinary people believed, and we are not bound to suppose that he himself believed everything that he chose to record. When he chose to record a Northumbrian legend about a meeting between Gregory (not yet Pope) and some Northumbrian boys in the market place in Rome, he did so because the story was widely believed by the faithful in Northumbria, not necessarily because he himself believed the event to have happened. He introduced the story with the words *nec silentio praetereunda opinio, quae de beato Gregorio traditione maiorum ad nos usque perlata est*, and as though to emphasise his belief that the story was no more than a tradition he added at the end of the tale the words *haec iuxta opinionem, quam ab antiquis accepimus, historiae nostrae ecclesiasticae inserere oportunum duximus* [9].

(7) *In Lucam*, ed. D. Hurst, *C.S.S.L.* CXX, 67.
(8) Ed. Migne, *Pat. Lat.*, 23, 197.
(9) *Hist. Ecc.*, II, 1.

The dismemberment of an articulated skeleton may be necessary for the detailed study of its individual bones. It is not difficult to apply this process to Bede's historical writings, particularly to the *Historia* itself, but if, after the process has been completed we find ourselves with a lot of seemingly unrelated pieces of information, we must remember that all that we have achieved is the dismemberment of what was Bede's creation. Bede did not view history as a series of isolated events unrelated to one another, but as an orderly chronological development extending over several millenia from the first creation of man, and when we argue about whether the year which Bede called 670 was the year which we would have called 671, we should not lose sight of this wider view.

Bede was deeply interested in number, not only as a vehicle of mystical symbolism, but also as a science which had practical application to the problems of daily life, as well as the problems of those who wrote history. In Bede's sight, the central fact of past history whose significance over-rode all other past events, was the Resurrection of Christ. Both his homilies and his biblical commentaries contain passages, some of them sublimely moving, in which he expounds the symbolical significance of darkness and light, and sets out his view that through the Resurrection the whole order of time had been reversed. From the moment of creation, with man fallen from the light of paradise into the tribulations of the world, the light of day had been followed by the darkness of night, but with the Resurrection of Christ during the darkness of the night the whole order of time had been so changed that man moved away from the darkness of night towards the light of the following day [10].

(10) See, for example, *Opera Homiletica*, II, 7, ed. HURST, 226-7.

Bede accepted the common view which recognised the superiority of the contemplative over the active life within the monastic community [11], yet his was indeed the active life, and his own essentially practical view of daily living raised a number of questions which were of the essence of his faith. On what day in each passing year was the Resurrection to be celebrated ? The kingdom of Northumbria lay on the frontier of differing theological views. Before his birth the monastery at Whitby, and during his own lifetime, his own monastery at Wearmouth and Jarrow, played a leading part in keeping the *Ecclesia Anglicana* in conformity with Rome, and in leading at least the more northerly parts of the Celtic church in Ireland and Scotland towards a similar conformity. His interest in chronology, perhaps first acquired from his teacher and abbot, Ceolfrith, would be greatly stimulated by the arguments which he would hear, and in which he would participate, during the later years of the seventh century when he was still a young man. He became sufficiently expert in all the mysteries of Easter Tables to be able himself to compile a double set of the great Paschal cycle of 532 years, one running from the Incarnation to 532, and the other looking ahead as far as 1063.

There were two other questions scarcely less important than the date of the Resurrection – when was Christ himself born and how old when he died ? Bede's interest in the first of these questions is reflected in his account of information brought to him by some monks from Wearmouth and Jarrow who had been in Rome in the year 701 of the Incarnation according to Dionysius. The monks had observed the practice of attaching inscribed labels to candles which were lit in the church at Rome at Chri-

(11) See *Op. Hom.*, I, 9, ed. HURST, 64-5.

stmas in honour of the Virgin Mary. The labels which they saw read:- « From the Passion of Our Lord Jesus Christ there are 668 years ». Bede remarks how in this way the Roman church professed its belief that Christ had lived in the flesh for a little more than 33 years, because the labels on its Christmas candles recorded a number which was less by 33 years than the number which Dionysius gave from the time of His Incarnation [12].

As a historian and as a member of what he called the *Ecclesia Catholica* Bede recorded and accepted the belief which his fellow-monks had witnessed in Rome. The Incarnation had been followed 33 years later by the Passion. But now there was a third question. What was the date of Creation itself ? The doctrine of the Six Ages of the World, with the beginning of the Sixth Age marked by the Incarnation, was of course a commonplace of Bede's time. He accepted the doctrine itself, but he was not prepared to accept at third or fourth hand opinions about the duration of the Five Ages preceding the Incarnation. He challenged the opinion of Isidore whose figures were derived from Jerome through Eusebius and rested ultimately on the Greek Septuagint. Using knowledge won from the years of Biblical study at Wearmouth and Jarrow which had culminated in the production of Abbot Ceolfrith's Bible, now represented by the *Codex Amiatinus* in the Biblioteca Laurenziano in Florence, he made his own independent calculations from what he regarded as the most authoritative source – what he called the *Hebraica Veritas*, that is to say Jerome's own translation from the Hebrew which we know as the Vulgate. Using this source, and with some help from Josephus,

---

(12) *De Temporum Ratione*, c. xlvii, ed. C. W. JONES, *Bedae Opera de Temporibus*, 266-7.

206

he challenged the long-established tradition which had given a figure of upwards of 5,000 years from the Creation to the Incarnation, and arrived at a figure of 3953 years as covering the whole of the first Five Ages. It was alleged by those who had not troubled to read carefully what he wrote, that he had stated that Christ was born not at the beginning of the Sixth Age, but in the middle of the Fifth, and, like other historians who have challenged accepted views by returning to primary sources of evidence, he was charged with heresy [13].

Given the chronology of the first Five Ages derived from the *Hebraica Veritas* and given the traditional dates for Christ's Incarnation and Passion as they were accepted in Rome, how was it possible to relate the events of the current Sixth Age, as they happened year by year, to events which had occurred at earlier times and in other countries ? We must not say that Bede was the first to use the Christian era as an infinitely cumulative method of reckoning the passage of time past and to come. The *Annus Incarnationis* or *Annus Domini* had been used by Dionysius Exiguus in his Easter tables in the sixth century. But Bede's *Historia Ecclesiastica* was the first major historical work in which this era was consistently used as the chronological framework, and it is not the least of his claims to originality that he set a fashion which subsequently became, and still remains, the universal practice of historians in the western world. Moreover, when Bede borrowed a passage from Orosius in which Orosius gives the *Annus ab Urbe Condita* as marking the consulship of Julius Caesar and Lucius Bibulus,

(13) C. W. JONES, op. cit. 132-3. For the *Epistola ad Pleguinam* in which Bede replied to the charge, see *ibid.* 307-15.

he equated this year with the 60th year *ante Incarnationis Dominicae Tempus* [14]. We cannot tell who it was that equated past events in the history of the English in Britain with the successive *Anni Incarnationis*, and since there are no surviving Easter tables from Bede's own monastery, we cannot tell whether their margins had been used for this purpose. Surviving continental fragments suggest that this may well have been so but there were other chronological systems in use in Bede's age in Northumbria. The inscription which records the dedication of the church at Jarrow to St. Paul makes no reference to the *Annus Incarnationis* but dates the event to the 15th year of King Ecgfrith and the 4th year of Abbot Ceolfrith [15]. A primitive chronicle found on folio 128*b* of the Moore Manuscript of Bede's *Historia Ecclesiastica* dates a short series of events by recording the number of years elapsed since the occurrence of each of them, e.g. *angli in britanniam ante annos ccxcii* [16]. While Bede may well have derived some of his dates from marginal entries in Easter Tables, we ought not to suppose that these were his only source of chronological information. When we reflect that Bede had to take account of the regnal years of seven or eight Anglo-Saxon kings who reigned contemporaneously and had succeeded to their several kingdoms at different, and usually unknown, dates of the month within a calendar year which may not have had a uniform beginning even within England itself – to say nothing of episcopal or abbatial years – we can have no cause for surprise if

(14) *Hist. Ecc.* I, 2 and V, 24.
(15) P. HUNTER BLAIR, *An Introduction to Anglo-Saxon England*, 156 and Pl. VI.
(16) P. HUNTER BLAIR, « The *Moore Memoranda* on Northumbrian History » in *The Early Cultures of North-West Europe*, ed. C. FOX and B. DICKINS, 245-57.

we should find signs of inconsistency or minor error. In
such a situation we should turn to Bede's commentary
on the First Book of Kings. Bede knew from Scripture
that Solomon began to build the temple in the 480th
year after the children of Israel came out of the land of
Egypt, and he could account for 423 of them from the
Book of Judges. There remained 57 years to be distributed
between Joshua, Samuel and Saul, but when he turned
to Josephus he found the total ascribed to these three
was 58. « We are not to worry », he wrote, « that there
is one superfluous year beyond the 480, for either Scripture, giving a round number in its usual way did not
trouble to add in the extra year, or else, as is much easier
to believe, through lack of care over a long period, the
Chronicle of Josephus has somewhere added an extra
year, as often happens »[17]. All of us who have struggled
with chronological problems will feel grateful to Bede for
allowing us this escape.

We shall never be able to trace the growth of Bede's
interest in history, and particularly in English history,
in any close detail, but we may fairly surmise that it
would be stimulated by reading those historical works
which reached the libraries of Jarrow and Wearmouth –
for example the *Historia Ecclesiastica* of Eusebius both
in Jerome's translation and in the version made by Ru-
finus, the *De Viris Illustribus* of Jerome, with the continuation by Gennadius, as well as some of the writings of
Orosius, Eutropius and Isidore of Seville. Touching the
history of Britain in particular, he knew the *De Excidio
et Conquestu Britanniae* written by the British monk
Gildas, and he used it extensively for his own *Historia
Ecclesiastica*. Writing in a context of c. 720, and with

(17) *Bedae Opera Exegetica, In I Samuelem*, ed. D. Hurst, *C.C.S.L.*, CXIX,
69.

a backward glance over several years, he remarks how in those times many Englishmen used to go to Rome, noblemen and common people, men and women, officers of government and ordinary citizens [18]. Some of these many travellers doubtless brought back books or information – such as the epitaph on the tomb of Gregory the Great in Rome [19] – which would ultimately reach Bede at Jarrow.

We can discern a little of Bede's growing knowledge of English history by comparing the chronicles of the Sixth Age which he appended to each of his two works on chronology. Most of the material in these chronicles [20] is of course derived from earlier works. In the chronicle at the end of the *De Temporibus* written in 703, there is only one entry which is specific to Britain. It reads: *Saxones in Britannia fidem Christi suscipiunt*. Since this event is assigned by Bede to the reign of the Emperor Phocas 602-10, we may perhaps infer that at this date, i.e. 703, Bede knew nothing about the mission sent by Gregory the Great to Britain under the leadership of Augustine in 596. But when we turn to the corresponding chronicle at the end of the *De Temporum Ratione*, completed 22 years later in 725, we find a very different situation. Not only did Bede include some quite detailed information about the activities of Augustine and his companions in Kent and of Paulinus in Northumbria, but he also referred to the arrival of Theodore and Hadrian, to St. Audrey, the foundress of the double monastery at Ely, to Willibrord who was preaching to the Frisians, and to St. Cuthbert whose *Vita* (says Bede) we have recently

(18) *Chron. Majora*, ed. MOMMSEN, *Mon. Ger. Hist.*, *Auct. Ant.*, XIII, 320.
(19) Recorded by Bede in the *Hist. Ecc.* II, 1.
(20) Ed. MOMMSEN, *Mon. Ger. Hist.*, *Auct. Ant.*, XIII, 247-327.

X

written in prose, and some years previously in hexameter verse.

Two significant points emerge from the contrast between these two chronicles of the Sixth Age. First, Bede's account of the Gregorian mission in the later of the two shows a knowledge of some of the works of Gregory the Great – the *Moralia* and the *Dialogi*, as well as a knowledge of the *Liber Pontificalis* and of a letter written by Gregory the Great to Augustine on 22 June 601 [21]. And we know from his prose *Vita Cuthberti* that Bede had also received before this date a copy of the *Libellus Responsionum* [22]. This newly-acquired knowledge enabled Bede to correct his earlier error about the date of the arrival of Christianity among the English by putting it back to the reign of Maurice, the predecessor of Phocas, but it is not clear whether Bede yet knew the exact date of Augustine's arrival in England or whether he knew that the missioners arrived in two separate groups, one headed by Augustine in 597 and the other by Mellitus in 601. Whether or not Bede had already begun to plan the *Historia Ecclesiastica* by 725, I think we may infer that some at least of the material which he would use was now being gathered at Jarrow.

The second significant point arising from the later Chronicle is the interest which it shows in the lives of saints – of Gregory himself, Paulinus, Theodore, Audrey and particularly Cuthbert. Bede's own *Historia Ecclesiastica Gentis Anglorum*, to give it its full title, is at bottom a history of the deeds done by individual men and women in the conversion of the English from paganism to Christianity and in the subsequent development of the

(21) *Ep.* XI, 39, reproduced by Bede in *Hist. Ecc.* I, 29.
(22) *C.* xvi, ed. B. COLGRAVE, *Two Lives of Saint Cuthbert*, 208.

Church in England. It is concerned with individual monks and nuns, rather than with the Monastic Order, with particular men who were bishops rather than with ecclesiastical government, with individual teachers of singing rather than with the chant and the liturgy in general, with particular kings who won or lost battles rather than with warfare between kingdoms. This is as much as to say that when we look at the *Historia* as a whole we find that it is in fact precisely what Bede tells us in the *Preface* that it is going to be – a work telling of the good deeds done by good men, and of the evil deeds done by wicked men. But who, in Bede's sight, were the wicked men ?

If we look at Bede's account of the history of Britain between the sack of Rome in 410 and the arrival of St. Augustine at Canterbury in 597, we find that it is based mainly upon two sources – the *Vita Germani* of Constantius and the *de Excidio et Conquestu Britanniae* of Gildas who is generally thought to have been writing c. 550. The amount of material which Bede borrowed from Gildas seems to show that he saw the conquest of Britain in much the same light as Gildas had seen it – the vengeance of God upon a people who had fallen from Christian virtues into every kind of corrupt and evil living. To the list of unspeakable crimes attributed to the Britons by their own historian, Gildas, Bede could add the further crime that the Britons never preached the Christian faith to the Angles and Saxons living among them in Britain. He repeated this charge near the end of the *Historia*[23], remarking that as the British had formerly been unwilling to teach the Christian faith to the heathen English, so now when the English were fully instructed *in regula*

(23) *Hist. Ecc.* V, 22.

X

212

fidei catholicae, the British still stubbornly persisted in
their old errors. Bede well knew that the purpose of the
visit paid by Germanus to Britain in 429 was to combat
the Pelagian heresy and to call the British church back
to the orthodox fold. In using the Constantius *Vita Germani*, representing the victory of Catholicism over Pelagianism, and the work of Gildas which bitterly attacked
the British clergy as well as the laity, Bede was certainly
influenced by his passionate devotion to the catholic
faith. It may also be that he looked upon the conti-
nuance of the British church in error as Divine retribu-
tion for the failure of their clergy to preach to the English [24].

In his attitude towards the British clergy Bede ex-
presses himself with an uncompromising vigour which
may seem distasteful to those who prefer that measure
of tolerance which is ready to admit that there may be
more than one point of view. We must not forget that,
when the monastery at Jarrow was founded, only half
a century had elapsed from that *infaustus annus* of apostasy following the death of Edwin, Northumbria's first
Christian king, at the hands of Cadwallon, the British,
and Christian, king of Gwynedd [25]. We must not forget
that, as Eddius tells us, British clergy had been driven
out of their churches and monasteries by the sword of
pagan English invaders [26]. Yet we cannot dismiss Bede's
remarks as the mere prejudice of an Englishman against
all Celts. Those who incline to do so should first read
what he wrote of Aidan of Lindisfarne [27], and then take

(24) I am indebted to Professor Whitelock for this point.
(25) *Hist. Ecc.* II, 20, III, 1.
(26) *The Life of Bishop Wilfrid by Eddius Stephanus*, ed. B. COLGRAVE, c.
XVII, 36.
(27) *Hist. Ecc.* III, 5.

note of one of the most vigorous condemnations in the *Historia* – the condemnation of the English king Ecgfrith for his attack on the Irish and the representation of Ecgfrith's death in battle against the Picts as Divine punishment for his sin [28] – and this was the same English king who gave their first endowments to Wearmouth and Jarrow.

Nor must we forget that when Bede wrote the *Historia*, of all the Christian communities in Britain only the British church had failed to conform to Roman usage in the observance of Easter. We do not need to read very deeply in Bede's Biblical commentaries to realise how much store he set by the maintenance of catholic orthodoxy. Departure from such orthodoxy was in his sight a grave sin upon which there could be no compromise. Our judgment about Bede's attitude towards the British church ought not to be based upon his failure to conform to our prejudices, but upon the extent to which he was true to his own beliefs, and we shall not understand the depth of those beliefs if we confine our reading to his historical works. Yet when we have taken all this into account, we are left with the impression that there may have been other factors operating during Bede's own lifetime of which we know nothing, but which contributed to the hardness of his attitude.

It is in his account of the Gregorian mission, at work first in the south-east of England and later in Northumbria, that Bede's *Historia Ecclesiastica* has come under heavy attack in recent years, an attack which in total seems to impugn the stature of his intellect and, perhaps even worse, his intellectual honesty. It has been said that he was wrong about the place of St. Augustine's

(28) *Hist. Ecc.* IV, 26.

214

consecration as archbishop, that he accepted as a genuine document a Canterbury forgery foisted upon him by Nothhelm, that he implied a false date for the conversion of King Ethelbert of Kent and that he deliberately suppressed the evidence which he knew would have shown him to be wrong [29], and that he was wrong about the date at which the mission extended its activities to Northumbria under Paulinus [30].

Bede's account of the Augustinian mission in Kent comprises eleven consecutive chapters in the first Book of the *Historia Ecclesiastica* [31]. A little more than two-thirds of the content of those eleven chapters consists of the direct reproduction of letters written by Gregory the Great. The remainder derives from Canterbury tradition which reached Bede from Albinus, abbot of what we now know as St. Augustine's monastery. Albinus himself had been educated in the school established by Theodore and Hadrian, and Bede says of him that he knew not a little Greek, and was as familiar with Latin as he was with English. Both Gregory the Great and Augustine were still alive when Theodore was born. With this background we may suppose that unwritten traditional information coming to Jarrow from Canterbury would be well-founded. And we know from Bede himself of two separate occasions when material was conveyed to him from Canterbury. The account which Bede gives of the church dedicated to St. Martin in which Bertha

(29) On these points see the detailed arguments expressed by S. BRECHTER, *Die Quellen zur Angelsachsenmission Gregors des Grossen.* See also Brechter's « Zur Bekehrungsgeschichte der Angelsachsen », *Settimane* XIV, Spoleto 1967, 191-215.

(30) See D. P. KIRBY, « Bede's Northumbrian Chronology », *English Historical Review*, LXXVIII (1963), 514-27. I hope to discuss this problem more fully elsewhere.

(31) *Hist. Ecc.* V, 20.

X

worshipped, and of the monastery founded by St. Augustine in which there were churches dedicated the one to SS Peter and Paul, and the other to St. Mary, is abundantly confirmed by surviving architectural remains, as well as by the discoveries made in the detailed excavation of the churches of St. Augustine's monastery [32]. We have found the burial places of the early archbishops of Canterbury precisely where Bede, on the strength of his Canterbury informants, describes them as lying. But the reason why Bede could be both detailed and accurate on this heading was because the churches themselves were still in use and the archbishops' tombs could still be seen.

What was the strength of Canterbury tradition touching matters of which no visible evidence remained when Bede was writing ? So far as we can tell no documents relating to the mission survived in Canterbury itself. Bede would naturally want to know the answer to a number of questions – when exactly did Augustine land in Kent ? – when and where was he consecrated bishop ? – when was King Ethelbert of Kent converted to Christianity ? It looks very much as if the answers to these questions were not to be found in Canterbury tradition as it reached Bede, and that he was dependent for his knowledge of the mission's chronology on the dating clauses of Gregory the Great's letters, copies of which were brought to him by Nothhelm who had travelled to Rome for the particular purpose of examining the papal register and bringing back copies of such documents as he thought would be of interest to Bede.

Bede knew that when Augustine set out from Rome for the second time, in or after July 596, he did so as an abbot. He also knew that when Gregory wrote to Brun-

hild in September 597 he referred to Augustine as *co-epi-
scopus*. He derived these facts from Gregory's letters.
What then was the source of Bede's statement that at
some unspecified date after his arrival in Britain Augustine went to Gaul and was consecrated bishop by Aetherius, archbishop of Arles [33] ? We know that in one
detail, Bede here fell into error, since the archbishop of
Arles was Vergilius, and not Aetherius who was bishop
of Lyons. One of our great difficulties is that we do not
know for certain how many of Gregory's letters Bede did
in fact see. He knew that Gregory had told the archbishop of Arles to give Augustine any help that he might
need. We know that Gregory had written to Vergilius
of Arles to the effect that if Augustine should come to
visit him about the delinquencies of priests or others, the
two were to discuss the cases together [34]. Yet there was
one particular letter of Gregory's which we can feel certain that Bede did not see. It was written on 29 July
598 to Eulogius patriarch of Alexandria [35]. In this letter
Gregory tells how Augustine, who was with his permission made a bishop of the Germanies, has reached England and how 10,000 Englishmen are reported to have
been baptised on Christmas Day in 597. If we read
Gregory's letter objectively, it is difficult not to infer that
Augustine's consecration as bishop had preceded his arrival in England. If this letter had been known either
in Canterbury or to Bede, it seems scarcely credible that
the scene of the mass baptisms on Christmas Day, authenticated by none other than Gregory the Great himself,
would not have had its dramatic potentialities exploited
to the full. The failure of any memory of this incident

(33) *Hist. Ecc.* I, 27.
(34) *Ep.* XI, 45.
(35) *Ep.* VIII, 29.

to have become enshrined in Canterbury tradition is most remarkable, as also is the seeming fact that Canterbury tradition did not even know the date of Augustine's death. It remains possible that Bede was right in saying that Augustine was consecrated bishop in Arles, but even if he was wrong, it is not difficult to see how either he or his Canterbury informant may have made a faulty inference from inadequate evidence [36].

Gregory's correspondence, our only contemporary source for Augustine's mission to the English, does not give the date of King Ethelbert's conversion. Bede himself makes no explicit statement about it either in the body of the *Historia* or in the chronological summary, but he implies that it occurred in 597 soon after the arrival of the missioners. It has been alleged that Ethelbert was still pagan in 601, that Bede became aware of this alleged fact c. 731 when he had already written his account of the mission and that he deliberately suppressed the inconvenient evidence which did not accord with the opinion which he had previously reached [37]. The charge has, to my mind, been effectively refuted by Dr. Markus [38], but its nature is so serious, and the refutation perhaps not so widely known, that no apology is needed for presenting a summary of the arguments first advanced by Dr. Markus.

The case against Bede's integrity rests on three legs. The first argument is that if Ethelbert had been converted by 598 Gregory would have mentioned the fact in the

(36) See P. MEYVAERT, *Bede and Gregory the Great*, Jarrow Lecture 1964, 12-13.

(37) S. BRECHTER, *op. cit.* 240-48.

(38) R. A. MARKUS, « The Chronology of the Gregorian Mission to England: Bede's Narrative and Gregory's Correspondence », *Journal of Ecclesiastical History* XIV (1963), 16-30. I have used Markus's translations of the relevant documents.

X

letter to Eulogius in July of that year. But why should
the Pope in Rome writing to a patriarch in Alexandria
have mentioned the name of an obscure king ruling a minute area of land lying on the very edge of the world ?
The purpose of the letter was to give Eulogius the joyful
news that a mission had set out from Rome, that it had
reached England and that it had met with success. The
second argument rests on a letter which Gregory wrote
to King Ethelbert himself on 22 June 601. The relevant
passage reads:-

« . . . . . and therefore illustrious son give earnest heed to keep the
grace which has been given you by God; be eager to spread the
Christian faith among the peoples whom you rule; redouble your
upright zeal in their conversion; drive out the worship of the
idols; overthrow the temple buildings » [39].

I can see no force in the argument that in this passage
« grace » need not here refer to the grace of baptism, but
may only refer to the grace of faith which the missioners
themselves have brought to England. Hitherto successive generations of historians have thought that a letter
written in such terms as these could only have been written to one who had already been converted, and I can
see no ground for departing from this view.

The third leg of the argument rests upon a letter
which Gregory wrote to Bertha, Ethelbert's queen, also
in June 601, or rests rather upon a part of the letter which
reads thus:-

« And indeed it was your duty this long time past by the excel-
lence of your prudence like a true Christian to have predisposed
the mind of our illustrious son, your consort, to follow the faith
which you cherish » [40].

(39) *Ep.*, XI, 37.
(40) *Ep.*, XI, 35.

I think we must all agree that in this passage Gregory was blaming Bertha for not having secured Ethelbert's conversion, but let us note the words « this long time past », and consider how the letter goes on:-

« And now that by God's good pleasure a fitting moment is come, be sure that you repair past neglect with interest by the help of divine grace. Confirm therefore the mind of your illustrious consort in his attachment to the Christian faith by constant exhortation; let your care pour into him an increased love of God, and inflame his soul for the complete conversion of the race of his subjects ».

Bertha was a Christian Frankish princess who brought a bishop with her from Gaul and who attended services in St. Martin's church in Canterbury – all this before the Gregorian mission reached Kent. We do not know how how long Bertha had been in Kent before Augustine arrived, but surely we can only interpret the letter – if we read all of it – as a rebuke to Bertha for not having used her past opportunities to convert her husband, and as an exhortation to confirm him in his attachment to the Christian faith. We have no proof that Bede ever saw this letter to Bertha and even if he did, would he not have interpreted it precisely in this way ? How can it be said that Bede suppressed the letter because it showed that Ethelbert was still pagan in 601, whilst he had already written his *Historia* with its implication that Ethelbert was converted in 597 ?

The charge that Bede was deceived by a forgery foisted upon him by Nothhelm concerns the authenticity of the *Libellus Responsionum* which was reproduced by Bede as Book I, chapter 27 of the *Historia*. It springs in part from a letter which Boniface wrote to Nothhelm [41],

(41) Ed. M. TANGL, *Mon. Ger. Hist.*, *Ep. Sel.* I, No. 33.

220

then archbishop of Canterbury, in 736, asking for an
assurance that what we now call the *Libellus* was a genuine Gregorian work since, when the archives of the
Roman church were searched, no copy of it could be found
among the other writings of Gregory. In its most extreme
form the charge represents this document as a forgery
perpetrated by Nothhelm himself and first taken to Bede
in 731. Part at least of the charge can be easily refuted,
since Bede quotes a passage from the *Libellus* in his *Vita
Cuthberti* which was written not later than 721, ten years
or more before its inclusion in the *Historia Ecclesiastica*.
This was time enough for Bede to be able to consider the
document and to satisfy himself of its authenticity. Moreover such a forgery could scarcely have been perpetrated in Canterbury without the knowledge of Albinus,
abbot of St. Augustine's monastery. From what we
know of their personal relationships it is not easy to envisage Albinus and Nothhelm deliberately setting out to
deceive Bede in this way, nor is it any easier to envisage
Bede being deceived so readily. That the *Libellus* could
not then, and cannot now, be found in the Register of
Gregory's letters is not a decisive argument since the
Libellus is not in fact a letter. The *Libellus* enjoyed a
very wide circulation as a complete document in itself
apart from its inclusion in the *Historia Ecclesiastica*. It
survives in a large number of manuscripts and much
further work remains to be done on it before any final
decision can be reached, but such as has been done lends
no support to the belief that it was a Canterbury forgery
first taken to Bede c. 731 [43].

(42) *C.* XVI.
(43) See further M. DEANESLY and P. GROSJEAN, « The Canterbury Edition
of the Answers of Pope Gregory I to St. Augustine », *Journal of Ecclesiastical
History*, 10 (1959), 1-49; P. MEYVAERT, « Les Responsiones de S. Grégoire le

X

The *Historia Ecclesiastica Gentis Anglorum* has now
been read for more than twelve centuries and therein
perhaps we may see adequate proof of its qualities. Although we cannot prove that any of the surviving manuscripts were written before Bede's death, there are several eighth-century copies and there is abundant evidence
of the great interest which it aroused in France and Ger-
many. It was prized by two famous English kings, Offa
of Mercia and Alfred the Great. Alcuin had a copy and
it was used also by Paul the Lombard. By the ninth
century it was known at Würzburg, St. Gall, Lorsch and
Murbach [44]. In all, more than 150 complete manuscripts
of the work still survive and it was still being copied by
hand in the 15th century when the first printed edition
appeared at Strasbourg in about 1475. Some may read
it as professional historians, finding in it the prime source
of information about the early history of Christianity
among the English. Others may be attracted by the
lucid style of its Latin which formed an excellent vehicle
for the remarkable narrative powers of its author, so
little removed in time from his pagan forebears. Others
may remember Bede's hope that his account of the past
might encourage men to imitate the good and shun the
evil. However much we may criticise in detail, we are
left in the end with a sense of wonder and admiration
that a man who lived in that *alter orbis* so far removed from
the ancient centres of civilisation, was yet able to acquire
a sense of historical vision which enabled him to see how
much was to be gained *ad instructionem posteritatis* from
a book which told of the conversion of a people from
paganism to Christianity.

Grand à S. Augustin de Cantorbery », *Revue d'Histoire ecclésiastique*, 54 (1959),
879-94; M. DEANESLY, « The Capitular Text of the *Responsiones* of Pope Gregory I to St. Augustine », *Journal of Ecclesiastical History*, 12 (1961), 231-4.
    (44) See D. WHITELOCK, *After Bede*, Jarrow Lecture 1960.

XI

The letters of Pope Boniface V and the mission of Paulinus to Northumbria

Paulinus is named, together with Mellitus, Justus and Rufinianus, as one of the leading members of the mission which left Rome for England in 601. His career in England lasted until his death forty-three years later and was, with the probable exception of that of his deacon, James,[1] by far the longest of any of the Roman missioners known to us by name. Yet nothing has been recorded about that career between 601 and 625, a period four times as long as the duration of his Northumbrian mission. Bede states that he was ordained bishop by Justus on 21 July 625 and went to Northumbria with Æthelberg, baptizing the infant princess Eanflæd in 626 and Edwin in 627 at York. He continued preaching for six years until Edwin's death, spending most of his time in Deira, but also visiting Bernicia. He baptized in the Glen at Old Yeavering and in the Swale near Catterick. He built a church in *Campodonum*, and went on a mission to the kingdom of Lindsey, building a church at Lincoln and baptizing in the Trent at Littleborough. He received a pallium from Pope Honorius, but after Edwin's death he withdrew to Kent, becoming bishop of Rochester, where he died on 10 October 644. All this information is derived from Bede's *Ecclesiastical History* which was completed rather more than eighty-five years after Paulinus's death.[2]

Among Gregory the Great's correspondents were four men called Paulinus, but three of them were already bishops when Gregory was writing to them. The fourth is mentioned in a letter written in February 591 to Anthemius, rector of a papal estate in Campania, and is described as *presbyter monasterii sancti Herasmi, quod in latere montis Repperi situm est.*[3] Since Anthemius was instructed in the letter to give this Paulinus some assistance we may infer that he was personally known to Gregory, but the whereabouts of the monastery itself is unknown save that it lay in Campania. Among the cities of Campania was Naples with whose neighbourhood the English church had connections in the seventh and eighth

---

[1] James survived until the 670s, see below, p. 12, but we do not know the date of his first arrival in England.

[2] HE I. 29; II. 14, 16, 17, 19 and 20; III. 14; and v. 24.

[3] *Gregorii I Papae Registrum Epistolarum, MGH, Epistolae* I, 27. For the three bishops called Paulinus, see *ibid.* II, 502.

centuries,[1] but Paulinus is a common name and a conjecture that the Campanian priest was the same as the later Northumbrian missionary would require better evidence than we possess. The notes about Gregory the Great found in the short collection of papal biographies known as the *Liber Pontificalis* make only brief reference to the English mission. They name Mellitus, Augustine and John, in that order, but they do not distinguish between the first group of missioners who set out from Rome under Augustine in 596 and the second group which reached England in 601 under the leadership of Mellitus. They do not mention Paulinus by name, though he may have been included among the *alios plures...* *monachos* who were of the party.[2] No reference to the mission is to be found in the biographies of any of Gregory the Great's successors.

There is no strictly contemporary written evidence about the activities of Paulinus in England. The nearest approach consists of letters written by Pope Boniface V and these, unlike Gregory the Great's letters, have not survived independently in the papal archive, but are known to us only from Bede's *History*.[3] There is no evidence for the survival either in Kent or in Northumbria of original documents relating to the earliest days of the Roman mission and it therefore seems probable that Bede's knowledge of Boniface's letters, as of those of Gregory the Great, derived from copies made in Rome in the eighth century by one of the many Englishmen who visited Rome at that time. Although, in his letter to Albinus, Bede refers specifically to Nothelm as bringing him written documents,[4] we should not overlook Hwætberht as a likely bearer to Jarrow of written documents secured in Rome. Hwætberht, who succeeded Ceolfrith as abbot in 716 and was still alive in 735 when Bede died, was in Rome with other monks from Wearmouth and Jarrow in 701, and Bede wrote of him *non paruo ibidem temporis spatio demoratus, quaeque sibi necessaria iudicabat, didicit, descripsit, retulit*.[5] Was it through the agency of Hwætberht, called Eusebius, whose literary interests are witnessed by the Latin riddles which he composed,[6] that the works of Gregory the Great were first brought to Northumbria?

[1] Neapolitan influence on the Lindisfarne Gospels has long been recognized. A scribal note on the Echternach Gospels, 222v, points to earlier connections with a book from the library of Eugippius (d. 535), abbot of Lucullanum near Naples; E. A. Lowe, *CLA* v, no. 578. Marginal additions in an eighth-century insular hand suggest that the *Diatessaron* written for Victor, bishop of Capua 541-54, may have been in England before it went to Fulda; Lowe, *ibid.* viii, no. 1196.

[2] *Liber Pontificalis, Pars Prior, MGH, Gesta Pontificum Romanorum* i, 161.

[3] William of Malmesbury gives a series of spurious letters written in support of Canterbury's claims vis-à-vis York. Among them is one supposedly written by Boniface V to Justus; *Councils* iii, 73-4.

[4] Plummer, *Bede* i, 3.

[5] *Historia Abbatum*, ed. Plummer, *Bede* i, 383; also *De Temporum Ratione*, ch. xlvii, *Bedae Opera de Temporibus*, ed. C. W. Jones (Cambridge, Mass., 1943), pp. 266-7.

[6] *Eusebius (Hwaetherhtus): Aenigmata*, ed. A. Ebert, *Sachsiche Gesellschaft der Wissenschaften* xxviii (1877), 20-56.

The letters of Pope Boniface V

The text of the *Ecclesiastical History* contains three letters written by Boniface V – one to Justus, one to Edwin and one to Æthelberg – but it is possible that Bede did not put into the *History* all the letters of Boniface that he had. Recording the appointment of Mellitus to Canterbury after the death of Lawrence, with Justus remaining at Rochester, Bede notes that Mellitus and Justus *susceperunt scripta exhortatoria a pontifice Romanae et apostolicae sedis Bonifatio qui post Deusdedit ecclesiae praefuit anno incarnationis dominicae DCXVIIII.*[1] Bede thus precisely identified the pope in question as Boniface V, 619–25, rather than Boniface IV, 608–15, but it is not quite clear whether we should take the date 619 as referring to the year of Boniface's succession or to the date of the letters, though the point is of little significance since we know nothing of the contents of the letters save that they were exhortatory.

After recording the death of Mellitus on 24 April 624, the succession of Justus to Canterbury and the consecration of Romanus to Rochester by Justus, Bede noted that Justus had received authority to ordain bishops from Pope Boniface – *cuius auctoritatis ista est forma* – and he then gave the text of a letter addressed *Dilectissimo fratri Iusto Bonifatius.*[2] Neither at the beginning nor at the end is there any dating clause and Bede himself does not say when the letter was written. In places the text is difficult to construe and Plummer,[3] noting the variation between *uos* and *uester* in its earlier part and *tu* and *tuus* in its later part, suggested that careless copying might have resulted in the joining together of two originally separate letters, one to Mellitus and one to Justus, but such a conjecture hardly seems necessary. In isolation from its context the letter is primarily one of exhortation and encouragement to Justus, but within the context of the *History* we can see that Bede inserted it in order to show by what authority Justus had consecrated Romanus as bishop of Rochester.

Setting aside the exhortation, the facts which emerge from the letter are that Pope Boniface has received a letter from Justus, that letters received from a king called *Aduluald* have shown him with what depth of scriptural learning Justus had brought that king to a true conversion, that, with the bearer of his letter to Justus, Boniface has sent a *pallium* which Justus may use in *sacrosanctis celebrandis mysteriis*, but not at any other time, and finally that Boniface has given Justus permission to ordain bishops as need might arise. The Moore manuscript of the *History* reads *filii nostri adulualdi regis*[4] and this reading of the king's name is supported with only minor variations by the other eighth-century manuscripts known to Plummer.[5] The Leningrad manuscript, not known to Plummer, also read originally *adulualdi*, but a later hand erased the first *u* and inserted a *b* partly over the second *u*, to

---

[1] *HE* ii. 7.   [2] *HE* ii. 8.   [3] *Bede* ii, 92–3.
[4] *The Moore Bede*, ed. P. Hunter Blair, EEMF 9 (Copenhagen, 1959), 33r.
[5] See Plummer's critical notes to *HE* ii. 8.

XI

give a reading something like *ad lbaldi*. A different and considerably later hand added *eadbaldi* in the upper margin.[1] These alterations and additions show that at a relatively early date it was assumed by some that *adulualdi* was an error for *eadbaldi* and that the reference in the letter is to that King Eadbald who ruled in Kent after the death of his father Æthelberht. All modern commentators seem to have made the same assumption, though without knowledge of the Leningrad manuscript. Yet the manuscript authority for the form *adulwald* is excellent, the name is a common one and it is quite distinct from Eadbald, as Bede himself undoubtedly knew. Recalling how little we know of the history of south-eastern England in the first decades of the seventh century, we should be wiser to accept the evidence of the letter at its face value and to believe that Justus did in fact secure the conversion of an otherwise unrecorded king called Æthelwald. Before going to Canterbury Justus was bishop in Rochester for twenty years from 604, and it is a fair inference that it was as bishop of Rochester that he secured King Æthelwald's conversion. The existence of the two Kentish bishoprics is part of a considerable body of evidence pointing to a real division between eastern and western Kent.[2] We know that at certain times in the seventh century there were two kings reigning at the same time in Kent, and that there were times when two, three or even four kings ruled together among both the South Saxons and the East Saxons.[3]

The sending of the pallium to Justus ought not to be regarded in the light of the significance attached to this vestment in later times. The pope stated specifically that it was to be used only in the celebration of the eucharist, and it would be unwise to suppose that already at this early date it had come to be regarded as particular to the archbishop of Canterbury. Mellitus, the predecessor of Justus at Canterbury, was a man of poor physical health[4] and it may well have seemed desirable to authorize Justus to consecrate bishops while Mellitus was still alive. We cannot assume that Boniface's letter was not written to Justus until he was already archbishop. Lacking other evidence we can say only that the letter was written in the years 619–25. It has no relevance to the date of King Eadbald's conversion nor to the date at which news of this event reached Rome.

The letters from Boniface V to Edwin and Æthelberg are given consecutively in the *History* and comprise the entire content of II. 10–11, saving only for brief introductory sentences. Each of the two is explicitly stated to be a copy (*exemplar*) of a letter written by Boniface, called in the one letter bishop of the apostolic see and in the other pope of the city of Rome. The letter to Edwin is a long exhortation to the observance of the true

[1] *The Leningrad Bede*, ed. O. Arngart, EEMF 2 (Copenhagen, 1952), 35v, col. 2.
[2] H. M. Chadwick, *Studies on Anglo-Saxon Institutions* (Cambridge, 1905), pp. 271–4.
[3] *Ibid.* pp. 270 and 275.   [4] *HE* II. 7.

8

The letters of Pope Boniface V

faith and the abandonment of all idolatry. It contains only one passage relating to specific events in England:

> We suppose that your highness, because of the proximity of place, has become thoroughly acquainted with what the mercy of the redeemer has wrought in the enlightenment of our glorious son, King Audubald, and the peoples subject to him. We therefore trust with assured hope that by heavenly long-suffering this wonderful gift is being bestowed upon you; since indeed we have learned that your illustrious consort, who is discerned to be part of your body, has been enlightened with the reward of eternity through the regeneration of holy baptism.

In later passages Boniface urges Edwin to receive the word of the preachers and the gospel of God of which they are the bearers. In his letter to Æthelberg Boniface refers to the gift of faith which has been bestowed upon her and continues: 'For we have learned from those who brought to us the news of the praiseworthy conversion of our glorious son King Audubald that your highness also, after receiving the wonderful sacrament of the Christian faith, perpetually shines forth in good works pleasing to God.' Urging Æthelberg to refrain from idolatry and the allurements of temples and sooth-saying, Boniface continues: 'and when of our fatherly love we had made enquiry of your glorious husband we learned that, hitherto serving the abomination of idolatry, he has delayed in showing his obedience by giving ear to the voice of the preachers.' Boniface was concerned because in this state the marriage could not be a complete union. *Scriptum namque est: Erunt duo in carne una.* Æthelberg must therefore be unceasing in her efforts to turn Edwin from the worship of idols and to kindle in him the warmth of divine faith.

The letters themselves contain no dating clauses and we have no means of knowing whether they were sent on separate occasions or both together. Bede did not attempt to date them more precisely than by introducing them with the indefinite *quo tempore*. Both letters were written after Boniface had heard of the conversion of King Eadbald (*Audubaldus*) and at a time when he believed that Æthelberg of Kent, though herself Christian, was married to Edwin who as yet remained unconverted. Eadbald's conversion is attributed by Bede to Lawrence whose successor, Mellitus, is said to have died on 24 April 624 after holding the archbishopric for five years.[1] On this evidence Eadbald's conversion should fall before April 619. The date of Æthelberg's conversion is unknown and Bede does not give a date in his reference to the marriage of Æthelberg and Edwin. We can say only that the two letters were written some time during Boniface's tenure of the papacy, i.e. between 619 and 25 October 625. Whether Bede knew this last date is uncertain.

---

[1] *HE* ii. 6 and 7.

Familiarity with Bede's account of the mission of Paulinus to Northumbria may lead us to forget that its value as historical evidence is that of a Northumbrian tradition whose oldest manuscript-witness dates from rather more than a century after the events to which it refers. The account is contained in six consecutive chapters of book II of the *History*, but is divided into two parts by the letters from Boniface V to Edwin and Æthelberg which fill two of those six chapters. The chapter preceding the two letters (II. 9) recounts Edwin's courting of Æthelberg, the consecration of Paulinus as bishop and his journey to Northumbria with Æthelberg, the attempt on Edwin's life by an assassin sent from Wessex, the birth and subsequent baptism of Æthelberg's child, Eanflæd, Edwin's punitive expedition against Wessex and his continuing reluctance to accept Christianity. Bede's chronology for this part of the tradition is precise: Paulinus was consecrated bishop *die XII Kalendarum Augustarum anno ab incarnatione Domini DCXXV*, that is 21 July 625 – the attempted assassination of Edwin occurred *anno sequente*, i.e. 626 – Eanflæd was born *nocte sacrosancta dominici paschae* and was baptized *die sancto pentecostes*, i.e. 31 March 626 for the birth and 19 May 626 for the baptism. The second half of the tradition, following the papal letters, occupies three chapters (II. 12–14) of which the first tells of Edwin's experiences in exile at Rædwald's court in East Anglia, the second of the famous debate in the Northumbrian witan and the third of Edwin's baptism at York and of the activities of Paulinus both in Bernicia and in Deira. Bede gives only one exact date in this part of the tradition – the baptism of Edwin which took place in the year *dominicae incarnationis DCXXVII...die sancto paschae pridie Iduum Aprilium*,[1] i.e. 12 April 627.

Bede wrote the *History ad instructionem posteritatis*[2] and he would surely find the story of the mission to Northumbria, in which Edwin rather than Paulinus is the hero, excellently suited to his purpose. Analysis of its different elements – exile and misfortune, the celestial comforter, escape from death, triumph in battle, ultimate conversion – is largely irrelevant. In Bede's view the duty of a historian was to give expression to the beliefs of common people – *opinionem uulgi exprimens, quae vera historiae lex est*, he wrote, in his commentary on Luke,[3] slightly adapting a phrase used by Jerome in his tract *Adversus Helvidium*.[4] Yet we must do Bede the justice of supposing him to be fully aware of the differing evidential value of the *opinio uulgi* on the one hand and the contemporary letters of popes on the other. He plainly signifies this awareness by repeating the texts of such letters verbatim and so leaving his readers to reach their own conclusions from their content. The two letters from Boniface V to Edwin and Æthel-

[1] *HE* II. 14.
[2] *HE Praefatio.*
[3] *In Lucam*, ed. D. Hurst, *CC* CXX, 67.
[4] Migne, *PL* XXIII, col. 197.

The letters of Pope Boniface V

berg are left to speak for themselves and are not intermingled with the content of the *opinio uulgi*. We cannot tell whether Bede himself was aware of a difficulty with which this method has confronted modern historians in the case of the Paulinus mission. We read first that Paulinus, after being consecrated bishop on 21 July 625, went to Edwin with Æthelberg, and we read next that Boniface V wrote letters both to Edwin and to Æthelberg in which he referred to Edwin's continuing refusal to accept Christianity. Knowing, as Bede may or may not have known, that Boniface V died on 25 October 625, we ask how it was possible for Paulinus to travel from Kent to Northumbria, attempt unsuccessfully to convert Edwin, write to the pope of his failure and for the pope himself to reply, all within the period between 21 July and 25 October of the same year. Though not totally impossible, we must admit that time seems short – a remark which may also apply to the birth of Eanflæd on 31 March 626 if Æthelberg did not set out from Kent on her first visit to Edwin until after 21 July 625.

One means of escape from this problem is to suggest that the letters were not written by Boniface V but by his successor Honorius.[1] Another is to assert that Bede was mistaken in bringing Paulinus to Northumbria with Æthelberg for the first time after 21 July 625.[2] In either case we are impugning the veracity of Bede, by supposing on the one hand that he was incapable of seeing that documents were copied accurately and on the other that he was ill-informed about what was for him perhaps the most important single event in the history of his own Northumbria. And we are implicitly accepting the greater reliability of the *opinio uulgi* as against the belief of a careful scholar. The difficulty has arisen from attempting to do what Bede himself was careful not to do, namely to amalgamate the contemporary document with the *opinio uulgi*. We have no right to assume, because Bede placed Boniface's letters after his account of the journey of Paulinus to Northumbria, that Boniface's letters were not in fact written until after 21 July 625. There was a period of fifteen to twenty years during the reign of Æthelfrith when Edwin was in exile. Some of that time he probably spent in Mercia, since he had children by a daughter of the Mercian royal family[3] – an episode which finds no place in the *opinio uulgi* where it would have reflected ill upon the saintliness of Edwin. Some of it he spent in East Anglia. How did it come about that he married into the Kentish royal family unless as a result of a sojourn in Kent? There is an equally long gap in our knowledge of the doings of Paulinus between his first arrival in England in 601 and his mission to Northumbria in 625. As Plummer pointed out,[4] a rational explanation of the celestial visitor at

[1] W. Bright, *Chapters on Early English Church History* (Oxford, 1878), p. 114. Plummer, *Bede* II, 97, advances an objection to this view.
[2] D. P. Kirby, 'Bede and Northumbrian Chronology', *EHR* LXXVIII (1963), 552–3.
[3] *HE* II. 14.   [4] *Bede* II, 93.

Rædwald's court would be to suppose that Paulinus had at some time been on a mission to East Anglia and had made an unsuccessful attempt to convert Edwin there. The *opinio uulgi* represents Paulinus as bringing the virgin Æthelberg to Edwin in Northumbria, but the scene is as much part of hagiography as history. We do not know when or where the marriage took place and it is not difficult to envisage a situation in which, after a marriage in Kent, Edwin returned to Northumbria still pagan. The letters of Boniface V would be wholly apt to such a situation, and the *opinio uulgi* that Paulinus later brought Æthelberg to Edwin in Northumbria would still be acceptable. Sanctified tradition would prefer to represent her as the unspotted virgin rather than as the already wedded wife. Moreover Pope Boniface had been at pains to point out in his letter to Æthelberg that a marriage between a Christian and a pagan could not result in a complete union.

Despite their best endeavours scholars have not been able to reach complete agreement about the exact date of a number of events in seventh-century England. When we reflect upon the formidable difficulties which faced Bede in seeking to establish a uniform chronology for a country divided into several kingdoms, the regnal dates of whose rulers were at best imperfectly known and sometimes not recorded at all, we need hardly be surprised if here and there we find signs of his failure to solve a problem which was in the last resort insoluble. But before we reject his chronology, we ought to consider carefully whether our own solution is likely to be better founded than his. The mission of Paulinus and the conversion of Edwin were events of outstanding importance in the history of Christianity among the English. If Bede had wished to give chronological precision to an *opinio uulgi*, how would he have set about doing so?

After leaving Northumbria on the death of Edwin, Paulinus went to Kent where he became bishop of Rochester. He died there on 10 October 644.[1] He left behind him in York his deacon, James, who was present at the Synod of Whitby in 664 and died *senex ac plenus dierum* after surviving, as Bede writes, *ad nostra usque tempora*.[2] On this evidence James the Deacon was still living when Bede was born and presumably did not die before the 670s. Hild, abbess of Whitby, was baptized by Paulinus at the same time as Edwin, i.e. 627, and she was aged sixty-six when she died at Whitby in 680,[3] when Bede was about nine. Aged about thirteen at the time of her baptism, Hild was old enough to have remembered something of the occasion and to have passed on her memories to the community at Whitby, where King Edwin himself was buried. Eanflæd, baptized by Paulinus on 19 May 626 in infancy, was taken to Kent by Paulinus but later returned to Northumbria as wife of King Oswiu. In 685, when Bede was about four-

---

[1] *HE* iii. 14.   [2] *HE* iii. 25, ii. 20 and ii. 16.   [3] *HE* iv. 23.

The letters of Pope Boniface V

teen, she was presiding jointly with her daughter, Ælfflæd, over the abbey of Whitby. Ælfflæd, *quae uixdum unius anni aetatem impleverat* when the battle at the Winwæd was fought in 655, died as abbess of Whitby, having reached the age of fifty-nine,[1] and on this evidence her death occurred *c.* 714 when Bede was aged about forty-two. We know that the works of Gregory the Great, author of the English mission, were studied at Whitby in the seventh century,[2] we know also that traditions about Paulinus were current there, and we may surely infer that the Easter dispute, culminating in the synod, would stimulate chronological studies. It is scarcely conceivable that the events which occurred in York in 626 and 627 were not remembered and discussed by Hild, Eanflæd and Ælfflæd. When we consider that Benedict Biscop, Ceolfrith and even Bede himself (though only as a boy) could have met and talked with James, the deacon of Paulinus, and when we consider also the kind of information which would have been available to Bede at Whitby, we shall not find it easy to believe that we are better placed than he was to know the truth about such an important event as the arrival of Paulinus in Northumbria.

[1] *HE* iii. 24.
[2] *The Earliest Life of Gregory the Great*, ed. B. Colgrave (Lawrence, 1968), p. 53.

XII

From Bede to Alcuin

Bede's *Historia Ecclesiastica Gentis Anglorum*, completed some three years before his death, ends on a hopeful note.[1] The times were peaceful and prosperous. The Saracens had been defeated in Gaul. The English kingdoms south of Humber were all subject to the supremacy of King Æthelbald of Mercia and were served by the ministrations of almost a dozen bishops all duly consecrated to their respective offices. North of Humber there were another four bishops. A scholarly king was reigning, The Picts and Scots lived peaceably and in friendship with the English. Only the British remained unrepentant in their hostility to the Catholic Church, and they were paying for their obstinacy by continuing to be in part subject to the rule of the English.[2] This spirit of hopefulness was surely justified in a work which had begun with Julius Caesar's invasion of Britain and had traced the origin and development of a Christian society from autumn sowing to summer flowering. Yet, if Bede leaves us with a sense of gratitude for the blessings which providence had bestowed upon his country, he leaves us with an even stronger sense of his uneasiness as he surveyed the present and looked towards the future. What happened to the kingdom of Northumbria in the years between the writing of Bede's letter to Egbert in the autumn of 734 and the appearance of the Northmen sixty years later? Did it fall into rapid political, ecclesiastical, and intellectual decay, overshadowed by its more powerful neighbour to the south?

A full answer to these questions would require first a detailed study of the reigns of its successive kings. Such a study would tend to confirm Bede's fears about the outcome of a flight from secular responsibilities to the more restricted world of monasteries.[3] We would read of two successive kings who abdicated and entered monasteries—Ceolwulf in Lindisfarne[4] and Eadberht in York.[5] Later in the century we would find parallels in the cases of Osbald who was successively ealdorman, king, and abbot, and of three other officers of government all of whom died as clerics.[6] Bede knew well enough that if society needed regiments of men and women to wage spiritual warfare within their monasteries, it had no less a need for those who could draw their swords on the battlefields of this world in defence of their own kingdom. We would find a second source of political weakness in disputed successions which often resulted in violent death and subsequent feuding. It is easy to point to the record of conspiracy, rebellion, and murder, but not all of the colours are sombre. King Alhred's interest in the mission to the Germans is marked by his letter to Lul, by the consecration in York of a missionary bishop to the Old Saxons, and by the summoning of a synod which resulted in the sending of Willehad, friend of Alcuin, to Friesland.[7] His reign—of nine years—was as long as Oswald's. A little later King Ælfwold, the victim of a murderer, is described as a pious and just king. A church was built on the site of his death and he was buried with great honour at Hexham.[8] In some ways the eighth century seems no more violent than the seventh, but whereas most of the seventh-century rulers died heroic deaths in battle against external enemies, those of the eighth were more likely to be victims of internal conspiracy. It is certainly true that the later Northumbrian kings seem small beer beside the great secular rules of Mercia in the same age, Æthelbald and Offa, but some of them were patrons of letters and protectors of the Church, leaving a good name behind them.

After examining the state of the kingdom we would need to make a similarly detailed study of the Church—of its internal organization, of its place in society, of the individuals who held office as bishops at York, Hexham, Lindisfarne, and Whithorn, not to say Mayo, and of its buildings, notably the great cathedral at York—a resplendent place of beauty as Alcuin called it, holding thirty altars with rich and varied furnishings.[9] There are materials to hand for such a study, notably Bede's *Letter* to his old pupil Egbert,[10] urging the need for a metropolitan at York, for more priests and teachers, for the suppression of spurious monasteries, and touching upon much else that was causing Bede anxiety, not least, perhaps, the corrupting power of the Church's wealth.[11] For the place of the Church in society we could turn to Archbishop Egbert's *Dialogus Ecclesiasticae Institutionis* which discusses many problems[12]—the value of the oath attaching to bishop, priest, and monk, accusations of heinous crime committed by the clergy, fugitive monks, the bequeathing of monasteries, the death of bishop, priest, or monk at the hands of laymen.

There is much here to illustrate Egbert's concern with securing the rights of the clergy within the lay society of Northumbria as a whole. And from the *Dialogus* we could turn to the report of the Legatine visitation of 786[13]—noting the emphasis laid upon the ordination of kings and the sanctity attaching to the king's person. 'No one shall seek to bring about the death of a king because he is the Lord's Annointed.' And we might wonder how much this phrase bears upon the realities of the situation in Northumbria at this date, and how much it is merely a reflection of the biblical and Mediterranean background of the legates themselves. And to remind us that we are still not so very far removed from barbarism we would find references here to priests approaching the altar with bare legs at the celebration of Mass, to pagans who scar and disfigure themselves, to the mutilation of horses by slitting their nostrils,[14] tying their ears back, and making them deaf. Here, too, are references to the settlements of lawsuits by the casting of lots and to the eating of horses, which, say the legates in their report, no Christian does in the East.

From the place of the Church in society we could turn next to the intellectual life of Northumbria during the two generations which followed Bede's death, using the contemporary letters of Boniface, Alcuin, and one or two others, discovering what particular works were being copied in the monastic *scriptoria* and asking what original work was being written in Northumbria during the middle and later years of the eighth century. Among this latter group of material we would find the poem about Ninian which the scholars of York sent to Alcuin,[15] Alcuin's own peom on the saints of York,[16] Æthelwulf's poem *De Abbatibus* recently edited and translated by Professor Campbell,[17] the metrical Kalendar from York,[18] the annals preserved by Symeon of Durham,[19] and perhaps the collection of riddles composed by Hwætberht, under the name of Eusebius,[20] though we do not know whether they were written before or after Bede's death. Thus to specify only some of the available material is enough to suggest a degree of intellectual activity which is hard to reconcile with the view that Northumbrian scholarship fell into rapid decay after 735.

Another line of approach is to ask whether there are indications of the arrival in Northumbria of any significant body of new learning such as had not been available to Bede. More specifically, are there any signs that the library of which Alcuin had charge at York was significantly richer in works of learning than Bede's library at

242

Wearmouth and Jarrow? This is the question to which I invite particular attention. Since there is no early booklist from either centre comparable with the eighth-century list from Würzburg now in the Bodleian library,[21] we must do as best we can to answer the question from inadequate means. Laistner's 'Catalogue of Authors and Works in Bede's Library',[22] which was published nearly forty years ago, can now be substantially lengthened, and although we might now be even more cautious than he was before assuming that a particular work cited by Bede was available to him at first hand, we have a fairly full picture of the library. The same method cannot be used effectively for the York library because the works known to have been written at York are so much fewer in number. On the other hand we have some guide to the York library of a kind that is not available for Wearmouth or Jarrow. In his poem on the bishops and saints of York Alcuin devotes twenty-seven lines to a description of the York library, and he names forty-one writers, grouping them broadly under the Christian Fathers and other biblical commentators, the ancient historians (*historici veteres*), the poets both Christian and pagan, and the grammarians.[23] When we find that Laistner's far from complete list of the authors certainly or possibly represented in Bede's library amounts to more than eighty, the York total seems rather unimpressive, but Alcuin makes it quite plain that he was not attempting to give a complete list of all the authors represented at York. He ends this section of his poem by telling his readers that they would have found there the works of a great many other scholars who had written very many volumes, but it would have taken too much space to include all the names within the compass of his poem. So the list is selective, and the inclusion or omission of this or that name may have been governed by so simple a matter as the demands of metrical scansion. On the other hand it is difficult to believe that the list is merely a poetic fiction. Alcuin had been educated in the school at York,[24] and in later years he himself had charge of both the school and the library. Moreover, something of the quality of the library is suggested in the letter which he wrote to Charlemagne in 796 or 797 from Tours, saying that he lacked there some of the choicer books of scholarly learning (*exquisitiores eruditionis scolasticae libelli*) which he had had in his native land and that to remedy this he was proposing to send some of his pupils (*ex pueris nostris*) to copy works and bring back the *flores Brittaniae* to France so that they might be available in Tours as well as in York.[25]

We are surely justified in believing that the authors named by Alcuin in the poem were indeed represented by some of their works. If Bede had been able to read Alcuin's list of authors he would have found himself familiar with most of them, but I think he would have paused at the line which follows the reference to Aldhelm and to *Beda magister* himself. Here he would have met a name which would, I believe, have been completely new to him—Boethius. And I think he would also have paused at the two lines which name 'the ancient historians': *Historici veteres, Pompeius, Plinius, ipse Acer Aristoteles, rhetor quoque Tullius ingens.*[26]

Then he would have been on familiar ground again with the Christian poets—Sedulius, Juvencus, Paulinus, Arator, and some others. This section is followed by a line with the names of three classical poets—Virgil, Statius, and Lucan—and finally there comes a list of eight grammarians, most and perhaps all of them certainly well known to Bede. Since Pompeius is named among the grammarians, the Pompeius named among the *historici veteres* must be some other. Was this Pompeius Saturninus, contemporary of Pliny the Younger by whom he was praised as a distinguished historian, or was it Pompeius Festus the lexicographer whose work was later abridged by Paul the Deacon and presented by him to Charlemagne? Bede was certainly familiar with some of Pliny at first hand, but there remain a number of names which invite further attention: Aristotle, Cicero, Lucan, Statius, and, from a later period, Boethius. None of these names figures in Laistner's list and so far as I am aware no scholar has ever claimed that Bede knew any of their writings at first hand. And if we indulge our imagination and allow ourselves to envisage Alcuin putting a direct question to Bede—'Which of Virgil's works did you have in your library at Jarrow?'—what would Bede have replied? 'He knows his Virgil well and quotes him frequently', wrote Plummer in 1896.[27] In 1933 Laistner wrote, 'The one poet of the classical period whom Bede can safely be said to have known at first hand was Virgil.'[28] And more recently still Colgrave wrote, 'The only classical authors with whom we may be sure that Bede was familiar are, first and foremost Virgil, as all his works bear witness, and Pliny's *Natural History*.'[29] The weight of authority is formidable, but when a French scholar as distinguished as Professor Jacques Fontaine at one time found himself reluctant to allow even Isidore of Seville a direct first-hand acquaintance with the works of Virgil,[30] perhaps we ought at least to ask the question, were the

Eclogues, the *Georgics*, and the twelve books of the *Aeneid* in Bede's library?

If we had asked the same question about Pliny, we could have answered it by pointing not only to Bede's lengthy quotations from certain books of the *Natural History*, but also to a manuscript of part of this work now at Leyden but originally written, Lowe claims, in the first half of the eighth century in the north of England.[31] We have no comparable evidence for Virgil. So far as I know there is no surviving manuscript which contains even a fragment of any of Virgil's writings and which is believed to have been written at an Anglo-Saxon *scriptorium* in the first half of the eighth century,[32] but when so much has been lost, negative evidence of this kind has no value and all that we can do is to look at the use which Bede made of Virgil's writings.

When we turn to the index of quotations in the Colgrave and Mynors edition of the *History*, we find that there are said to be seven from the writings of Virgil, comprising two from the *Eclogues* and five from the *Aeneid*. One of these, however, is not a quotation at all, but is regarded by the editors as no more than 'possibly echoing' a passage from *Eclogue* I, 66.[33] Only one of the remaining six amounts to a complete line. Describing how a man possessed was healed by contact with soil which had itself been in contact with Oswald's relics, Bede writes, *Conticuere omnes intentique ora tenebant*. This is the opening line of Book II of the *Aeneid*.[34] A search through the grammarians[35] shows that this same line was used to illustrate grammatical points by Charisius,[36] twice by Priscian,[37] by Macrobius,[38] Atilius Fortunatus,[39] Marius Plotius,[40] and in the *Fragmenta Bobiensia*.[41] In other words this line is part of the grammarians' stock-in-trade, a Virgilian cliché which will have been familiar to every schoolboy. Describing the overthrow of the heathen temple at Goodmanham, Bede tells how Coifi destroyed the altars which he himself had consecrated—*quas ipse sacrauerat aras*[42]—and the words seem close to *Aeneid* II, 502—*quos ipse sacrauerat ignis*. After telling of Ecgfrith's defeat and death in battle in 685, Bede writes in a familiar passage that from this time forth the hopes and strength of the English kingdom began to ebb and fall away—*fluere ac retro sublapsa referri*,[43] these five words deriving from *Aeneid* II, 169. I have not found either of these Virgilian passages in the works of the grammarians, but both of them occur in one and the same chapter of a work with which Bede was very familiar, Augustine's *De Civitate*

Dei.[44] In *HE* v.1 we find the words *tumida aequora placauit* which compare with *Aeneid* I, 142, *tumida aequora placat.* The phrase is used by Priscian[45] and Arusianus Messius.[46] In *HE* v.12 we read *sola sub nocte per umbras* which derives from *Aenid* VI, 268 where the received text reads *umbram* for Bede's *umbras.* This same phrase is used by Priscian.[47] So that of the seven apparent Virgilian quotations in the *History,* one is doubtfully an echo at best, two are used by Augustine, and three are found in the works of the grammarians. In the seventh passage Bede writes of the aged abbess Torhtgyth that she was so wasted away that her bones scarcely held together—*uix ossibus hereret.*[48] In *Eclogues* III, 102 we find the words *uix ossibus haerent.* Is this a quotation, an echo, or merely Bede himself?

The results of looking at the antecedents of the Virgilian quotations in the *History* suggest that it may be worthwhile making a similar approach to Bede's other writings. The efficacy of an approach of this kind does of course depend on trustworthy critical editions of the works involved. Such editions exist for the *De Arte Metrica,* the *De Orthographia,* and the *De Schematibus et Tropis,* for the *Opera de Temporibus,* and now also for the *De Natura Rerum.*[49] We also have modern editions for the historical works, the homilies, and several of the biblical commentaries.[50] We can probably assume that in the case of works for which we are still dependent on the texts of Giles or Migne the Virgilian quotations which comprise one or more lines have all been recognized, but it seems likely that there may still be some as yet unrecognized quotations of three or four words. If, for purposes of convenience, we define a quotation as comprising a passage of not less than three consecutive words, it is possible to assemble a total of 106 passages in which Bede quotes from the *Eclogues,* the *Georgics,* or the *Aeneid.*[51] At first sight the case for the view expressed by Plummer, Laistner, and Colgrave seems overwhelmingly strong, but it is not enough to accept this figure without some further analysis. Some of Bede's works depended mainly on particular points being illustrated by passages from suitable authors, while others did not, though they might be embellished by them. It is commonly held that Bede's three school treatises were written at an early stage in his scholarly life, probably within a few years of 700. The examples which he used to illustrate points in the *De Schematibus et Tropis* are all taken from Christian literature and the treatise therefore yields no evidence to our purpose. The *De Arte Metrica* contains 34 quotations from Virgil and the *De Orthographia* which is of much the same length contains 44. Out of this total of 78 yielded by these two relatively short works, we find that 11 come from the *Eclogues*, 17 from the *Georgics*, and 50 from the *Aeneid*. And out of this same total of 78, 39 consist of a complete line or more and 39 of less than a complete line.

These figures can leave no possible doubt that Bede drew heavily upon the works of Virgil, especially the *Aeneid*, for illustrations of the points of metre and orthography which form the subject-matter of the two treatises, but Bede was not opening up a new field of study in the writing of elementary grammatical works. He holds a place in a long list of writers—Agroecius, Donatus, Charisius, Diomedes, Priscian, Probus, Servius, and a great many more. Even the surviving works of the grammarians fill seven large volumes of Keil's *Grammatici Latini* and there are many references to other grammarians whose works have not survived independently. Particularly in the fourth and fifth centuries the grammarians swarmed like bees upon the works of the great classical authors, and especially upon Virgil's. We may surely suppose that the surviving grammatical treatises represent only a small fraction of a large mass of ephemeral literature which formed the schoolbooks of the day. In the *De Schematibus et Tropis* Bede was at pains to show that Christian literature could be used to provide the examples that the grammarians needed, but in the other two school treatises he followed the footsteps of his predecessors.

Returning to figures, it can be shown that out of the 78 quotations from Virgil in the two school treatises, 71 are used by grammarians or others whose work still survives.[52] In many instances we find that a passage quoted by Bede has already been quoted by half a dozen grammarians, frequently by 10, 11, or 12 and in one case, a passage from *Aeneid* III, 211, no fewer than 23 times.[53] Of the seven quotations in these two treatises which I have not so far found in other sources, it is interesting to note that three of them are found within a space of ten lines in cap. xvi of the *De Arte Metrica*.[54] The implication seems to be that Bede was here drawing upon one of the grammatical treatises which have not survived. In many instances it is possible to relate some of the quotations directly or indirectly to a particular grammarian. For example, in the *De Orthographia* there is a passage of several lines which includes two Virgilian quotations, one from the *Georgics* and the other from the *Aeneid*. Both quotations occur in the same order in the *Ars De Orthographia* of Agroecius, from whom Bede seems also to have taken many other Virgilian quotations.[55] Sometimes we find that Bede's version of a passage from Virgil differs from the received text. He quotes, for example, *Aeneid* IX, 503 of which the received text reads: *At tuba terribilem sonitum procul aere canoro.*[56] This is one of the most popular lines among the grammarians and we can find it quoted in whole or in part no less than 18 times. But where the received text ends *procul aere canoro* Bede's version has *procul excitat horrida*, thus ending with a dactyl instead of a spondee. Most of the eighteen grammarians known to have used the line have the received text, but, while there are one or two other minor variations, Victorinus[57] and Audax[58] both agree with Bede. Evidently this particular line had become corrupted in circulation and had reached Bede in a corrupt form, but he seems to have thought it better to repeat the line as he found it rather than attempt emendation, even though this did result in a faulty hexameter in his own *De Arte Metrica.*[59] Other examples of this kind could be given, but perhaps the point has been laboured enough. It seems clear beyond all doubt that the 78 Virgilian quotations in the school treatises were all derived directly or indirectly from the grammarians and not from Virgil's own works.

Yet we are still a long way from being able to guess at the answer which Bede would have given to Alcuin's question. If Bede depended entirely upon the grammarians for his schoolbook use of Virgil *c.* 700, may not the situation have been very different thirty years later? So far as I am myself aware, there are no quotations from Virgil in any of the following of Bede's works:[60] *De Temporibus, De Natura Rerum*, In Ezram et Neemiam, De Tobia*, In Cant. Habacum*, In Lucam, Expositio Actuum et Retractationes, In Apocalypsin*, Vita Cuthberti, Historia Abbatum, Homiliae et Opera Rhythmica.* In the remaining works I am aware of 28 such quotations dispersed as follows: *In Genesim* 3, *In I Samuhelem* 1, *In Regum XXX Quaestiones* 1, *De Tabernaculo* 1, *De Templo* 1, *In Proverbia Salomonis** 1, *In Canticum Canticorum** 4, *In Marcum* 1, *In Epistolas Catholicas** 1, *Historia Ecclesiastica* 5, *De Temporum Ratione* 8, *Epistola ad Wicthedum* 1. In this total of 28, there are two instances in which the same passage from Virgil is quoted twice, so that the real total is reduced to 26. We must now examine these quotations, and it will be convenient to do so by setting out the evidence in three lists. *List A* contains the passages which are found in identical form in other sources known to have been available to Bede. *List B* contains the passages which are found in part in other sources known to have been

248

available to Bede. *List C* contains the passages which I have not so far located in other sources.

LIST A

1. *In Genesim* iii.68–70 (pp. 143–4): a passage from *Georg.* II, 117 and also from *Aen.* I, 417. Both are used by Jerome *Hebraicae Quaestiones in Libro Geneseos, CCSL* lxxii, 12.

2. *De Tabernaculo* i, 304–5 (p. 12): all but one word of two lines from *Aen.* VI, 731–2. The same passage is used by Augustine *De Civitate Dei* XIV, 3, *CCSL* xlviii, 417.

3. *In Proverbia Salomonis PL* xci, 1019: a line from *Eclog.* II, 22. The same line is used by Probus *K* IV, 7, 6 and Consentius *K* V, 348, 21.

4. *In Canticum Canticorum PL* xci, 1167: a line from *Eclog.* III, 63. The complete line is used by Priscian *K* III, 172, 10 and the second half of it by Charisius *K* I, 136, 6.

5. *In Marcum* ii.516 (p. 502): the last five words of *Aen.* II, 54. The line is used by Diomedes *K* I, 438, 12.

6. *De Temporum Ratione* 7.6–7 (p. 193): a line and a half from *Aen.* II, 250–1. The same passage is used by Isidore *Etymol.* v, 31, 3. *PL* lxxxii, 218.

7. *De Temp. Rat.* 7.61 (p. 195): a line from *Aen.* I, 374. The line is also used by Isidore, *Etymol.* v, 31, 5. *PL* lxxxii, 218.

8. *De Temp. Rat.* 29. 24–5 (p. 233): a line and a half from *Georg. II,* 479–80. The same passage is used by Augustine *Enchiridion* V, 16. 8–9, ed. O. Scheel (Tübingen 1903), p. 10, lines 3–4.

9. *De Temp. Rat.* 34.54–5 (p. 245): a line and a half from *Georg.* I, 237–8. The same passage is used by Isidore *De Natura Rerum* x, 4. *PL* lxxxiii, 979.

We have already examined the Virgilian quotations in the *History* and have found that two are used by Augustine and three by the grammarians. Adding these five to the nine set out above, we reach a total of fourteen passages in which the Virgilian quotations used by Bede are used in identical form by other authors known to have been available to him.

LIST B

1. *In Genesim* i.435 (p. 16): a line from *Aen.* VIII, 97. Bede used this line again in *De Temp. Rat.* 32. 20 (p. 240). The first half of the line is used by Probus *K* IV, 224.3.

2. *In Cant. Cant. PL* xci, 1065; two lines from *Eclog.* III, 92–3. Half of the first of these two lines is used by Arusianus Messius, *K* VII, 477, 31.

3. *In Cant. Cant. PL* xci, 1189: two lines from *Aen.* I, 723–4: the whole of the second of these two lines is used by Isidore *Etymol.* xx, 5, 3. *PL* lxxxii, 716, and part of the second line is used by Pompeius *K* V, 307. 3.

4. *De Temp. Rat.* 16.61–2 (p. 215): two lines from *Georg.* I, 231.2. Bede used these same lines again in his *Epistola ad Wicthedum,* ed. Jones, *Op. de Temp.* p. 321. The second of the two lines is used by Consentius *K* V, 401, 16.

5. *De Temp. Rat.* 34.43–4 (p. 245); two lines from *Georg.* I, 233–4. Part of the first line is used by Isidore *De Natura Rerum* x, 1. *PL* lxxxiii, 978, and parts of both the first and the second line are found in *De Dubiis Nominibus K* V, 573, 17–18.

LIST C

1. *In Genesim* i.904–5 (p. 30): one line from *Georg.* III, 537. Placed within its context the passage runs: *patet quia nec ipsae aves raptu infirmorum alitum uiuebant, nec lupus insidias explorabat ouilia circum, nec serpenti puluis panis eius erat.* . . . The passage *nec lupus* . . . *circum* is from *Georg.* III, 537 and the words *serpenti* . . . *erat* derive from Isaiah 65.25. But where the received text of *Georg.* III, 537 reads *explorat,* Bede has *explorabat.* The resultant destruction of the metre leads one to wonder whether Bede even knew that this was a Virgilian hexameter or whether he had simply derived the line in this form from some other so far unidentified source.

2. *In I Samuhelem* III, 461 (p. 148): one line from *Aen.* III, 467.

3. *In Regum XXX Quaestiones* 8.19 (p. 302): one line from *Aen.* XII, 84.

4. *De Templo* i.378–9 (p. 156): two lines from *Aen.* III, 126–7. Where the last word of the second line reads *terris* in the received text, Bede has *uentis.*

5. *In Cant. Cant. PL* xci, 1101; two lines from *Georg.* III, 414–15, but where the received text has *odoratam* . . . *galbaneo* . . . *chelydros,* Bede has *odorantem* . . . *galbano* . . . *chilindros,* but these variations may simply reflect the inadequacies of Migne's text of *In Cant. Cant.*

6. *In Epistolas Catholicas PL* xciii, 74; a passage of four words from *Aen.* X, 640.

7. *De Temp. Rat.* 34.48–9 (p. 245): two lines from *Georg.* I, 235–6.

Let us now look again at the figures. We began with a total of 106 passages in which Bede quotes from the *Eclogues*, the *Georgics*, or the *Aeneid*. We have seen that 78 of these occur in the *De Arte Metrica* or the *De Orthographia* and I have argued that because 71 of these can still be shown to have been used by the grammarians, it seems reasonable to suppose that the remaining seven were derived at second hand from similar sources. We have examined the antecedents of the remaining 28 passages in Bede's other works. In two cases (*List B* 1 and 4) Bede uses the same passage in each of two works thus reducing the total to 26. Of these 26 there are 14 (*List A*) in which the same passage occurs in identical form in works available to Bede and there are another five (*List B*) in which the same passage is similarly quoted in part. There remain the seven passages in *List C*. One of these consists of only four words (no. 6). The rest comprise three passages in each of which one line is quoted and three passages in each of which two lines are quoted, yielding between them a total of nine lines. Can we now feel quite so sure that the works of Virgil were in Bede's library? On the one hand, it seems likely that there may be some Virgilian quotations yet to be identified and that my own figure of 106 will prove too low. On the other hand, we can hardly doubt that many minor grammatical treatises and *florilegia* containing extracts from the classical poets have perished since Bede's day. Moreover my own searches in patristic literature and in the works of other early Christian writers have been limited and it may well be that a scholar more at home in what is to me an unfamiliar field would be able to trace elsewhere some if not all of the quotations referred to in *List C*. As the evidence stands at the moment. I venture to think that Bede would have replied to Alcuin: 'All that I knew of Virgil was what I could read in other men's writings.'[61]

Suppose that we allow Bede to turn the question back to Alcuin: 'And you? Did you and your fellow-scholars at York read Virgil?' We could examine Alcuin's writings as we have examined Bede's, but the need seems not to arise. Several times in his letters Alcuin refers to the *Virgilii mendacia*—and perhaps we do best to follow those who interpret *mendacium* in this context as meaning imaginative fiction rather than literal falsehood.[62] The anonymous author of the *Vita Alcuini*, writing shortly before 830, tells a tale of Alcuin's boyhood, how he alone slept on when he should have been at the night vigils, how he was visited by a supernatural being, was rebuked, and was duly penitent.[63] The charge brought against him was that

he loved Virgil more than the Psalms. A later passage in the same
work[64] shows Alcuin telling his pupils that the sacred poets are
sufficient for them and that there is no reason why they should be
corrupted by the luxuriance of Virgil's language. From the biographer
we can turn to the letter which Alcuin wrote to a former pupil c.
791–2, Richbod, abbot of Lorsch and bishop of Trier:

> Has love of Maro made you forget me? Would that my name was
> Virgil that I might always disport myself before thine eyes. . . .
> Flaccus has gone away. Virgil has come and Maro is building a
> nest in his master's place. . . . O that the four Gospels and not the
> twelve books of the Aenied may fill thy breast![65]

There is also some manuscript evidence which seems to be relevant.
Some forty years ago Beeson commented on three early manuscripts
of the *Interpretationes Virgilianae* of Tiberius Claudius Donatus,[66]
noting certain insular characteristics both of orthography and in the
form of abbreviations. He wrote: 'All are descended from the same
archetype, which was undoubtedly written in insular script.'[67] Three
years previously Rand had associated all three manuscripts with
Tours.[68] One of these three manuscripts seems to invite particular
attention. It is now in Florence, Laurenziana XLV, 15, and Rand,
writing in 1929, described it as an *édition-de-luxe* of a pagan author,
showing a great reverence for Virgil and his commentators'.[69] In 1938
Lowe attributed it to the second half of the eighth century and located
it at Tours.[70] The particular interest of the manuscript is that it falls
into two distinct parts characterized by differences of handwriting.
The first 56 folios, approximately one third of the whole, are written,
to quote Lowe, 'in a calligraphic Anglo-Saxon minuscule by an expert hand'. The remainder of the book, folios 57–160, is written in an
early Carolingian minuscule of a kind which Lowe claims to be
characteristic of the Tours *scriptorium*.

We know that when Alcuin was at York Donatus was among the
authors represented in the library. We know that when he was at
Tours he lacked some of the books which had been available at York
and that he sent some of his pupils there to make copies and bring
them back to Tours. We have seen evidence enough to be certain of
Alcuin's devotion to Virgil. When we find a manuscript of the commentary of Donatus on Virgil written partly in an expert Anglo-
Saxon minuscule and partly in a Carolingian minuscule characteristic
of Tours, the whole being attributed on palaeographical grounds to

the second half of the eighth century, we may well wonder if this manuscript might not be one of those which was copied in York by some of Alcuin's pupils and brought back to Tours. Perhaps it is overbold for a historian thus to speculate in palaeographical fields, but the temptation is great, for if the speculation could be substantiated we would then have a notable example of the minuscule hand written at York in the second half of the eighth century, if, that is, folios 1–56 were written by a York scribe.[71]

If any further proof of Alcuin's familiarity with Virgil were needed we might turn to the Berne manuscript of the poet's works which is known on internal evidence to have been at Tours in, or very soon after, Alcuin's time.[72] Whatever we may think about the answer which Bede would have given to Alcuin's question, we can hardly be in any doubt about Alcuin's reply to Bede, and we can only regret the lack of any present opportunity of listening to the subsequent discussion about the wisdom of reading the *Virgilii mendacia*. Before leaving Virgil and the suggestive York-Tours link, it seems worth glancing at another geographical link, that between York and Worcester. Now in the Vatican library, there is a manuscript of Virgil which Bishop attributes to the second half of the tenth century and which he thinks was probably written at Worcester.[73] Of its script, Bishop remarks that it contains 'more instances of the typical Insular spellings than are common in English Caroline even of the tenth century'.[74] Whence came this Virgil to Worcester? And what was the ancestry of the manuscript of Statius now at Worcester but held to have been copied from a Tours exemplar?[75] We may recall Alcuin's claim that Statius was among the authors represented at York. In the second half of the tenth century the bishops of Worcester were also archbishops of York. We know that Wulfstan was able to get copies of Alcuin's letters since the collection of these letters found in British Museum MS. Cotton Vespasian A.XIV contains annotations and corrections made in Wulfstan's own hand.[76] There is no reason why Alcuin's letters should have been kept at Worcester and we can only suppose that Wulfstan was able to get copies from York. Were the Virgil, and perhaps ultimately the Statius, descended from exemplars which had come from York?

While there is evidence enough to allow some discussion of the Virgil problem, the case is different with Aristotle, Cicero, Lucan, Statius, and Boethius. Bede's school treatises contain a very small number of quotations from Cicero and Lucan, but certainly not enough to suggest any first-hand knowledge of any of their works. Turning to Bede's other writings, I am not aware of any quotations from Aristotle, Cicero, Lucan, Statius, or Boethius. I have not had the opportunity of looking at Alcuin's use of the writings of Aristotle, Lucan, or Statius. As for his use of Cicero, this surely needs no arguing. Alcuin's *De Rhetorica* depends for some 80 per cent of its dialogue on Cicero's *De Inventione* and Julius Victor's *Ars Rhetorica*, with the borrowings from Cicero being some four times as great as those from Julius Victor.[77] The importance of training in rhetoric at the York school is amply witnessed by the rhetorical skills which Alcuin deploys so freely in his own writings. As late as 852, a bare fifteen years before the Danish attack on York, the great Carolingian scholar, Lupus of Ferrières, wrote to Abbot Ealdsige of York asking him to send the twelve books of Quintilian's *De Institutione Oratorica* so that he could have them copied.[78] Quintilian's name does not figure in Alcuin's list of authors, but if this work was in fact in the York library it is unlikely to have arrived there later than *c*. 800 when the Viking raids were beginning to interrupt scholarly communication.

Perhaps the most important, and tantalizing, case is that of Boethius and the *De Consolatione Philosophiae*. No quotation from Boethius has ever been found in any of Bede's works and I take it as certain that he did not know the *Consolatio*. Since the work itself was written when Boethius was in prison its early circulation will presumably have been clandestine. The name of Boethius does not figure in any volume of *Codices Latini Antiquiores* and so far as I know there is no surviving fragment of the work of pre-Carolingian date.[79] A French scholar has remarked that at the very moment when interest in Augustine's *Confessions* was beginning to wane the *Consolatio* of Boethius was discovered and immediately became a dazzling success. The man responsible for this success, he says, was Alcuin.[80] And it is Alcuin who tells us that Boethius was in the library at York. Although I can contribute nothing to the problem of the early circulation of the *Consolatio*, I can draw attention to some neglected evidence for the association of Boethius with York or thereabouts before the Viking attack. The compiler of the first part of the *Historia Regum* attributed to Symeon of Durham shows a fondness for interlarding his work with passages in verse borrowed from other authors. Among these borrowed passages we find no fewer than thirteen separate quotations amounting in all to forty-six lines from

254

the verse sections of the *Consolatio*. There is also at least one from the prose section.[81] I have set out my reasons elsewhere[82] for thinking that the compiler of this section of the *Historia Regum* was working either in or fairly close to York and I suggest that he found there a copy of the *De Consolatione Philosophiae*.

The evidence seems to me to indicate that the library at York came to possess a range of books which was significantly broader than had been available to Bede at Jarrow, and that in particular the presence there of some at least of the works of Virgil, Cicero, and Boethius gave it a colouring less narrowly monastic and more widely humanistic. The significance of this wider spread for the general intellectual life of Anglo-Saxon England lies outside the limits of my topic, though perhaps it may seem relevant to those who think that they can detect Virgilian influences on *Beowulf*. But if the York library was thus enriched, whose was the achievement and whence came the books?

The archbishopric of York was held for a period of close on fifty years (732–80) by only two men, Egbert and Æthelbert. Egbert, at first bishop from 732 and then archbishop from 735, held his office till 766. A man of royal birth, brother to the king, he is described by Alcuin as *rector clarissimus* and *egregius doctor*[83] and praised by him for his generosity and his devotion to the poor, for his gifts of treasure to the church at York and for the attention which he paid to the singing. We know also that he visited Rome and had been interested in the service-books which he found in use at St Peter's.[84] The *Vita Alcuini*[85] tells of his qualities as a teacher in worthy succession to Cuthbert, Theodore, and Bede. Alcuin was aged about thirty when Archbishop Egbert died and no doubt he will have been among his younger pupils. While Alcuin devoted forty lines of his poem to Archbishop Egbert,[86] he gave more than five times as many to his successor, Æthelbert.[87] Moreover he thought it appropriate to include his account of the York library within this part of his poem rather than in the parts dealing with either Æthelbert's predecessor, Egbert, or his successor, Eanbald. He leaves us in no doubt that, although Egbert might be called *egregius doctor*, it was Æthelbert whom he regarded as the outstanding scholar under whose guidance the school at York reached its greatest heights of intellectual attainment. Æthelbert, said to have been a kinsman of Archbishop Egbert, was sent by his parents to a monastery for his early education. He was distinguished at an early age for his intellectual ability and, after becoming deacon and then priest, he was made master of the school at York while Egbert was still holding the archbishopric. His range of learning, Alcuin tells us, covered grammar, rhetoric, law, music, poetry, astronomy, natural philosophy, and mathematics. While he was master of the school he travelled more than once to foreign lands 'led on by his love of wisdom to see if perchance he could discover in those lands any new books or branches of learning which he might bring back with him'.[88] We know that these journeys were made before he became archbishop in 766 and that in the course of them he visited Rome. I think that it is not going beyond the evidence given by Alcuin to see Magister Æthelbert travelling through Gaul to Italy in search of books for his York library in much the same way as Benedict Biscop had done for Wearmouth and Jarrow some seventy-five years earlier, and to believe that behind Alcuin's lines— *Si quid forte novi librorum seu studiorum quod secum ferret, terris reperiret in illis*—there lies the story of the arrival at York of many of the works of Virgil, Cicero, Statius, Lucan, perhaps also Aristotle, and almost certainly Boethius. How right, then, for Alcuin to have brought to its close his own song in praise of the great teacher and scholar with the line which he took from the fifth Eclogue: *Semper honos nomenque tuum, laudesque manebunt.*

NOTES

1 Hereafter I refer to this work in the text as Bede's *History* and in footnotes as *HE*, with references by book and chapter to *Bede's Ecclesiastical History of the English People*, ed. B. Colgrave and R. A. B. Mynors (Oxford 1969).

2 *HE* v. 23.

3 *Epistola ad Ecgbertum Episcopum*, ed. C. Plummer, *Venerabilis Baedae Opera Historica* (Oxford 1896), I, 415.

4 Ceolwulf's abdication is recorded by Symeon of Durham, *Historia Regum*, ed. T. Arnold, Rolls Series (London 1885) under 737, and this date is supported by *Baedae Continuatio*, ed. Plummer, op. cit., I, 362. Arnold's text conceals the fact that the entry in the *Historia Regum* recording Ceolwulf's abdication and withdrawal to Lindisfarne is a marginal addition not earlier than the twelfth century; see Corpus Christi College, Cambridge, MS. 139, f. 60b, col. 1, but the content of the entry is supported by other Durham sources. According to Symeon,

Hist. Reg., Ceolwulf died in 764 as a monk, but the D and E texts of the *Anglo-Saxon Chronicle* recorded his death under 760.

5 Symeon, *Hist. Reg.* and *Baed. Con.*, date Eadbert's abdication to 758, but texts D and E of the *Anglo-Saxon Chronicle* give 757. Symeon dates Eadbert's death to 20 August 768. The *Chronicle* agrees as to the year, but text E gives 19 August.

6 For Osbald called *dux*, *rex*, and then *abbas* see Symeon, *Hist. Reg.* 799; see ibid. 794 for Ethelheard called *dux*, then *clericus*; 796 for Alric called *dux*, then *clericus*; 801 for Edwine called *dux*, then *abbas*. Osbald, Ethelheard, and Alric all died in York. Edwine was buried in his own monastery at Gainford.

7 *Monumenta Germaniae Historica, Epistolae Selectae* I, ed. M. Tangl, No. 121; Symeon, *Hist. Reg.* 767; *Vita Willehadi* c. 1, ed. G. H. Pertz, *MGH Scriptores* II, 380.

8 Symeon, *Hist. Reg.*, 779, 788.

9 *Alcuini Versus de Patribus Regibus et Sanctis Euboricensis Ecclesiae*, ed. E. Dümmler, *MGH Poet. Lat. Car. Aev.* I (1881), 169–206, hereafter referred to as Alcuin, *Versus*. The new cathedral is described in lines 1506–13.

10 Ed. Plummer, op. cit. n. 3 above, I, 405–23.

11 See J. Campbell, 'The First Century of Christianity in England', *Ampleforth Journal* lxxvi pt. i (1971), esp. pp. 13–16.

12 *Councils and Ecclesiastical Documents relating to Great Britain and Ireland*, ed. A. W. Haddan and W. Stubbs, III (Oxford 1871), 403–13. The *Dialogus* takes the form of sixteen questions with explanatory answers, like the *Libellus Responsionum* in *HE* i.27.

13 Ed. E. Dümmler, *MGH Ep. Car. Aev.* II (1895), 20–9, also Haddan and Stubbs, III, 447–61.

14 The expanded nostrils on some cruciform brooches with horse-head terminals may reflect this practice. See, e.g., the brooch from Londesborough, Yorks, *The Arts in Early England*, G. Baldwin Brown, III (London 1915), pl. xliv.

15 Alcuin, *Epist.* No. 273, ed. Dümmler, *MGH Epist.* IV, 431. The poem was edited by K. Strecker, *MGH Poet. Lat. Car. Aev.* IV, 943–62. See also W. Levison, 'An Eighth-century Poem on St. Ninian', *Antiquity* xiv (1940), pp. 280–91.

16 See above n. 9.

17 *Æthelwulf, De Abbatibus*, ed. A. Campbell (Oxford 1967).

18 A. Wilmart, '*Un témoin Anglo-Saxon du calendrier métrique d'York*', *Revue Bénédictine* xlvi (1934), pp. 41–69.

19 P. Hunter Blair, 'Some Observations on the *Historia Regum* attributed to Symeon of Durham', *Celt and Saxon*, ed. N. K. Chadwick (Cambridge 1963), pp. 63–118. See also H. S. Offler, 'Hexham and the *Historia Regum*', *Trans. Architect. and Archaeol. Soc. of Durham and Northumberland* ii (1970), pp. 51–62.

20 Ed. Maria de Marco, *Tatuini Opera Omnia*, *CCSL* cxxxiii (1968), *Aenigmata Eusebii* pp. 207–71, with tr. by Erika von Erhardt-Siebold.

21 E. A. Lowe, 'An Eighth-century List of Books in a Bodleian Manuscript

from Würzburg and its Probable Relation to the Laudian Acts',
Palaeographical Papers 1907–65, ed. L. Bieler (Oxford 1972), I, pp. 239–
250 (reprinted from *Speculum* iii (1928), pp. 3–15).

[22] *Bede: His Life, Times, and Writings*, ed. A. Hamilton Thompson
(Oxford 1935), pp. 263–6.

[23] Alcuin, *Versus* ll. 1535–61.

[24] For a survey of the subjects taught there see V. R. Stallbaumer, 'The
York Cathedral School', *American Benedictine Review* xxii (1971),
pp. 286–97.

[25] Alcuin, *Epist.* no. 121.

[26] *Versus* ll. 1548–9.

[27] *Baed. Op. Hist.* I, liii.

[28] *The Intellectual Heritage of the Early Middle Ages; Selected Essays by
M. L. W. Laistner*, ed. C. G. Starr (New York 1957), p. 97. See also
J. D. A. Ogilvy, *Books Known to the English, 597–1066* (Cambridge,
Mass. 1967), p. 258.

[29] Op. cit., n. 1 above, p. xxvi.

[30] J. Fontaine, *Isidore de Séville et la culture classique dans l'Espagne
wisigothique* (Paris 1959), II, p. 759.

[31] *C.L.A.* x, no. 1578.

[32] I refer of course to manuscripts purporting to be direct copies of Virgil's
own works, not to those which merely contain illustrative quotations.

[33] *HE* i.8.

[34] *HE* iii.11. All references to Virgil's works are to the edition of R. A. B.
Mynors, *P. Vergili Maronis Opera, Scriptorum Classicorum Bibliotheca
Oxoniensis* (Oxford 1969).

[35] H. Keil, *Grammatici Latini*, 7 vols. (Leipzig 1857–80) has proved an
indispensable tool. Hereafter I refer to this work as *K*, followed by
references to volume, page, and line.

[36] *K* I, 175, 16.

[37] *K* III, 113, 14 and 469, 14.

[38] *K* V, 632, 4.

[39] *K* VI, 285, 13.

[40] *K* VI, 505, 4.

[41] *K* VI, 623, 12.

[42] *HE* ii.13.

[43] *HE* iv.26.

[44] *dCD* I, 2, ed. Dombart and Kalb, *CCSL* xlvii (1955), 3.

[45] *K* II, 542, 10.

[46] *K* VII, 463, 6.

[47] *K* III, 54, 11.

[48] *HE* iv.9.

[49] For *De Arte Metrica* and *De Orthographia* see *K* VII, 219–94; *De
Schematibus et Tropis*, C. Halm, *Rhetores Latini Minores* (Leipzig 1863),
pp. 607–18; *Opera de Temporibus*, ed. C. W. Jones (Cambridge, Mass.
1943). New texts of Bede's *Opera Didascalica* came too late for use in
this paper. See Addendum, p. 260 below.

[50] The works now available in *Corpus Christianorum Series Latina* are *In*

258

Genesim, ed. C. W. Jones (vol. cxviiiA, 1967); *In I Samuhelis* and *In Reges*, ed. D. Hurst (vol. cxix, 1962); *De Tabernaculo, De Templo*, and *In Ezram et Neemiam*, ed. D. Hurst (vol. cxixA, 1969); *In Lucam* and *In Marcum*, ed. D. Hurst (vol. cxx, 1960); *Opera homiletica et rhythmica*, ed. D. Hurst (vol. cxxii, 1965). To these we must add *Expositio Actuum Apostolorum et Retractatio*, ed. M. L. W. Laistner (Cambridge, Mass. 1939), *Vita Sancti Cuthberti*, ed. B. Colgrave (Cambridge 1940), *Metrische Vita Sancti Cuthberti*, ed. W. Jaager, *Palaestra* 198 (Leipzig 1935), *Historia Abbatum*, ed. C. Plummer (Oxford 1896). Where no more recent edition is available I refer to the texts found in Migne *Patrologia Latina*.

51 I do not claim that this is the complete total, but only that, if space permitted, I could give references for this number.

52 To substantiate this claim would require a long and detailed appendix. A reader interested enough to undertake the labour can check my figures by using Keil's *Index Auctorum*. Should his results differ from my figures by one or two, they will hardly invalidate the general significance of the totals.

53 The passage consists of the words *insulae Ionio in magno* in *De Arte Metrica*, *K* VII, 232, 9. The same passage is used by Charisius (twice), Diomedes, Priscian, Probus, Donatus, Servius, Sergius, Cledonius, Pompeius (twice), Consentius, Marius Victorinus (six times), Maximus Victorinus (twice), Terentianus, Marius Plotius, and Mallius Theodorus. Again to save space I must leave the reader to make his own check from Keil's *Index Auctorum*. I am not of course claiming that all these grammarians were available to Bede, but wish merely to demonstrate how the bees swarmed.

54 Three of the seven are *De Orthographia K* VII, 267, 21–2 = *Georg.* I, 173; *K* VII, 271, 15 = *Eclog.* IX, 23; *K* VII, 268, 8 = *Aen.* IV, 687. The remaining four are *De Arte Metrica K* VII, 231, 24 = *Aen.* V, 189; *K* VII, 253, 22 = *Georg.* I, 352; *K* VII, 253, 24–5 = *Georg.* III, 384–5; *K* VII, 254, 1 = *Georg.* I, 4.

55 *K* VII, 272, 23–6, cf. with *K* VII, 125, 9–14.

56 *De Arte Metrica, K* VII, 253, 7.

57 *K* VI, 213, 8.

58 *K* VII, 340, 5.

59 For the care with which Bede, or his amanuensis, copied from written sources even to the inclusion of their errors, see Colgrave and Mynors, *Bede's Ecclesiastical History*, xxxix–xl.

60 An asterisk indicates that there is no satisfactory modern edition of the work in question. For the editions used see n. 50 above.

61 It is worth noting that in the *De Temporum Ratione* Bede quotes in separate places four couplets from *Georg.* I and that these four couplets cover eight consecutive lines of the poem, lines 231–8. One of these couplets is used in full by Isidore—*List A*, 9 above. Two of the couplets are used in part by other authors—*List B*, 4 and 5 above. The fourth couplet I have not traced elsewhere—*List C*, 7 above. Of the seven Virgilian quotations in the schoolbooks which I have not located else-

where, three come from *Georg*. I—see note 54 above—but these three
are not in sequence either with themselves or with the eight lines in the
De Temporum Ratione. Perhaps Bede may have had a copy of *Georg*. I
or at least a work with longish extracts from it.

[62] E. M. Sanford, 'Alcuin and the Classics', *Classical J*. xx (1924–5), pp.
526–33; A. Balise, *Dictionaire latin-francais des auteurs chrétiens* (Turn-
hout 1954), s.v. *mendacium*.

[63] *V. Alc*. c. 2, ed. W. Arndt, *MGH SS* XV, i, p. 185.

[64] Ibid., c. 16 (p. 193).

[65] *Ep. Alc*. no. 13, ed. E. Dümmler, *MGH, Ep. Kar. Aev*. II (1895), pp.
38–9.

[66] C. H. Beeson, 'Insular Symptoms in the Commentaries on Vergil',
Studi Medievali, N.S. v (1932), pp. 81–100.

[67] Ibid., pp. 81.

[68] E. K. Rand, *A Survey of the Manuscripts of Tours* (Cambridge, Mass.,
Medieval, 1929), Vol. I, nos. 8, 9, 89.

[69] Ibid., I, 91.

[70] *CLA* III, 297 *a* and *b*.

[71] As Professor T. J. Brown has remarked to me, the fact that the whole
manuscript is written on parchment prepared in the continental rather
than the insular manner is not decisive either way. Parchment was
valuable and scribes from Tours might have taken their own supply.
Since Servius is named by Alcuin, *Versus* 1556, as being represented in
the York Library it may be that his *Commentary* on Virgil was also
there. Florence *Laurenziana* XLV, 14 contains a complete copy and one
of Tours provenance from the first half of the ninth century is found in
Paris *Bibl. Nat. Lat.* 7959; see Valerie Edden, 'Early Manuscripts of
Virgiliana' *The Library, Trans. Bibliog. Soc*. xxviii (1973), pp. 14–25,
esp. p. 21, nos. 5 and 6.

[72] Berne *Stadtbibliothek* 165, see Edden, op. cit., p. 16 and E. Chatelain,
Paléographie des classiques latin (Paris 1884–92), I, *Pl*. 67.

[73] Vatican *Bibl. Apost. Reg. Lat.* 1671. See T. A. M. Bishop, *English
Caroline Miniscule* (Oxford 1971), *Pl*. XVII, no. 19, p. 17.

[74] Ibid., p. 17.

[75] Bishop, op. cit., *Pl*. XVIII no. 20, p. 18.

[76] N. R. Ker, *Catalogue of Manuscripts containing Anglo-Saxon* (Oxford
1957), no. 204; also id., 'The Handwriting of Archbishop Wulfstan',
England before the Conquest, ed. P. Clemoes and K. Hughes (Cambridge
1971), pp. 315–31, esp. 326–7.

[77] W. S. Howell, *The Rhetoric of Alcuin and Charlemagne*, (New York
1965), pp. 24–5.

[78] Ed. E. Perels, *MGH Ep. Car. Aev*. IV (1925), no. 62, p. 62.

[79] See *Beothii Philosophiae Consolatio*, ed. L. Bieler, *CCSL* xciv (1957),
p. xxvii for list of MSS.

[80] P. Courcelle, '*La Survie comparée des Confessions augustiniennes et de la
Consolation boécienne*' in *Classical Influences on European Culture
A.D. 500–1500*, ed. R. R. Bolgar (Cambridge 1971), p. 133.

[81] *Historia Regum*, ed. Arnold, p. 74, last three lines *beatas . . . sapientiae*

260

contigisset are from Boethius I, pr. 5, ed. Bieler, p. 7, lines 15–17. The same passage is used again in *Hist. Reg.*, ed. Arnold, p. 81 top.
[82] Op. cit., n. 19 above.
[83] *Versus* 1258–9.
[84] *Dialogus*, ed. Haddan and Stubbs, III, 412.
[85] C. 4.
[86] *Versus* 1247–86.
[87] *Versus* 1393–1595.
[88] *Versus* 1455–6.

ADDENDUM

Corpus Christianorum Series Latina CXXIII A, *Bedae Venerabilis Opera, Pars I, Opera Didascalica* (Tvrnholti 1975), contains new editions of *De Orthographia* (ed. C. W. Jones), *De Arte Metrica* and *De Schematibus et Tropis* (ed. C. B. Kendall) and *De Natura Rerum* (ed: C. W. Jones).

INDEX